TABLE OF CONTENTS

Acknowledgements iv
Introduction v
East Coast Producers Panel 1
Part One: Inspiration 17
    Glen Ballard 18
Part Two: Roots 27
    Al Schmitt 28
    Arif Mardin 36
    Brian Wilson 40
    Phil Ramone 49
    Elliot Scheiner 57
    Humberto Gatica 62
Part Three: Meanwhile, on the Other Side of the Atlantic... 69
    George Martin 70
    Geoff Emerick 83
    John Leckie 99
    Alan Parsons 110
    Steve Churchyard 121
    Eddie Kramer 130
    Andy Johns 137
    Tony Visconti 142
Part Four: Back in the States 155
    Jack Douglas 156
    Thom Panunzio 162
    George Massenburg 171
    Nile Rodgers 175
    Keith Olsen 186
    Frank Filipetti 193
    Mitchell Froom 202
    Ed Cherney 208
    Mike Clink 215
Part Five: Across the Pond Again 223
    Craig Leon 225
    Mick Glossop 233
    Mike Hedges 246
    Stephen Hague 252
    Steve Levine 260
Part Six: Young Guns 265
    Walter Afanasieff 266
    Chuck Ainlay 277
    Ralph Sutton 289
    Sylvia Massy Shivy 295
    Danny Saber 304
West Coast Producers Panel 313

Acknowledgements

riting *Behind the Glass* has truly been a labor of love. It represents almost three years' worth of work, and it could never have come to fruition without the help of a whole lot of good people.

First and foremost, I would like to express my sincere appreciation to all the phenomenally talented men and women who agreed to be interviewed for this project. All of you have very special gifts, and I feel privileged to have met you. Thank you for giving so much of yourselves.

I am deeply indebted to Bob Doerschuk, my editor at *Musician* magazine and one of the finest journalists on the planet. Bob was the person who finally let me out of the cage after years of writing solely technical articles and product reviews, shoving me, blinking, into the bright light of music journalism. "But I've never interviewed a *person* before," I stammered as he gave me my first assignment. "Don't worry—I have a feeling you'll be good at it," was his reply as he pushed me out the door. Bob, I hope I've justified your faith in me.

Special thanks also to Hector LaTorre and Mitch Gallagher, my editors at *EQ* magazine, for their encouragement and direction, and for allowing me to continue the series in their pages after *Musician* ceased publication in early 1999. Managing editor Tony Savona has done a yeoman's job in both editing and rounding up photographs, and I'd like to express my appreciation to Matt Kelsey and Dorothy Cox for giving me the opportunity to release this body of work in book form.

Three terrific people were key in helping me connect up with many of the producers featured here. Rory Kaplan, executive producer at DTS, became my guardian angel, often even going so far as to make the introductory phone call himself. Tim Heile and Sam Chates of the MPGA (now the NARAS Producers and Engineers Wing) were also extremely helpful in that regard, with Tim heroically and single-handedly making the arrangements for the two group interviews. Thanks, guys—drinks are on me!

I'm also most grateful to Linda Law for her editorial input and transcription help—often the most difficult part of the process—and to my good friend Tim Sanders for numerous kindnesses, including putting a roof over my head during my visits to London and those frequent late-night chats that provided me with invaluable feedback and inspiration.

Last but not least, special thanks to JoAnne Antonucci, Jennifer Ballyntine, Angelo Biasi, Stephen Budd, Peter Chaikin, Rose Mann Cherney, Joe D'Ambrosio, Mike D'Amore, Corey Davidson, Jill Dell'Abate, David Dunton, Kathleen Ervin, Peter Fields, Matthew Freeman, Alastair Gavin, Michael Gelfand, Laurie Jakobsen, Barbara Mathieson, Frank McDonough, Gary Montalvo, Shannon O'Shea, Kristen Ochs, Eric Olsen, Frank Papalardo, Steve Parr, Richard Pinto, Marty Porter, Mac Randall, Sharon Rose, Dr. Robin Oshman, Mark Rowland, Chris Scapaletti, Ed Sengstack, Jean Sievers, Dr. Barney Spivack, David Snow, Mark Vail, Paul Verna, Emma Walden, Monique Ward, Sharon Weisz, Melinda Wilson, and anyone else who helped me along the way but was inadvertently omitted from this list. As a certain First Lady once (almost) said, it takes a village to write a book!

(((Behind the Glass)))

TOP RECORD PRODUCERS TELL HOW THEY CRAFT THE HITS

**HOWARD
MASSEY**

Backbeat
Books
San Francisco

Published by Backbeat Books
(formerly Miller Freeman Books)
600 Harrison Street, San Francisco, CA 94107
www.backbeatbooks.com
Email: books@musicplayer.com
An imprint of Music Player Network
United Entertainment Media, Inc.
Publishers of *EQ* magazine and MusicPlayer.com

Distributed to the book trade in the U.S. and Canada
by Publishers Group West
1700 Fourth Street, Berkeley, CA 94710

Distributed to the music trade in the U.S. and Canada
by Hal Leonard Publishing
P.O. Box 13819, Milwaukee, WE 53213

Cover design by Saroyan Humphrey

Front cover photo by David Goggin

Text Composition by Gary Montalvo

Library of Congress Cataloging-in-Publication Data

Massey, Howard.
    Behind the glass: top record producers tell how they craft the
    hits/Howard Massey.
        p. cm
    "[Interviews] originally conducted for a feature series in Musician
    Magazine call "First Take" (later continued in EQ magazine in the 'From
    the Desk' series)" -- Introd. ISBN 0-87930-614-9 (alk. paper)
    1. Sound recording executives and producers--Interviews. 2. Sound
    recordings--Production and direction. 3. Popular music--History and
    criticism. 4. Sound recording industry. I. Title

    ML3790.M352 2000
    781.64'149--dc 21

                                        00-056052

    05   8 7

Introduction

How is a hit record made? What makes a great record producer? For many people, record production seems to be a kind of black art, imbued with an almost mystical secrecy. After all, it's easy to understand the roles of pretty much everyone else involved in making a CD: the songwriter creates the music; the artist (who is sometimes the same person) interprets and performs it; and the engineer is responsible for getting the sound successfully on tape or to hard disk by looking after the faders, knobs, meters and other technical aspects. But then there's that other person—the one hovering in the background, often engaged in deep conversation with the musicians and the engineer. What exactly is he (or she) doing?

That's what this book sets out to answer.

Originally conducted for a feature series in *Musician* magazine called "First Take" (later continued in *EQ* magazine in the "From the Desk" series), the interviews you'll read in these pages give a fascinating perspective on what it takes to be a successful record producer and provide a wealth of real-world tips and techniques that every musician and student of the recording arts can add to their arsenal of creative tools. Today, of course, every musician has the capability of creating a hit record in the comfort of his or her bedroom—witness Alanis Morissette's wildly successful *Jagged Little Pill*, recorded in producer Glen Ballard's home studio (a process he recounts in great detail in his interview). That makes the collective wisdom presented here even more relevant for the latest generation of artists, who, more and more, find themselves wearing the hats of engineer and producer as well.

Making hit records is, of course, an international phenomenon, not something that's restricted to America. In particular, ever since the so-called "British invasion" of the '60s, English records have had a strong influence on American tastes (just as American records have always had a major impact on English artists and producers). As a result, I interviewed almost as many British producers as American ones (as well as a few Americans who made their careers in England, and vice versa). I also wanted to take advantage of the unique interplay that can occur when you get several creative people to attack a question at the same time and bounce ideas off each other, so I decided to conduct two group interviews—one in New York and one in Los Angeles. Beyond revealing some interesting cultural differences between the two coasts, the resulting dialog was every bit as entertaining as it was illuminating.

While all thirty-four producers interviewed here have much in common—for example, their deep, abiding love of music and a heartfelt passion for their work—they also have very distinctive personalities and opinions. Some come from a musical background, others from an engineering background. In their interviews, some chose to focus on technical aspects; others preferred to take a more philosophical approach. Phil Ramone talks about room treatments; Geoff Emerick reveals the secrets of McCartney's *Sgt. Pepper* era bass sound; Tony Visconti provides an illuminating primer on the power of psychoacoustics. But you'll also find Arif Mardin describing how to go about selecting the best key for a song, George Martin reflecting on randomness and the Chaos Theory, and Nile Rodgers dissecting the meaning of "groove."

As you go through these pages, you'll notice that I sometimes ask the same questions of different producers. I assure you that this was not due to laziness or lack of imagination on my part; instead, this was done purposefully so that the reader could compare and contrast the responses. Some answers varied greatly from producer to producer; others were much more homogenous, lending credence to the theory that perhaps there are some universal factors to making hit records—for example, starting with a strong song and eliciting an emotional performance from the artist. To be sure, there are at least as many intangible variables, but that's the voodoo—the magic "fairy-dust"—of record-making.

Some wag once said that talking about music is about the same as listening to a painting, but creating a great record is equal parts craft and art. As creative and open as the process is, there's much that *can* be articulated, and a great deal that can be gained from listening to the voices of those who have achieved the pinnacle of success. Meeting and interviewing these gifted, talented people was an amazing experience for me, and I know that *I* learned a lot. I hope that you get as much out of reading their words.

One last note—we're already thinking about future editions of *Behind the Glass*, so please e-mail me at BehindTG@aol.com with your comments and suggestions for other producers that you'd like to see included. I can't promise to answer every e-mail, but I do promise to read them all. Thanks!

Howard Massey
March, 2000

East Coast Producers Panel

Five Producers and a Loudmouth

Panelists: Elliot Scheiner, Frank Filipetti, Tony Visconti, Ed Cherney, Ralph Sutton

Get five producers in one room and you'll get five different approaches to making records. Beyond the common ground of their immense talents and undeniable track records, Elliot Scheiner, Frank Filipetti, Tony Visconti, Ed Cherney, and Ralph Sutton have strong—and sometimes conflicting—views on the art of being a record producer. Comrades in arms yet friendly competitors, the interplay between them in this panel discussion was fast, furious, and more than a little controversial—but always interesting.

Get *four* producers in a room (Elliot Scheiner had to leave early) and you may also be lucky enough to witness four different problem-solving techniques. Midway through our discussion, we were interrupted by an unwanted visit from a colleague who will go unnamed here. Pleasant as this chap may be in normal circumstances, on this particular evening he had one beer too many to drink and one chip too many on his shoulder. Ignoring the fact that there was work going on (not to mention the presence of a journalist and tape recorder), he sat down and proceeded to essentially pick a fight with our four panelists, arguing vehemently (and rather incoherently) about what he alleged was his God-given right to sample records without making royalty payments to either the producer, artist, or record company.

Interestingly, the four panelists took four entirely different approaches to dealing with the interloper. One argued strenuously with him; another tried to gently reason with him. A third studiously ignored him, furiously scanning a trade magazine and avoiding all eye contact. And the fourth—perhaps the one you'd least expect—kept his counsel, fixing the besotted loudmouth with a steely glare, but without uttering a word. Until he'd had enough, that is, at which point he addressed the gate-crasher in no uncertain terms, announcing in a quiet yet firm voice, "You've said your peace. Now leave. Get out of here." Needless to say, this induced an alcohol-laden flow of testosterone in the provocateur, who staggered to his feet and delivered the timeless playground rejoinder, "Yeah? Who's going to make me?" Standing up, our man of the hour looked him straight in the eye and, carefully raising the level of his voice several decibels, delivered the answer: "Me. Now get the fuck out of here before I throw you out." Needless to say, this silenced everyone in the room (even producer #3 stopped flipping through his magazine), including the scoundrel, who instinctively went into the classic bully response, slinking out of the room with his tail between his legs. End of interruption, back to business.

So which producer was which? Sorry, the secret will go to the grave with me. But I urge you to keep this story in mind as you read the following interview; the fun will come in the guessing.

Let's start by asking the most basic question: Does every artist need a producer?

ES: Some people probably are already doing a great job on their own; it's not everybody that does need a producer.

FF: I'd say that the majority of artists need a producer. There are very few artists that I've admired over the course of their careers that are self-produced. Occasionally, you have a Prince or a Paula Cole; there are some that can do this, but, for the most part, there aren't that many people that have that objectivity. You need someone to bounce ideas off of. I think that's why engineer/producers started to happen; the artist wanted to be the producer, but they started to work with the engineer—you need an engineer, obviously—and started to realize that many engineers have a good musical background. So they started bouncing ideas off of them and realized that this is something that they need. Being an artist once myself, I know from experience that it's very difficult when you're standing in front of a microphone singing a vocal. I would go into the control room and say, "I really nailed that last take; it was really happening," and then the producer would say, "No, the first take was the one." I'd say, "No, it can't be—I was thinking about the subway ride coming in," and yet that was the one. There's a certain emotional attachment sometimes that an artist may have to a certain performance or a particular chord progression or the way they wrote the song: "No, I can't change the song because I wrote this about my boyfriend, blah, blah, blah." You need someone to bounce an idea off of and say, "No, that chorus just isn't working; if you listen to it objectively, you're not saying what you think you're saying, you're not finishing that statement, you're not paying off in the chorus." When you're involved in the writing and the performance, there are things that you just don't have the objectivity for. I'd say that the majority of the time—in 80 to 85 percent of the cases—you need someone to get that from.

TV: You know, the best business to be in these days is probably the music retail business. You see ad after ad in the newspaper saying, if you buy this, you're basically going to get a record deal. (laughs) People are walking out of Sam Ash and the Guitar Center every day with boxes of stuff that they are convinced are going to turn them into great artists. But the one thing you can't buy is a record producer. As Frank says, it's that objectivity that comes encapsulated in another person who has been through this so many times that they know the difference between a good vocal and a bad vocal, the difference between an inspired guitar solo and just a run-of-the-mill running of your fingers up and down the fretboard. A producer's got to have great ears and a great mind. You can't buy him in Sam Ash; that's really the icing on the cake of any great production. You might want to pose the question: Why does a football team need a coach? It's the same thing. It's the way the world is set up—you just can't do these things objectively, you need another outside mind.

FF: Take an artist like a James Taylor. He doesn't need me as a producer; James can go with anybody that he wants, and he's going to come out with a brilliant record. But even a great artist like James needs *someone*. And the fact is that what we do, we do day in and day out. We don't deal with one artist at a time—we'll do one album and we'll move onto another, so we deal with a whole cross section of music. Those of us that are good at what we do bring much more than just even objectivity—we've had hit records, we know how they sound, we know how they operate. We're the one that deals on a day-to-day basis with the A&R people; we know many times what the record company is looking for; we are often the liaison between the artist and the record company, trying to sort all that out. Even the mundane matters, like budgets, making the deals, hiring the right musicians. The artist is touring around the country most of the time; they don't know who to hire when a mandolin player is needed for a track. They have to have someone they can count on to come up with these ideas—people that live in the community, that work in the community and know the musicians that are available. The producer is the one who kind of puts all that together. Now, obviously, if you're sitting in your home studio and you're playing all the instruments, a producer is not going to add a whole lot to what you're doing. On the other hand, a producer would probably be saying, "You shouldn't be playing the drums on that, you should get a drummer to do that." (laughs)

How do you address the concerns of a new artist who's worried about a producer tampering with their vision? I'm thinking specifically about an artist that wants to set new boundaries and not adhere to old rules—someone who doesn't want the "Frank Filipetti sound" or the "Elliot Scheiner sound."

FF: Well, I think bringing the Elliott Scheiner sound to a record is not a bad idea! (laughs)

EC: It's very important that an artist speaks to a lot of different producers and spends enough time with them so that they know they're with someone who's empathetic to what they're doing. That's really important. There's a lot of different hats that a producer wears, and it changes, depending on the kind of artist you're working with and what your artist needs. There are some artists that can play everything and can write the song and perform it, and maybe they need you to work out the budget and decide what you're going to have for dinner. There are other artists where you have to take something that was hammered out on an out-of-tune acoustic guitar, and you have to craft the whole song: put in a space, find a hook, create a chorus, maybe eliminate two bridges so there's only one. As an artist, you have to make sure you're with someone who understands what it is you're trying to say and is going to clear the way for you so you can create the music that you're trying to create.

ES: Also, any artist that believes any one of us would tamper with their music is mistaken. An artist has to change their perspective in order to work with a producer. You can't come in thinking, well, my stuff is golden, and it can't be changed; that's just not the way it works. If an artist believes that that's the way it is, then they should just go and make the record by themselves. Everybody has to be prepared to sacrifice. There's always compromise, but any time I've had a big record, there was a lot of conflict in the process; anything that went smoothly was usually a disaster.

FF: My feeling is that it depends on what the artist wants to do. If they feel that their material is inspired by something and that they don't want to change it, they probably don't belong in this situation anyway. On the other hand, if what the artist is looking for—or if what the record company who brought you the artist is looking for—is to make a hit record in a very competitive market, that's what we do. My job is to point out the options to the artist I'm working with, to say, "Look, I don't think this song is strong enough, I think we're going to run into trouble here," or, "Instead of doing the standard string thing, let's try something slightly different." My job is to bring the musical sensibility to this thing that may put a new twist on it that they may not have thought of. On the other hand, if the artist feels really strongly that their vision is going to be tampered with, we all make compromises. If an artist really feels that a suggestion you make is going to be to the detriment of the song, then you go along with them and abandon the idea. Again, it depends on who you're working with. If you're working with a brand-new artist who doesn't know the ropes and hasn't been around, they may need more guidance than a more established artist. If someone is making their fourteenth record, they generally understand those things. But there are many aspects to this, and it always involves the art of compromise. One of the most interesting producer's jobs is being that person in the middle of conflict between musicians. I've worked with many bands with inner working conflicts, and part of your job, many times, is to be the guy to say, "OK, let's just chill out for awhile." The producer's job is very encompassing. It requires not only musical talent but also means that you have to have a good working relationship with people.

> *"My job is to bring the musical sensibility to [a song] that may put a new twist on it that the artist may not have thought of."*
> — Frank Filipetti

EC: You need good people skills.

FF: Absolutely. A lot of it is people skills.

TV: I'm actually quite excited when an artist has a concept, when they have a vision. While an artist might think that so-called tampering might impede them, it's quite the reverse. Usually, if an artist has a vision, any number of a hundred things can go wrong without people on the team who know how to get these things, these effects, or the sound. For instance, if an artist says, "I write songs this way; I'm really into the Lennon vocal sound," you have to have somebody on the team who knows how to approach the sound. Just putting an artist in the studio with an engineer—or just with an ADAT machine—these things will not happen out of thin air. It's hard enough to be the musician and the singer. Does that person want the responsibility of getting the quality of sound? Do they want to be responsible for mixing it? Do they want to be responsible for marketing it? These are simply too many jobs for one person to do, so you want to get people on your team who are sympathetic with your vision. Sure, there are people who will tam-

From Left to Right: Ed Cherney, Frank Filipetti, Ralph Sutton

per with your vision, because they have an agenda of their own. But I come from the point of view where I want to work with people who have a vision. It's boring to work with a person who lies back in the bed and says, "Do me." (laughs)

ES: (mock surprise) You don't like that?

TV: No, not really. Do *me!* (laughs)

How is the connection made between you and new artists?

ES: It's very difficult to find new artists. People don't know how to get in touch with us necessarily. I used to get a lot of tapes because they'd come from within the industry, come from the record company. I'm convinced that's not the key anymore. The key is really to have some guy from Charleston, South Carolina send you a tape. There's a lot of music out there that we're not getting to hear, that nobody's getting to hear.

EC: I just started working with a young band from Fresno. My wife—who happens to be president of the Record Plant—for some reason happened to send them my discography, she just faxed it out to a hundred people.

FF: Yeah, I was wondering why she sent me a copy. (laughs)

EC: Anyway, a lawyer saw it and said, "Oh, I have this friend who represents a band in Fresno,"

> *"I used to get a lot of tapes from within the industry, but I'm convinced that's not the key anymore."*
> *— Elliott Scheiner*

and they sent me a tape, and I really liked it. I met with them and saw them play, and I thought they were pretty good. They don't have a deal yet, but I'm working with them.

ES: Perhaps the trade magazines should make it possible for musicians to get tapes to producers.

FF: There's a type of producer that I admire— the guys who are doing the club circuit two, three, four times a week checking out the new bands. A friend of mine—Ron St. Germain—is always telling me about this great new band, and I don't know who the hell he's talking about. He's out there, on the street, all the time looking at the stuff, and I wish I could do that. I don't have the time—between the work that I do and my family, it's very difficult. I wish I could go out there and see what's going on; in a certain sense, I feel like I'm missing something by not being able to do that. We're here in New York—one of the great cities in the world—and there's always new things coming up; L.A. is probably *the* premiere place for new bands. But the fact is that there's all this music always going on, and if I had the time, I would love to go out there and do that. I don't, so all of my stuff now comes through the record company. I'm also lucky in the sense that I'm not strictly a music producer; I don't just produce records; I also engineer, and I actually enjoy just engineering records. So many times, I'll work with an act through a producer that comes to me and asks me to engineer for him.

But you're all always looking for new artists.

ES: Always looking.

TV: I'm doing this game for thirty years now. In that thirty years time, I've witnessed only one occasion where a tape came in the mail and the person eventually became a star. That person was Joe Cocker. I was in my London office with my mentor, Denny Cordell, the day that thing arrived. I remember ripping open the envelope, we put it on, and there was Joe Cocker singing on tape. We said, "Get that guy on the phone immediately!" In thirty years, I haven't had a feeling like that. I got one or two tapes that were really great; I phoned the people up and did a little bit of work with them, but the problem is that I don't think that our stars of tomorrow are going to come from people making tapes in their bedroom. I think there's a certain rite of passage you have to go through; there are several steps before a person can get to people like us. I hate to say this—it's not elitism, it's just the way the whole world is set up. Take Guns N' Roses—they didn't happen overnight, they didn't make tapes in their bedroom. They played gigs for years, every night. They had a fan base. The record company was bright enough to say, "If these guys are killing a fan base of 5,000, night after night, getting to these people, think of what they can do nationwide." That's the rite of passage every star goes through; every star has a history of live performing and turning on people somewhere, be it a small club or a local television show. On some level, you are proving that you can entertain people, that people like you.

FF: I've actually had the experience where I've worked with writers or musicians that sent me a tape that I thought was fantastic. I said I'd get behind them, and we'd do a couple of things. Then I made the unfortunate mistake of not seeing them live first. I set up this one fellow, we did some songs in the studio, then I set up the record company thing at a live gig, and I myself

> **"I want to work with people who have a vision. It's boring to work with a person who lies back in the bed and says, 'Do me.'"**
> **— Tony Visconti**

hadn't seen them live before. The gig was OK, but it just wasn't good enough. Record companies are looking for stars. They're not looking for songwriters. *Publishers* are looking for songwriters. But record companies want someone who's going to go up there and be a star. And this is the problem—in an incredibly competitive market, it's the live performance right now; that's the important thing. A friend took me to a club one night and we saw Cyndi Lauper playing with her cover band. We said, "This is it, she's a star," and we actually signed her to a production deal. But you don't see that very often.

RS: The clubs have changed, also. In L.A., we have a lot of "pay-to-play" clubs, and that's not good; we're losing that energy. The Troubadour used to be the spot in L.A.; now you have to pay to play there, so we're not seeing as much live musicianship as we used to see, either. I don't know what that's really due to.

TV: I had a situation recently where my manager said, "Go to the Bottom Line tonight; there's this great band playing. Go down there, I think you'll get along with them. They're into T. Rex and Bowie and all that, and they'll love you. They know you're coming." And I think, "Great, I've got this one, I've got this gig." So I go down there, and I see Frank in the audience, and I see a lot of my colleagues, a lot of my peers in the audience! So if a band is hot, they are hot. Here I thought they're putting this show on for me, and I see five record companies, eight record producers! (laughs) Everyone wants to get into the act when a band is hot. That's how I get acts; as I said, it's a rite of passage. I get a lot of beautiful-sounding demos in the mail now; I'd say I get about five or ten a week. They sound great, because the equipment you buy in Sam Ash is getting better. The quality of the demos is getting better and better, but you don't hear the star quality. That's very, very elusive.

Do demos ever make for good records? Or maybe I should ask the converse—do you ever lose something when you create the master?

ES: We've all played chase the demo, that's true.

TV: We've all been through that.

EC: And I've got to tell you something, in all honesty: There are producers that will decide to work with an artist based on the song demos that come with them. And I won't name names, but I know two specific people that have made great careers copping great demos, line for line, lick for lick.

ES: Has anyone here actually used a demo on a record?

EC: Well, you might take stuff from the home recording, a guitar part or something.

TV: I've used parts of demos, flying in a part or two. If the musician says, "I can't do it," you get the 16-track tape...

ES: ...or fly it in from Pro Tools.

FF: About five years ago I was working with an artist named Beth Neilson Chapman, out of Nashville. This woman sings in her home unbelievably well. She'll sit at the piano, writing a song, and she sings it into a cassette. One song in particular, called "Rage On Rage"—it made you cry, just listening to the cassette. And I sat there in the studio trying to recreate this. If we had ADATs or DA-88s back then, and if she could have put that performance on one of those machines, I would have definitely used it, because there was no way I was ever going to get that in the studio. We ended up getting something that was very good, but I don't know that we ever really matched the intensity of that performance. The good news is that now, at least if an artist does do something like that in their home, there is the capability of downloading it into Pro Tools and making a professional recording that will stand up as a professional recording. But I'd say that's more the exception than the rule.

EC: If I'm working with an artist doing a demo at their home, I'll spend a lot of time building a drum loop, creating a rhythm track for them to sing to in tempo. A lot of times I'll end up keeping that loop and using that as the cornerstone and building around that. A lot of times that happens.

RS: More so than it used to...

FF: Because now you can do it. You go in there with an 02R and a DA-88—and with someone who knows what they're doing, you can get a professional recording in a bedroom. Let's face it: What we do is all smoke and mirrors, in the sense that the worst, most sterile environment that you can ever place a performer into is the studio. For someone who's used to either doing it on their own or being in front of a huge stadium of people and getting the energy off that—you don't put them in a room like a studio, with people with headphones on, and say, "Give me everything you've got." It is a really difficult environment for the artist.

ES: But the stuff that comes out of bedrooms is so, well, unmoving. You know it was recorded in somebody's bedroom with a bunch of machines, and it's probably just one guy sitting there doing everything, and you can't be inspired by it. But you remember the days in the studio when the whole room was filled with candles and incense and it was the band's first day in the studio and they were just going, "Ahh, this is the shit!" (laughs) You know, they were psyched to be there. I agree that their environment is the arena, but they love being in the studio too.

TV: Some do, anyway.

(At this point Elliott Scheiner has to depart and the contretemps with the uninvited guest described earlier takes place. After a short break, the panel resumes.)

What sort of reasonable expectations can a new artist have of their producer? What sort of expectations are unreasonable?

FF: They can expect a well-executed, professional-sounding record that, according to our contract, will be a "commercially viable, marketable product."

EC: Basically, the record company can shit-can it if they want to, though.

FF: Yeah, we have no control over what the record company does. Once the record is done, it's out of our hands; it's in the hands of marketing and promotions. Hopefully, what an artist can do with a very good, reasonably sensitive producer is, they can get the album they always hoped for. They will get something they will be proud of, and hopefully we will have added enough beyond the expertise that we bring to it because of our abilities. But also they will have something that they feel realizes their vision. But beyond that, there are just no guarantees. I've worked with artists who are the darlings of the record company, and they're going to go out there and do something, and then at the last minute, the manager does something stupid, and God knows what will happen. There's just no way to guarantee a hit that I know of.

So it's unreasonable to expect that if you hook up with a certain producer, you'll have a hit record.

FF: Let's put it this way: If you hook up with a good producer, your chances have vastly improved.

But this is still a chance, it's not a certainty. I'll do seven or eight records a year—because I mix records as well as produce them—and maybe five of them are viable on the charts; they reach the charts, and they reach a certain chart position. And then there will be three that I think are really wonderful records, and you just don't hear from. There's just so many things that influence that; there's just no way to tell.

RS: The public is very fickle, too.

EC: Well, it's not that. You've got big problems if it's a new artist: Radio playlists are very, very narrow. They have room for one or two new acts a month, maybe—and there's probably four thousand records coming out each month. And I don't think it's the artist's idea that you're going in to make a hit. You're going in to represent what the artist is doing, to be as honest as you can, and hope for the best—hopefully make something where business and commerce and art meet, all at the same intersection. Hopefully you can do that, but all you can do is do your best, have a good time, and create music; hopefully the rest will take care of itself. That's the only expectation that you can have, to go in and make a great record, great music.

> **"You're going in to represent what the artist is doing, to be as honest as you can, and hope for the best—hopefully make something where business and commerce and art meet, all at the same intersection."**
> **— Ed Cherney**

FF: And have a good time doing it. I know that when you're dealing with a more established artist, it's not quite the same, but when you're dealing with a new artist, I find that many times just going into the studio and getting them working with someone or with a band they really admire takes the edge off. Instead of being really nervous about the session, they have a great time, because they get to play with people that they never expected to.

I was going to ask what the top two or three things are that an artist should look for in a producer, but I think you've already answered that. So let me turn the question around: What are the top two or three warning signs that a particular producer may not be right for an artist?

EC: When he says, I-I-I-I-I-I-I!!! (laughs)

TV: I've heard of groups that have been very turned off by arrogant record producers who say they're going to change everything. That's a signal right there. It's as if he's saying, "You guys aren't cutting it, I know all the answers." You might know a lot of the answers, but you'll never play that card in the first day! (laughs)

RS: Right, exactly. But, you know, I think a lot of times, talent looks for that. They challenge you, they test you: "Well, I don't like that." They're just seeing if you're really going to stand behind your idea. If it's a great idea, it's a great idea. And they'll say, "Let's say we don't like it." I work with a lot of R&B acts, and they actually challenge me a lot of times: "We don't like the way that sounds, Ralph." And they'll conspire, just to see if I'm going to change. And we stick by it, and then they say, "Oh, we were only fucking with you."

FF: The thing is that you're dealing in a creative process, and, when you're dealing with a creative process, there's always ego involved; no one can leave it totally at the door. So when it comes to working in the studio, I have one philosophy, and that is, I never want to get into an argument or discuss how something is going to sound. No one is ever going to win an argument with me by telling me ahead of time how something is going to sound. Yes, sometimes you can tell ahead of time if something is going to work, but nine times out of ten, once you hear it, then everybody can hear it immediately. I've had people sit there and tell me why putting the backgrounds in the first chorus isn't going to work, and they'll expound on that for thirty minutes, when all you've got to do is play the damn thing, and then you'll hear it. And more times than not, everybody agrees, once they hear it. But they'll sit there and they'll argue this thing out without listening to it. So if an artist asks me, "So what do you think about this?" my answer is, "Let's hear it, let's just try it." That's the only way for me to tell. You can intellectualize all this stuff until you're blue in the face, but the end result is the way it sounds. And that can really surprise you sometimes. There have been times when I thought I was absolutely right in this logic of my argument, and then I listen to it, and I have to admit, "Jeez, that actually sounds pretty good." Once you get to that stage where you say, "Let's just play it," it's really amazing how everybody kind of hears the same thing all of a sudden. And it takes that ego thing out of it, too.

EC: It saves time, too. Working as an engineer, I've seen artists say, let's try this or that, and I've seen the producer go into a half-hour discussion about why it won't work. But you know what? In ten minutes we could have cut it five different ways, so you can actually take it and put it in the palm of your hand and look at it.

What sort of business arrangements should artists expect to make with their producer? What's a ripoff, and what's a reasonable deal?

TV: The bottom line is what the record company is putting out as the budget. The producer's going to get anywhere from a third to half of that budget for their services. If it's an eight-to ten-week job, you've got to earn a reasonable amount for your time. If a record company's going to say, we only have $50,000 to make the album, what are you going to do? Probably if the producer really loves the gig, he'll eat it; he'll say, "I'll do it, I love this group. I've got to do it even if I'm going to lose money." But every single project is a special case.

EC: It also depends on where the producer is in their career. If you get a producer that has a big name, the record company will pay him a couple of hundred thousand dollars to produce the record, well knowing that he has a following, and people will buy the record, and they can get all this press and a jumping-off point because of this guy's name. He puts his name on it— a Phil Ramone, a Don Was, a Nile Rodgers, a Babyface—so you have those situations where it goes like that.

What's the range of points that the producer will typically get?

EC: Typically a producer will get three points, but you can negotiate bumps—a half a point bump when it hits 500,000 or another half a point when it goes platinum.

FF: Mixers are getting points now; you've got artists that are looking for larger slices of the pie; there's just so many factors now.

EC: And the points will depend on the deal. You can take what they call an advance—how much you take on the front end. Or you can do the record for a lot less, and if you believe in the artist, it's going to cost less money to physically make the record at that moment, but if it's successful, your share will be proportionally larger with the risk that you took.

TV: And the pie has been traditionally expanding since the '50s. There was no reason on earth why an artist in the '50s should get two percent, three percent—the producer usually got a salary. Our cut of the pie has been getting greater and greater, and when you look at it logically, that's where all the troubles are in the business. This slice of the pie—why is it so narrow? Even though it's getting bigger, I think it's still too narrow. I for one am happy to see mixers getting a cut of the pie, a percentage. I'd like to see everyone involved in making a record get something from that pie. Why is the cut so narrow?

FF: The pie stops at about 19 percent, 20 percent. And the rest of that pie goes, guess where? To the record company. Not only that, but I remember when CDs first came out and record companies were charging fourteen, fifteen dollars for them because it was costing them nine or ten dollars per CD to make them. And people kept saying, once they sell a lot of them, the price is going to come down, obviously. Well, now it costs them about a nickel per CD, and they're still charging fourteen or fifteen dollars a CD! And, on top of that, the producer royalties are paid after the album is recouped—but it's not the recoupment of the album per unit sales. For example, let's say the album cost $400,000 to make. It's not after the record has made $400,000 [that you get paid], it's after the record has made $400,000 after being filtered through the artist's fourteen points. So actually the record has to sell something like $2,500,000 before it starts getting recouped! So this whole thing is really skewed, and then there's this little trickle that comes out at the bottom.

EC: And you have to recoup the advance that you were paid, also.

RS: Exactly, and the artist's advance comes out of that, too.

EC: Typically, most producers don't see any royalties on most of their records.

TV: That's true.

FF: That's what my lawyer says! (laughs)

EC: If you see royalties from one out of ten or two out of ten, you're doing pretty well.

What's your advice for those who aspire to be professional record producers? What's the best career path to take?

EC: When I came up, there was no prescribed way to become an engineer. There weren't schools to go to; a lot of the gear was homemade, so every studio was different and had its own personality. So you would get a job that was basically an apprenticeship: you would start cleaning toilets, vacuuming the floors, cleaning the headphones, repairing cables. But you'd learn it from the very bottom and take years to learn it—but you'd be brought up by people that knew something, that would mentor you and bring you along and fill you in. So people that weren't that committed would fall by the wayside. At the end of a long period of time, only the people that were most committed to doing it and most loved and most compelled to do it were the ones left doing it. Right now, there's a proliferation of schools. For thirty, forty thousand dollars a year you can go to all these different schools and be taught about gear—and not know a goddamn thing when you get out. People come out and get jobs as assistant engineers in studios, or may have to become runners in studios.

FF: What I think the schools are good for, actually, is giving kids a basic fundamental knowledge of music: reading, writing, and notation. I enjoy doing a rock and roll date one day and an orchestral date the next day. And being able to read music, being able to understand musical concepts, is important. That's not to say that there aren't great engineers who don't understand music necessarily. But the down side is that many of these kids come out of these schools after investing forty or sixty thousand dollars thinking, "OK, here I am!" And what happens is, regardless of all that school training, you still go into the studio and you start cleaning the toilets, because that's the way the system is. You don't come out of a school and suddenly become a second engineer. In most of the studios I work at, for the first year, you're the gofer: you handle the phones and you go out and do the errands. After you've been there for a year, if you've shown some perseverance and you've gotten things right, then you start second engineering. But there's a real crusade that I'm on, and here's what these schools really should be teaching: You used to work at one studio all the time; the second engineer would know you, you'd know them. There was a procedure in terms of how the tapes were labeled, and everyone would know it. But now, inside of twenty days, I'll be in fifteen different studios on two or three different projects, and suddenly how the notes are taken, how the mixes are written down, how the tapes are labeled, becomes incredibly important, because six months later, you don't remember how these things were done. This is what I think some of these schools should be teaching, because that's the thing that's really going to be useful to the students when they get into a studio.

EC: Those are very important skills, and those are the skills that you build on to be able to record big dates. Those are the building blocks—knowing what's going on, understanding what you're doing there, understanding why that was a good take, we want to keep that. Putting it together and having that kind of studio sense—I don't think you can learn that in a school.

TV: Maybe you could if the curriculum was right.

Thirty, forty years ago—as you pointed out—a lot of the gear was hand-built. Today, though, you can go into a music store and buy low-cost gear that's much more sophisticated, and a lot of people are doing that—buying gear, figuring it out for themselves, and recording their friends at home. Isn't that a viable way to learn to become an engineer or producer?

FF: Whatever works for whoever it is—like I said before, let's hear it. Everyone has their own way. I started as a singer/songwriter working in my basement, recording myself on a 4-track reel-to-reel. It was just simply a tool for me to put my music down, but when the singer/songwriter thing stopped happening, I used to get a lot of comments that my demos sounded pretty good. It never entered into my mind that I was going to be an engineer or a producer. I was just using whatever I had to make my song demos.

EC: It wasn't a career option then, either. Being a recording engineer or a record producer— what the hell was that? That was some mysterious thing. And the recording studio was this place, somewhere, where this mysterious thing happened. If you wanted to record music, you would have to go there; you couldn't do it anywhere else—you would have to go to this mysterious place.

So what advice would you give to the next generation of kids who want to become record producers?

EC: In this life, you need to be a well-rounded human being. You can get this gear and know how an ADAT works and how a sampler works, but if you want to make your living being a recording engineer, you've got to know how to use microphones; you have to know what a microphone sounds like, and you have to be able to record an opera, or record a grunge metal band, or record hip-hop, or do anything. You have to be able to do those things to be well-versed, to have a lasting career.

TV: A common mistake that's being made today is getting the order of protocol reversed. People think, have, do, be: If I have this equipment, I can do it, and I can be it. That's not the way it works: It's be, do, have. Everyone says, "How do I get a great guitar sound?" It's really simple: You put the amp there, you tweak, you play, you put the mic there—and a microphone is pretty much a mirror—you put the mic in front of that great guitar sound. That's where you have to do it in the first place. So many people think that, if they get all this gear, it's going to make them sound great, but the opposite is true. I know that things are going to change—30 years from now, I don't know *what* we'll be recording on. Maybe a tomato, I don't know. (laughs) But it doesn't matter—certain principles will always apply. They applied two hundred years ago when Mozart was alive—you have to really be an artist. And being an artist means that you have to woodshed, you have to put time in, you have to practice. That is where good sounds will always come from—how you record them is irrelevant. A great performance transcends all that.

FF: But also what you have to do is you have to trust your ears.

TV: But, Frank, you have to *train* your ears.

FF: Well, I can't tell you how many times I've sat and watched sessions go on where the artist will come in and say, jeez, you know, this or that doesn't sound right, and the engineer will just sit there and start tweaking things and won't go out and listen to it in the room. And I've gone out, and I've listened to it in the room, and sometimes it really sounds horrible! So the microphone is not a magician—it's not going to change things. Sometimes you get isolated in this, but the fact is that the best thing you ever do is to go out there whenever anything's being played in the room. The first thing I do is to walk out in the room—I just want to see what it sounds like out there. Then I go inside, and now I know where to start. Then if the artist or producer says to me, "The snare sounds thin," then I can say, "Well, it sounds thin out there." Or they say, "Oh, there's a buzz on the piano," so you go out there and listen and there *is* a buzz on the piano! (laughs)

TV: That's the type of training that may be kind of old-fashioned, but it's really critical that you go out there and listen to the source of the sound. That's the secret.

FF: That's it. What you were saying is that people are getting used to hearing these things coming through equipment. They get used to hearing samplers, and they get used to devices that make their own sounds, and they forget that there are acoustical instruments that live in an environment. They forget that these instruments were developed over hundreds, even thousands of years to make the most of the acoustical environment. You have to be true to that; you have to pay attention to that. There are certain things you learn, like not putting a trumpet against a glass window—unless that's what you're looking for. You've got to sit down, and you've got to make the proper adjustments.

RS: What I'm finding a lot nowadays is that the musicians that I'm working with don't understand what they're going for. They'll listen to a CD, they'll take a snippet out of it, and they'll say, "I want the snare to sound like that." They'll call their cousin or a friend who has only a piccolo, [snare] and he comes in and he hits it, and the artist will say, "Make that sound like the Earth, Wind & Fire snare." Well, that's a deep snare—that's not a piccolo snare—and they're not grasping this, because they're not going through this process of learning, of dinking around.

FF: Well, they're used to having a bass drum sample on track 1, a snare sample on track 2, and a highhat sample on track 3—all pristine, with no leakage. But if you put a live kit out there, and there's leakage of the snare onto the bass drum, they don't know how to deal with it. And one of the things a good engineer will always do is to listen to the leakage, because it can really screw you up—or it can really help you out, be your friend. The only way to know that is to know how these things sound live, in their natural environment.

EC: Learning how to listen objectively is an acquired skill. It takes a long time to learn how to sit in front of music and listen to it and be able to pick out the balances and the timbre and the interplay between the instruments, to make sense out of it. The important thing about my apprenticeship—I worked for Bruce Swedien as his assistant for a long time—was that I learned how to listen through someone else's ears. I would sit behind him and listen through his ears through every turn of the knob, through every reverb, every mic change. Over a period of twenty years, you start to get the hang of it. That's how you learn how to make great-sounding records consistently, outing after outing.

FF: When I first started, I was a drummer. I always inherently knew the relationships of the drums, so whenever I'd work with drums, I'd get the balances. But, to me, that guitar was a one-mic thing—you put a mic in front of it, and a guitar's a guitar, you know? But when I started to work with artists, I started to realize how wrong I was. I remember the first sessions I did with Kiss—I'd started putting mics in front of the guitars, and I'd walk back into the control room, and Gene Simmons or Paul Stanley would say, "No, it's missing some of that edge, I'm not quite hearing it all there." And I'd say, "C'mon, it's a guitar! What are you talking about?" But then I started to listen through their ears, and I began to realize that all those nuances that I was picking up on the drums—about the high hat being a little bit out of balance and that overtone on the cymbal—that's happening on the guitar, that's happening on the piano. And all these musicians are hearing that. The piano player's hearing all these overtones, and you've got to listen to them. When he says, "You're not quite getting the sound on that," you have to listen. You know, initially, my first response was, "C'mon, it sounds great, now let's go!" (laughs) The most important of all is the singer. When a great singer starts saying, "There's something not happening here on the top" or "It seems like I'm pushing against something" or whatever it is they say—even if what you're hearing sounds amazing—you have to stop. Many times, you need to take a step back and stop thinking like an engineer. Your engineer chops may be saying, "This vocal sounds great—I don't care what she says," but if you actually listen, you can hear that they *are* hearing something. And then you can actually make it better. So it's important to listen through other people and to understand what they're thinking—it gives you a whole new perspective on things.

TV: As a drummer, where do you put the high hat in the mix?

FF: It's funny—for my first four years or so of engineering, I set it up like it is in front of me, but now everything I do is audience perspective.

EC: Except when the assistant reverses your room mics. (laughs)

FF: You know what the trend seems to be in England? I've come across at least three or four different projects where the toms are drummer's perspective, and the overheads are audience perspective.

TV: I know. I went through that for years.

RS: What's that about?

FF: I don't know. What is it? I don't get it.

TV: I think it's just a fuck-up. (laughs)

FF: No, I've actually asked a couple of English engineers, and they've said, "I meant to do that, that's my sound."

RS: They've got that psychedelic thing going.

TV: For years, I thought I was a fuck-up because I wasn't sure—you know, am I behind the kit? Am I in front of the kit? And then sometimes I would be in both places at once! (laughs)

FF: What's lovely about the drummer's perspective is that the toms go from left to right when you do a fill. Unfortunately, that's the only thing that works—everything else is wrong. Of course, when these guys do the sampling thing, they can put it anywhere they please.

RS: And that goes back to what a producer does. People depend on us to come up with the proper thing. We know the song, and we stick to the game plan, even though in some cases, artists will go off on tangents—they will get creative on you, and they'll try to change the original game plan that you've all agreed to. They depend on us to keep them in that box. Because they will stretch: "Let me call so-and-so and have him sing here..."

But you're feeding right into a fear that many new artists have when you use that phrase, "They will get creative on you." A producer should also be willing to go with the flow.

RS: Yes and no. Within reason.

FF: But if you've got a new artist that's got, at most, a $150,000 budget, there's not a whole lot of time for experimentation. If you're in there with Sting or U2, you can sit and you can play around, spend an afternoon trying a new approach. But especially with a new artist, you get your preproduction game plan—you sit there, you work this stuff out, there ain't a whole lot of time to start playing around.

EC: But with all the technical equipment we have now, if the artist wants to try some things, I can make them an ADAT or a DA-88, and they can go home and knock around, come back with something that's cool. That's really great, because we haven't eaten up a lot of studio time or a lot of money.

TV: One of the nice things that came out of the home studio revolution is that new artists know a lot more nowadays than new artists knew in the '70s.

EC: Recording was a mystery then.

TV: You'd get one or two guys in a group in the '70s saying, "What does this box do? What does that box do?" And you'd have to audition every goddamn sound for these guys as a courtesy; you don't want to freak them out. But nowadays a lot of kids understand how every reverb is made, how ADT, phasing, flanging, chorusing work. In some ways, that's created shortcuts for me—they've been around the block at least once, and it helps.

FF: It helps until you start hearing them say, "Can you give me half a dB of 300 on the voice?" (laughs)

EC: That's when I say, "There's the equalizer right there."

TV: But you never let an artist touch the board. It's the end of the production the day that happens.

FF: For the new artist—and we all have to go back to when *we* were starting out—there are a lot of fears. But we've all been through this. This is not something that we just started doing the other day. We've worked with the artists that are supposedly the terrors, we've worked with new artists, and, as we said before, part of this whole thing is people skills, being able to understand when someone's really getting nervous.

EC: You've got to relate to the artist, and you have to know how to react. This is a business where people are going to be mad at you—people who are powerful. I had Keith Richards in my face, cutting me a new asshole, and you've got to react in the right way. Fortunately, I was invited back to do a couple more records, but if you flip out or take it the wrong way, you're on the street on your ass.

TV: You have to understand that these people are in a very vulnerable place. I never forget that. If you're thinking of ripping a new asshole...well, you do whatever it takes, but the producer cannot lose his temper. Everybody's in a vulnerable state, they're worried about their career, there's a lot of money at stake. I call it the blues. It happens at the end of the album, in the middle of the mix, just before the mix. The artist looks at you and says, "It's a total piece of shit, it's all wrong." Then you have to sit and spend hours showing them all the possibilities. The producer is not allowed that luxury, but every artist goes through it.

EC: Well, you are allowed that luxury on the drive home, when you can ask yourself, "What was I thinking?" (laughs)

TV: But it happens. That's when you have to use your people skills, if you have any, or if you think you have any. That's where they come in. That's the part that's not musical, it's not technical.

EC: It takes a lot of courage to get through an album. For the artist, there's a lot of money involved, there's a lot of pressure brought to bear; people's lives are at stake. As the producer or the engineer, you're probably going to be able to go ahead and work again, but the artist may not have that luxury.

RS: It's interesting that you would say that, because we're not allowed to make mistakes! If I miss a punch after twelve hours, you would think that I unleashed a fucking nuclear weapon! (laughs)

EC: So how many engineers does it take to change a light bulb? None—the assistant did it the night before.

Part One

Inspiration

Glen Ballard

In 1995, a young Canadian singer burst upon the scene, releasing an album that forever changed the landscape of the music business. Her name was Alanis Morissette,
and the album was *Jagged Little Pill.* Not only did it yield three hit singles and dominate the charts for close to a year, it ended up selling over 15 million copies worldwide, setting
an all-time record for a debut recording.

Oh, and did we mention that it was recorded on ADATs in a home studio?

Glen Ballard was Morissette's producer and collaborator on that fateful album and on the
follow-up *Supposed Former Infatuation Junkie* a few years later. A protégé of famed producer/arranger
Quincy Jones, Ballard already had a long and distinguished track record on the day that
Morissette appeared at the door of his home studio with a sheaf of lyrics and an idea about making a new kind of record. He was the man behind the board for the '90s female trio Wilson Philips,
crafting their hit "Hold On" as well as a string of successful albums and singles for a diverse crop
of artists, ranging from Teddy Pendergrass to Curtis Stigers, and from Barbra Streisand to Paula
Abdul. An accomplished instrumentalist, arranger, and songwriter, he had already written hits
for the likes of Michael Jackson, Aretha Franklin, Al Jarreau, George Strait, and Earth, Wind &
Fire. Today he heads up his own label—Java Records—where he maintains an active schedule
and continues to work with both established and new artists. But Ballard will forever be known
as the man who, in true harmony with an artist of rare vision and talent, guided a record from
a home studio to the top of the charts, proving once and for all that, yes, it can be done.

How much of *Jagged Little Pill* was actually recorded in a home studio?

It was 75 percent done in my home studio, which certainly is a professional situation, but
is not a commercial studio. The entire genesis of every track was done there, so everything was
created in that environment, just with the two of us. When we overdubbed drums and other
musicians, that was kind of postproduction, almost.

All of it was recorded on black-face 16-bit ADATs, and it was never bounced to any oth-
er format—it was mixed off the ADATs. We even used the ADAT's onboard A/D converters.
There were no upgrades, no extras, no nothing—it was just off the rack. And I have to tell you,
I think those original ADATs sounded amazing; in some ways, I miss the sound. I can't tell
you why, but it just jumps out at me. I listen to "Jagged Little Pill," and, God, it sounds alive.
At the time, I liked the way it sounded, and I like the way it sounds right now. These days,

I'm working with Pro Tools, but that was ADAT—give it its due.

Was it mixed in a professional studio?

We did some overdubs on one song at Westlake, but the entire album was mixed in my studio on a Euphonix console.

It's a recording that proves that the magic comes from the talent of the artist and the producer and not from the equipment.

Well, I have a couple of analog multitrack machines, and I didn't use them on the record, because I wanted the freedom to be able to move things around and to edit. With analog, you're further removed from being able to do that—you've either got to move it to another platform or cut tape, which I'm really not interested in doing now.

Did you also edit directly on the ADATs?

Yeah, the only edits we did were from ADAT to ADAT. It was usually just arrangement, maybe adding another four bars of guitar, or whatever. We would just do offsets; we got really good at that! It's much easier now on a Pro Tools system, but we certainly accomplished the same thing and were able to stay in the digital domain through the light-pipe optical cabling.

So there was only the one analog-to-digital conversion—through the ADAT's onboard converters—and then it stayed digital all the way through.

Yeah. I think one of the big positive factors was having a great mic for Alanis to sing through—a vintage C12—going into a Demeter preamp, into an LA-2A, and then straight to tape. So we had a pretty nice analog stage for a lot of the stuff before we got it to ADAT.

So there was no equalization on the vocal on the way in?

None. Occasionally, with some of the guitar stuff, there might be a little bit of board EQ. I also have a Pultec equalizer, which I'd sometimes use lightly on the bass. I also have a Massenburg stereo EQ, which we'd occasionally put across the mix [bus].

Was the vocal chain you used with Alanis developed after a lot of experimentation with different mics and preamps?

Well, I have a pretty decent selection of tube mics—I've got a C12, an M 49, a U 47, and a U 67. The first time I heard this particular C12, I thought it had incredible top end, and yet it was really warm in the lower mids. So it's got this wonderful combination of brilliant highs and still a real warm, tube thing. I always loved that mic, although it's not right for every singer. But the first time Alanis sang with me, I just put it up because I thought this would be the right mic for her, and I've never changed.

So you didn't audition other mics on her?

No, I didn't. I just loved the way she sounded on it so much—it was right. At one point, the capsule fried, so I used the U 67 on her, and it was much inferior. So I got the C12 fixed really quickly! (laughs) It's a delicate baby—it's older than I am!

How much compression do you apply to Alanis's vocal?

It was just under medium compression, and I was riding the level to tape with my left hand at the same time. Her voice has an incredible dynamic range, and I usually have one or two chances to get it on tape—she's a one-take singer—so it was a heightened experience for me! (laughs) And after cutting a track all day, engineering everything, it could get pretty interesting.

On "You Oughta Know," I definitely scorched the vocal—the preamp was too high, and it was distorting—but there it is! (laughs) It was literally a one-take vocal, and it was so stunning, that was it. I knew I had a couple of scorch marks on that one, but nobody seemed to mind. Certainly she had the courage to say, "I love this—let's not take all the life out of it by redoing and sanitizing," and I certainly enjoyed that kind of attitude of, "Let's put it on tape with energy and leave it there."

It's the same kind of attitude you find on some of the old jazz recordings of the '50s and early '60s.

In some ways it really was, except that it was just me playing by myself. I would sequence the basic track and the drum track and toss it on tape and put a couple of guitars on—basically create the whole track before she sang, even though I knew what she was going to be singing, because we'd been writing it. It was usually one or two takes for me, too. She was really interested in it being in that moment, so I didn't really fix much of anything. It shows my deficiencies as a guitar player, but I think on some level, whatever style I have is apparent, because I wasn't thinking about it too hard—I was hoping I was in tune, and go.

Paul McCartney has said that there's something to be said about the immediacy of making a record—how it can be productive to not have too long to think about what you're doing. I imagine he was referring to The Beatles' first album, which was done in a day, but then, of course, they went on to longer studio projects, like _Sgt. Pepper_.

There's something to be said for both [approaches]. For something to really work on a spontaneous level, you have to be prepared—you have to have prepared yourself to get to the moment where you can credibly get something together and have it work and not sound completely naive. The interesting thing is that Alanis as a singer had done her homework. She had made a couple of albums when she was in high school; she even made a record when she was ten years old. So at the age of nineteen and twenty, she was really coming into it with a skill set that most nineteen or twenty-year-olds would not have, and certainly I've made a lot of records, done a lot of arranging and a lot of programming—sort of the whole gamut. I've made my share of records that take three to six to eight months—I've been through that—and when we got together, I think we were both prepared to take the craft that we had incorporated from our past experiences and really apply it in a much more spontaneous way. It certainly was the backup that enabled us to make a record in a day—write it and make it—and then do the same thing the next day.

That's probably what makes _Jagged Little Pill_ so unique.

Well, I've never been able to blast through three weeks and have seven or eight songs, and then do another three or four weeks and have another seven or eight songs, all essentially done. So there was certainly a high tide for both of us at that time, to really tap into something special, something that was greater than the sum of our parts.

And it was really a true collaboration, too.

It was the best collaboration I've ever had. Not that it diminishes anything I'm doing now or anything I've done before, but certainly that first record was ideal, in terms of the collaboration. We were completely in sync, and we were each bringing something to the party that wouldn't be there without the other. That's what you hope for in a creative relationship.

You've said in an interview that you and Alanis realized early on that you were both pre-

pared to go where you *felt* things should go as opposed to where you *thought* things should go. What's the distinction between the two?

I was talking about immediacy and trying to achieve this kind of visceral connection with the music without analyzing it the second it's created. I think we were simply trying to create something that we liked, and we weren't thinking about the marketplace. We were just trying to have fun with it and satisfy our own tastes and really kind of remove it from the whole process of making a "commercial record." I certainly had done my share of that, and she had done some of that, too, in terms of making records that weren't necessarily an artistic expression for her but were great places to learn how to make records. Being in that moment, being able to feel it rather than analyze it, was why we were able to just go into this trance and let it guide the process, as opposed to thinking our way through and calculating it. There were no expectations that we were trying to fulfill, other than our own taste at the moment. I was doing it for the fun of it and for the love of it, because it did feel so good to me. It was a really innocent, joyous time for both of us. I hear it on there now; I listen to it, and I

> **"So much of what's really good about what an artist does comes from outside himself."**

think, gosh, we were definitely having fun, and we were definitely in another zone. We didn't know exactly what we were doing, but I can hear how we were satisfying our own tastes.

It's almost like you were connecting with some kind of higher energy, as New Age as that sounds.

I certainly feel that. And I'm a very practical, down-to-earth person who works very hard every day making records and writing and arranging and running a record company. But I'm also humble enough to know that so much of what's really good about what an artist does comes from outside himself. Or at least what he or she's got on the inside taps into something from the outside, and suddenly you get this through line, and there's this inspired kind of connection. I certainly felt it on that record; it was very palpable to me.

There was a moment early on in the process—it was probably in June of '95, and we were working in my studio; it's a very calm environment with lots of trees and windows you can see out, and you don't even really know where you are; you feel like you're in the country. The longest day of the year is June 21st, and I remember we were writing a song that day, and the light was so amazingly lambent. It was one of those long days, and we were writing a song that we really loved, and it was like, gosh, there's something definitely going on here! I'll never forget that moment—the light was perfect, and there was something surreal about it. That light, I think it infuses that whole first record, for me.

How did that contrast with the experience of recording *Supposed Former Infatuation Junkie*, after Alanis had been on the road and had a chance to enjoy the fruits of her success? Was the collaborative process different the second time around?

I think it was different. It was probably a little less satisfying for me and a little more satisfying for her. I love the record, but I think that she really was interested in expanding the form of what she did. She wanted to take a more dense lyrical approach and wanted the freedom to kind of smudge the boundaries a little bit in terms of structure, in terms of how much you could actually say in a song. There was a real desire for her to break out of a more conventional song structure and to really let that be the predicate for what we were doing. I have such respect for her as an artist and as a singer and as a writer—for the words that she pulls out of her soul—that there was no question that that was the way we were going to do it. But because there are literally more words, it was a bit more of a challenge for me to try to incorporate all that, though I think we pulled it off.

Alanis has such a deep and abiding intellectual curiosity and artistic vision. I think she really did want to say, "OK, *Jagged Little Pill*—that was then, and this is where I am right now, and I can't really even refer to that record." I always told her, "Whatever you want to do is what we're going to do. We're not going to revisit *Jagged Little Pill* and try to write it sideways and somehow suddenly start listening to that to inspire us for this next record." She took time off to really let the well fill up again; she wasn't just doing it because it was time to make another record or because the marketplace was demanding it.

It's a glossier production, too. I gather it wasn't done on ADATs the second time around.

Well, you know, it was! (laughs) It was done on the 20-bit ADATs, but it was one of the last things I did on ADAT, because once the 24-bit Pro Tools came along, it was, just, how can I not go there? I didn't like the way the 16-bit Pro Tools sounded—I much preferred the ADAT sound to that—but clearly the platform offers so many advantages, it's a disadvantage not to use it now.

Were you still using the ADAT's onboard converters?

Yep. Same vocal chain, same mixer—the Euphonix at my studio. Like *Jagged Little Pill*, it was mixed there, too. We went to DAT and to half inch analog, and, like *Jagged Little Pill*, I think about two-thirds of the final mixes came off the analog half inch, and a couple of the mixes, we just liked the way they sounded on DAT. So it was pretty much the same setup—the only difference was that it was 20-bit ADAT.

It's a denser recording, though. Did you use more tracks on the second album?

It's denser, yeah. Again, we started with everything just the way we did it before—the two of us in my studio. Then we took it into Royaltone, which is a wonderful, big commercial studio, and the band played along with the basic tracks that we had. So there's a lot more of her band involved on that record than on the first record; it's really more of an ensemble.

At Royaltone, were the overdubs also recorded on ADATs?

Yeah, everything. We just kept it in that format. But we probably didn't go beyond 32 tracks on any song. On *Jagged Little Pill*, I don't think we went beyond 20, ever, and some songs had just 9 tracks. *Infatuation Junkie* is denser; it has more tracks, more words, more backgrounds, more everything. (laughs) And because it's denser, it takes up more room sonically.

It's more of a hi-fi album, for want of a better word.

Yeah, I think you're right.

What's the story behind the guitar hum on "That I Would Be Good"?

(laughs) That was a complete accident. That's a 60-cycle hum with some reverb on it. I played the song on my Telecaster, and it's got this single-coil pickup, so it's a noisy guitar unless you're sitting just right. But because I was recording it myself, I couldn't really do anything about it— I just hit record, jumped over and grabbed the guitar and started playing on it; I was sitting on the floor with Alanis, and she was actually singing it while I was playing it. I listened back to it and thought, gosh, that hum has got to go. Later, she went home, and before she came in the next day, I replayed the guitar and cleaned it up. When she came back in, she freaked out, saying, "What happened to that guitar? " I said, "I didn't erase the original, I promise!" So she made me put it back.

The hum almost sounds like it's changing pitch along with the chord changes.

It's an aural illusion, a harmonic accident. I know I'm blowing my street credibility here, but it was a complete accident! (laughs) Not only that, but I was trying to get rid of it! I was saying, "We can't live with this," but she always fights for the authenticity of the moment, and she's always right. I guess that giving yourself the opportunity is what's important—being willing to go with it. We're big on just, "let's do it."

I don't think the listener cares about perfection. They just want to feel the emotion of the communication. That comes in many forms, but what we sometimes do in the studio is we spend 90 percent of our time on stuff that's worth about 10 percent—the absolute detail of everything that, at the end of the day, probably doesn't matter. It doesn't mean that we don't obsess over it and try to make it perfect—or at least as good as it can be—but sometimes it's almost like it's either there or it's not. It's got to be there as a basic thrust, or a lot of the other stuff doesn't matter. It's just got to feel right, and if it doesn't feel right, it's probably never going to be right.

> *"What we sometimes do in the studio is we spend 90 percent of our time on stuff that's worth about 10 percent."*

And the real art of the producer is knowing when it *is* right, having the courage of your convictions.

With the technology that's available to us now, it's very easy to do a couple of things. First of all, it's very easy to postpone any kind of decision-making, because you can literally record as many takes as you want and keep everything. So you can postpone what you should really be deciding on right then and there. Secondly, you can obviously clean up everything: You can tune vocals, you can time-adjust everything—you can really make it all perfect, on paper. That technology is available to anybody that wants to make a reasonably modest investment. So, given that fact, the real challenge is to know when *not* to use all of that stuff, and really to find out the essence of what it is you're trying to accomplish. You can make it perfect—that's easy, the tools are there—but that's not what we're doing here. We're trying to get the magic, and the magic is none of those things. Those tools can help, but more than ever, you've got to feel it—it's almost like you have to not think about it and really be emotional with your approach, because that's still at the heart of it.

That sounds like the kind of thing you would have learned from Quincy Jones.

Absolutely. Anything that's worth knowing about making records and about dealing with artists, I would give him full credit for. Starting with his deep love of music and how deeply he *feels* music, even as he's deeply educated in all forms of music. He probably has the deepest knowledge of music of anyone that I know, whether it's the origin of African rhythms and talking drums, whether it's orchestral, or jazz, or pop—he's fluent in all the musical areas. To him, it's all about the feeling of it—creating an atmosphere where people feel safe and creative and warm and want to give it up out of joy and love. So certainly he's been the biggest influence on me in that regard, and I love him like a father.

Did he impart technical skills to you as well?

Well, he's not really a technical guy. He's a musical guy, and he didn't spend a lot of time on the technical stuff. Bruce Swedien was his longtime engineer, and he let Bruce do his thing—and Bruce is a meticulous, brilliant recorder. Quincy was much more interested in getting performances. Certainly, if he didn't like the way something sounded, he would say so, but otherwise he was not into sitting down and EQing something on his own. He was very good at delegating that—much better than I am, because I'm such a hands-on person.

I have to laugh sometimes when I'm with a real engineer, because I'm constantly messing up levels! (laughs) Pretty soon they have to back everything down because I end up pushing all the faders up—it's just my enthusiasm. So I'm no master engineer. I do understand it, and I've certainly learned from great engineers like Bruce and Jack Joseph Puig, guys that really know what they're doing—Bill Schnee and people like that who really do get it and know it from the ground floor up. But that part of it was never Quincy's thing; to him, it was always, if it's feeling good, then it's right. But he was always highly interested in the music, the minutiae of the arrangement, for sure.

What sort of common mistakes are you hearing in the tapes you hear that are coming out of project studios?

I guess if I have any complaint, it's that people tend to over-sing stuff right now. I like hearing a melody first and then a variation on that melody, and I think there's kind of a trend right now for people to start off with licks, and then they sing more licks—vocal gymnastics—and it seems a little bit of an overkill to me. If it's a good melody, I don't think it needs to be embellished in the first verse, but that's just personal taste; I think people have become used to singers showing off vocally.

I love hearing people be inventive, and I hear a lot of incredible programming going on out there, but I still love to hear real instruments wherever possible. I sit around and I program all day long, but there's still something wonderful about having a couple of people play together, which I don't think you get any other way, other than having them do that.

Is a strong melody the key for you? Is that what it takes on a demo to get your attention?

Not necessarily. I think, ultimately, if a song is going to mean anything outside of just zeitgeist, it has to have melody. And ten years from now, when we look back, I think the songs people will remember are the ones that have melodies. But sometimes it's just the feeling; sometimes it's just the groove; sometimes it can be just one simple thing in a track that makes it work.

It's also melody in context with the harmonic structure, because the color of a melody is always determined by the chords under it. For me, as a musician, it's always fun to find out how you can really change the emotional context of a melody with different chords.

That was another hallmark of your collaboration with Alanis—unexpected chord changes under a melody, or unexpected melody over a standard chord change.

Well, we were just firing on all cylinders. I remember, when we were writing "You Oughta Know," it's in F# minor for the verse, and then we go to F# major for the chorus, which is a bit unusual. I remember that I hit the major third, and she went right there—it was just like, wow! So, yeah, we definitely had some fun. We did a couple of tricky things and hopefully you don't even know that it's tricky, but I think within the pop music form, we did have some fun with melody and harmonic structure, which I always love to do. Coming from the Quincy Jones school, he's such a master musician, he always appreciated that in me—that there was an element of harmonic sophistication.

And musical surprise—things not necessarily going where the ear is expecting them to go.

Well, I'm usually just trying to get myself off on that regard, and when people feel it, I'm just thrilled.

One of the hardest things for the home recordist is dealing with the low end—getting it tight and full without it being flabby and woofy. Any advice there?

Absolutely: Get a Minimoog! (laughs) Ninety percent of the bass I do is Minimoog. I think it's the best way to solve low-end problems—that and being real careful with the pattern of the kick drum. Because the Minimoog has three oscillators, you can cover so much ground with it, and there are MIDIable versions of them now, so you can sequence with them. I've always had such great luck with that as my bass, and you can get an infinite variety of sounds with it— the filtering can be incredible, you can adjust the sustain. It has so many colors, and yet it's about the richest bottom end harmonic element that I've ever come across. The Minimoog is just such a workhorse for me—I can't do without it.

Do you compress it when you record it?

Not very much. It depends on the part. Sometimes I do and, again, I might go through the Pultec for a little EQ and then to the LA-2A. But usually not—it just has such a satisfying resonance. It's warm, and yet it can be very defined. It just has an infinite number of applications for me.

On many of your records, it sounds like the kick drum is sitting above the bass, with a toppier sound.

That's probably because I cover so much ground with the Minimoog, since I usually have one of the oscillators down an octave. One of the first things I do with any track—and all of the Alanis stuff, certainly—is to get the bass and drum pattern pretty much locked, and that's usually where I start. It's not a conscious decision—it's just the way I hear it.

When you mix, do you start with those two elements?

I don't do that much mixing. The only thing I mixed on her record was "Hand In My Pocket," and that was strictly by accident. It was the end of the night, and it was, just, OK, this is it. And we could never beat it.

Chris Fogel mixed both of those records, and I think he just pushes up the faders and tries to hear the song first and then starts defining what needs to be defined. I think the best mixers listen to it as a song first, because you can spend all this time on the kick and the snare and the bass and it's perfect—and then you get everything else in and it's completely different. You've got to keep it in context as often as you can. If you're [spending] five hours on the kick drum, then you're in trouble.

But the key is the interplay between the bass part and the kick drum; it's all about that. If you've got that right, it's going to have exponentially more impact and definition, so I really try to keep those things in sync. The impact of a Minimoog and the right kick drum pattern—jeez, it's remarkable.

What advice do you have for the reader who wants to be the next Glen Ballard?

I think the best advice is to get hands-on with everything you can. Learn Pro Tools, because you can accomplish so much in that one box now—you don't really need anything else. At the same time, learn as much music as you can to go with it, because one without the other isn't enough. I started out as a musician and I learned engineering and programming just because it was an easier and more efficient way for me to express myself as a musician and as an arranger. But if you have both of those things, you're in good shape.

And learn to be sensitive to artists; if you're working with other artists, give them an extra measure of patience and encouragement. It's kind of like tending your garden—it can be very satisfying.

You know, I'm always studying. It seems like I'm getting software updates every two weeks for everything I've got, and I'm still studying music; I'm still trying to make up for my days as a music student, when I wasn't such a great student. So it's a constant learning process, and if you learn one thing every day, at the end of the year you'll be a lot smarter, I promise.

Selected Listening:
Alanis Morisette: *Jagged Little Pill*, Maverick, 1995; *Supposed Former Infatuation Junkie*, Maverick, 1998
Wilson Phillips: *Wilson Phillips*, SBK, 1990; *Shadows And Light*, Gold Rush, 1992
Paula Abdul: *Forever Your Girl*, Atlantic, 1990
Corrs: *Talk On Corners*, Atlantic, 1998
Barbra Streisand: *Till I Loved You*, Columbia, 1988
Teddy Pendergrass: *Workin' It Back*, Asylum, 1985

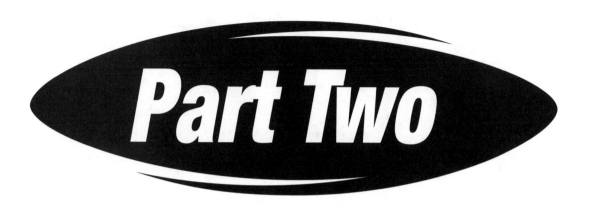

Roots

Al Schmitt

Legendary is a word that is often bandied about too freely. But what else could you say about a man whose first session was for the Duke Ellington Orchestra and whose work continues to dominate the charts? After more than half a century behind the board, Schmitt is universally acknowledged as being one of the absolute masters of his trade, a fact that is reflected in the multitude of Grammys he has won and in the more than 150 gold and platinum records he has produced, engineered, and/or mixed for an incredibly wide range of artists: from Henry Mancini to Steely Dan; from Frank Sinatra to Jefferson Airplane; from Eddie Fisher to Duane Eddy; from Barbra Streisand to Neil Young. Soft-spoken yet intense, Schmitt took some time out to talk with us in between sessions for Diana Krall's *When I Look In Your Eyes*—a project that has since won him the 1999 Grammy for Best Engineered Album of the year.

How do you feel the rise of the home studio has impacted on how records are made today?

In general, the demos that I get now sound better than a lot of records that were made 15, 20 years ago. A lot of it comes from the sharing of information between musicians and the fact that they loan one another gear. I do a lot less work on overdubbing things like guitars and keyboards and synth parts than I used to do, because a majority of it now is being done at home. So I work with an artist, and we'll do the basic tracks; when everything's done, we'll transfer stuff over to ADATs or DA-88s, and they'll take that home and put all the other stuff on that we used to spend hours in the studio doing. When they get all the overdubs done, we bring it in, we dump it back in, do whatever finessing we have to do, and then we mix it. So it's helping with budgets and so forth.

Is it possible to make a good acoustic recording without a top-of-the-line microphone?

I'm a microphone freak, and I know that a lot of the microphone companies are getting into making microphones for less than a thousand dollars that are great. The one that kills me is the Neumann 103—that's a fabulous microphone. Audio-Technica is also making some good microphones for reasonable amounts of money. I've been using the Neumann for dates—and it's rare for me to use a cheap microphone on dates—but I've been using it on guitar on an album I just finished, and I used it on trumpet in a section. It sounded fabulous.

If you're working with an inexpensive mic versus a $10,000 mic, is the placement the same or different?

The placement is pretty much the same. Even with real expensive microphones, no two microphones sound exactly alike; I don't care what anybody tells you.

But will you put them in the same place?

Yeah, I would start out that way, but that doesn't mean I'm going to leave it that way. First of all, it depends on the player and how he plays. Moving the mic an inch can make all the difference in the world. The most important thing is to stand out there when the guy's playing. Whether it's trombone or trumpet or violin, listen to what it sounds like, then try to place the mic where you think it should be placed. One of the best gauges is the guy that's playing the instrument himself. The player can give you a general idea of where the best place is for the sound that they put out, so you should start in that direction. The best friend an engineer has in the studio is the musician. You've *got* to be friends with the musician—you've got to get out there, you've got to make his life easier, because he's going to make *your* life easier. The more comfortable they are, the better they play, and the easier it is to make records.

> "The best friend an engineer has in the studio is the musician."

Do you ever experiment with miking at the musician's ears?

I've tried that a few times. It doesn't always work, and it also depends on what else is going on. If you're just overdubbing a musician, maybe you can do that, but if you get other things going on in the same room, in the same vicinity, it doesn't always work that well. You've got to have some sort of separation; you can't have what's playing three or four feet away louder in the mic than the guy that you're trying to mic. Except that you do want to capture the ambience and the leakage, because that's what makes the thing sound big. You have to keep that in mind when you're placing microphones—and also when you're positioning the musicians. Most guys who have studios at home are usually doing one instrument at a time—it's usually an overdubbing thing. They usually don't have a rhythm section in there, so they won't have that problem.

How do you generally mic acoustic guitars?

It depends on what kind of guitar it is. If it's a round hole guitar, I'll usually put the microphone off the hole, maybe 18 inches away. And I'll have the mic up a little, facing down towards the hole. We just did some acoustic guitar on this Diana Krall record, and I used a C12. It's a $10,000 microphone, and it sounded wonderful. But you can get by with AKG 451s; certain Schoeps are good. I've also tried this new Neumann 103 that sounded great on acoustic guitar, and we were very happy with that.

So you work down by the hole, not up by the frets?

No, down at the hole. Sometimes I use two microphones—I may have one up on the frets and one down by the hole. But the hole is there for a reason. It's like when you're miking a bass—you don't put the mic way up on top on the bass, you put the mic down where the F-hole is. I'll put up a tube U 47, and it usually just sounds wonderful. I had a guy in just recently, and with the tube 47 the bottom end of the bass was great, but I wasn't getting that nice top, so I took a Schoeps and I put it up where his left hand would be—I had it up high—and I just touched a little of it in there, but it gave me that top end, and the bass sounded great. The bass player was thrilled because he said he never gets that kind of sound.

If you're using two mics on an acoustic guitar, would you record it in stereo?

If I have the availability of tracks, yes. If not, I'll blend them together.

But will you look for a stereo image?

Not really. You may get a little bit of imaging, but I wouldn't try to get a real broad stereo image on it—maybe just a little bit. And even if I was going to pan it off center, it would just be a little off—a little left and a little right of center—just to give it a little bit of stereo.

How do you approach electric guitar amp miking?

I learned a long time ago that 99 percent of the time a [Shure] 57 works. I'll put up good microphones, and the musician will usually say, "That's not quite what I really want to hear," so then I'll stick a 57 up and they'll say, "That's it!" So I'll do that, and then I'll put a really good mic up—maybe a Neumann U 67 or an M 50—for the room

How far away would the room mic be placed?

It depends on the room. It could be anywhere from 15 to 20 feet.

And the close mic, is that on axis?

Yes, on axis, and a little off the center of the cone, on axis.

When you record electric bass, do you typically use some amp, or is it always just DI?

I use a Demeter tube DI, and my chain on that is, it goes into the Demeter, into a Summit. I'll limit maybe a dB—I want to get the tube sound—and that's it. No EQ.

So you don't typically use bass amps at all.

Very, very rarely. And if I do, then I'll try maybe a FET 47 on the bass amp. But very rarely do we do that anymore; I don't get the call for it much.

What's your approach to recording acoustic piano?

I know that Ed Cherney says the most difficult thing in the world to record is the human voice; I say the piano is the most difficult instrument to record well. I've been doing so many piano records—I work with Joe Sample, Bill Evans, on and on and on. Lately, I've been using the new Neumann M 149s on piano. If it's a solo instrument—and by that I mean if the artist is not singing—I'll use an AKG C24 stereo microphone, off the piano. So I'll have the two M 149s close in on the piano, and then off the piano—if you open the piano lid, just where it curves—I'll have the C24 right up in there. If I have the tracks, I'll use four tracks, and then I can blend them in however I want to.

Where do you place the close mics?

The close mics are usually a couple of feet off the high end and a couple of feet off the low end, kind of at 45 degree angles to each other. And then you move them around a little bit. Again, it depends on the player, it depends on the instrument. Again, I'm lucky in that I'm working with the kind of artists where we rent nine-foot German Steinways, so the pianos all sound good.

Have you done much recording of upright pianos?

Sure. I used to do all that stuff with Mancini years ago—there were a lot of upright pianos. I used to put two mics behind the piano, off the sounding board. You've got to place the mics where they pick up all 88 keys.

So you'd work in stereo.

Yes, but if a guy's doing an effect where he's just playing something up on the high end, then you just worry about that part of it, just zero in on that section.

Do you often re-amp DI signals?

I do that all the time when I'm mixing—I'll feed signal through really good speakers out in the room and then put some mics up reasonably close to the speakers and then maybe some mics further back. I might even use a little bit of delay on it.

What's your take on the resurgence of tube gear over the last few years?

Well, for me, it's not a resurgence, since tube gear is all I ever use! (laughs) I like old boards—Neve consoles and APIs—and I use all-tube microphones on my sessions. If you walk in on one of my sessions when I'm doing a big orchestra date, there might be thirty mics out there, and they'll all be tube microphones—and 95 percent of them will be Neumanns.

I think my all-time favorite mic ever made—for a microphone that does anything—is the [U] 67. I use it on strings; I'm using it on Diana's vocals; you can use it on upright bass; you can use it on saxes, trombones, trumpets. To me, it's the most flexible mic made that sounds really good. If I was going to buy one mic, that would be the one I would buy, although now they're very expensive. I'm sorry I didn't buy all those mics for $300–400 apiece when I had the opportunity!

You mentioned that you sometimes use a little light limiting when you're recording bass.

Yeah, but I mostly do hand limiting, where on the vocals you ride the fader; I still do that a lot. When I use a limiter or compression, it'll be for sound or for an effect. Maybe I'll squash the hell out of a sound if I'm looking for a certain effect on it, but in general I use very little EQ and very little limiting.

I know that, in recording, you get sounds from mic placement rather than from EQ, but do you use very little EQ on your mixes too?

Yeah—I almost try to turn it off. If you look over my shoulder at the board, you'll see very few EQs.

Do you find yourself using more compression on mixing than during tracking, or do you still keep it very light?

Very light. If a compressor is [affecting] 2 or 3 dB, for me, that's an awful lot.

So I guess I shouldn't even ask if you ever strap one across the stereo bus.

You know, I've done that; in fact, I just did that recently on [a project where] we were trying to match something that was done in Japan, and it needed a little bit of compression overall. I wound up using an old SSL stereo limiter, and it sounded pretty good, but I only did like a dB and a half on it. It did work.

Do you do a lot of digital recording, or are you still sticking with analog?

I stick with analog mostly, but I do some digital. Digital is getting better and better, but I still prefer analog. At some point, there won't be any more analog; someday we won't have tape machines any more—it will all be going into the computer, they'll have the sound down so well. Hopefully, I'll be out fishing when that comes about! (laughs)

What's the most common problem that you hear in tapes coming out of project studios?

The biggest mistakes that happen in project studios are the result of the monitoring systems. I get stuff where 90 percent of the time it's overloaded with low end for some reason; I think they try to overcompensate for [monitoring deficiencies] in some way.

> **"The biggest mistakes that happen in project studios are the result of the monitoring systems."**

So I guess the assumption has to be that some of the monitors that people are using in project studios are bass light.

They're either bass light, or something's going on [acoustically] in the rooms they are in. I've got to say that, in general, I'm really impressed with stuff coming out of project studios. But no matter how good the equipment is, or how good the speakers are or anything else, a big part of it depends on the guy that's putting it together—the engineer/producer/musician or whoever is doing it. A lot of guys don't know how to balance things, so what sounds right to them may be totally wrong to me.

What are your personal favorite monitors?

I use the Mastering Lab monitors—the hybrid that they put together with the Tannoy 10. I have four of those; I'm trying to get another one so I can do my surround mixes on them. But I did [Natalie Cole's] *Unforgettable* on NS10s. My wife is an audiophile, and she rarely ever comes to the studio, but she came to this studio and she saw the NS10s and she just gave me a working over about, how can you do this? (laughs) You've got $50,000 worth of musicians out there playing their hearts out, and you're listening on this $300 crap, you know? (laughs) But it's just what you get used to.

So are you recommending that people stick with NS10s in their project studios?

In an oblique way, I am. The reason why NS10s got so popular was that every studio had them. Years ago it was the Big Reds with the crossover networks and all that. When it got down to the nearfields, in every studio there was a pair of Auratones, the "Horrortones," as we used to call them. Now, with the advent of all these great new nearfield speakers, you walk in the studio and everybody's got different monitors.

In what order do you bring faders up during a mix?

I start from the bottom up, like building a house—I put the foundation down. So it's the bass, the kick, the drums, then getting my echoes set—I have certain kinds of echoes I like to use on things. Then maybe I'll put the guitar or keyboard in. When I get the rhythm section set, then I may stick the vocal in for awhile and just kind of get that comfortable, get my echoes right. Then I'll take the vocal out and start adding other things in—violins or wood-winds or brass. Then I'll pump the vocal back in just to make sure we've got a relationship, and I'll take the vocal back out again and fine tune things, work on my echoes. I don't use a lot of echo, but I use a lot of *different* echoes. I may use as many as eight different chambers on a mix—sometimes more, all at different lengths. I try not to overburden the chamber with too many things going in.

So you only send one or two sources to each echo.

Right. And that's pretty much it. I mix fast, so I can usually do a couple of mixes a day; I've done as many as four or five in a day on jazz albums. In general, even if it's large orchestral things and vocals, I'll always get two a day. But I work on the rhythm, getting that foundation first, making sure that's right and making sure the vocal is sitting in the right spot and with the right echo. If I'm working at Capitol, I try to get that live chamber on vocals as much as I can—that's a great chamber. If I'm not mixing there, I use the old EMT250 plate—the R2D2—on vocals or my [TC Electronics] M5000, or I may use a combination of the two of them. I'll just finesse that for awhile—I may spend 20 minutes just working on that, setting different blends, decay times and so forth, until I get exactly what I want. And that's all that will go to the vocal—those chambers will *only* be used for that; I won't put anything else in there. But on each tune it will be different—I won't use the same setup on each song.

What sort of tricks have you come up with to get a problematic vocal track to sit in a mix?

You've got to equalize and set it right, though you don't want to overdo that. Again, you should do hand limiting to make sure that you even the vocal out, because if you overdo a limiter, squashing it is not quite the same. Even taking a vocal [track] and putting it into a speaker in the room; sometimes just adding in a tiny bit of that—almost inaudible—will help give it a little depth and help it sit better. But fixing things in the mix usually doesn't work. (laughs)

What is your general approach to recording vocals?

Well, you've got to use a good windscreen, certainly—you've got to make sure that the artist isn't swallowing the mic. That's one mistake that a lot of people make—they get too close on top of the mic, and the diaphragm just doesn't work right when you're that close. My recommendation is that you stick your thumb to your nose and then spread your fingers out; you shouldn't be any closer than that. In general, try to keep the singer anywhere from nine inches to a foot away from the microphone.

Do you usually use a large diaphragm condenser mic for vocals?

Yes, but even if you're not, you still don't want the singer to swallow the mic.

Do you mic vocals directly on axis?

It depends on the artist. Some people have a lot of sibilance problems, and you're going to try to adjust for that; others have major pop problems, even with wind screens. Sometimes if a person sings down, I'll have the mic below them so they are singing into it; sometimes they sing up, and I'll have the mic up. The chain I normally use is the microphone to a really good preamp. I've been using the Martech [preamp] lately or the Mastering Lab preamp—I like both of those a lot, so it's one or the other. Then I'll go into the Summit, compress it a dB or so, and that's it—I hand limit the rest. But when you're doing it at home, try to keep things on axis. Also, there's a reason that there's red on the meter; it means be careful. You don't want to slam stuff unless you're looking for some sort of saturation; try to keep things relatively close to zero, and get your cleanest sound.

What mics do you favor for percussion overdubs?

I always try to use a nice, really bright microphone—C12s or the M149s, but a lot of times I'll use AKGs or Sennheisers. When I'm doing congas, I only use two mics and I try to XY them over the player's head. I usually place them at head level, pretty much where his ears are but out over the instruments. For tambourines and shakers, the room determines where you put the mic; you just move it around until you're happy with what you get. There I'll use EQ sometimes, but if I do, it's usually air. A lot of the home boards don't have that, but a lot of professional boards allow me to add 20,000 cycles. I can add 4 or 6 dB up there, which gives it some air; I try to do that as much as I can.

What's the single most important piece of equipment in the project studio? Where would you spend the most money if you were starting out building a modest room?

Personally, microphones are the most important thing to me, but you've also got to have a good [mixing] board and a good monitoring system. The nice thing about using [modular recording systems] in project studios is that, as you get a little more successful and get a little more money, you can add on.

What sort of features should the project studio owner look for in a mixing console?

It's got to have some good EQ, because, usually if you're recording at home, the acoustics in the rooms may not be as good [as in a professional studio] and you're going to have to use some EQ to do things. I like in-line boards so I can see what's happening straight up.

How important is the quality of the mic preamps?

That's the most important thing. I would try to spend some money on some good preamps—buy one and maybe later on, buy another. That makes a big difference as far as warmth, because a lot of the digital boards, while they sound OK, they sound digital. They don't add that warmth you look for, and that's why a good tube preamp is so important. Save up enough money, and get one at a time, and buy microphones when you can save up enough to get a decent microphone. They're always going to go up in value; these things don't lose their value, so a good microphone is a good investment if you can afford it. I know that, unfortunately, a lot of project studio guys are working 9 to 5, and they're also trying to make these records at home, but when they can—if they're going to invest in themselves and their studio—they should try to do it with some good preamps and some good microphones. You really can't lose on those, because you can always find somebody who'll buy it from you if you have to get rid of it.

What are the things you listen for in a demo when you're considering working with an artist?

The most important thing to me is the song—that's number one. If I'm judging the artist, I want to hear that material, because a mediocre singer can have a hit with a great song, but even a really good singer will rarely have a hit with a mediocre piece of material. So the first thing I listen for is the material, the song. The second thing is the vocal. If the vocal knocks me out and the song is mediocre, I'll still say, "Well, wait a minute; there's something happening here vocally. Now all we've got to do is find the right material and we could have something good here." Those are the most important things.

Can bad engineering obscure a good song?

Sure it can. And really good engineering can make a mediocre song or artist sound pretty damn good. I've had that happen. You say, "Wow, this is great," and then as you listen further on you realize that it's not so great; it was just a good mix with good effects.

Do you have any advice for the reader who wants to become the next Al Schmitt?

Well, if you're investing money and time in your own studio, you must love what you're doing, so just persevere. Don't let anybody beat you up, don't let anybody tell you that what you are doing is shitty. Stick with doing what you're doing; hang in there and keep doing it. Believe in yourself. I can't tell you how many times guys get turned down and rejected and battered about and then, all of a sudden, wham!—they just pop through. I don't know a better way to enjoy your life than making a living doing something you really love to do. I'm blessed that way, so it can happen to anybody! If you love doing something, you're going to do it well, and if you do it well, you'll make money from it and have a good life.

Selected Listening:
Steely Dan: *Aja*, MCA, 1977; *FM (No Static At All)*, MCA, 1978
Natalie Cole: *Unforgettable*, Elektra, 1991
George Benson: *Breezin'*, Warner Bros., 1976
Jefferson Airplane: *After Bathing At Baxter's*, RCA, 1967; *Crown Of Creation*, RCA, 1968; *Bless Its Pointed Little Head*, RCA, 1969; *Volunteers*, RCA, 1970
Neil Young: *On The Beach*, Reprise, 1974
Diana Krall: *When I Look In Your Eyes*, GRP, 1998

Arif Mardin

sk Arif Mardin a question about music—any question at all—and his eyes light up. Despite his near-exalted status as one of the prime architects of contemporary music for more than four decades, he still exudes the sheer delight of a child in a candy store when talking about the art of composing, arranging, and producing records. It's obvious that this is a man who enjoys his work.

A skilled pianist, arranger and composer, Mardin's discography reads like a who's who in the history of rock, soul, and rhythm and blues: Young Rascals, Aretha Franklin, Barbra Streisand, Patti LaBelle, Bee Gees (yes, he's the producer who first got Maurice Gibb to sing in falsetto), Average White Band, Hall and Oates, Roberta Flack, Bette Midler, Chaka Khan, Phil Collins, Culture Club, Scritti Politti, and Howard Jones, to name just a few.

He's also a perfect gentleman. Sophisticated, erudite, and self-effacing, Mardin took time out from his busy schedule to share his thoughts with me on the rise of the home studio and today's rapidly changing technologies.

Do you have a home studio yourself, or do you do all your arranging and preproduction work at a piano?

I do of course use a piano, but I also have a real-time system. I have a lot of good synthesizers, and I play and I fill up my multitrack. Once I start tweaking and playing with the sounds, I waste a lot of time but I love it! I do appreciate the new developments in technology. A creative person can get up at four o'clock in the morning and get an idea, put it down, take it to the studio and transfer the idea to a multi and turn it into a master. That's really great, and I like that idea.

Do you find it more satisfying working that way than just doing standard arrangements at the piano?

You know, the other day I wrote something, and I asked myself, in the old days how would I have come up with this idea without hearing the overdubs? How did the great nineteenth century composers writing in the moonlight in their attic with a quill come up with all these incredible counterpoints and lines? It's easy when you hear all those parts, so yes, it's a new way of composing.

Do you think Lennon and McCartney would have written better songs if they had used computers instead of acoustic guitars?

The easy answer is that geniuses don't need a lot of technology. At the same time, I bet Bach

would have loved to use a sequencer—can you imagine that?

It's wonderful to think about what a Bach or an Ellington might have been able to do with this technology.

In the early days, when I was at Berklee College of Music, after I wrote an arrangement, I would copy the parts myself all night and go to the rehearsal in the morning and pass out the parts and savor the sounds—ah, that's what I wrote! It was the anticipation of hearing what you wrote that was great. This kind of computerization, hearing your demo before it is played, spoils the fun—a little bit. That is, the fun and excitement of hearing your music played by real musicians.

It's gratification versus anticipation.

Exactly.

I'm interested in getting your thoughts on the work you did with Howard Jones—kind of an atypical project for you—and the approach you took to using synthesizers and heavily processed instruments.

First of all, Howard Jones—and it comes through his music, too—Howard is such a soulful person, sensitive, romantic. Even though the music is sequenced, for me that soulfulness comes through. That was a period in my musical journey where I had just worked with Scritti Politti, and it was a world of precision, like a Swiss clock—things move; parts, counterpoints, and stabs come in—and I was very intrigued by that. So when I started work with Howard, I had the experience and desire to work like that. And we had a lot of good times working that way.

In a technical sense, there seems to always be a sheen, a polish to your productions. This is especially apparent to me on some of your more recent work, where artists are using different producers for different songs. Your tracks have a sound of their own.

I hope "sheen" doesn't mean overpolished or slick.

No, it's not a slickness, it's a clarity.

A luster, perhaps.

Exactly. It's present in your lush string orchestrations and in the way you record the orchestra. Granted, you can't bring an orchestra into a home studio, but how can some of that sheen be accomplished in home recordings?

You know, music education is so important. You have to know your chords, you have to know your scales. You can't just get a drum beat going and put stuff on it without knowing what you're doing. I think there should be a love of melody. Musicians are falling into cliches. A lot of hip-hop or dance beats are the same, with that little skip in the bass drum. Still, there are great hip-hop records which rise way above the mediocre. Maybe people don't have time to listen and analyze and feel it. Someone pointed out to me recently that some people think they know Italian if they can say "marinara." In the same way, some people think they know music. No, you have to know the language.

> ## "Some people think they know Italian if they can say 'marinara'. In the same way, some people think they know music."

There's the point of view that technology has on the one hand enabled the democratization of music, making it possible for more people than ever before to make music, but has on the other hand also made it possible for more bad music to be made than ever before, making it harder for the cream to rise to the top.

I hate elitist attitudes, but I kind of see the point. Although if one genius or one accomplished composer or arranger or musician finds prominence or recognition through the democratization of music, well at least that person was given a chance. So even if just one percent is able to achieve their musical goals, then it's a good thing.

So you're saying the glass is half full, not half empty.

Sure. But even if technology wasn't that prevalent, you would have bad musicians.

Have you used ISDN yet for long-distance mix approvals?

Sure. EdNet saved our lives—Barbra Streisand loved it. We did five mixes in seven days with her, approved, because she had an EdNet system in her living room in Los Angeles that was compatible with what we had in the studio. She would call and say, could I have a little more violins here or can you do such-and-such to my voice, and we'd have the mix recalled in ten minutes, make the changes, and she'd listen to it as we do it, and approve it in real time.

That's technology at its best, I suppose, albeit expensive.

But it also saved a tremendous amount of money. She [Barbra] was so happy; she was saying, "I'm looking at the ocean, and I'm listening to your mixes."

As a producer, do you tend to go for take after take, polishing until every note is correct or do you go for "feel," stopping when you get a good performance, even if there's a mistake or two?

I'm in between. Of course, the artists I tend to work with are perfectionists, too. But they also leave a lot of room for corrections, and I will correct, for example, instances in an arrangement where a certain section is not defined enough, or where it is not clear how to get to a certain section. Whether another instrument needs to go there, or a level raised, or things like that. Usually I spend two or three days on a basic track, then maybe a day for vocal overdubs, then a day and a half for a mix. I usually mix two songs in three days. In all, I spend about a week on a single. But if I'm doing a live recording, then it's a different situation—if it sounds great, I say correct only the important mistakes and leave the rest the way it is.

What advice can you give struggling young musicians who have home studios and are trying to come up with demos that will land them a record deal?

First, read the lyrics of the song. Ask yourself, what are you trying to present to the listener? What is the song about? What kind of musical setting is required by the melody? Think about what genre (country, R & B, hip-hop) you want to use to present the song. Secondly, the producer must get together with the singer and find out how he or she sounds when performing that song. It's very mundane, but the selection of the key is very important. A song may sound fantastic in a key that forces the singer to strain, but it may sound terribly unimportant when the singer is very comfortable in a lower register—or vice versa. Barry White songs, for example, may sound awful in a high key. For me, a record is almost like a minifilm—you have to invoke imagery.

"For me, a record is almost like a minifilm—you have to invoke imagery."

It sounds like you take a very holistic approach, looking at what you're trying to accomplish with a song.

Right. I also almost like advertising techniques, adding sounds and colors under certain lyrics to make the song kind of come alive, even if the listener doesn't know why. Of course, tempo is very important, especially if you're doing a dance thing. You've got to know the tempo du jour, the bpm of the month.

Although records that have a completely steady tempo throughout can be almost intolerable to listen to.

I agree. Even if we're doing music that's sequenced, we use a lot of subliminal tempo changes.

Do you prefer analog recording to digital?

I'm no purist—I go with whatever sounds good. In the early days of digital, of course, the machines sounded awful, but today's digital machines sound fine. We always mix to both analog and DAT, then listen carefully to both and decide which to use for mastering, on a project by project basis. A lot has to do with mic placement and the talent of the artists. I've heard incredible classical recordings made with just a single microphone. Sure, the microphone has to be in just the right place, but the conductor has to know what he's doing, too.

Selected Listening:
Any Aretha Franklin recording from 1968 - 1974
Any Chaka Khan recording from 1978 - 1986
Barbra Streisand: *Higher Ground*, Columbia, 1997
Bee Gees: *Main Course*, RSO, 1975; *Nights On Broadway*, RSO, 1975
Young Rascals: *Good Lovin'*, Atlantic, 1966; *I've Been Lonely Too Long*, Atlantic, 1967
Average White Band: *Pick Up The Pieces*, Atlantic, 1975
Howard Jones: *One To One*, Elektra, 1986

Brian Wilson

Brian Wilson is the ultimate survivor. Best-known, of course, as the founder, lead singer and songwriter for The Beach Boys, he almost single-handedly crafted the "California sound"—a genre that has inspired thousands of musicians and has lasted through generations. His soaring falsettos, relentlessly catchy melodies and sophisticated harmony structures are forever intermingled with rose-colored images of sun, surf, and innocence in an era gone by. But there's a deeper, darker side to the man, too—a side that, for better or worse, has been well-publicized over the past couple of decades. Once dubbed "the most famous crazy guy in the world" by some irreverent journalist, Brian's struggles with mental illness and drugs and alcohol almost pale beside the abuses he has endured— as a child and teen from his over-critical, underachieving father; as a young man at the height of his creative powers from a grasping record company and, sadly, even from some of his bandmates; and, in middle age, from a questionable Svengali/therapist who brought him back from the depths of despair in exchange for a hefty piece of the action.

"Nature is slow to heal," Brian sings on his 1998 solo album, *Imagination*. "Oh, God, please let me feel." Little wonder that the man's emotional state is in tatters, what with the enormous burden of living up to the "genius" tag (make no mistake, he is one) while struggling with petty intergroup rivalries and the tortuous, alcohol-laden disintegration and death of brother and fellow Beach Boy Dennis Wilson. In recent years Brian has suffered through the passing of his mother and youngest brother Carl, the mainstay of the band and Brian's closest ally. But still he keeps plugging away, keeps cranking out those hooky tunes and staggeringly sophisticated arrangements. 1999 saw another major accomplishment—his first ever solo tour. While limited in scope and size, the gigs were critically acclaimed and provided him with the opportunity to showcase his formidable talents before a new generation of fans.

The scenario for both interviews I conducted with Brian in late 1999 was basically the same: Seated strategically on a sofa in his living room so that his good left ear faces me (he's been deaf in his right ear since early childhood), he seems oblivious to the cacophony generated by his two infant daughters and unknown number of dogs elsewhere in the house. Sometimes he even spaces out completely, apparently departing the mortal plane for a moment or two, eyes closed, before reappearing and politely asking, "What was the question again?" There's no rockstar attitude here—in contrast, his gee-whiz innocence is downright charming—but, apart from a few isolated moments when he comes to life and flashes his boyish grin, he seems present more in body than in spirit. But despite all this—despite the taciturnity and the awkwardness and the lack of engagement—what Brian *does* have to say is thoughtful, insightful, and sometimes more than a little surprising.

Do you remember your first recording session back in 1961?

Sure. The first recording session we ever did was in a place that was basically for movie soundtracks—it wasn't actually a recording studio used for music.

In that first session, were you already starting to think of the studio as an instrument?

Yeah, I learned from a friend of mine named Gary Usher. He taught me how to record, and of course Phil Spector's records came along, and I learned everything there was to learn about records.

Do you remember the first time you heard a Phil Spector record?

That was "Be My Baby", which I heard on the radio, and I pulled over to the side of the road. I was so blown out by the sound of the record that I had to pull over and listen to it! Me and my girlfriend were going nuts, we couldn't believe how great it sounded. We'd never heard anything like it before.

Where do you think Spector got his influence from?

I think he's just an innovator. Where did Bach get his inspiration? Bach was a total innovator.

You met Phil Spector at one point, didn't you?

Oh yeah, I met him a couple of times.

You even did a session once with him.

I was pulled off! He put me on the piano and he pulled me off because he said I wasn't playing the rhythm right. But I didn't care. I was just honored to be there. I didn't care whether he pulled me off or not.

Did you learn anything that night, just being there and observing how he worked?

Yeah, he told me to play hard, and I thought, oh, that's how he gets that sound—he has his musicians playing hard!

What's your definition of record production?

It's an overall feeling—you have this overall feeling for music, and you try to get the overall feel on tape; the total is greater than the sum of the parts.

Certainly that was the case in terms of the way you combined instruments.

Yeah, there were certain combinations that would make a third sound. I learned that from Phil Spector.

It's like you took his "wall of sound" concept and took it a step further.

Right. I tried to bring it into more focus.

It also became a more modern sound, with more emphasis on the vocals and more separation between the vocals and the backing track.

Yes, the Beach Boys were really all about vocals.

As you make records, do you have a sound in your head and work towards achieving that as a goal?

I can hear an *arrangement* in my head—I can't hear the sound. Other producers are able to hear the sound in their head, but I can't do that. When I get into the studio, as the record is being made, then I can hear it.

Were there ever records you made that ended up being very different from the way you first envisioned them?

Well, take "Good Vibrations," for example. We started out in one studio, doing a little bit, and then moved to a different studio, because we didn't know what we weren't into until the very last part of it. It was kind of a surprise for us to see how it evolved into a record.

You took more of a classical approach on that record than a pop approach, taking a theme and restating it. Was that a conscious decision—were you listening to classical music at the time?

No, I wasn't. It just took on a life of its own.

But you had a sense of how it would all piece together.

As I went, yeah. I didn't know what the end result was going to be, but as I went, I knew what I was doing. We just kept trying different things. We would edit different parts together, take out parts we didn't need, and we ended up with "Good Vibrations."

When you say "we," are you referring to yourself and the engineer [Chuck Britz]?

Yes.

Is it true that the other guys in the group had no idea how it was going to turn out?

That's right. But it was one of the most exciting projects I ever had anything to do with.

***Pet Sounds* and *Sgt. Pepper* are arguably the two greatest rock albums ever made...**

Among some of the greatest, yeah.

I think most people would agree that they're certainly among the top three or four. Why do you think *Sgt. Pepper* was embraced immediately, while it took twenty years or more for people to really understand and appreciate *Pet Sounds*?

I think it was that it was Phil Spector-oriented kind of tracks, you know, with Beach Boy vocals, so it was more or less our ode to Phil Spector, and then we threw in our two cents artistically.

But why did it take people so long to get it? It wasn't a big success when it first came out.

No, it didn't sell too well.

Do you have any explanation or idea why?

I don't know. I can't figure it out. It was such a great album, you'd think it would have been a smash. And it wasn't. (long pause)

Most people feel that the hardest thing for an artist is to produce themselves—very few artists have pulled that off successfully.

I can do that.

You're one of the very few—even The Beatles needed George Martin.

I was someone who had the arrangement, the vocal, the production all together in my head.

But generally the producer is supposed to be the person with the objective set of ears. How can you do that when you *are* the artist?

I just learned to do it. It's a trick—you have to learn to do it, learn to get it together.

So you have to kind of step into another set of shoes?

Exactly. When I was in my singing mode, I would sing. When I was in my production

mode, I would produce.

And you're able to view things objectively?

Yeah, I am. Most songwriters and artists need producers.

Recently, though, you've been working with coproducers as opposed to being the sole producer. Is there a reason for that?

It's because I needed to have the springboard of ideas between two people. Because I'd run out of ideas—I had writer's and producer's block, and I've had it for the past year and a half, two years.

Were you doing that with Carl on the later Beach Boys albums? Did he effectively serve as a coproducer with you?

Yeah, he was a great producer.

Well, he learned from a master, let's face it.

Yeah, he learned from me—a lot.

But from what I understand, he didn't have the Phil Spector influence in his background.

He was in a Chuck Berry mode.

So he brought more of a rock influence to your records, which was an interesting marriage.

Right, yeah. Very much so.

In the Beach Boys, you treated the voices very much as another instrument. Did you see their voices as paralleling acoustic instruments—Carl as flute, Mike as trombone?

I used their voices in textures. Usually we had five-part harmonies, and each guy would contribute to that harmony. Because we were a family, our vocal cords had similar qualities, so that was the secret of the Beach Boys, that they were a family.

But Dennis' voice had a different timbre to your voice and Carl's, which were very similar.

Yeah, Dennis had a little more husky, harsh voice.

He also sung in a lower register.

Yeah.

Did you try swapping parts around to see whose voice would suit which part best?

No, I knew instinctively which parts would work—I was able to tell the guys right away who would sing what. It was all planned out beforehand.

So you knew right away, this is Bruce's part, this is Carl's part?

Yeah, I did.

There were times when you tried out different guys on a lead vocal. Was there ever that same kind of experimentation with the harmony parts?

It was an adventure to try to get the guys to do it twice, to match up their harmonies on an overdub to give it a fatter and more resilient sound. It was a very interesting concept.

When you'd double the backing vocals, did they always sing the same parts again, or did you have them switch parts?

No, it was always the same part twice.

Did you ever try having them swap parts on the overdub?

No, I never did try that. It's interesting that you say that, I never tried that.

It might have made for an interesting texture on the double-track.

You know, you're right. I never thought of that.

What is the difference between a record and a song demo?

> *"A record frames the song. The arrangement and the orchestration frames the vocal, just like you'd have a frame around a pictures."*

A record frames the song. The arrangement and the orchestration frames the vocal, just like you'd have a frame around a picture.

But how do you know when a record's done, when to stop painting?

You know it instinctively.

But, especially with the Phil Spector approach, there's a very thin line between a record being produced and overproduced.

Yeah, you're right.

How do you know when you've gone up to that line and not crossed it?

It's certainly an instinctual thing. You just *know* when you have it right, when it's cool.

That's the hardest lesson for most people getting into record production—knowing when enough is enough.

You just know, like when you're eating and you've had enough. You know when you're through eating, and you know when you're through producing.

Like all the great producers—Spector, Martin—you actually used the studio itself as an instrument. Was that a conscious decision, and if so, when did you learn to take that approach?

1965.

What was the event?

"California Girls." I thought that was a very full record, a very full, happy record. Up until then, I hadn't known that. It took two years of listening to Phil Spector's music to get that notion and to get it right. "California Girls" was my turning point; that was a great production.

I understand that you were never completely satisfied with Mike Love's lead vocal on that track.

Mike flatted in a couple places in the first verse, but it was raw and real. His flat was like a real thing, it was a great lead.

I gather there were no punch-ins on that.

No, he just kicked butt on that.

What do think it was about "I Get Around" that got it all the way to #1 while none of the previous releases quite got there?

It had a nice competitive feel about it, an up feel. It was an up-on-your toes production, that's what I think was the reason why it was #1. It was like a male version of, what's that group that did that Carole King song...(sings)

The Chiffons?

I can't remember the name, but it was a girl group from out of New York. The Beach Boys were like their male alter ego...Their record had a great background sound, and so did we.

Speaking of alter ego, when I grew up in Brooklyn, there were constant fierce debates in my school about which group was cooler, the Beach Boys or the Four Seasons. It seemed as if the Four Seasons were the New York version of the Beach Boys.

There was a great rivalry going out there—east and west.

It's well-known that you viewed The Beatles competitively. Did you view the Four Seasons that way, too?

A little bit, yeah. I think so, more so than I had realized. I was young, and I was a little bit naive, you know. But they were really a very special group, and they meant a lot to us. They were the first group to put a really high voice like that [out front], although "The Lion Sleeps Tonight" did that, too. But the Four Seasons were the first to really lay the falsetto on thick.

That's what seemed to be the common theme between the two groups.

Yeah, and they spoke well, they were really great at it.

But their productions weren't as full as Beach Boys productions.

No, their tracks were very clean. They weren't like that Phil Spector, echo chamber, throw everything in that you can there kind of thing.

Did you always sing backing vocals around one mic?

Yes, we did it all around one mic.

So if you needed to do a punch-in, it had to be of all of you.

Yeah, right.

Was the backing track always bounced down from one machine onto another in mono so that you'd have lots of open tracks for vocals?

We used to do a lot of bouncing, yeah; that was one of the most important things.

Those were, of course, the days before 24-track.

Right.

The fact that you can only hear in one ear forced you to work in mono throughout your whole career.

Mono's the only thing I know; I never could hear stereo, because of my right ear. So I was fucked out of hearing sound depth, hearing something over here, something over there. I don't get to hear that dimension; I only have one-dimensional hearing.

But you use reverbs and echoes to get depth in your mono mixes.

I got a good sound, but I can't hear what other people hear. It's a weird thing; I can do a production, but I can't hear it the way other people hear it. It's a really strange trip for me, really weird.

Even though you don't have left-right, you do have forward-back, so it makes reverb even more important.

Right.

I gather the echo chamber at Western Studios was a big part of the Beach Boys sound.

It was a very special chamber, especially for instruments. It gave a depth and an eternal sound to the instrument. So you have an eternity in music; in sound and in voice, it sounds like forever.

I understand that even in *Imagination*, which was recorded in Chicago, you were flying tapes back to L.A. so the tracks could be fed through the echo chamber at Western.

Right. It's amazing how the two can be a perfect marriage—a marriage between a voice and an echo chamber.

Did you ever experiment with chambers in other studios?

Well, Gold Star had two chambers at once, two echo chambers that you could bring into the board at one time. That was the secret of Phil Spector's records; he had all that echo at his disposal.

So he had two chambers while other people were using one.

Yeah.

Did you ever get into using echo plates or digital reverbs?

No, just acoustic ones.

And even in your latest records, you're still using them; that's the fairy-dust.

Yes. (laughs)

You worked a lot with [engineer] Chuck Britz in the Beach Boys days. Did you ever get

involved with mic selection and placement, or did you leave that up to him?

No, I left that up to him; he was a genius at that. He knew what he was doing; I didn't know how to mic instruments, so he did all the miking himself. He'd have young kids set up the room for him, and he'd experiment with where to put the microphones. That's how we got that California Girls sound.

On the *Pet Sounds* box set, you can hear instances where you're instructing the musicians to move in closer or further to the mic, so you must have been doing the acoustic balancing.

Right. I'd listen to their sound and mix them together. Back in the days of "California Girls," we would work in 4-track. I'd put the whole background orchestration on one track, then I'd do sets of background voices and bounce that over [to mono] so we'd have two lead vocals, double-tracked.

So you bounced things within one machine, double-tracking both the lead and the backing vocals. The balancing, then, was a matter of you getting the guys closer or further from the single mic.

Right. Get on mic and stay on mic, then stay in that same place until you were done singing.

But you were always around one mic? You didn't have individual mics for each vocalist?

Just in the last few years. Most of the Beach Boys hit records were done all around one mic.

Did you get involved in the EQ or the compression/limiting?

No, that was all Chuck's work. He would EQ it, put the sound together, make a wall of sound.

And vocal effects were basically just live chambers, gluing the sound together.

It's called 'swimming.' They used to swim in echo.

Obviously, Spector was a huge influence on you...

Oh, yeah.

But as you got into the mid-'60s and Spector eased off, were you listening to other hit records of the day?

You mean was I copying them?

No, you obviously didn't copy them because you had your own distinctive sound. I was wondering if you were studying them, perhaps trying to consciously avoid their sounds.

Yeah, I studied their music, but I studied Phil Spector way more than The Beatles or any other music.

But you were still conscious of the production techniques of the time.

Right.

Do you listen to a lot of contemporary music today?

I try to listen to oldies, to get those oldies but goodies in my soul. My soul feels a little bit weird sometimes, so I need music to help it out.

"If you have an idea, don't go 50 percent of the way on it and then junk it. Go 100 percent and get it done."

Do you feel that technological advances have changed production values?

Production values have changed immensely, with the coming of 24- and 48-track, 72-track machines. Because you can lay down one thing and get it just right, then lay down another thing and blend the two together. You have much more control over the overall sound than when you record all the instruments onto one track and have to mix it as you're going.

With the coming of the new machines, you can do it one at a time and mix it all together by computer.

Having more tracks allows you to put off decisions until the very end.

Right, and you have a computer to help you. The computer remembers all the settings of the knobs, turning tracks on and off. It really helps in the production.

Is there any advice you'd like to pass on to the next generation of musicians?

Yes. Follow through on your ideas. If you have an idea, don't go 50 percent of the way on it and then junk it. Go 100 percent and get it done. Follow through with what you start. That's a very good lesson in life. Sometimes you poop out halfway through, but not me—I go all the way through.

Selected Listening:
Any Beach Boys recording prior to 1968, especially the *Pet Sounds* album and the "I Get Around," "California Girls," "Sloop John B," "Good Vibrations," and "Heroes and Villains" singles (all on Capitol). Other standout tracks: "Until I Die" and "Surf's Up" (both from the 1971 *Surf's Up* album) and "Sail On Sailor" (from the 1973 *Holland* album), both on Reprise.
Solo Albums: *Brian Wilson*, Sire/Reprise, 1988; *Imagination*, Giant, 1998

Phil Ramone

Talking with famed producer Phil Ramone is a little like hopping on a high-speed roller-coaster. His thoughts flow so quickly, they have a tendency to actually interrupt his sentences in mid-speech, and you've got to be pretty well-focused to keep up. It's a safe bet the recording engineers he works with drink a lot of coffee.

Of course, if anyone's got a right to be-bop like that, Ramone does. This is the guy about whom the phrase, "been there, done that" was invented. From Billy Joel to Barbra Streisand, from Paul McCartney to Frank Sinatra, from Paul Simon to Gloria Estefan, Ramone has helped define mainstream music for more than three decades. Even when the guy was just starting out in the '60s in primitive Tin Pan Alley studios, Ramone had the engineering chops to make an indelible mark on such timeless classics as "The Girl From Ipanema," "Raindrops Keep Falling On My Head," and "Alice's Restaurant." Sure, he's been around forever, but make no mistake about it—the guy isn't living off past glories. Ramone has made an entire career of embracing new technologies, from digital recording to Dolby surround to EDNet (used for long-distance collaboration on the Sinatra *Duets* sessions). Indeed, in his most recent venture—advisor to Lucent Technologies' Audio Initiatives —Ramone is behind the highest quality audio compression technology called EPAC.

A child prodigy, a classically trained violinist, a leader, an innovator, Phil Ramone—the "Pope of Pop"—has become no less than an icon in the subculture of professional producers and engineers.

What's the single most important thing the typical home recordist needs to learn?

I started a studio way back when I was a kid. I went through that growth stage of building kits, building mixers, preamps. I worked in a demo studio when I started—you know, four microphones in a living room. Room acoustics is one thing, but [mic] placement is another. No matter what grandiose console you're using, it still comes down to, first of all, [mic] technique. Technique is a lost art in my book—there's no decision making when you've got tons of microphones and you put them all over the place.

When you don't have any money, you've got to make a decision and you've got to bounce tracks together so they survive. The key is a good preamp, a good microphone, and a good limiter. Give me those and, hello, I'm a hero.

I guess you've got to make all the mistakes in order to learn from them.

Well, the guy who taught me said you've got to cut the disk first so you know what the problems are before you put a mic in front of an artist. If you can't cut the lacquer, it means you don't understand the principle behind what you're doing. And if you don't understand the wiring from here to there, you won't understand what it means. So you'll open an expensive mic and you won't know what to do with it, where to put it, or why.

> **"The key is a good preamp, a good microphone, and a good limiter. Give me those and, hello, I'm a hero."**

You work with what you're given. There are situations, such as in bad weather, where you'll want to use Shure SM57s instead of expensive condenser mics. I've taught courses where I've had kids record material to a multitrack using inexpensive Shure mics through Shure mic mixers at the same time that a pro was recording through an expensive console and, believe me, the tracks the kids recorded sounded pretty damn good. Not ideal, yet pretty close to ideal. You make do sometimes; I think you have to stop being an audio snob.

Also, a home recordist has so much of an advantage today with all the home equipment out there. The quality of the demo is so important these days—you can't go anywhere with a piano/voice demo or a guitar/voice demo. You can't do that anymore.

Most A&R people would deny that, of course.

But it's not true. It's like me coming in with [an album] cover made on a cheap camera. You'd better come in with an exact image, not a simple instant photo. With all the digital advantages, all the things that are a part of us right now, engineers need to understand what you're putting together, and how to utilize it. You have to *listen*, first and foremost. There are a lot of subtleties you can work with. You have to understand your equipment. You, as the engineer, have to share in the painting with the artist.

One important consideration is how you're going to master a piece, how you're going to finish it. Information laid down on tracks doesn't tell you you've got a finished idea. And I always like the idea of painting the big picture as quickly as possible, because if I like the rhythm date, maybe I won't put an extra guitar in. I like the idea of really making myself work hard at the time I'm doing a basic idea.

To that end, will you do things like print effects?

I will, though not necessarily every day. I [generally] don't do it on vocals, though with Sinatra [on *Duets*], I knew that I wasn't going to get him back in the room. He and chamber seven at Capitol were a marriage made in heaven. It was the old sound —- the *right* sound. There was no way I was going to get that any other way, so I printed it separately, and it paid off handsomely later when I needed a little less or a little more to match against the other vocals. But if you know that a certain type of short reverb really smacks with the drums, sure, print it. One of the hardest things to recreate, you know, is the day, the moon, the moment, the fader [setting].

Do you ever find yourself in a million-dollar facility turning to low-end project-studio gear by choice?

All the time, all the time. From day one, I've never stopped using crazy things. Billy Joel used to love to sing to effects. He said it helped him sing. So I built this little device with stupid

things like Echoplexes, MXR phasers, and flangers, and I'd put it on the keyboard. I'd give him like eight switches labeled "Elvis," you know, so the guy could at least have a good time while he was recording.

We're talking about insanity here, we're talking about air and space and things that go along with sound. There's nothing worse than a guy putting on his headphones, about to inspire himself, and the engineer puts his voice in a drywell or somewhere under the ocean. That's bull. You need to be there. For example, I like to use tape delays on reverb sends. It just sounds different than using digital predelays. I never, ever stopped buying funky gear.

> **"We're talking about insanity here, we're talking about air and space and things that go along with sound."**

When guitar pedals came in, let's face it—they had better sounds than what the engineer was able to produce.

Although engineers may swear the pedals don't sound as good as the expensive box in the rack.

That's just job security. I always blamed the engineer for being so stupid about it. To put an expensive delay device and a very expensive compressor on a guitar? Come on, remember where the signal comes from. Think about what a guitar pickup is! A guitar does buzz and it does crackle. It's only in recent years that they finally have a way to make the mic and the pickup on an acoustic bass sound like a bass. Otherwise, it always sounded like some thin piece of rubber being stretched between two steel cans.

Audio technology these days seems to be going simultaneously forward and backward. You've got all this movement towards high-end digital, and at the same time you've got the vintage tube craze. Do you find yourself these days working with a lot of the same gear you were using 35 years ago?

(laughs) It's scary. I mean, it's nice, but it's like taking a Sunday drive in a '36 Packard! Some of the gear is interesting, but the condition of them worries me—tubes are not the same. Now that we've broken the wall down between [the U.S. and] East Germany and Russia, there are tubes back in the circuits.

Yeah, the same tubes we shipped over to them 30 years ago.

Of course. They were four bucks apiece or eight bucks for a very expensive pair. Now I don't even want to think about what it costs. But I think maintenance is one problem, especially with the older consoles. Vintage consoles have corrosion no matter what you do. There's just so many years something can work.

That's what turned people around when solid-state first came out. Solid-state made things sound as ice-cold as they could be compared with the tube. No question, not having the tube fry on you during an important moment was good, but then there was this different noise, this hissy, crappy thing that came with the invention of solid-state. So every period—including digital—has its ugliness.

But, put together in the larger picture, there's nothing better than all the mix [of gear]. The palette for the painter is, I'll use oil here and I'll use something else here, so, absolutely, there's no question that you should mix and match.

And when you record, I wonder about putting a very expensive microphone by a guitar amp—are you accomplishing anything? What mic is right? That's where the money doesn't count—it's how you record that damn amp that worries me. I had a guitar built for me a while ago. Each string was fed to a separate amp, six strings, six amps. I put compressors across every string, and panpots—I wanted to get the ultimate guitar sound. I used it in a session with Michael Sembello once for three days. He passed a pawn shop and found an old Vox. Michael picked it up, took it to the studio and, just for a test, we plugged it in. It scared the hell out of us, it was so good, so simple. We said, no wonder the Beatles sounded great! Everybody forgot! (laughs) It had three knobs, maybe there was a midrange, just bass, treble, thank you very much. But there's a mixture of the two that goes together that makes you a hero if you use the right stuff. If you don't have the right stuff, having the most expensive antique mic won't help you at all. This is just pure subtlety; playing with it until your ears say, "I like that." You've got to be an adventurer, you can't just say I won't do this unless I have my new "zonk."

If you're working on a limited budget, what's the most important component in the signal chain? Where would you invest the most money?

The preamp. I can get miracles if I've got a good, clean preamp. I can always screw it up [later], but I can't go backwards. If I can't get the microphone to speak on a vocal, it doesn't matter. If the preamp sucks, you've got problems. So you've got to go from where the microphone source is.

And it's not just a question of how many microphones you have. If I were recording a drum set in a small space, I'd put two microphones just above the ears of the drummer. I'd figure, if it sounded good to him when he tuned it before he put the headphones on…

If I gave him that pair of mics in his phones, it would be the most natural balance for him. Obviously, kick and snare [have to be worked on separately], but for the rest of the kit, I'd never hear a complaint. This is not tricky, over-the-top stuff; it's just two microphones at the exact spacing of his head. We all know that a good set of tuned drums will give you what you're looking for, but you can over-mic it. Here's where the limitations of a home studio can actually help. It's like tracks: when you think you don't have enough, you can combine the toms and the overhead, and then use equalization to get more of one or the other if necessary. So why not make that decision? I used to hate locking multitracks, so I'd do that—record all the drums on four tracks, two tracks in the beginning. My big thing when we got to three tracks was to record the kick separately. People used to wonder why, but I could control the only thing that was the heart factor in rock and roll.

You're talking about the interplay between the bass and the kick drum.

Yeah, and I could never get that marriage until, a lot of times, afterwards. Because a lot of basses in the early days of rock and roll didn't sound good, especially direct. So you'd use different kinds of amplifiers, but you'd never get the miking right because you never had room for the thing. You'd stuff it in a closet and put a mic on it. I screwed around with omni mics more than most people do. That's another technique you can definitely bring to the home studio.

An omnidirectional microphone gives you less problems if you use it in the proper place— if you've got a wandering singer, or if you don't have the proper acoustics. I guarantee you I'll get a good vocal [in a dead room], but I'll probably get you a better one with an omni because it will be just a little bit broader, and it won't have a lot of bounce off the walls. It's a good technique, especially if you [use a mic with] a variable capsule—it's a home run.

A common theme in many of your recordings is a sense of spaciousness. A lot of home recordings, though, tend to sound cramped. How can the home recordist get that big sound even when working in a small room?

A lot of it has to do with the way you record, your attitude. When I started, I worked in an apartment-kind of setting. The control room was behind a sliding door that looked into the living room—and it wasn't a big living room. But the reason that room sounded so big was the echo chamber, which was a small bedroom, maybe 11 by 17—but we lacquered the hell out of the walls and put a microphone and two speakers in there. Later we changed to two microphones, two omnis. That, with a delay out of the tape machine, was just enough to put a little edge around a voice or around the piano. That studio got more work because it had that great chamber or "the room sound," as people called it. I never forgot that.

The first studio I built [A&R Recording] was terrifyingly dead, compared to the big rooms that were around in the early '60s. So I learned more about the challenge [of making a small room sound big] because of the clumsiness and klutziness of the room I was in. You can do that at home. You can take a small room, take wood shades or shutters, and lacquer them while putting styrofoam, drape, or deadening material on the other side of them. It helps also to work in a nonsquared room—that gets rid of standing waves.

If an artist is going to sing, the hardest thing in the world is to tell an artist you should sing with the microphone a handful away. They just don't believe you when you say that. So some-

"The ultimate feeling of a good record [is] having various spaces that you feel you're in."

times you have to use two mics—one close, one out, like you do on drums and other things. Why not think about that? There's a balance between the two. An omni and a directional mic can give you another attitude. I never had enough inputs, never had enough plates, so I decided that the best way to create space was to work constantly to find an environment that sounded like there was an environment. I'd use two plates, one with just a short delay for vocals and another one for the rhythm sound. To me, that's the ultimate feeling of a good record—having various spaces that you feel you're in.

Your choices and varieties of reverbs always seem well thought out.

It's probably the most important thing to me. Once you know the basics, it's easy to record, but the second half of that is the cleanliness with which the chamber responds.

If it doesn't respond cleanly, why would you expect the signal to be married to the original? One of the hardest things to teach somebody is to listen to the device itself. Take out the source and listen to the device. You'd be amazed how crummy some of these things sound! They flange, they phase, there's cancellation all over the place. And you really should listen to it in mono to make sure that what you're hearing is what you get. That's why a lot of television shows get so screwed up. They come in with these great effects, but when they check in mono, half the signal goes away or half the reverb goes away…which is worse.

If you had sixteen instruments and they were all [recorded] isolated, does that give you a better space? No. You'd think that would be ideal, but it isn't. You can record things separately for the engineer, but do you get anything musical? I don't think so. So space is what you have to create, and reverb is the only place to get it. In 90 percent of the rooms I work in, it's rare when I actually hear the strings sounding good. Now you can double acoustic instruments with synths, but you still have to find the space for the synth. [A synth] is not just a device you can plug in and say, here we are, because you have to create a space for its echo. That's part of why those that have built-in echo don't sound good. Part of the mystique is gone; they've taken out the better part of what you need to work with.

You also seem to be a stickler for the "little things" that make a record a record. Things that are so subtle that they may go by the average listener—underpinnings like triangles, hand-claps, tambourines. How can these be brought out in the home studio?

The little things do sound better if you pay attention. Handclaps have been on records for a long, long time, but you've got to equalize them, to work them into a track. A triangle is hard to put on a record, but along with handclaps, it was a favorite thing in many early [rock and roll] records. And the right sound of a kick drum. That's the hard-core part of the sound—what are you going to do on top?

Cymbals were always a key thing for me, because they tended to wipe the record out when you needed that big splash. Then there's the shaker.

And how do you record a shaker? Ninety percent of the people I know over-record them. They over-modulate on it, they're afraid to let the preamp work, to let the tape work.

They're watching the meters instead of listening.

They're not listening. They're always too close. You can go over to a percussionist and say, "I'll crank it up in your headphones so you can hear better, but please don't come any closer to that mic, it would help me." You know, this is a relationship you have with people, that's part of the whole thing in big studios. In your home studio, you better do it right! There are no choices—there's no excuse, either. But if you bring in an outside percussionist to do overdubs, make sure you understand the subtleties. I don't want to use the word under-record, but not over-modulating and not entering distortion. You don't have to be a technical genius to know that; you've got to use your ears. We've all gotten lazy, and everybody puts the mic two inches away from everything, but that doesn't help you.

Take tambourines—when I started out, tambourines were the most important things to make a record hot. It wasn't the reverb as much as it was how that thing would slam. You had to find a better way to give it air, and part of that was to move the microphone into the right place. Those are the little highlights inside of a record. They're not all close-miked. They're miked in a specific way or two ways to get me a place in the record when the moment stops—the point where, if the record's been pumping, going really loud, it suddenly drops to a space. You have to come back, your ear will not adjust quick enough, so how loud do you put that? That's the subtlety of the mix, that's really what counts. But you should be more careful at home.

Another thing you can do is to put limiters on the headphones so they sound good. You make an artist happy, they play better. It's like protection on your speakers, it allows you to run the headphones louder. And I've seen players who want it so loud their ears bleed. Most of the stuff is not subtle, it's really about getting you there. It's about, what do you want? Do you want to whisper down a mic?

Yeah, you can whisper down a mic. I've recorded singers with a voice that was so tiny, up against huge bands. Mic technique is really important, knowing that in some sections you need to step in and in other sections you need to get two inches away so we don't break up. It's not that my hands aren't fast enough [riding the faders] or that the limiter's not fast enough, I just don't like limiters [on vocals]. They're not healthy. It means you're losing your skills. It's like automatic pilot, c'mon, you can fly the plane. If you can't do that, you shouldn't be in the cockpit.

Paul Simon has said that you were always more inclined to getting the feel right, and if you got the performance right, you'd make the sound do. What sort of things would you do to "make the sound do"?

The perfect example is that we rehearsed "Loves Me Like A Rock" sitting around a single mic in the middle and a guitar mic, feet tapping, with me running a rehearsal multitrack. The next day, we come in, everybody's miked, everything's correct, but we never got home to where Paul liked it. From my experience, I hated when people just ran a cassette. I always ran a tape, 2-track, something, because you never know if you can turn it around. Experience tells you, never waste your time by not recording. I'm famous for this because every engineer I've ever worked with knows I'm going to walk in and just hit "record." I don't care what the tape costs.

I mean, how can it be compared to the [right] mood? No one in the annals of history will write down whether your preamp was set right or too low or too high. Even if it's crapping out and you have to make adjustment halfway through, maybe you can use the rest of it. I always tell singers and musicians, "Don't stop, please don't stop once you're in and the mood is here." I mean, I've had microphones fall over, I've had everything that can happen in the studio happen to me in the middle of takes I've ended up using—and forget about live recording!

That's what Paul was referring to. You make do only because that's all you've got. But you make do; you don't just sit there and cry in your beer. You make it happen.

So many great records have been made—like [Dylan's] *Blood On The Tracks*—from run-throughs, not even takes. *Rock of Ages*, with The Band, was mostly from the rehearsal night. We're taping, you hear guys talking, you hear mics falling over. Eighty percent of the album was from that first night; the New Year's Eve night is not nearly as good. That's my battle training: Thou Shalt Always Be Prepared. So something's distorted—don't stand there and wait until the take is over. I run out in the middle of the room. I've got a take with me adjusting mics in the middle of the take and changing the high end of the mics on the drums and me moving a whole guitar rig over, and it's in the record! It was the best take! And how did I compensate? I didn't have the drummer replay it—I figured it out: pull up these faders while you pull others down to put the drummer in the right dimension. I've had stuff happen where there are shorts, things breaking up, tape dropouts—but the band went on. What are you going to do? I think it's great to come to work and think something can happen in the first take, before you start the day. How about rolling when they're first warming up, while everybody's checking their headphones? I've heard some great music made during those moments.

Selected Listening:
Any Billy Joel recording from 1978 – 1986
Paul Simon: *There Goes Rhymin' Simon*, Columbia, 1973; *Still Crazy After All These Years*, Warner Bros., 1975
Bob Dylan: *Blood On The Tracks*, 1975
The Band: *Rock Of Ages*, Capitol, 1972
Barbra Streisand: *A Star Is Born*, Columbia, 1977
Simon and Garfunkel: *The Concert In Central Park*, 1981
Julian Lennon: *Valotte*, Atlantic, 1984
Sinead O'Connor: *Am I Not Your Girl?* 1992
Frank Sinatra: *Duets*, Capitol, 1993; *Duets II*, Capitol, 1994
Dave Grusin: *West Side Story*, N2K Encoded Music, 1997

Elliot Scheiner

You'd be hard-pressed to find a producer/engineer more associated with the "American sound" than Elliot Scheiner—a name long linked with such red-white-and-blue mainstays as Steely Dan, Fleetwood Mac, The Eagles, Toto, John Fogerty, Bruce Hornsby, Dan Fogelberg, and Jimmy Buffett. The irony of this is not lost on Scheiner, who recalls in this interview that his first big break came from working with Irish singer Van Morrison!

Scheiner started at the famed A&R Studios in New York in 1967, working under Phil Ramone, and eventually becoming the first engineer in New York to go freelance. As Scheiner's client list and reputation grew, the work began streaming in. Steely Dan's Donald Fagen and Walter Becker hired him to do the tracking for *The Royal Scam*, and the rest is history. Nominated for a staggering 11 Grammys (and winner of two of them), Scheiner is clearly one of the most respected and in-demand engineer/producers in the business. These days, Scheiner is establishing himself as one of the premier 5.1 remixers, having completed projects for Steely Dan (*Gaucho*), The Eagles (*Hell Freezes Over*), Sting (*Brand New Day*), and MTV mixes for Fleetwood Mac and John Fogerty. Warm and personable yet technically savvy, the reasons for his popularity and critical acclaim became apparent within minutes of our conversation.

How did you make the transition from engineering to production?

My first production was an obscure artist named Don Cooper, signed to Roulette Records. But with Van Morrison's *Moondance* record, we were getting ready to mix it. It was around Christmastime, and Van said, "I'm not gonna be here, I'm going home to Woodstock to be with my family, so why don't you mix it and just send it to me?" So [drummer] Gary Malabar and I ended up mixing it by ourselves, and we sent it up to him, and that was it. He didn't change anything, he loved it. So I felt that was really the beginning of my production career. When the next album came around (*Band & Street Choir*), I was supposed to coproduce that with Van, and we started it, then it ended up not happening.

Have you ever done any producing where you didn't engineer at the same time?

I did that once in my career, and it actually was very good—the engineer I used was great. But when it got down to mixing, I couldn't let it go. I probably should have, I should have let the guy who recorded it mix it. And I didn't, and consequently I did a bad job, so it was a bad experience for me. I love engineering, though. That's where I started, and I love that art form. It would be hard for me to put that down. I'm probably going to hire somebody to do certain stuff for me, like vocal overdubs or guitar overdubs. I don't have to sit behind the console for that stuff. But for tracking and for mixing, I feel like I need to be there, I need to be a part of it.

What are your thoughts about the rise of home recording?

Well, I've mixed a bunch of things from home studios, and what I generally notice is that there's not enough care taken. It's one thing if you're doing a demo and you're just going for a vibe; anything goes, there aren't any rules. For a demo, you have to get the correct vibe of a song, the attitude of a singer, on tape. And that's all that's important. That's all that's *ever* important—the music. Back in the '50s and '60s, they placed mics in a room, and they weren't worried about anything except vibe. That's all that matters. Steve Albini's attitude towards making records is phenomenal to me; he doesn't care, he just wants to get the band to perform. He's done things like putting up a couple of mics and seeing if he can gather the whole thing through a couple of mics—that's pretty incredible to me.

> **"What I generally notice [about home recordings] is that there's not enough care taken."**

What do you mean exactly by "not enough care taken"?

Things like punch-ins, like making sure that machines are locked before going into record—which is especially important when using ADATs and DA-88s. You're trying to figure out why you're hearing these wow-y kinds of things, and you realize it's because, when the track was recorded, the machines weren't yet locked together. People have got all this technology, but they really don't know how to use it yet.

What common mistakes do you hear in tapes that come out of home studios?

Obviously some people overproduce their things. They've got every synth in the world in their home studio, and they're going to put strings and horns everywhere. Most tapes I hear out of home studios sound pretty good, though.

Is it possible to get a big room sound out of a small room?

You can make it sound a little more live by finding a sweet spot in the room and placing ambient mics there. In a small room, you may be better off not recording drums with close mics. Just use a pair of stereo mics, and see if you can find a sweet spot in the room.

Where should the home recordist on a small fixed budget allocate the greatest amount of money?

On microphones and mic preamps. You can literally bypass that portion of the console altogether if you have quality mics and preamps, so you can buy a much less expensive console. One of my favorite mic pres is the GML. You can probably get a pair of GMLs for about $1,700, which is kind of pricey but well worth it; it's one of the sweetest mic pres ever. As far as mics go, Audio-Technica have been coming up with some very, very good-sounding mics at very reasonable prices. I've been using them for vocals in live situations. They're low-end in terms of price but not in terms of fidelity.

How do you generally record vocals?

I work on axis, but I generally like the singer to stand back about six or eight inches, facing straight on. I'll keep the mic raised above lip level to try to cut down on plosives. Ideally, I won't use a screen, so I'll sometimes raise the mic straight, keep it above the lips, closer to the nose, and then tilt it on an angle towards the floor. Not severely, but at a 35-40 degree angle.

That will cut down on the pops as well.

Do you tend to record vocals with compressors/limiters, or do you ride gain manually?

I used to ride gain manually; now I can't a lot of times because singers are so unpredictable. Back in the '60s and the '70s, a singer knew when to back off the microphone; today, it's not so common. So I'll put a limiter in the line, but barely touching it; it will only kick in if something terrible happens, like overloading.

Do you ever experiment with different polar patterns other than cardioid?

I don't use figure-eights for anything anymore. It's an interesting sound to use an omni for a solo singer; sometimes that works out very well. But there are so many subjective things here, it's hard to generalize. An omni may sound great on one particular singer in one particular room, but you change rooms, and it doesn't sound so good. In a home studio, it's much less of a problem, because you're not moving around, so once you find something you like, you're set. Obviously, the way to go is to experiment, especially since you're not paying anyone for their time. Get a singer in there, try the mic in omni, see how it sounds. Do it a number of different ways, and see what sounds best to you.

What sort of miking techniques do you use for acoustic guitars?

I have a couple of different techniques, depending on whether somebody's picking or strumming. For strumming rhythm parts, I'll use a [Shure] SM81; that's what I used with the Eagles. I'll position it just a little bit up towards the neck, but barely. For picking parts, I tend to use a Neumann U 47, also positioned a little towards the neck, but backed off quite a bit. For electric guitars, I use the same thing I always have—a [Shure] SM57. I'll find the best speaker in the stack and go right up against the grill, but not necessarily off axis; sometimes I'll have another mic in the room for ambience.

Any specific techniques for miking bass amps?

I wish someone could tell me! (laughs)

So you're a DI guy.

Yeah. With Fleetwood, John McVie had an iso box made up for his amp so we could mic it with no leakage. I used it, but still ended up using 80 percent DI and only 20 percent amp. The amp signal just doesn't have enough definition; it just contributes a lot of low end.

Do you record bass with compression?

No. I record with minimal compression, sometimes none. It really depends on the bass player; you can't apply the same technique to every situation. I generally use compression on the bass during mixdown, however.

How do approach the diplomatic aspects of being an engineer/producer?

You've got to respect certain issues; you can't infringe upon the player. The idea is to create as little interference as possible, to make it as comfortable as possible for a player to perform. You don't want to be the focus of attention; you want to be as inconspicuous as possible. That's what I've always tried to do—I don't want you to think about the microphones, just give me the performance. If something's no good, I'll fix it.

So how do you go about fixing something that's no good?

Well, you can't undo distortion; that's impossible—at least, so far. But pitch is easy to fix now; there are all these new automatic pitch correction devices. As far as level corrections, that's fairly easy—you either do it with your hand or you use a compressor. A compressor can also impart a fairly interesting sound; it may be exactly what you're looking for.

How do you approach using reverbs? Do you prefer to apply a different reverb to each sound source, or do you just use a couple of master reverbs?

Generally, I like to have a couple of master reverbs; I like to think that the band played in the same room at the same time, so I'll try and create an environment for those players. I'll use other reverbs for more specific things—those things that weren't tracked at the same time or need to have some other kind of thing happening.

What would be typical settings you'd use for the master reverbs?

> **"I'm tired of reverbs; for too long now we've been putting reverbs on in rooms that don't have natural reverb."**

To be honest, right now I'm in a mode where I'm trying not to use *any* reverb. I'm trying to make things a little more organic. Personally, I'm tired of reverbs. We're putting reverbs on in rooms that don't have natural reverb, and I'm trying to get away from it. If I'm going to use a reverb, I want it to be inconspicuous, so I don't use bright reverbs any more; my reverbs are generally darker. I'll set one longer and one shorter—anywhere from 2.8 to 3.8 seconds on the long end, and 1.5 to 2 seconds on the short end.

Do you generally delay sends to reverbs to separate them out from the main signal?

Oh yes, absolutely. I'm working on a song now where I have to use reverb because I'm trying to match an old mix, and I've got a 200 ms delay on [the send to] a very long chamber. It creates an ambience, but separate from the singer, so you can maintain the notes and not have it all wash together.

Let's talk some more about this "organic" approach to making records.

The idea is to use no reverb at all, not even using the room sound, necessarily. Just dry. That's the way we generally hear things. If somebody was playing guitar in your living room, you'd hear it bone dry. A great example of this is Sheryl Crow's *Tuesday Night Music Club*. That was a phenomenal job to me; there was no reverb at all, and it was a great-sounding record. But I want to do a project that way, and I'm determined to.

Does this approach dictate everything being close-miked, with no ambient mics in the room?

I'd probably record some ambient mics in the room, but whether I'd use them or not [in the mix], I don't know. When I record now, I'm recording with 5.1 in mind, so I'll set up ambient mics around the room, just for the possible eventuality of DVD.

Where do you start when you're doing a mix?

I start by playing each instrument by itself and determine a basic sound for it, something I find pleasing when I just listen to the instrument by itself. Once I've done that for everything, then I start putting everything together and see what's working and what's not working—what you need to EQ a little more to have it come out, or whether level changes alone will work. Everybody mixes differently; there's no right or wrong approach. I always work with the bass and drums for awhile to get a sound.

Is the separation between bass guitar and kick drum important at that stage?

Not necessarily. I just want to make sure that you can hear both and pick each one out; it's important that you hear the notes of the bass guitar and feel the kick drum. I'll work with them for awhile until I get something I'm happy with. Then I'll start bringing in the other instruments, first guitars and keyboards and then whatever extra stuff there is. The last thing I put in is vocals. I make sure the track is sitting the way I want it to sit before I bring them in.

What can you do to help get a problematic vocal track to "sit" in the backing tracks?

Well, it *should* sit there. Somebody sang to this track. It had to sit there at one point. Maybe it's an indication that you've done too much EQing, so you might want to back off the EQ and see if it sits any better. But you've got to remember that the vocal *was* recorded to this track, and if it's a good performance then it should sit there somehow.

So maybe this is a barometer, saying you've gone too far, you've done something wrong in the mix.

That's possible. Or maybe it's just screaming for the vocal to sit on top of the track.

Selected Listening:
Steely Dan: *Two Against Nature*, Warner Bros., 2000; *Gaucho*, MCA, 1980; *Aja*, MCA, 1977; *Royal Scam*, MCA, 1976
Donald Fagen: *Night Fly*, Warner Bros., 1982
Van Morrison: *Moondance*, Warner Bros., 1970; *Street Band & Choir*, Warner Bros., 1970
The Eagles: *Hell Freezes Over*, Geffen, 1994
Fleetwood Mac: *The Dance*, Reprise, 1997
Bruce Hornsby: *The Way It Is*, RCA, 1986

Humberto Gatica

OK, trivia fans, try this one on for size: who was the engineer for the most complex recording session of the twentieth century? Hint: The session in question was 1985's *We Are The World* produced by Quincy Jones and featuring Michael Jackson, Lionel Richie, Bruce Springsteen, and what seemed to be a cast of thousands. The answer, of course, is the name at the top of this page—the supremely talented Humberto Gatica.

These days, Gatica is best-known as Celine Dion's producer, but he has enjoyed a long and illustrious career spanning more than three decades. Needless to say, Gatica has earned a reputation as one of L.A.'s leading specialists in vocal recording; in addition to Celine, he has worked with many other equally demanding artists, including Barbra Streisand, Gloria Estafan, Julio Iglesias, Tina Turner, Marilyn McCoo, Bette Midler, Taylor Dayne, R Kelly, and Cher (Gatica mixed her 1999 hit, "Believe"). As impressive as that list is, it's really only the tip of the iceberg, considering the wealth of material he engineers and produces for the Latino market (yes, he's worked with Ricky Martin) and his movie soundtrack and production work, which puts him with everyone from Chicago to Kenny G and from Johnny Mathis to Coolio.

With a track record like this, you might expect that the man would be somewhat unapproachable, but nothing could be further from the truth. Warm, gracious, and unassuming, it's easy to see why he's so popular among the staff at L.A.'s Record Plant ("my home away from home," as he describes it). During a break between sessions, he talked with us about his philosophy towards engineering and production as well as sharing some inside tips about the sublime "Celine Dion sound."

How would you summarize the reasons for your longevity and success?

I'm just a pure and artistic person who knows how to use the tools that are available, and I apply and make them work to create what I think my sound is. I have gained the respect and the trust of many artists, and there is something that got me to work with them. Hey, I've been in the business for three generations, and that is what's keeping me pretty busy!

I'd like to ask you to comment on the track ["Here, There and Everywhere"] that Celine recorded for George Martin's 1998 solo album [*In My Life*, MCA]. It's a beautiful production, but it's qualitatively different than the tracks you've done with her.

Sir George Martin is the nicest human being in the business that I have ever met. He's a legend, so just being next to him was an unbelievable experience. I actually recorded the vocal for "Here, There and Everywhere," collaborating with him. He allowed me to do what I do, and that was an amazing experience. So it's interesting that you say it's different...

Maybe it's because the mix is different.

The mix *is* different. I was asked to do the mix but time did not permit me. The approach they took toward Celine's vocal was that they interpreted it literally, which is somewhat differently than we usually do and the way she usually likes to hear it. Not that it was wrong; it was just a bit different.

What were the specific differences?

The way he approached the 'verb on her. She's an artist who has a certain 'verb sound, where it's not swimming in 'verb, where the definition of her is right in your face, but then there's a cool trail that notes sort of sustain to.

Do you achieve that with a delay?

No. I use an AMS RMX16, which I think is the best 'verb for vocals. There are certain programs that I use and certain ways I apply them—sometimes post[fader], sometimes pre—depending on what I'm looking for. Sometimes I route the pre[fader signal] through a delay device, and then I combine the direct signal and the presignal to create a certain effect that is triggered according to how loud or soft the artist is singing.

I think that Mr. Martin used a very short, dry, straight-ahead [reverb]. I don't think it was crafted the way we craft the vocal in reference to how she performs—all those little things that pay at the end of the day. Not that it's wrong, it's just different. And you were able to see the difference. If you compare it to, say, the "Because You Love Me" vocal, you'll see it's a tremendous difference. You know, it's like any artist. Through the years, for instance, Phil Collins had a certain sound that was based on this cool room-y sort of Harmonizer kind of placement in the mix, and it worked for him. If you took it out and instead put in compression and a straight echo, you'd say—whoa, that's not him, what's wrong with the sound?

Can you tell us about the approach you take to recording Celine's vocals?

Celine is an artist who has one of the greatest voices in the business. Through the years, we have developed a particular so-called Celine Dion sound. Sometimes that sound runs completely through a song; other times we have to sort of accommodate it because it's a different type of track or a different type of song. But overall, it's a consistent sound. I use a Telefunken 251 microphone that has been modified by a very, very talented young man named Steven Paul. He helped me locate this microphone and proceeded to modify it. I route the 251 to a custom mic preamp, one that I have used for the past 10 years. It was custom-built by a friend of mine, a very intelligent, very gifted sound engineer. I think the first time I ever used that mic pre was when I recorded "The Way of the World," which was a big challenge for me because we had twelve individuals and twelve different timbres and qualities. But this particular mic pre could really allow me to be consistent. I have never been able to use anything else, unless there was an emergency. I don't think there's anything in the market right now that is in my opinion able to surpass the quality of this mic pre.

I then route the signal through a GML equalizer, which I think is the most musical equalizer that anybody can have access to. Then I use an old 160 dbx limiter/compressor and, in terms of 'verb, an AMS RMX16 with an ambience program. That's the basic aspect of what

Celine Dion's sound is all about, and when you add in an amazing voice, it all comes together.

We work real hard on vocals; she's very demanding in terms of what she likes to hear when she sings, because that allows her to project. Doing vocals with her is a process, a big production—but it works; the end results are great. Basically, the sound you hear is established at the recording, not in the mixing. I'm a guy who believes in commitment. If you like something, you sort of think a little bit toward the future where it's going to end up [in the mix]. What's going to be in front of this voice, what's going to be against it, that sort of thing. You make a decision and commit to it, and it's done. Come time to do the mix, it's already there.

In terms of the headphone mix, does Celine tend to go for less of herself in the cans so that she will project more?

The way she describes it to me is, "I want to be able to hear when I'm singing very soft and when I'm singing very loud." So what I give to her on the phones is a sound—it's not a mix— a sound that allows her to really hear every little thing that she's doing, and she likes to hear it very loud.

Do you strap a limiter across the headphones to protect her ears?

No. I never put a limiter on the phones because, when she opens up, she will be over-singing, she'll be trying to fight the limiter. But I put another GML across the headphone mix, and I create an EQ curve just for the phones. I don't care how good they are, at the end of the day they are these little things that are just blowing volume up your ears. I use Sony headphones—I'm not sure of the model number—because they don't give me problems with feedback, even at close proximity. You have to understand that this mic I use [the Telefunken 251] is so hot, sometimes I tell Celine, "I can even hear your thoughts!" But even when she opens up, instead of the mic thinning her out, it just responds incredibly. I do want to make sure that the headphones are being driven by a very powerful set of amplifiers so they don't clip. Celine can hear the slightest little increment of compression or overloading, even in the midst of a loud playback where you go gee, how is she ever able to hear this? So the headphone mix is pretty clean; her voice is very defined in the phones, and the music takes a very second place.

Through the whole process of recording her voice, I'm constantly creating a kind of mini-mix; sometimes I have to hold her back just a little bit so she doesn't go over the top. We have an amazing rapport; there are a lot of visual things, a lot of signs and signals that she's giving me between takes or between lines. Or she'll just look at me and, without even saying anything, I'll know she's telling me to do something that might help. It's just a very trusting sort of thing that we have.

[Barbra] Streisand is a bit different. Streisand's one basic comment is: "I'm happy." That's it. Celine says, "I'm happy, but maybe on this line you're going to help me here, right?" So I might do something like change around the mix so she can hear more definition.

When you're recording Celine's vocals, are you monitoring the headphone mix in the control room?

She hears exactly what I'm hearing, but I don't monitor the EQed mix. Occasionally, after the sound is established, I'll put the phones on and I'll evaluate where she's at; what exactly is she hearing? And then sort of relate and make my differences so when I listen to the big mon-

itors, I know exactly where she's at. It works, and that is all part of her sound. I try to establish this from day one, so when it comes to mixing and the final record, that's it.

Celine is powerful; she has a lot of range and a tremendous amount of energy. She's a person who is very mindful of what is done, and she definitely knows how to work the mic!

I guess what you're saying is, find the signal chain that works for you.

Exactly. Find what works best. It's funny, because the other day I was going through some tapes. I was looking for a specific sound in my library, and I ran into a DAT that was recorded during the *We Are The World* sessions. This tape had vocals only, from one of the passes—we did five passes that night—and it was completely unEQed and unprocessed. It just had a good balance between one artist and the next. I was surprised because the quality and presence of the vocals—every one of those individuals—was pretty unbelievable.

At the end of the day, in any kind of music, it's about how the artist feels, about how good you make the artist sound. You can have an amazing-sounding track, you can have an amazing balance, but if the quality and the presence and the placement of the vocals is not right—if the artist is not comfortable—you're going to end up with a record that has something wrong with it. Learn through the years where to place the vocal, and then you can process it; you can effect it, any way you want.

Start with a great, substantial, healthy foundation of rhythm, add a great-sounding vocal, and establish a great relationship between the two. When I begin my mixes, I start by establishing the rhythm, regardless of the kind of music, then I add the vocal. If I am mixing and I come to the point where I feel comfortable and have established the relationship that makes it fall in place,

> *"At the end of the day, in any kind of music, its about how the artist feels, about how good you make the artist sound."*

it will be painless. The artist comes in or the producer comes in, and it's an amazing feeling when you know the vocal is right. At that point, you can always lift things up, or take things out. But many times, certain panning or equalization can hinder that definition and clarity in the vocal, even if it's recorded correctly.

Another important thing to understand is that it's OK to take things down in a disciplined way; for example, trying to clear the air space that's been invaded by certain instruments. I want to hear things in my face sometimes, yes, but I also want to hear the vocal! And when I'm playing it loud, in the parts where the vocalist is also singing loud, I don't want it to be piercing my ear, either. Sometimes I hear CDs where all of a sudden the music builds, and the artist begins to get thin and small, and all you hear is this frequency that just sticks out, even though it's not really having any impact. It's weird, it truly is.

So you're saying that you need to maintain emotional intensity, whether the music's going up or going down.

You've got to maintain it. Pretend you're singing, and you're there behind the mic, killing yourself, right? You're trying to deliver a performance that people will believe in, even though they're not watching you moving or doing anything. Now I can hinder that very easily in the mix, even if I record you incredibly. To me, a great mix is when you have accomplished a tremendous feeling about the music being played, a tremendous feedback of whatever you're getting from the artist, whoever is motivating your emotion. The whole idea of a great producer is to create a performance that's believable, and the engineer's job is to capitalize on that and put down on tape the best quality possible. When the quality is good, the emotions come out.

> **"The whole idea of a great producer is to create a performance that's believable, and the engineer's job is to capitalize on that and put down on tape the best quality possible."**

You have to listen to the individual. Ask yourself, am I creating a tense feeling when they are singing by over-compressing? Sometimes it's kind of cool, but other times, at the end of the day, when you put everything around [it], it's not cool; all of a sudden there's a sound, but the emotion goes down to nothing.

It's important to use a good mic. The Telefunken is one of my all-time favorite mics; it lets me accomplish what *I* like to hear. And don't be afraid to use equalization; there's nothing wrong with that. A lot of people say everything should be flat. Well, I've heard a lot of things that are flat, natural, but still sound pretty bad. Equipment has been designed to use in moderation.

Do you ever find yourself equalizing a vocal differently during the course of a song? Actually tweaking settings during the choruses and the verses?

I've developed a pretty consistent format of equalization that I use on most artists that I work with. If I have to record an artist where I don't have access to certain equipment, like a GML equalizer, maybe then I would just do it flat. But I just use my experience and whatever my ears tell me—my ears are the only tool that I completely trust.

How about in the mixing stage?

In the mixing stage, there are times where I may have to thin the vocal out, because of the nature of the singing or the key the person is singing in. Sometimes I mult the vocal and have the verse processed one way and the chorus another way; sometimes I use the 'verb aspect to change it a little bit. And that's great; if you have access to do that, it's wonderful. I don't do that all the time, but, with some artists, I do it maybe 60 percent of the time. Many times when Celine opens up in the chorus, I need to warm the sound up a bit, so I process it a little differently—I take away some air, and I may add it back perhaps on the verses.

But you're emphasizing the importance of using good equalization circuitry.

It's very important. You want to make sure your signal is clean and that you're not damaging the signal chain in any shape or way. Sometimes, processors are not correctly aligned, so when you use an outboard compressor and equalizer along with whatever console you are using, they may not like each other. I usually don't use console equalizers; my whole vocal thing is done from outside equipment.

I used an SSL 9000 to mix five songs on the new Barbra Streisand album. In a few places she said to me, "I can hear the compilations of performance, and that bothers me sometimes." I can totally respect that in an artist; she can see the different emotional stages when we come in and comp the vocal.

Sure, you can't be in the same mood every time...

Exactly. And she can tell better than anyone, so she says, "Well, I was a little soft here, I was a bit angry there, and it bothers me..." To the average ear, no one would hear it, but I can really relate to her, so it was easy for me. But instead of doing a level thing [to compensate], I used EQ to take away some frequencies, and the SSL allows you to program the EQ and pop it in and out and save a lot of anxiety.

How long do you typically spend on a mix?

In 90 percent of the mixes that I do—whether it's a 24-track, 48-track, or two 48-tracks linked together—I will build a mix in eight hours. Sometimes, though, maybe you are a little fatigued, and if you're smart, you say, "Let's just come back tomorrow." And tomorrow, in one or two good clean hours, I can kill this. That's my theory. After the mix is done, my assistant and I dissect it from many different points of view.

For instance, right now I'm mixing Celine Dion's *Greatest Hits*. We're doing about eight or nine songs, and then out of the nine, we'll select the best six. On this project, I'm working with many different producers—David Foster, Rick Wake, Mutt Lange, Max Martin, the guy who does all the Backstreet Boys. My job right now is getting all the producers to where they are 100 percent satisfied and happy. In their hearts and in their minds, they know that when it comes to the vocal—and, of course they have an opinion, they can say anything they like—they know that department is taken care of by Celine and myself, in that order. So usually they're very happy about where the vocal is. When it's all done, that's when I play all the mixes for her. She's very sensitive about the emotion that she puts down. Meaning, every little breath, every little thing in between breaths, every little pickup of a line where sometimes you have to help, matters. For example, she'll sing, "The way I *love* you." I exaggerate it; I make sure that "L" is so divine that it really delivered what she meant to say. She's very into that; that's what she likes about working with us.

Do you take a different approach when producing music for the Latino market?

No, I just apply what I know. The language itself...sometimes that permits you to do things a little differently. But it's very limited—you have very little room to move.

I produce a girl from South America named Myriam Hernandez, a very successful artist, one of the greatest female singers in that part of the world. I consider her to be the Celine Dion of Latino music, and I use the same sort of tricks and approach in terms of recording her vocals. But the Latino market, especially now, is so hip. And let me tell you, there are a lot of great-sounding Latino records recorded by Latino engineers, produced by Latino guys.

So technically, there's no qualitative difference.

No. Though sometimes you'll notice a bit of a difference in the way you equalize things, because there's a little more rhythm in the Spanish language; extra vowels, you know. They're different, so it's a different sound, and therefore certain EQ doesn't work. Same thing in French. Celine has done two French records, and I have to tell myself to EQ her differently when she sings in French. A million things change because of the nature of the language; one dB in a certain frequency can make all the difference in the world. Certain languages do require certain crafts.

Do you have any general advice for someone just starting out in this field, someone who's got their own little home studio and aspires to be the next Humberto Gatica?

Just be yourself, don't hold back, and be open-minded to both criticism and advice. Be open to trying things, and you will find your sound. At the end of the day, you can only teach an individual so much; at the end of the day, it's what you think sounds good and what feels good to you. It might be in line with other people who will want to work with you because they love the way you hear things. Or it might work against you because they don't like what you do.

You're going to make mistakes. The important thing is to learn from them, to tell yourself, "Oh my God, that sounds horrible, I will never do that again." And then when you find yourself in the same position, you have to remember and to go, "No, I'm not going to do what I did before." You learn because that's how it is; you've got to make mistakes. You correct yourself, and then you balance it so the good overrules the bad. And you go on from there.

Selected Listening:
Any Celine Dion recording from 1990 – 2000
Various Artists: *We Are The World*, Polygram/Mercury, 1985
Michael Jackson: *Thriller*, Epic, 1982; *Bad*, Epic, 1987
Barbra Streisand: *Back To Broadway*, Columbia, 1993; *The Mirror Has Two Faces*, Sony, 1996; *Higher Ground*, Columbia, 1997
Julio Iglesias: *Non Stop*, Columbia, 1988; *Un Hombre Solo*, Sony, 1989; *Crazy*, Sony, 1994; *La Carretera*, Sony, 1995; *Tango*, Columbia, 1996
Ricky Martin: *Vuelve*, Sony, 1998
Cher: *Believe*, Warner Bros., 1998

Part Three

Meanwhile, on the Other Side of the Atlantic...

George Martin

T
he New York weather in February, 1964 was brutal. Though I was five months shy of my eleventh birthday, the massive snowdrifts and bitter cold are still indelibly etched in my mind. But the most memorable thing about that bleak winter was that it marked the first time I ever heard a Beatles record.

"The Beatles are coming! The Beatles are coming!" shouted the hysterical DJ, interrupting "I Want To Hold Your Hand" every thirty seconds, but so transfixed was I with the *sound* I was hearing, I hardly paid any notice. What the hell was this?? It was so different, so much bigger than life than any record I had ever heard before. I listened to it over and over again on my crappy transistor radio (pick a station, any station—it was being played more or less continuously), finally deciding I had to experience it on something a bit better (which in this case was my plastic monaural record player, with its *five*-inch speaker). Scraping together the better part of a week's allowance, I bundled up, made the trek to my neighborhood record store and bought my first-ever 45.

I still remember trundling home and excitedly examining my new purchase. The faces on the sleeve were familiar, all right—the Ed Sullivan appearances were coming up, and the Fab Four's publicity machine was grinding away in high gear—but on the label there was a name and a job title that was unfamiliar to me. "Produced by George Martin," it said as it spun around endlessly on my turntable. "So he must be the guy that made it sound this way," I thought. "I wonder how he does it…"

Fast-forward nearly thirty-five years into the future. The precocious ten year old is now a grown man, sitting somewhat nervously in the lounge of a London recording studio, waiting to—at long last—meet the name on the label. He's pretty sure he knows what record producers do—he's met plenty of them and even produced a few records himself—but he's still in awe, still wondering how George Martin actually crafted that amazing sound all those years ago. In a few minutes, he hopes to find out.

Best known, of course, as the man who signed The Beatles after every other record label in England turned them down—and as the gifted, resourceful producer of every one of their records—Martin has also had a long and illustrious pre- and post-Beatles career, working with artists as diverse as Peter Sellers, Jeff Beck, America, Mahavishnu Orchestra, Cheap Trick, Dire Straits, Ultravox, and Elton John. In 1998, after nearly half a century of been-there-done-that, Sir George (yes, he's been tapped on the shoulder by the Queen) announced his retirement.

Determined to call the shots to the very end, he literally orchestrated his departure with the release of *In My Life*, a self-described album of "friends and heroes" that not only showcased his formidable production abilities but at the same time paid homage to the four lads from Liverpool who put him on the map. Recorded mainly at his new North London studio (Air Lyndhurst—a converted nineteenth century church) and aided ably by his son Giles, *In My Life* gives you a good sense of what went into making those classic Beatles records as well as an intriguing glimpse into how they might have sounded if they had been recorded with today's technology. On that level, it succeeds far more than Jeff Lynne and the surviving group members' 1996 reworking of Lennon's "Free As A Bird" and "Real Love."

In the summer of 1998—all these years, all these miles later—I found myself awkwardly shaking George Martin's hand and following him up a flight of stairs to the converted rectory in Air Lyndhurst where we were to be convening. There's no question that Sir George means business—as soon as he settled his lanky frame into a chair, he issued the first direction of the day to me: "Right then, off you go." Feeling somewhat like a novice singer entering a vocal booth for the first time, I cleared my throat and started the interview, with the sounds of February 1964 still ringing loudly in my ears.

It's hard to believe that *In My Life* is really your last record.

This *is* the last album I'll ever make, for several good reasons. One is that I'm very old, and I think it's about time I stopped—I've been making records for 48 years, and it's a long time. Secondly, my hearing isn't very good now because I damaged it when I was younger, and old age affects it too. So I know I'm not as good as I used to be. But in making a final album, I decided I would make one I could enjoy. It's not a Beatles record, it's a record of friends and heroes. For a hook to hang it on, we used Beatles songs. It could equally have been Cole Porter, or Gershwin, or Jerome Kern.

What's most clearly conveyed in this album is the sheer pleasure that the artists were taking in participating.

A lot of the people involved were old friends, people like Phil Collins, Jeff Beck, John Williams—they're old pals, and it was just like having a real get-together. But there were a lot of people who were heroes of mine, people I hadn't met before—Goldie Hawn, Robin Williams, Jim Carrey. Of course, the danger of doing a thing like this is that you get so enamored of each other that you forget about the audience. But I don't think we did; I think we really tried to make it a good record, too.

On some of the tracks, you stick very closely with the original arrangement, and on others you change the feel radically.

Well, the obvious one [that follows the original arrangement] is Phil Collins' version of "Golden Slumbers." That is such a special piece of music to me, I didn't want to change it, though we did make the drum solo longer. Obviously, with Goldie Hawn, "A Hard Day's Night" had to be a different kind of score. And if you're doing a thing with Celine Dion, you've got to write something that's going to work for her, rather than the way we did "Here, There and Everywhere" with Paul. Those decisions were easy. It was more difficult to decide to stick with a score than to change it, because we knew people were going to say, "Why did he do it that way? Why didn't he do something new?" But the only valid reason must be, because the original way was the right way to do it. To change it, you've got to have a good reason.

"I Am The Walrus" uses the original score, but because everything is recorded with '90s technology, you can hear all the individual instruments much more clearly.

Jim [Carrey] wanted very much to do that one, and he was so used to the original, which did seem to work well. I have very fond memories of when John first brought me the song. We always had the same routine—I would sit on a high stool and he would stand in front of me with his acoustic guitar and just sing it through. When I heard him do "Strawberry Fields" [that way], I fell in love with it—enormously—but when he first ran through "I Am The Walrus" for me, I said to him, "What the hell is *that*?" (laughs) I asked him, "What are we going to do with it?" and he replied, "Couldn't you do a score?" I mean, when you hear it with just guitar, it's really weird.

Sure, there's not much to it, melodically.

Really. So I said, "Well, what do you have in mind, John?" Because John was never very articulate about orchestration; he'd never sit down with you and say, "I'd like some brass to come in here, or some cellos to do that," as Paul would. He would just say, "Do something good." So I went away and thought about it, and I wrote with four cellos and some trumpets in mind. But then I knew that we had to have kooky effects, so I engaged a twelve-piece choir—the Mike Sammes Singers—who were the kind of regular, dare I say, hack singers of radio and television. They were very proficient—they could read music just like that, and they had good voices, but they weren't who you normally would pick for The Beatles. But I needed those kind of people, because I actually wrote into the score the "whoooo's" (demonstrates) and "ha ha ha hee hee hee's," all those kinds of things. When we recorded it, John had no idea I'd done this, (laughs) and when they started doing their little bits and pieces, they were really so professional about it, so serious, you know, counting off, one, two, three, "whoooo!" That in itself was hysterical, everything was barlined and John fell around laughing, saying, "What the hell have you done?" I said, "Well, I think it's going to work," and he agreed: "Yeah, it sounds great." So it did work very well, it went extraordinarily well. In the outro, Jim says something about ruining a masterpiece...

"I have defiled a timeless piece of art!" I believe are his exact words.

Yes, that's right. We filmed the whole thing, you know. Jim was playing to the cameras a lot, doing all of his funny faces, and he was very amusing, but eventually I had to get rid of the cameras because we had to think of what we were going to sound like.

The odd thing about the original recording is that you have this wild score juxtaposed against Lennon's vocal delivery, which is very restrained, delivering these nonsense lyrics in a very dry, almost acerbic way. Here, you've taken a completely different vocal approach.

I knew we needed someone crazy, and Jim was the right choice, I think.

And he can sing, too.

Yes, he's a very good singer, he really is. I didn't realize how good he was until I worked with him, actually. Getting your tongue around those words is quite tricky; there's some weird stuff there.

Jeff Beck was offered his choice of songs, and it was his decision to do "A Day In The Life." Why was he the only artist allowed to pick his song?

Generally, people don't like being given completely free rein— people like to be guided a little bit. So in most cases, I did actually assign the song. With Celine [Dion], for example, I didn't want any big buildups. My first thought was "Blackbird," but then I thought "Here, There and Everywhere" would be a good one, and she went along with that.

Which Beatles song would you have asked Hendrix to cover?

Probably "Revolution #9," I would think. (laughs)

You would have had to score it, though...

I don't know about that...(laughs) Actually, there's one other one I'd like to have done— and Hendrix would have done a great job on it—and that's "Yer Blue*s*." I love the meter of it, I love the quirky time changes. I thought that Jeff [Beck] would do something like that. I was surprised when he chose "A Day In The Life." Hendrix was a fantastic player. Jeff knew him—I never did. Jeff once said to me, "You know, I found out that Hendrix uses very, very thick strings— almost like piano wire—and they're very difficult to bend." But he had enormously powerful hands; his fingers were like steel, he could bend those great notes. Jeff told me, "I couldn't do it, not the way his guitar was strung."

The album contains only two McCartney songs—all the others except "Here Comes The Sun" are Lennon songs.

I love Paul's songs, but, as I've told him, "The trouble with you is that you've written all the popular ones, and I don't want this album to be full of songs that everybody knows backwards!" I didn't want to do "Fool On The Hill" and "Michelle" and "Yesterday" and "Let It Be." The thing is, if you analyze Lennon-McCartney songs on the [total] number of performances— and I'm quite sure somebody has—then you would find that Paul's songs probably form 70% of performances. John actually said to me once, about the popularity of his songs—and sometimes he was a bit irritated with the fact that Paul's songs were so popular—he said, "Let's face it, George, I don't expect to walk into a bar in Spain and hear someone whistling 'I Am The Walrus.'" (laughs) That's the reason why there aren't too many of Paul's songs on my record. It wasn't a question of taste, and Paul understands that.

Most Lennon songs have a much simpler melodic content—they don't operate over such a wide range of notes, they have more to do with the lyrics and how the chords are changing under the melody.

That's right, but I think that the similarities between John and Paul were greater than the differences. Most people tend to regard Paul as being the softie, and John as being the rebel and rocker. But Paul was pretty rebellious and pretty rocky—look at "Helter Skelter." And, don't forget, Paul was the avant-garde man—he used to hang around arty places in London and loved Stockhausen, while John would go back to his place in Weybridge with his wife and have coffee by the fire. So the public image of them isn't exactly true. John was just as capable of writing a soft song as Paul—"Julia," "Good Night"—that was a great song.

With the announcement of your retirement, people are already talking about who will be the "next George Martin." You've singled out Brian Eno as a producer you admire.

The thing I like about Brian is that he's a lateral thinker. He doesn't go directly to the target—he thinks about it a great deal and goes around the sides, contributing something that's quite refreshing. I think that his musical work has always been stimulating, always been interesting. He doesn't just follow the herd, like most people do. That's why I admire him very much.

> **"It's difficult to be innovative and yet be solidly commercially successful."**

It's difficult to be innovative and yet be solidly commercially successful. I've tried to combine the two things—to be inventive and different, and at the same time not to leave the public behind. It's quite tricky to strike that balance.

Eno also uses a lot of random elements in his approach to music. Do you think randomness is an important component in creating innovative music?

Randomness is good, up to a point, but it can be chaotic. Mind you, some people like chaos. In fact, some people think it's the answer to *everything*—look at the chaos theory of the universe. But the idea of doing a lottery with music, just bringing in sounds at random—well, sometimes it works, but most of the time it doesn't. The Beatles were into randomness when we were doing "I Am The Walrus." When we were mixing it, we brought in a radio set and God smiled on us that day because there happened to be a Shakespearian play on, and that did work. But it could just as easily have been just rubbish.

Paul used to spend a lot of time putting on a record and then [simultaneously] watching a movie. He was interested in the random juxtaposition of images with unrelated music. He once came to me and said, "You know, it's remarkable how things do actually work out well in randomness." He was quite right, but if you do that, then five percent of the time you'll have the music hitting particular spots, and you'll say, "Wow—that brings it to life!" But, of course, the other 95 percent of the time it doesn't, and you tend to forget that.

But it was also randomness that brought together two of the greatest songwriters of the century—growing up within a couple miles of each other, within a few years of each other, meeting, sticking together despite adversity, and then eventually connecting up with you. Surely, if the three of you hadn't found each other, the music would not have been as good.

But that's life. That's like saying, "What would have happened if Hitler hadn't invaded Poland?" or "What would have happened if I hadn't met my wife?—my children wouldn't have been born." There's the "if" factor. But randomness is what life is about; life *is* random.

So randomness has its place in music, too.

Yes, but art is also human endeavor and human desire. You can put a lot of colors into a blender and come up with something, or you can put a lot of sounds into a mixing board and come up with something, but if it's not designed—if it's chaotic and random—then it's not necessarily good. It could be good, but it's more likely to be awful.

Your greatest influence on popular music may have been that, after *Sgt. Pepper*, pop musicians wanted to be taken seriously. Before then, the genre was just light entertainment— afterwards, it became an art form.

I've never subscribed to the view that pop music is trivial, though it's ephemeral in many cases. There have been great moments in popular music, as there have been great moments in classical music.

When we were doing *Pepper*, we seemed to stumble upon something which was a little bit more lasting. The combination of using classical influences with rock and roll seemed to me a very good one, and I thought we were doing something which was actually bringing the disparate worlds together. I'd always resented the snobbishness of classical musicians towards rock and roll, and rock and roll musicians towards classical music—the people who had musical blinkers, who could only see what they saw in front of them; they couldn't see either side. I thought, how crazy. Music is a wonderful, big world; why limit yourself to one thing? I liked this combination of classical influences, and I tried to persuade The Beatles that this was a way forward. Paul was pretty interested, and he kind of went along with it. George wanted his own little things, but John was very resistant. John said, "No. Rock and roll is rock and roll. I'm a Teddy Boy, you know, let it all hang out." As a result, as we went from *Pepper* through *All You Need Is Love*, through *Magical Mystery Tour* and the *White Album*, we moved further and further away from that concept [of integrating classical influences]. And what killed it, momentarily and inevitably, was the rise of punk rock—suddenly music became little boys dropping their trousers. That was the opposite end of the bell. But also, John really didn't like it. One of the problems with the *Let It Be* album was that he was rebelling against production. He said to me, "I don't want any of your production crap on this record."

(laughs) That's reassuring...

I asked him, "What do you mean by that?" He replied, "I want it to be an honest record. What we do, we should do it for real. We shouldn't do any overdubs. We should sing live, with the band." And it didn't succeed—it couldn't succeed. Because with new music, you're experimenting, and each performance is going to be different. They said, "We'll get it," but of course they didn't. We went on, and it became very boring. Take 52, well, maybe the bass had a bit of a blip in it, though you've got a great vocal or whatever. You'd never get the perfect match. Alongside that were all the other problems they had at that time. Eventually, *Let It Be* was put on a shelf and left. I made up a version of it with Glyn Johns which was warts and all, like a documentary, and that was it—left on a shelf.

Then they came back to me and said, "Would you come back and make another record?" My reply was, "Not really. I don't like that game." And they said, "No, no, really, produce it the way you used to." So we made *Abbey Road*, and it was then that I went back to my idea, and I suggested to Paul, "Think symphonically. Bring some of your tunes back as certain subjects, work them contrapuntally, put them in different keys. Think in terms of *any* instrument— you've got the world, you can have whatever sound you like. We can wrap this into something that's really worthwhile." So it became a piecemeal assembly into the side that ends up with my favorite song, "Golden Slumbers." Funnily enough, John actually went along with that to a limited extent, he actually contributed some of his songs, "Hey, I've got something that can go in here, what about it?" But as a compromise, the other side had to be single tracks, and what great single tracks they were. Out of that came "Come Together," and "Because." "Because" was amazing; that was a complete flip for John.

Did you write the vocal arrangement for "Because?"

Yes. The way it worked was that John had this arpeggio-type accompaniment he played on guitar. I learned all the notes he was playing, and I duplicated them on electric harpsichord so we played in unison, and Paul played bass; that was the original track. We had to keep ourselves together because it had to be *exactly* right, and I'm not the greatest time player in the world— the others were much better ensemble players than I was. We had no such things as click tracks or drum machines in those days—they didn't exist. So we got a drum machine of our own, which was Ringo Starr. We put him in a little corner of the room, we surrounded him with screens and pads, and locked him up. And he just sat there playing quarter notes on the high hat [demonstrates] while we played—he enabled us to keep together. Then we started adding voices, with the three of them together. They were so good at singing, so good at working together, that we'd lay down one track and then I'd say to them, "OK, let's do another track with slightly different harmonies." We did three tracks altogether, so we had nine voices. It worked well.

I gather there were still a lot of tensions in the band at the time of Abbey Road

Much less than during [the recording of] *Let It Be*. I think probably we all knew it was the last record. Sure, there were tensions, because John was still very, well...the John and Yoko scene was the one that pulled everything away. When Yoko was ill, they brought her bed into the studio, that kind of thing. It was very odd...

How did you deal with those tensions?

Well, there were two alternatives you had. Either you walked out or you stuck it out, and I wasn't one for walking out. I just hoped it would change. During the making of *Abbey Road*, it was okay, it was much happier. The music, too, was good, which made it all worthwhile. But I think we all knew it was the last one. John had gone through a tremendous upheaval in his private life, and he was a very odd person at times, he wasn't at all himself. There was the famous interview he did for *Rolling Stone*, which has been reprinted many times, in which he says many unfair and untrue things, slagged everybody off, including me. I took him to task over it later on, asking him, "Why did you say all those things? It wasn't very nice..." He said, "Oh, I was just stoned out of my head." That was his only apology, really. Unfortunately, that has become history now; it's accepted as the Bible.

You've stated that you learned as much from The Beatles as they did from you. What exactly did you learn from them?

The main thing was never to accept the obvious, never to accept second-best, and always to look beyond what's there. They were intensely curious and very demanding, and they often wanted something that wasn't possible. But that, in a way, was also good because it spurred me on to doing better things; I did better work because of them. If they had been lesser people, my work wouldn't have been as good. I'm sure of that.

> *"[The Beatles] were intensely curious and very demanding, and they often wanted something that wasn't possible. But that spurred me on to doing better things; I did better work because of them."*

I think I opened their eyes to a few things, too. They were very difficult people at times. They expected so much that when they got something that was really good, they thought it was normal.

What did you think of the so-called "classic rock" bands of the '70s —bands of classically trained musicians like Yes, or Emerson, Lake and Palmer? Did you feel that you'd created a monster?

(laughs) I think it was quite healthy—I don't think it was a monster! I've never believed that a little bit of learning does any harm; on the contrary, it's quite beneficial. A lot of pop musicians are concerned that, if they learn music "properly," it might rob them of inspiration, of creation. I don't hold with that view. Any inhibition that might arise from that is something you can control. The more you find out about things, the better you're likely to be. Ignorance—which is quoted as a virtue by some people—is not a virtue. Indeed, it can be a hindrance, and people who are really brilliant would be even more brilliant if they weren't ignorant.

Were you familiar with the records that influenced The Beatles so much in their early years? Had you listened to Chuck Berry and Little Richard before you met The Beatles?

I'd listened to Chuck Berry and Little Richard, but I wasn't aware of most of the Motown stuff. They generally got hold of that stuff earlier than most people. I was aware of the mainstream artists of the day, people like Jerry Lee Lewis. The Beatles exposed me to the more sophisticated records, like the stuff coming out of Motown. It was quite interesting, and I loved it.

So you weren't really familiar with some of the originals before you recorded the cover versions.

Not really, no.

As you were working with The Beatles in the early years, were you actively listening to the contemporary producers of the day and studying their techniques?

No. The fact of the matter was that I was too busy to listen to much of *anything*. I was really working all hours of the day. When The Beatles came along, I already had a full roster of artists, I was head of the label [Parlophone], and I was making most of the records on that label. When you're working that hard, you don't get time to go and look for recordings. If something comes your way, you listen to it, but you don't start actively looking for what's happening elsewhere; you're too busy with what you're doing.

But in the '50s, you visited Capitol Studios in L.A. to study American recording techniques.

I think we're talking about 1954 or 1955; Abbey Road was pretty crappy in those days. I'd gone to America with Ron Goodwin; I'd had a minor hit with him in the States called "Swinging Sweetheart," and we took the opportunity to go to Capitol and see what they were doing. They were recording on Ampex 3-track half-inch [tape]; we were recording on mono quarter-inch, though our classical people were using stereo quarter-inch. We never used stereo in the pop world—stereo pop records didn't exist in England at the time. I went to a Sinatra session, and they recorded five titles in four hours. I sat in the control booth, and I was enormously impressed with the professionalism of everybody as well as with the technical side of things. This 3-track Ampex meant that you could record the band in stereo on the outside tracks, put the voice in the center track, and you had the freedom to balance them afterwards, after everybody had gone home. And that wasn't the end of it. The microphones they were using were better, and the compression and limiting was infinitely better [than at Abbey Road]. It was my first experience with the Fairchild limiter, which we still use to this day. We didn't have them at Abbey Road, we had nothing like that, so we weren't able to make records that were so dynamic, so brilliant. I came back from America telling everybody in England, "We've got to do something about this, we've got to re-equip the studio, because without it, we're not going to make any good records, ever." And that was a kind of turning point; Abbey Road started getting its act together. It wasn't until the '60s that people started saying, "Wow, they're making good sounds."

The first Beatles album was essentially a snapshot of their stage performance. Did the technology of the time allow you to accurately capture the sound of the band live or did the studio's limitations change their sound?

[The first album] was a mono recording done on a stereo machine separated into twin tracks. It was all done live; I put all the instruments on one track and all the voices on the other. That was to give me the separation that Sinatra had. But it was a live recording in the studio, so it was like doing a radio broadcast. I knew the pieces, I knew their repertoire from The Cavern. We set up the balance and we just ran through the repertoire during the day. We started in the morning, and we finished up about 11 o'clock at night, and we had an album.

But what a phenomenal day...

It was hard work. We deliberately kept "Twist and Shout" for the last track, because I knew John would never do more than one take. We did two takes, actually, but we used the first one. But it was really like doing a broadcast.

The Beatles certainly benefited from having a producer who was musically literate, as opposed to a technical engineer/producer. But these days a lot of producers come up through the engineering ranks and have limited musical knowledge. Are there ever times when an artist will benefit more from having that kind of producer as opposed to a musically-oriented one?

It depends how much the artist is in control of their own product. A technical producer will help them to bring out the sounds that they want. A musical producer will be able to give them extra sounds, will be able to feed them other ideas. Generally speaking, I'd say that you can always get a good technician, you can always get a good engineer to do what you want, so it's useful to have someone who can contribute musically as well. But, by definition, engineers who want to be producers want to be more than engineers: Hugh Padgham, for instance, or Glyn Johns. There are a lot of people who are good producers who provide a musical input as well. Phil Ramone was a technician who was also a fine musician. I think you've got to be specially talented to think of all those things. It's useful for an engineer to concentrate on the technical aspect, and for a producer to concentrate on the musical aspect.

These days, everything is becoming very self-contained, and a lot of musicians are engineering and producing themselves in home studios. Do you see that as a healthy trend?

I think home recording can be very limited, and slightly illusory too, because a lot of young musicians know about nothing else. Personally, I like mixing with different talents all the time. To be cocooned in one particular place is not my style. I like working with lots of different people. I get bored very easily, anyway, which is why I've done so many different kinds of recording.

You've stated that *Sgt. Pepper* would not have sounded as good if it had been recorded on a 24-track, that it was the limitations of 4-track recording that actually acted as a stimulant to creativity.

I do believe that. There's a curious thing here, because what 4-track imposed on us was, firstly, you had to think ahead as to what you were going to do. Secondly, you had to get things right at the time; you couldn't just say, "OK, let's leave that because we can fix it in the mix." All those kinds of decisions, that kind of discipline, imposes constraints on you, but it also makes you focus much more, makes you think. It put a strain on the performers, too. It made them perform—they *had* to be good.

For example, in the case of "She's Leaving Home," I luxuriously used four tracks for the orchestral tracks, and then I mixed those down to two on another 4-track [recorder]. I knew the song, and I knew Paul and John would be singing together, and I did want to double-track them, but I didn't really want to go to another generation. So I made them sing live, the two of them together, on two mics. When John sang the counter-melody ("We gave them most of our lives..."), he had to be further back and he had to have a different echo, which we fixed at the time. They had to get it right the first time, the two of them together—then they had to do it *exactly* the same on the second track.

Would you extend that as a general principle for younger musicians starting out: to work in fewer tracks and force yourself to really get the performances right?

It's difficult to tell people to do that nowadays, because the equipment is so available. All I'm saying is, because we had nothing else in those days, that's what we had to do. And I do believe that if we had had more, the result would have been less.

One of the classical musicians who played on *Sgt. Pepper* **has described the sessions this way: "They would make changes all the time, sort of cutting and pasting as they went along." This, of course, is the way that people use digital editing today, proving, I suppose, that you were 25 years ahead of your time!**

If I'd had today's technology [available for the *Pepper* sessions], I would have loved it. The techniques we used were just a way to create interesting sounds. We had no synthesizers or computers, so we made up our own sounds. The only synthesizer we had in those days was a Mellotron. We actually had a Moog Series III by the time *Abbey Road* came along, but that was pretty primitive too.

A lot of the signal processing you were doing in those days consisted of tape varispeed, which is a lost art today.

We used it a great deal, to alter drum sounds and vocal textures, that kind of thing. We used to varispeed the machines for tape echo, too. The original ADT [Automatic Double-Tracking] we did was developed as a result of my continually saying to the Abbey Road people, "We've got to do something about this." It was Ken Townshend who came up with a way of taking the signal off the sync head and then delaying it through other varispeeded recorders, so the gap between the two could be adjusted. If you got it slightly out, you got phasing. But if you got it out to about 25 to 30 msec, it became a form of ADT. If you took it way out to about 80 msec, you got an Elvis Presley "Heartbreak Hotel" kind of sound. All those variations were on a knob on a tape machine. It was better because it was so unstable—someone had to monitor it all the time to make sure the tape speed was correct, which is why it was so good. Now, if you press a button, once it's there, even if it's scanned a little bit, it's still a little bit mechanical. John Lennon rang me up from New York while he was doing vocals with ADT on *Double Fantasy*, and he said, "It doesn't sound as good as we used to get!" I said, "You're right, John, it doesn't!"

What do you see as having been the most important technological advances in recording and production over the past half century?

Unquestionably, the digital revolution is the most sensational thing that's happened, and it's still not perfect. It's getting there now, with the 24 bits and so on. But the very fact that it is digital is changing the way we think about music altogether. That's a revolutionary thing, though everybody still hankers for the analog sound—me, too. But the new digital gear is getting pretty close to that.

Was *In My Life* **recorded digitally?**

Yes, I'm afraid so. (laughs) But, you know, I don't think technological advances have helped production very much. What I welcome in production is the fact that you can create synthetic sounds much more easily than you used to, which is useful. But I'm a great traditionalist—I still like orchestras, I still like people playing together. I hate putting down a drum track and then a bass track. Almost everything I've done—even now, on the new album—is done with musicians playing together.

In some of the orchestrations you did for The Beatles, you'd be asking highly-trained musicians to play very simple parts—often unisons—or you'd be asking them to break the rules altogether, for instance, telling them not to listen to one another. How did the classical musicians react to this? Did you encounter any resistance?

Not often, no. The most radical thing was on "A Day In The Life," when I asked them to do that climb without copying the musician next to them. Here, they had learned all their lives, especially the string players, to play as one man, and I was asking them *not* to play as one man, to play as 40 people. So that was a bit of a shock to them. But some of the things we asked them to do were very difficult. I think the most disappointing thing for those people was when it wasn't acknowledged how difficult it was—when the piccolo trumpet that David Mason played [in "Penny Lane"] was accepted as normal. I remember Paul asking David to play that solo over again. I said to Paul, "You can't ask a man to do that again, it's fantastic." And the guy, red-faced, said, "I can't do it any better." I felt embarrassed for him, because they were so demanding; they didn't understand.

Paul McCartney once said, "There may be some sort of correlation between the speed of making a record and how good it is. I think there is some sort of secret in not having too long to think."

Paul said that?

Yes. Then he qualifies things by pointing out that there are no hard and fast rules, with *Sgt. Pepper* as a case in point. But is faster usually better than slower? Is it usually counterproductive to keep pushing and dragging things out?

We're talking about variables here. First of all, I think the "raw" factor is something you have to consider. There are cases where you go on so many times that everybody gets sick to death of the bloody thing, and they don't give good performances. This happened during *Let It Be*, when we were doing take after take after take, and it started turning into mud, and you started sinking up to your knees. That's when you mustn't go on, and there *is* a certain timeframe where you should complete everything. It's not fixed, you can't say, "I've got to do this in three hours," it's just a question of reading the emotions. There's a kind of curve where you start from nothing, you learn the piece and gradually get better and better at it until you reach a peak—then you start to go down. You need to catch people at that peak.

"There's a kind of curve where you start from nothing, you learn the piece and gradually get better and better at it until you reach a peak— then you start to go down. You need to catch people at that peak."

With the benefit of your 48 years of experience, what do you think is the single most constructive thing a band just starting out can do to help themselves?

Write a bloody good song. The song is what's the most important thing. Without a good song, they're nowhere.

What's the single most destructive thing a band can do to hurt themselves?
Take drugs.

Some people might say, though, that Lennon and McCartney's involvement with acid— the fact that they were in a little world all their own—may have added something unique to *Sgt. Pepper*.

I don't believe that. I think that *Sgt. Pepper* would have been just as good without them doing what they did. Anyway, John was the [main] one who was into LSD. Their principle criminal offense up to that time was in smoking marijuana. They used to go down to the canteen, have a puff and come back, looking seraphic, all smiles, thinking I didn't know. But they slowed up after that. They didn't write on drugs, the material was already there. No, I think that drugs are very destructive.

On a more philosophical note, you've observed that music is the one art form that needs time to develop, that it can't exist without someone at the other end to listen to it.

Well, you can't look at it and say, "What a nice piece of music that is." You've got to spend a bit of your life in order to appreciate it. Every time you listen to a symphony, you invest forty minutes of your life. You've only got a finite amount of time on this earth, and you've just spent forty minutes of it listening to a symphony, or to an album!

The fact is that music doesn't exist at all without time; time is the dimension which makes it work. I suppose that's true of dance, also, but music is the most sublime of all the arts. It's the most intangible, it's a mystery, and it's been with us since we were primeval. Human beings were making music 80,000 years ago, before they could talk. I think it's the most fundamental part of our lives; in fact, without rhythm, we wouldn't exist. Your heart is pumping out a rhythm, and when it stops, you don't live anymore, so rhythm is actually the difference between life and death. Everything has a rhythm—the sun, the moon, the stars. It really makes you think...

Selected listening:
Any Beatles recording (Capitol/Parlophone/Apple)
Paul McCartney: *Tug Of War*, Columbia, 1982; *Pipes Of Peace*, Parlophone/CBS, 1983
America: *History*, Warner Bros., 1975
Jeff Beck: *Blow By Blow*, Epic, 1975
Seatrain: *Marblehead Messenger*, One Way, 1971; *Seatrain*, Capitol, 1971
Ultravox: *Quartet*, Chrysalis, 1983

Geoff Emerick

Most Beatles scholars agree that George Martin provided the musical polish which made complete the towering, raw talent of John Lennon and Paul McCartney. But perhaps the secret weapon in the group's legacy of recorded music was engineer Geoff Emerick. As the man behind some of the most innovative sounds ever put down on tape, Emerick was the inventor of many recording techniques still in use today. Joining Abbey Road studios as a mere teenager, he quickly developed a reputation as a maverick—as someone who was willing to experiment, unafraid to challenge the staid ways of the past. Incredibly, he was promoted to full engineer a few months shy of his twentieth birthday and shortly thereafter was awarded the coveted job of becoming The Beatles' full-time engineer, replacing Norman Smith.

Emerick was behind the board for The Beatles' most adventurous forays, including the legendary *Revolver, Sgt. Pepper,* and *Magical Mystery Tour* albums, as well as the "Paperback Writer"/"Rain" single [which premiered McCartney's new bold bass sound and was also the group's first experiment with backwards tapes], the live worldwide TV broadcast of "All You Need Is Love" [the first time such a feat was ever attempted], and what was perhaps the greatest double-sided single of all time: "Penny Lane"/"Strawberry Fields Forever." In the face of growing tensions within the band, Emerick departed halfway through the recording of the *White Album*, only to return for what many consider The Beatles' crowning glory—*Abbey Road*.

In the thirty years since the dissolution of the group, Emerick has forged an active career as an engineer/producer, working with Paul McCartney on many of his solo efforts (including his acclaimed *Band On The Run*) as well as with other major artists such as Elvis Costello, Art Garfunkel, Cheap Trick, Badfinger, John McLaughlin, Robin Trower, America, Jeff Beck, Split Enz, and Ultravox. Mild-mannered, unassuming, and soft-spoken, not only is Emerick one of the most respected, experienced, and knowledgeable engineers on the planet, he's also one of the nicest people in the business.

How did you land your first job in engineering?

As a kid, I used to like listening to records at home, and I used to think, well, if I were involved with making that record, I'd have done this or that, lifted up the trumpet line or the string line. In those days, there were only four major recording studios in London: EMI, Decca, Pye, and Phillips; there were no independent studios as such. So just prior to leaving school, I'd written to EMI at Abbey Road requesting a job and I got a rejection. It was actually the youth employment officer that got me an interview at Abbey Road. I started there in 1962, roughly the same month that The Beatles went in for their first recording test.

You assisted for Norman Smith on some early Beatles sessions. Did he share his recording techniques with you, or was he secretive?

> *"I've always described [engineering] as painting a picture with sounds; I think of microphones as lenses."*

There were no secrets, because there was nothing to be secretive about. The main concept that Norman introduced me to was that it's got to happen in the studio, above all. He'd say, "You can open one mic and you'll know whether you've got a hit record or not." So it was more of an artistic slant than a technical slant. I was never that technically minded, but I had sounds in my head. I've always described the job as painting a picture with sounds; I think of microphones as lenses. Engineering is such a wrong term for music mixing, really.

For instance, when you're mixing, you may see strings as a silver shimmer, something else as golden, something else as dark, something as green, something as red. That's the way I hear things.

That's an interesting point: Laymen tend to think of sounds in visual terms. A technical person would hear something and think, that sound's got lots of 150 Hz; a nontechnical person would think, that sound is dark.

That's right. When I was younger, I had this thing with the maintenance people at Abbey Road. I'd do something, and they'd say, "You can't do that because...." They'd go on about so many nanowebers of this and so many nanowebers of that, and I wouldn't even know what they were talking about! All I'd know is that I'd hear something, and it would sound right to me.

So the training you received was just a matter of sitting back and observing?

Just observing. There was another good engineer at Abbey Road named Stuart Eltham, and I learned a lot from Stuart. But there was no actual training; it was up to you to pick up what you could. You can't really train anyone, anyway—it's like trying to train someone to paint a picture. If you can't paint, you can't paint.

George Martin has talked about a trip he made to America in the '50s to sit in on some Sinatra sessions and take note of the gear being used. When he came back, he told the Abbey Road management that they needed to purchase this equipment to stay competitive with the American studios.

That's right, but they were totally against anything like that. Later on, when the first Telefunken and Studer multitracks began appearing, every piece of outside equipment that went into Abbey Road, the technicians stripped it down to every last nut and bolt and rebuilt it.

Why would they do that?

I don't know. It was just the way things had to be done. When we started *Revolver*, we had two 4-track rooms, which were remote from the studios because there were only two 4-track machines but there were three studios. So the 4-track machines were never in the control room—they were always remote. For drop-ins, you had to do it remotely over an intercom; from the control room, you'd say "drop in now," and the guy upstairs would drop in but would only be able to monitor one track at a time—it was just impossible.

Because of the complexity of recording *Revolver*—doing backwards stuff and all that—we wanted the 4-track machine put into the control room, which meant wheeling it up the corridor and through a door. But we were told this was impossible because all the azimuth was going to go out, and other things were going to go wrong. In the end, they relented, but they brought in four technical people from the research establishment down at Hayes. So six people watched how it was transported up the corridor.

Were they wearing lab coats?

Yeah! (laughs) It was unbelievable. The poor man who wheeled it wore a brown coat, because the people wearing the brown coats swept the floors and put the chairs out and wheeled the machinery around. So the five people in the white coats were watching the one man in the brown coat wheel the machine down the corridor. (laughs)

Why do you think you got promoted to this tremendously responsible job—engineer to The Beatles, top of the pyramid—over some of your peers?

Well, first of all, I used to work well with Norman. Second engineering then—being the assistant—was purely operating the tape machine. You didn't put the mics out or anything—someone else did that. But it was quite an important job because most sessions were straight stereo, and if anything went wrong, there was no comeback; it couldn't be mixed again. And if you've got a whole orchestra there, it's a very expensive thing to bring everyone back. So it was important that the tape machines were working perfectly, that the heads were cleaned and everything was pristine. If you pressed the wrong button, you wiped something and that was it.

Anyway, Norman wanted to leave to be a producer, and I believe he said to George Martin, "Can I still engineer for The Beatles?" and I think George said to Norman, "No, you can't do both jobs." So there was a promotion for someone to replace Norman. In those days, you were never going to be a recording engineer [at Abbey Road] until you were forty years old. That was your ultimate goal, and it was such an unattainable job that you couldn't attain that goal until you were forty years old. After a few months as an assistant engineer, I went on to cutting lacquers, which was a promotion. We didn't have cassettes in those days to give to artists for demonstration purposes—you had to cut onto seven inch acetate. So there would be an order from the three studios for the day's work—six copies of this title, six copies of that one. And the next step in the promotion chain was actually cutting the master discs, which I also did, for about eighteen months. All this happened in the space of four years, so everyone thought, how can this young kid do such an important job? Looking back on it, I guess I had to fight for it, but I was so naive I didn't realize that people were against it.

I think the first session I ever did in Studio 2—it was a young band called Go West—I had an idea in my head for a different sound. The studio had a hard end and a carpeted end. Normally, the rhythm section was up on the carpeted end and the strings were on the hard end, but I decided to change everything around. Of course, the next day everybody was saying, "Oh, why did you have to do that? You shouldn't do that—we've been doing things like this quite alright for the last ten years, you know." [They were complaining] because it meant extra work for them if the producer came in and said, "I want to do it like that." I didn't realize at the time that this was creating a bit of a problem.

Maybe you got the promotion for just that reason—because you were perceived as a maverick.

That, plus the fact that I was listening to American records, records from outside EMI. There were certain sounds I was hearing that we didn't have at EMI, so I was thinking, "How do you do that?" As an example, we took the front skin off the bass drum for the first time and put the mic close in to get that dead sound. We may have then put the front skin back on and stuffed it with a sweater. In fact, I think it was that sweater from one of the early Beatles promotional pictures, the one that had four necks in it—that was the one that was inside the bass drum. Anyway, I decided to put the microphone nearer than two feet, and I had to get a letter of authority to be able to do it, because the fear was that the air pressure would damage the diaphragm! I was permitted to do it, but only on Beatles sessions. There were these little hurdles to deal with all the time.

Do you think your nontechnical background played a part in your getting the promotion?

I don't think so, because the management at Abbey Road were dead set against someone so young being promoted into that engineering spot. But there was no one else, it was as simple as that. Obviously, George [Martin] had said, "We want Geoff to become the new Beatles engineer," because I had done some engineering prior to that. My memory is a little vague, but I think the first record I engineered that was a hit was *Pretty Flamingo* by Manfred Mann. I put the dobro guitar on that record through a Fairchild [limiter] and that was the other bit of equipment that we had. I just fell in love with Fairchild 660 limiters.

You mentioned that the assistant engineers were purely tape operators, so who set up the microphones?

The maintenance people would usually do that. The balance engineer would draw a plan, and the maintenance people used to put the mics out, roughly position them and plug them all in. The balance engineer could then move the mics, but if he wanted a mic changed from, say, fader 5 to fader 6, he wasn't allowed to do that. He had to phone up for someone to come and do that.

Someone, presumably, wearing a white coat.

That's right. (laughs)

Some engineers maintain that moving a mic a fraction of an inch can make a world of difference...

Well, in some instances, yes, but I'm not so convinced of that.

But if the assistants weren't out there moving the mics, how did they learn about the subtleties of mic placement?

They learned by comments the engineer might make, or you'd see the engineer go out there and move the mic, and then you'd hear the difference.

How did you feel during that very first session with The Beatles, recording "Tomorrow Never Knows"?

Terrible! I had already been promoted to engineer, but I hadn't been asked to do The Beatles; I was doing other acts. I remember going up to the studio manager's office and them saying, "Do you want to do The Beatles?" They were explaining why, that Norman was leaving, that you're so young, blah, blah, blah. George [Martin] was there and a few other people. I was playing an eenie, meenie, minie, moe game in my mind, thinking, no, I can't do this, but if it stops on yes, I'll just say yes. What did I have to lose, really?

Did The Beatles accept you in your new role right away, or was there a period of initiation?

They accepted me, more or less. I think Paul was OK; it was a little funny with the others. But it was alright after a week or so. Being young and somewhat innovative in my outlook, I guess I could really relate to George Martin. Although Norman would try things, there were certain things George would ask other engineers to do, and they would say, "No, it's impossible, you can't do that." At least, together, we'd try things, so that opened up a whole new world; we could do anything he wanted, because I was willing to do it.

The *Beatles Anthologies* includes that first take of "Tomorrow Never Knows," recorded your first day behind the board, and, to my ears, it has the classic Norman Smith sound.

That's right, the mics were set up the same.

But then, as the recording for the album progressed, each day's work yielded sounds that strayed further and further away, eventually moving into whole new areas.

Yeah. Every day we'd try something new. We were listening to American records, and the bass was so good. I remember thinking, how the hell did they do that? We wanted to get more clarity into Paul's bass sound, and we tried everything, even to the extent of using a loudspeaker as a microphone! The theory was, if you can push signal out of a loudspeaker, you can use it to receive signal, and it should push it out with a bigger sound. I believe we used that on two tracks on *Revolver*, but I can't remember which ones.

What did you think of all the tape loops and *music concrete* techniques that The Beatles began getting into during the *Revolver* sessions?

I thought it was great. It wasn't new to me, because when I first started at Abbey Road I'd second engineered sessions for a woman named Fiona Bentley who had a book club kind of thing, but spoken books on record, with great actors like Laurence Olivier reading the parts. They used to have someone who made up the music to go behind all the dialog, and he used to add all these weird sounds, *music concrete* kind of stuff. I really got into that—it was really good. He was possibly the first person to do this kind of thing commercially. This club did things like *The Bible*, which took about three years to record! (laughs)

What was the secret behind those incredibly rich, creamy bass sounds on *Sgt. Pepper*?

Even though we were working on 4-track—sometimes doing one or two reductions onto another machine—by the time we got halfway through *Revolver*, we always opened up one track that was purely for bass. Before, we were cutting the bass and drums together onto one track. The thinking was that if we later wanted more bass, we could turn up the bass EQ and if we wanted a bit more drums, we could turn up the treble EQ.

On *Pepper*, I was bringing Paul's bass amp out of the baffles because it was being done as an overdub. We'd do it late at night when everybody else had gone, and we'd spend quite a bit of time on it. I've actually seen Paul's fingers bleeding from pulling out the notes, getting a note to speak properly. I used a tube C12 mic and put it about six or eight feet away from the speaker cabinet and put it on figure of eight; I also used an Altech compressor, though I don't remember the model number. And that was it, basically.

So you didn't take a DI signal from the bass?

Never, ever. I've never DI'd Paul's bass.

Do you remember what his bass amp was?

It was probably a Vox.

Were there a lot of bass punch-ins?

Oh, no. It was a performance. On those 4-track machines, you couldn't do quick drop-ins; bass drop-ins were especially hard to do.

Although he changed from the Hofner to the Rickenbacker at around that time, I don't think it was so much the bass guitar he used. I think it was having the mic on figure of eight. With the studio empty, you could actually hear a little bit of the ambience of the room around the bass, which seemed to help. At one time on *Revolver*, I was trying to get extra definition on the bass, so I used to put a little chamber [reverb] on it—just a touch. Paul always detected it and hated it, so nine times out of ten I ended up taking it off; occasionally, it got through. But that gave the sound a certain roundness and put it in its own space, and that's what I was looking for. We had no electronic gimmick boxes—everything was organic, if that's the right word. We could do phasing mechanically, and also we were the first ones to do flanging, but there was only so much we could do.

The sound you crafted transformed the bass from a supporting rhythm instrument into a lead instrument.

It surely did, unbelievably so.

It's a compressed sound, but it's not overcompressed, not squashed.

That was the Altech compressor. The Fairchild couldn't take the bass signal, because the attack time was too fast.

The other thing I used to do when I was mixing—and Norman Smith taught me this —was that the last instrument that you bring in is the bass. So, at least through *Pepper*, everything was mixed without hearing the bass. I used to bring everything to -2 on the VU meter and then bring the bass in and make it go to 0, so it meant the bass was 2 dB louder than anything on the record; it was way out in front, the loudest thing on the record.

On *Rain*, I may have compressed the bass two or even three times, just to give it no dynamic range whatsoever and get it way out front.

Would that recompression happen during the mix?

No, it would have been done during recording. The song would have been overall compressed during mixing because we were going to vinyl, so there were problems in mastering albums. It also had to be well in phase, because it helped make the end product sound good on vinyl.

When you were recording McCartney's bass, did you typically use EQ on the board?

The EQ on the board was just treble and bass—with no selectable frequencies—so I had very little control in the control room; I can't even remember what frequencies they were set at. I can remember it taking up to an hour to get a bass sound, doing most of the EQ from the guitar and the amps. Most of the sound originated in the studio.

Let's talk a little bit about the approach you took to drum sounds and drum miking.

Norman used to sometimes use the STC 4038 ribbon mic—a BBC design—which is a fantastic mic. If the kit's well-tuned, you just have to put in some top EQ, and you get the most unbelievable drum sound. But I was looking for new drum sounds, so I started close miking all the toms and also putting a mic underneath the snare as well as a top mic. The top mic normally was an AKG D19C, which they've stopped making; it was a very cheap mic, made for talkback on the desks, but for some reason it sounded good on drums. We used to use an AKG 56 or 54 condenser underneath, though often the capsules would go. At some point, we started taking the bottom skin off the toms and put a D19C underneath each of the toms, just to get a bit of tone. That was pretty much it—underneath and overheads on the toms [both D19Cs], left and right overheads [STC 4038s] for the cymbals, over and under the snare, high hat, and bass drum [AKG D20].

So you had about a dozen mics or so on the kit.

By the time we got to the recording of *Abbey Road*, yes. You've got to remember also that all the equipment in the control room was tube, not transistor. The first transistorized equipment came in halfway through the *White Album*. When I went back and did the *Abbey Road* album, that was the first project that was done through the transistorized desk, which gave us more inputs. Prior to using that desk, we pretty much just used a single overhead mic on the drums, plus close mics on the snare, toms, and bass drum—I may have used both over and under mics on the snare, because I think there was a way of getting both into the desk using a little switch.

Did you compress the snare drum?

We used to compress *all* the drums—including the snare drum—through a single Fairchild, at least up to the recording of *Abbey Road*. On those early transistorized desks, there was a good-quality compressor and limiter on every fader, which was a luxury. I mixed the *Anthologies* on that board—it was as near as I could get to the original sound, and I didn't want to color those tapes at all.

Having the tubes was a big part of it. I remember when I started the *Abbey Road* album I couldn't get the same bass drum or snare drum sound that I'd gotten on the other records. The transistors wouldn't let the low-end distortion go through—everything was clipped.

Did Ringo tune his own kit?

Yes, and he always used to have a half-empty soft packet of Lark cigarettes on the top of the snare, which gave it a certain sound. I think it was Lark—you could put a soft packet of Peter Stuyvesants on there and it wouldn't sound the same! (laughs) No, I'm sure it was Lark—the Stuyvesants never sounded the same. It just shows you how sensitive all that stuff is. We used to use tea towels on top of the drums, too, just mopping-up cloths.

***Revolver* in particular has such a wide range of drum sounds. Did Ringo use different kits, or would you set up the mics differently on different tracks?**

I think it was a case of, "We've had that drum sound on that track, so let's have a different drum sound on this track." Hence the tea towels may have started to come out, or I may have started to put mics under the toms.

Did the kit get moved into different areas of the studio for different tracks?

No, it was always in a locked position. A lot of *Revolver* was done in the smallest of the Abbey Road rooms, so there weren't a lot of options for drum placement.

What prompted you to move on from the basic three-mic setup to start experimenting with additional mics on the drums?

Everyone had always just put those mics there, but, for me, it was a question of putting your ear near instruments and hearing what they really sounded like. Plus, the request on certain tracks was, "I know that I'm playing piano, but I don't want it to sound like a piano," or, "I don't want this guitar overdub to sound like a guitar." So it ended up with me wandering around everything and putting my ear in different places and wondering, what would it sound like if the mic were a quarter-inch away from the skin? Or if the cymbal were miked at the edge rather than on the top? If you do it from the edge you get this low rumble going, which is really amazing.

So that's why it always sounded like Ringo had a 40 inch crash cymbal that was 2 inches thick!

Yeah, but a lot of that was the Fairchild sound, too. Remember that, up until *Abbey Road*, we never had stereo drums—they were always mono drums. That's because we were way behind in England; stereo came much later than it did in America. When we were making *Sgt. Pepper*, we only ever monitored on one speaker. Because most of Ringo's drum patterns started with the bass drum hitting, then releasing, it often made the cymbals sound as though they were going backwards. That's because the bass drum hit was triggering the limiter, shutting the cymbals down, and then when the bass drum released, the cymbals were coming back up in volume.

Some of the *Anthology* cuts show just how immaculately the drums were recorded in the backing tracks, though much of the subtleties tended to get lost by the time you got to the final mix, which would often be three or four generations later. Was that a constant source of frustration for you, knowing how much was being lost?

Sure it was, but there was nothing we could do about it, it was an accepted fact. Don't forget that we worked on one-inch 4-track, so each track was a quarter of an inch wide. When you go to one track of a two-inch 24-track, each track is only one-twelfth of an inch wide. If you were to record a bass drum or snare drum on one track of each format and A/B it, you can bet you'd hear a tremendous difference, even if both tapes are lined up with the same tones.

It's like the difference between mixing to analog half inch versus quarter inch.

Exactly. When we started working on *Anthologies*, we started pulling out tapes that hadn't been out of their boxes for 25 or 30 years. The saving grace was that we recorded on EMI tape—they were in pristine condition. They didn't shed, some of them still had lineup tones on them, which just locked bang on to zero, and they were just in pristine form. If they were recorded on a different brand of tape, they never would have remained in that condition. It was unbelievable to start lifting those tapes out of their boxes and start playing them.

In particular, the difference in quality between the backing track and the final mix of "I Am The Walrus" is tremendous. It's probably only because they were recorded so well initially that they survived as well as they did, even four generations down.

That's true. Pete Cobbin, who remixed *Yellow Submarine* for DVD, commented on how incredible the original tapes sounded. You probably couldn't get anywhere near to that sound today, because with all the technical advancement, with things getting more and more miniature, the sound actually is getting more and more miniature! But if you listen to a lot of the big band records from the '50s and '60s, which were done through tube equipment, and compare them with big band records that have been done through transistorized equipment, brass sounds in particular are totally different. It's very hard to put your finger on it, but some of those old big band recordings even sound 5 or 6 dB louder. It's unbelievable.

The bottom end of some fifties rock and roll records—some of the Elvis stuff, for example—also sounds totally different. It's just a slap bass with a microphone a few feet away, but it was a big microphone, and the signal was recorded through tubes and onto a big bit of tape.

Exactly.

Did you ever use a pair of linked compressors to duck the instrumental background during vocals?

No, we never did that, certainly not intentionally. But any time you put a stereo compressor across a stereo mix, the instruments will be knocked down whenever the voice comes in, because it's the loudest thing. The only time we used a compressor sidechain input was on *Abbey Road*, on "Octopus's Garden." You know that funny wobbly sound on that record? The voice went through the compressor and we fed a pulse signal into the sidechain input, which pulsed the compressor.

What tricks did you come up with for transforming keyboard and guitar sounds? Were you the first person to put a guitar through a Leslie?

Yes, I was. I can also remember miking the piano soundboard from underneath sometimes. And on the piano solo in "Lovely Rita," there's a wobbly echo in the back of that; we stuck tons of editing tape around all the tape guides on the echo machine that was feeding the chamber. That wobbled the tape all over the place, with lots of wow and flutter, but it put a weird sort of shimmer on the echo. Then ADT and flange came along, and we used to play around with that.

Did you develop any special guitar miking techniques?

Not really. The tube equipment could handle a lot more [signal], so you could move mics pretty close in. The tolerance within the desk, the headroom, was a lot higher. On "Revolution," for example, the fuzz guitar was created by overloading the inputs to the mic amps in the desk. You can't do that through transistorized amps; the sound gets all thin and tizzy. But tubes distort all the way down into the bass end.

You recorded a lot of acoustic keyboards—pianos, harmoniums, harpsichords—as opposed to purely electronic ones. Did you come up with any special miking techniques for those?

Basically, it was a matter of using your ear and finding the right spot. There was normally only one place to mic a harmonium, and I used a pair of Neumann 56s over the place where the flaps open on the back of that particular harmonium. My favorite piano miking was to use two D19s, but down into the sound holes on the top; everything was a variance on that, really. George Martin had one of these small keyboards with very thin, fine strings—I think it was called a virginal—and we used to tape condenser mics onto the soundboard, stuff like that.

You also recorded one of the first uses of a synthesizer, on *Abbey Road*.

Yeah, that was the big modular Moog. I remember we used it for the french horn sounds on "Because."

How did you create the infamous overbright, overcompressed piano sound of "Lady Madonna"?

That was just the sound of the Fairchild, driven a bit more than usual. I used the same mic technique—two D19s, down in the sound holes.

John Lennon was renowned for never wanting his voice to sound like his voice.

Yes. For instance, on "Tomorrow Never Knows," he wanted to sound like the Dalai Lama, so we put his voice through a Leslie.

Is there truth to the rumor that he wanted to be swung around on the ceiling while singing?

Oh, yeah, just for the sheer hell of it. The idea was, he'd swing around the microphone on a rope in order to sound like a Leslie speaker.

Rather than swing the microphone.

(laughs) Yeah. He was so naive about all this stuff. He said to George Martin once that he couldn't understand why we couldn't directly inject his voice. George said, "Well, you'd have to have an operation first so we could implant a jack socket in your throat." He couldn't grasp that, he didn't even know what it really meant.

They weren't interested in technicalities; they were artists. Paul, even today, is not really interested in technical things. You start talking technicalities to any artist, and they don't want to know.

According to [producer] Jack Douglas, Lennon always complained that the ADT at the Record Plant didn't sound as good as it did at Abbey Road.

No, it wouldn't, and I'll tell you why. Because it was tube equipment, we used a sweep oscillator, going from 20 cycles up to about 80 cycles. That changed the voltage of the rectifiers that went into the motor of the machine; it was a huge piece of equipment. But it also meant that you could actually play the guitar note with the varispeed, following the string bends. I used to play the varispeed to Lennon's voice to get that ADT sound, and you can't do that with the tiny vernier scale knob you'd find on more modern varispeeds. Also, each tape track was one-quarter inch wide, so you could get absolutely perfect phasing. Everything had to be perfectly lined up to get that sound, but it lends itself to being a musical effect.

What was the standard Lennon vocal slapback echo?

It was just a straight tape echo at the ordinary 15 ips or 7 1/2 ips speeds. But don't forget that the length of the echo depends upon the gap between the record and replay heads, which is different on every machine. We used big EMI machines, so there was a considerably bigger gap than on today's smaller machines, hence a longer echo.

Jack Douglas has also talked about Lennon "working" the mic, singing certain words to the back or sides of the mic and flashing his esses by waving his hand.

That was a technique that they developed over the years. When artists used to come in for their first artist test—and Lennon must have gone through it—they were given certain instructions. For example, they were told to pronounce the letter *p* as a *b* so you don't get the pop, and they were taught to lean back on loud phrases. Flashing the esses, I'm not so sure about that. Paul's got a good mic technique as well.

What vocal mics did you use?

Mostly [Neumann] U 47s and U 67s. I'm sure we also used other mics, because there was this thing about, "Oh, it's the same old vocal sound." I remember, on one of John's vocals, getting a glass milk bottle and getting a very thin condenser mic and putting the mic in a plastic bag inside the bottle, then filling the bottle with water. The condenser mic, of course, had power within the capsule, so if water had gotten in, God knows what could have happened—the whole thing could have ended in death and disaster. But John sang to the milk bottle, so it was actually picking up the vibration of the glass, through the water, into the mic. I can't remember which song that was on, but it was one of the songs on *Sgt. Pepper*. We'd do anything to be different.

Were vocals typically routed through the Fairchild?

Always. Just the sound of the amplifier, even if you didn't do any limiting, it just added a certain presence. We used it on guitars, too.

The lead vocal in "I Am The Walrus" sounds like it was sung through a fuzz pedal. Were there fuzz pedals available then?

Yeah, there were, but that was a bit of overload, as well as the way John was singing it. Those mic amps were like their own fuzz pedal—it wasn't a nasty distortion, it kind of helped the signal.

Did you come up with any specific mixing techniques during your years with The Beatles?

Well, everything was monitored in mono. If you're working in stereo, and you have two electric guitars, one left and one right, it's very easy to pick them out. But if they're both coming out of the same loudspeaker, they each need their own character, so you have to spend a lot of time getting the sound right, placing each one individually in its own space. You wouldn't do all that extra work if you were mixing in stereo—that's the easy way out. I'd be filtering out various frequencies, so there was no interference. For example, the only bass content would be coming from the bass guitar. That's why the sound has got so much definition, because there's nothing interfering with it.

So even the kick drum doesn't have a lot of low end; the bass guitar is actually below it.

That's right.

Did you have that in mind when you were recording the kick drum and bass guitar?

Not really. It was because, in the final mix, everything was coming from one single sound source. When we did give ourselves a treat and monitored in stereo, it really sounded fantastic because of all the work that had gone into the individual sounds.

When mixing, what sort of things did you do to differentiate Lennon's guitar from Harrison's?

It was just basically EQ and maybe a slight bit of one echo chamber on one guitar and a different chamber on the other. We very rarely used an EMT plate; we almost always used live chambers instead.

George Martin has said that *Sgt. Pepper* wouldn't have been as good had it been recorded in 24-track, that necessity had been the mother of invention.

I agree. We were put on the spot, and that was the sound you made at the moment. You had to put the right echo on, the right EQ; the vocal had to be right. It made things easier in a way, because otherwise there are too many variables, and what's the point? Where do you go? To me, that's why there's no great product today. There's good product, but nothing great.

Do you ever think there will be another Beatles, another artist that will so completely dominate the music scene?

No, because of the way record companies function now; they're purely a money-making machine. When I started, there was more of a focus on artistic considerations. Sometimes it didn't matter if the record made money, as long as the artistic aspect was put out to the public.

Do you think that's because there's so much competition today?

No, it's just what record companies want. You have these manufactured bands like the Spice Girls, and the record companies don't have to spend all their money. At one time, it used to be a career for the artist; that was going to be their livelihood for the rest of their lives, they were going to be an entertainer for twenty, thirty years. Things have changed, and it's a shame.

How did you feel about making the transition from engineer to producer? You did it for awhile, then you seemed to return to engineering.

Well, over the years, young producers used to come in and rely on me to do most of it, but of course you got no credit for it.

But when you were producing records, were you approaching things differently?

No, I couldn't give 100 percent input when I was both producing and engineering; I found it very hard. For instance, doing Elvis Costello's albums—when it came to recording his vocals, there was no way I could do them. I let the second engineer, Jon Jacobs, look after the recording of the vocals, for the simple reason that if you're worried about levels and pops and esses and Elvis asks you, "Was it in tune?" you wouldn't know. That was impossible, so Jon used to look after the physical recording of it.

Elvis's *Imperial Bedrooms* is considered by many to be his best work. How did you approach the production of that record?

To me, listening to the old Elvis Costello product, I thought it would be better if we could hear more vocal, because of his great lyrics. You never really could before, so on *Imperial Bedrooms* there's a lot more voice, which he really couldn't come to terms with. He hated it, having so much voice in the mix, but eventually he came around to thinking that way.

There are certainly a lot of adventurous sounds on that record.

Yeah, but a lot of them weren't planned out; they just sort of happened. Because you have to capture the moment with Elvis, you can't labor anything. If he wants to do a vocal, that's it—you do the vocal. You can't mess around, saying, "Give us ten minutes to get a sound." Same with Paul—sometimes you go and do a vocal, put it in and that's it, away we go. It's just capturing the mood and the moment with Elvis, because the man is exploding with output and one performance of a song can be so different from the next one—the timing, anything. So that really was the approach. I think we cut about fourteen tracks in a couple of days on that record.

But it also sounds like a real production, as opposed to a documentation of a band playing.

I agree. Because Elvis was pushing all this stuff out, asking me questions about pitch and tempo; that's where the production end of things kicked in. It was hard. But in the end, when he sort of calmed down and we'd cut these tracks, a couple of people [heard them and] said, "Oh, that's good." Then he got some confidence in what we were doing, and we spent a bit more time thinking about what we should do. Vocally, I was trying to do new things. In one of the tracks, we have vocals left, right, and center, and one of them actually overlaps, even though he said, "Oh, you can't do that because I can't sing it for real."

I think you're thinking of the song "Pidgin English," where there are completely different vocal treatments—different EQ and compression, not just panning—on each vocal part.

Yes, that's right. A lot of that came quite fast, because it had to. You just had to pull all the stops out and say, "Although it might sound stupid, do it." If you'd have thought about it, you wouldn't have done it.

Because the sound on that album is so immaculate, it sounds like it took a long time to record and polish.

I don't think it took very long at all. [Keyboardist] Steve Nieve wrote some string arrangements, and I got George Martin to come in and have a chat with him, to talk about how it worked. In one track, he had written an arrangement for eighteen violas instead of violins—which would have been the norm—and the tricky thing was getting eighteen good viola players!

A lot of the sounds on that record hark back to the *Revolver* days—prepared pianos, backwards reverbs, one instrument transforming into another.

Right. But again, we worked completely in analog, so we could do proper tape phasing. Nothing was a problem. We mixed at 15 ips, no Dolby—I never used Dolby. So it was all mechanics, really—all those sort of sounds were easy.

Were you involved in producing other Apple artists?

I produced Mary Hopkin for a while when I was at Apple. I engineered "Those Were The Days" while Paul produced it. So while I was trying to feel my way through things, I said to Paul, "I wouldn't mind producing Mary." I think we did a couple of titles at Trident. But that sort of fizzled out. I don't know what happened; Mary ended up leaving Apple. After I built the studio [at Apple], I engineered some of the acts. I did an album with Tim Hardin, the Stealers Wheel album, which Lieber and Stoller produced, an album with a girl band named Fanny, which Richard Perry produced, and a few other bits and pieces. That was in the throes of trying to run the place.

You must have some classic Magic Alex stories from that era.

Well, they're not classic. I mean, his studio was not acceptable. We gutted the whole thing—it took us three years to rebuild it and do it properly. And once it was reopened, it was never empty. Plus, the [Apple] mastering room was the best one in London—Malcolm Davis came over from Abbey Road, and he was a great, great mastering engineer. So we had that, we mastered practically every hit record that was around then.

Was there much done in the mastering stage to The Beatles' tracks that you worked on?

No, and there's another little story here. When I finished *Pepper*, I wrote on the box, "Please transfer flat," because mastering engineers would sometimes add a little EQ, even though they weren't supposed to. But we were so used to hearing *Pepper* with every little nuance in it, so we didn't want anything touched. So I wrote, "Please transfer flat," and all hell broke loose! The manager of the mastering department said, "How dare you write on the box? You're telling my people their job!" All this even though I was a mastering engineer myself at one time! A terrible row blew up because I wanted to be allowed to be in the room when he mastered it—and in those days, the producer and engineer weren't allowed in the room during mastering. So I got permission to sit in the room while Harry Moss mastered it, because he had to do that little thing on the concentric. *(Note for readers under the age of 30: on the vinyl release of* Sgt. Pepper, *The Beatles placed a nonsense loop and high-frequency "treat for dogs" on the spin-out groove)* I think it took him about nine attempts—he had to master the entire album nine times to get that concentric to work out, because it was dependent on where the point went down at the beginning of the cut. So if the concentric didn't work out at the end, he had to cut the whole album again.

So he did transfer it flat in the end.

Well, I think he made a couple of little EQ things, which I agreed to do. But that led to the first collaboration between a mastering engineer and a recording engineer.

By the time of the *Abbey Road* album, though, were you able to attend mastering sessions and provide input to the mastering engineer?

Well, I'm pretty sure that was cut at Apple, so things were a lot better than they were during the *Pepper* days. Malcolm Davis would have done it, and I trusted him, so anything Malcolm would have done would have been fine with me.

There's another story that goes with that, because Malcolm was good friends with John [Lennon], so John gave him the master of "Imagine" to cut. But there was so much tape hiss on it, so on the beginning, during the piano introduction, Malcolm took about 10 dB of the top out to get rid of the hiss. That warm, wooly piano sets the mood of the song; then he slowly brought the top back in as the song progressed.

I always thought that was just a really badly recorded piano...

No, that was Malcolm getting rid of the tape hiss. He said to John that he was going to have to do this, and John trusted Malcolm's opinion. But when "Imagine" was remastered at Abbey Road a few years ago for an album, no one knew this story, no one kept any notes. So they left all the top in at the beginning, and it sounds like a different record. You hear all the hiss, but it also sounds like a different record, because that piano introduction sets the mood of the song.

When we remastered *Band On The Run* recently, we found the mastering notes from when I'd done the original [mastering]. Greg Calbi at Sterling Sound in New York did that. That record sounds really fantastic, really great. The remaster is about 6 dB louder than it was on the original CD, and we took it from the original master tape, played back on a tube machine.

Elvis Costello has described your work with him as a collaboration, with you looking after the sounds and him looking after the music. Was that similar to the role you had with George Martin, who wasn't technically oriented either?

Well, we both weren't that technical, but the great thing was, because George and I worked together for so long, there wasn't much conversation taking place between us. I knew what George was thinking and wanted, and he knew what I was wanting, if he needed to have changed anything in the studio. A lot of people couldn't understand that, but because we worked together for so long, we could basically read each other's minds.

Did you have that experience with anybody else you worked with?

No, not really. [It was] because we worked together all those years, you know?

The bass sound on Paul McCartney's solo albums—even on the ones you engineered— is qualitatively different than it was on Beatles records. Any idea why?

Well, on *Band On The Run*, we were working in a very different room, in Africa. It was no more then a shed, actually. Because there were no acoustic screens in the studio, we had to get a carpenter to make some screens. There was no drum booth, the band had split up the day they flew out, so it was only Denny Laine, Paul, and Linda. It was an EMI studio, but the 8-track multitrack only had four sync amps in it, so we had to keep changing the sync amps around everytime we wanted to do an overdub. So basically that was the sound of the studio in Nigeria. But it turned out great, it was a good sound. When we asked, "What mics have you got?" they just gave us a big cardboard box full of mics and that was it. The funny thing was, there was a door at the back of the studio, and when you opened it, that was the pressing plant. All these guys pressing records, and there was all this water and mess all over the floor—it was terrible! (laughs) They were actually pressing records out in the back!

Plus Paul got robbed at one point, and his demos got stolen. So a lot of material on that album was written at the time of being there. Paul said he couldn't remember the material he had demoed, so rather than try to remember, he just wrote new material. We mixed the album at Kingsway Studios in London, in just three days, because I had been double-booked. On the third day of mixing, I finished at 5 a.m. and had to start at 10 a.m. with this other band. So we only had three days to mix it.

> **"The primary role of the producer is to pull the most talent out of the artist, to inspire the very best performance, even to the point of frustration if necessary."**

Sometimes that kind of pressure is what's needed, though.

Yeah, and that's a nice album.

How do you see the role of producer as differing from that of the engineer?

The primary role of the producer is to pull the most talent out of the artist, to inspire the very best performance, even to the point of frustration if necessary.

What's your take on the impact of the home studio?

Well, the way I was taught is that different people look after different aspects of making a record. Being a producer, arranger, writer, engineer, artist—there's five people. And now the artist is trying to do it all himself. It might be good, but why take it all on yourself?

What are your thoughts on 5.1?

Well, I've just done my first 5.1 mix, so I'm certainly aware of it. The approach is somewhat similar to the approach we took when we were mixing for quad. If you're relying on compressors left and right for sounds, you can't do that anymore. For instance, on Paul's *Run Devil Run* tracks, I relied a lot on overall compression to get that sound; in 5.1 it's going to be a little bit harder to recreate something like that. I'm wondering whether 5.1 is really advantageous to the sound of music or whether it opens up a whole new thing where you're hearing a funny little thing in the guitar, where it's maybe not going to help. Most of Paul's album was recorded live, which brings out the genius in Paul—and I know he hates that word. But the vocals are done live, as is the bass playing, and the bass is playing a completely different musical pattern from the vocal.

If you had to pick one single track that you were most proud of—in terms of your role as engineer—which would it be?

(pauses) I don't know. That's a tough one because there are so many. Probably "Tomorrow Never Knows." Or maybe "All You Need Is Love," because it was such a nightmare, doing it live and via satellite. Or "Eleanor Rigby," because of the string sound. I was also very proud of the work I did with John McLaughlin (*Apocalypse*, 1974).

Selected Listening:
The Beatles: *Revolver*, Capitol/Parlophone, 1966; *Sgt. Pepper's Lonely Heart's Club Band*, Capitol/Parlophone, 1967; *Magical Mystery Tour*, Capitol/Parlophone, 1968; *Abbey Road*, Apple, 1969
Paul McCartney: *Band On The Run*, Apple, 1973; *Flaming Pie*, Capitol, 1997; *Run Devil Run*, Capitol, 1999
Elvis Costello: *Imperial Bedroom*, Columbia, 1982
Badfinger: *No Dice*, Apple, 1970
John McLaughlin: *Apocalypse*, Columbia, 1974

John Leckie

Every Englishman worthy of the name has a "local"—a neighborhood pub that they patronize regularly, sort of like the bar in "Cheers." John Leckie's local is the canteen at London's famed Abbey Road studios.

Hardly surprising, actually, when you consider that Leckie's career began at Abbey Road in the early 1970s, assisting on John Lennon's *Plastic Ono Band* and George Harrison's *All Things Must Pass* before going on to engineer Paul McCartney's *Red Rose Speedway* and Pink Floyd's pre-Dark Side album *Meddle*. In the late 1970s, he made the transition to producer, working with some of the premier post-punk bands of the time, including Be-Bop Deluxe, Magazine, Human League, Simple Minds, and XTC. By the late '80s, Leckie was working with "second wave" bands like the Stone Roses, Gene Loves Jezebel, and The Verve. In 1994, he hooked up with Radiohead, going on to engineer and produce their critically acclaimed album *The Bends*. Personable, insightful, and clearly dedicated to his craft, Leckie was kind enough to invite me to his local one evening not long ago, where he expounded on his philosophy and techniques over a pint of Guinness or two.

What do you feel have been the most significant changes in audio technology during the years you've been making records?

I've actually been reading about the *entire* history of recorded music recently, and it's fascinating, absolutely fascinating. We take sound reproduction for granted, but we don't remember that just 100 years ago, the only time you could hear music was in the present, when musicians were actually performing. When the performance was over, it was gone.

Obviously, the technology has changed in terms of the number of tracks you can use, therefore in the amount of isolation you can give each instrument. But it's still a recording of a performance; the performance is the thing that lasts. At the end of it all—no matter what technology you've used—the signal comes out of a speaker, and it's a piece of music that you can listen to.

But there are two different approaches to making a record. One is to stimulate and capture the best performance—kind of like taking a photograph—and the other is to construct a fantasy that could never be performed, like an impressionistic painter working with a blank canvas.

I tend to view it as a photograph, but it really depends on the artist I'm working with. If the artist has a very strong personality and the musical sense is highly developed—perhaps they've already been performing the songs live for years—then it would be crazy for me to develop a fantasy sound picture. In that case, they've hired me to present them in their best light. Making a record is really all about presentation, so I think it's up to me to take the best picture rather than to create an artificial thing. The worst thing about that approach is that it takes forever,

"Making a record is really all about presentation."

and you have to be totally into it, every day for months and months and months. The possibility of losing focus is high, and the possibility of having a life outside of the studio is low; that's the price you're going to have to pay. It's also very difficult to do within a limited budget and time period. Many artists destroy themselves by spending so much time making records, because they've got so much more to offer. If an artist spends a year, two years, three years in the studio, when they come out, their life has really changed—I know my life changes when I haven't been out of the studio for a long time. They find it hard because they lose the connection they have with their audience. The artist only exists because of his connection with the audience; they can't exist on their own.

But there are bands that show up with a completely blank slate, expecting to create in the studio.

Yeah, and their records are usually shit. It's very difficult to get out of the experimental nature. A lot of times in the studio, ideas come up that are interesting experiments: what will happen if we plug this piece of gear in here? Sure, you can do that—though it can be quite time-consuming—but in the end, when you're trying to mix it, trying to make it part of the song, it can often come across as a studio experiment. Of course, it's clever, and you're really proud of it because it's taken you days, weeks to do, but what has it really added to the song? That's where experience comes in, knowing when you're going too far with an experiment, whether it's worth it.

Sometimes, for example, a bass player will have an idea like putting the drums through a wah-wah pedal; it'll just be an academic idea he's got in his head, not one he's come up with for the sake of the song. That's part of being a producer; if the band didn't have a producer, they may go that route and spend three months on something that is totally unnecessary.

That's the biggest problem for people working on their own in project studios—knowing when enough is enough. What criteria do you use to make that decision?

I think you have to be aware of the people who are going to buy your records. If you're sending out demos and not getting any response, it's probably because you're not making your recordings for other people, you're making them for yourself. Very often, bands will take an obstinate stance: "This is our third album, and we're going to make this record for ourselves. We're not going to have any singles, fuck the record company, we're going to do this for us." And usually it's shit. Sometimes it's interesting or off the wall, but that's as far as it goes.

But there's also something to be said for being true to yourself, staying true to your artistic goals.

Sure, it's a fine line. But if you want success—if you want to take it a little bit further—you have to be aware of your audience, too. You have to ask yourself, what is it you want to do? Do you really want a record deal? Because if you get a record deal, your life's going to change. People working in home studios need to ask themselves if they really want to do this, or if they just want a CD in a cardboard box that they can give to their friends and family. If you just want that, it's easy to do, and you don't need a record company. But if not, you need to ask yourself a lot of tough questions: Do you really want to go further? Do you really want to seek out management? Do you really want to change your hair color, or sit through a photo session, or make a video?

Because if you sign a record deal, you don't just go into a studio and do records. You're expected to be a video film star, you've got to look good in photos, you've got to be controversial in interviews, speak sense and yet relate to the kids. And right at the bottom of the list, oh, by the way, you're expected to write songs as well. You've got to have a great voice, you've got to have a great band of musicians, you've got to have your business all together, all that stuff. Just writing the songs is a very small part of it.

Is the quality of the demo related to the degree of success an artist may or may not attain?

Not at all. Demos are what they are; they're a demonstration of the song or the talent of the artist. But it depends on what the purpose of the demo is. Some people go into the studio to make good demos, so you get this funny compromise between a demo and a master. You end up with something that's quite good, but everyone's apologizing for it because it's a demo! (laughs) The worst thing is playing someone a piece of music and making apologies—"Oh, it's a demo, the drum parts aren't right, maybe the vocal intro needs sorting, but listen to it anyway." You hear it, and it's the most amazing-sounding thing on earth, it sounds like it was recorded at Abbey Road and Trevor Horn spent a week mixing it—but it's a demo! So for whatever reason—maybe the drums are shit, or the song is shit, or it obviously needs arranging, or it needs a new bridge section written—the whole purpose of this amazing-sounding thing is wasted.

Most bands I work with, I'm quite happy to listen to a rehearsal room recording. From that, I can tell whether or not I want to work with them. Just a Walkman demo in a rehearsal hall.

What are you listening for in that rehearsal tape?

I'm listening for character, attitude, songs, strength of character in the vocal. It has to be an in-tune vocal; I can't stand out-of-tune vocals. I know you can tune them up nowadays very well, but I can't stand singers that are off-key. If the vocalist is out of tune, he needs singing lessons. In fact, one thing I'd recommend to all vocalists across the board: Do not be ashamed to seek out singing lessons. After just three weeks of lessons, you'll be amazed at what it does to your voice—it will give you strength and a sense of pitch. It won't change your voice—you won't come out a different person, with a different sound—but the intervals and notes you are singing will be correct, much more pleasing to the ear. At the end of the day, you'll sell more records, because an out-of-tune vocal always sounds angry and gives the wrong impression.

When you record backing tracks, are you just going for a good drum track, with the idea that all the other parts will be replaced later?

No, I like to get as many people as possible playing together, with the attitude that what they're playing is for keeps. You don't want to set up a situation where a bass player, for example, is thinking, it really doesn't matter if I make mistakes or if I lay back, as long as the drum part is OK. If I'm not confident that the band can do that, then they need further rehearsal to get things tightened up so that they can play, at least, bass, drums, rhythm guitar, and a guide vocal together. If they can't do that reasonably well, ready to be recorded, they should still be in the rehearsal room.

It's very important, when you're doing a guide vocal, to have the attitude of the vocal. You should almost be going for a keeper on the guide vocal. If you're going to do a guide vocal that doesn't have attitude, that's going to be lazy and not relate to the song, you might as well just count bars. I know it can be difficult after four, five, ten takes, and I know we're really just trying to get the drum track, but the drummer is influenced by everything the singer is doing. If the singer sounds bored in the drummer's headphones, the drummer is not going to play so well.

So you set up the guide vocal as if it's going to be a keeper?

Oh, yeah, of course. I'd say in 50 percent of the tracks I record, I use the guide vocal.

Do you use leakage as a creative tool?

No, I try to avoid leakage. I might create a leakage track, route an ambient mic somewhere. It's better if you have two tracks available so you can record it in stereo. It's interesting to put microphones in different places, like on the floor or half an inch from the wall, pointed at the wall. Crazy things like that—microphones in pipes or in tubes while the band is playing. Another thing I've done is to put an acoustic guitar in an open tuning in the key of the part and lean it up against the bass amp, then mic it.

So presumably you typically record a bass amp track.

Always both, along with a DI. In 90 percent of the tracks I do, I use both. The amp is usually an Ampeg SVT with a D12 mic placed very close on one speaker; sometimes I'll use an RE20 or a U 47 instead.

Do you use the DI for the attack and the amp for the bottom end?

Yes, usually it's the amp that provides the bottom end part of the signal, even with the 10 inch speakers in the SVT cabinet. That's because the D12 is very responsive to bass signal. The DI is funny, because on its own, it's usually terrible. But when you add it to an amp signal, it adds this invisible punch. But you've got to be careful, because the DI will sound like shit on its own—thin and woody or metallic, if you've got a fret buzz.

I record them on separate tracks so that, when it comes to the mix, you can vary the levels. It's amazing how, if you have a great sound on the amp, just by adding the slightest little bit of the DI—you can have it down at -20 [dB], -15 [dB]. The difference can be like turning lots of EQ knobs. And you can mess around with the phase, too. So having two tracks of bass—one amp, one DI—is a creative tool.

Do you typically record both with compression?

No, I don't, actually. Very often I go into a studio and the engineer straps a dbx 160x across the bass with the needles kicking—sometimes without even listening to it, strangely enough. I tend to use a little bit of compression but not much—I like to hear all the notes, the full range of it. It's very dangerous to squash a bass in the recording stage, because you never get it back. In the mixing stage, of course, you can do whatever you want. But even in mixing, I use very subtle, small amounts—very low ratios like 1:1.5 and a very slow attack.

Do you compress kick or snare drums during recording?

No, never.

Do you use analog tape saturation on them?

No, never. (laughs) Well, sometimes, but not really; I'm always a bit scared of abusing it. The drummer only needs to hit a little harder or something, and you never get it back. I still usually just use a [Shure] SM57 on top of the snare; I very rarely use an underneath mic—it's very dangerous. Sometimes I substitute an AKG 451 with the pad in if the drummer is playing with brushes or is playing lightly; then it's better to use a condenser mic, but you do need to pad it down. It gives you more of a sizzle thing happening.

I will use a good whack of EQ on the snare drum, though. A broad boost at 8 k for a general brightness—I'm a great believer in adding general brightness at the recording stage, general bass and treble. At the recording stage, that's all you should work with, really—broadband EQ and bass and treble shelving. Fiddling around with fine EQ is OK if you're searching for something on an overdub, but the key to getting a good sound quickly on a backing track is to just consider it as bass and treble. Don't go endlessly fiddling with parametrics on bass drums, compressors, and all that shit. You should just be able to put the microphones up, pull the faders up, and it should sound good. If it doesn't sound good, you need to go out into the studio and change it there. Go out and get another kit or another snare drum, tune the drums, or get the gaffer tape out. Change the bass amp, get another guitar, get another bass player in. Before you reach for any EQ or outboard gear, you have to know when things need to be changed in the studio.

Plus, you shouldn't always believe in what the musicians are giving you from the studio, because very often the guitarist has got his amp cranked up, and it's all around the room because he's used to hearing it loud. In the control room, of course, it sounds terrible—it sounds just like a fuzz box with a dead battery. That's always a bit of a problem—that reaction that bands have when they're used to playing live at very loud volumes. They come into a small control room, listening on NS10s or something, and you have to make the sound so it sounds like them onstage. That's what they're reacting to, and they're used to hearing their music onstage or in the rehearsal room.

So what steps can you take to recreate that big, live sound even when playing it back through NS10s?

You keep it as simple as possible. You treat it almost like recording classical music, where you set up the mics, pull up the faders, and the sound is there; if something needs to be changed, it's almost always changed in the studio, not the control room. Some people are shocked by the simplicity of the technique, but it should be simple. A lot of people use stuff in the studio because it's there, not because it's necessary. If you have a 90-piece orchestra in, it doesn't mean to say you need to have 90 microphones, or 24 microphones, or even two microphones. Same thing with a band; there's nothing that says you have to record a

"A lot of people use stuff in the studio because it's there, not because it's necessary."

kit of drums with one ambient mic, and there's also nothing that says you have to record it with 24 mics all over the place. You use what's needed to capture the moment. The focus has to remain on the artist; that's what you're there for. You're not there to fiddle about with knobs, at least not in a professional studio.

For many artists, though, the project studio is both a blessing and a curse. The blessing is that there's all this great gear and the clock isn't ticking, and the curse is that there's all this great gear and the clock isn't ticking.

Yeah, there's every possibility; in fact, there are too many possibilities.

How do you generally mic kick drums?

Kick drums give a big stamp on the sound, so it's very important to make that work. It's funny—a dull thud can make the band sound more serious, but as soon as you make the kick drum sound slappy and bright, it makes the band sound kind of younger somehow. I usually use the old [AKG] D12; sometimes I use a mix of the D12 and a Sennheiser 421. I used to take the front head off, with a cushion inside, but now I prefer to leave the front head on, but with a hole cut in it; it sounds a bit more contained. You can't be frightened to add high end to a kick drum; some 7 k can really brighten it up, give it more presence without it being too slappy. The trade-off is that it may give you a bit more leakage from the cymbals or the rack toms.

If the front head is on, it will sound more resonant, so you'll have to mic from a distance. Sometimes I put an RCA 44DX [ribbon mic] about three feet away, in front of the bass drum, but then you have to watch for cymbals and other spillage.

In general, I tend to close mic drums, and I'm a bit against the idea that you have to record drums in a big room. The idea is bollocks, really; if you want a big drum sound, you're far better off recording them in a small, contained space—it doesn't have to be cramped, but a normal-sized room with an 8- or 10-foot ceiling, and it can be quite a dead space. If you think about it, some of the best drum sounds are those dead sounds, if they're crisp and present. But if you're in a big room, you can never get rid of that big room ambience—it's always there. So my preference is to record in a smaller, deader room, where the drummers are sweating! Usually the drum sounds are great because they're very contained; in the mix, they're not taking up the whole sound picture. They're a lot easier to vary, also—you can add things, you can even add an artificial room sound if you like. I think a lot of people are embarrassed today by some of the drum sounds of the '80s, which, at the time, people thought were sensational.

But recording drums is down to the drum kit, really. If the drums sound shit, you should get another drum kit. And it doesn't have to be a big, new expensive kit, either—sometimes there's more character in a beat-up old kit with heads that need changing. Because that's what you're looking for in the recording: character. But it's important to make the drum sound part of the band sound. The two things that identify a record are the vocal and the snare drum. That's what people hear as soon as the record comes on the radio. Snare drums, again, can have all sorts of tones—big, heavy, small, crisp. When you're doing a recording, the snare drum sound has to be EQable in the mix; it's no good having a snare drum that you can't do anything with, because when you do come to the mix, you're going to want to play around with it to mold it into the track. So you do need a full-range snare drum sound.

Sometimes the drums sound spectacular, but it's not what you want, because you want the guitar to be spectacular, and you can't have spectacular everything! (laughs) Then you wonder why the mix doesn't sound good, because everything's crowding everything else. When you solo the instruments, everything sounds good, but when it's all put together, it's a jumbled-up mess, so something's got to give way, and you don't want it to be the vocal.

How do you go about recording spectacular guitar sounds?

First of all, I tend to use an SM58 instead of the more usual SM57. 57s tend to be that little bit brighter than the 58, which really isn't what you want when you're miking up an electric guitar amp. You really want to pick up a flat signal, an unstimulated signal, I suppose is the word. So you need to use a microphone that is pretty flat and pretty direct. I'll put the 58 up close to the speaker, just off-center, and I'll also put a Neumann U 67—not an 87—right up close, touching the speaker cloth. Both mics will be on the same speaker of the same amp. Then I'll make a balance between those two mics. The 58 gives you a very clear, focused, slightly thinner, harder sound, while the 67 gives you the warmth and a broader sound. If you brighten up the 67, it's totally different to brightening up the 58, so sometimes I'll add a little brightness to the 67 and a little compression. But between that combination, I find that I can get pretty much everything I need. Again, they rarely are used at equal level; sometimes I'll favor the 58 with the 67 at 10 or 15 dB down. Even 20 or 30 dB down, just bringing it in, it's amazing the different color you get—how much the tone of the guitar changes. Again, it's down to decisions; even if you decide to record the two mics on separate tracks, you've got to decide how you're going to monitor the signal, where the position of those two faders are.

Making records is about making decisions. All the time, you're making decisions. If you delay those decisions, you pay the price of having to sort them out later. And they mount up, so the sooner you make them, the better. So generally I'll record both mics onto one track and decide there and then how much the 67 is going to add to the 58, make the balance. I'll devote a lot of care and attention to doing that, even if it's the first rhythm guitar. Because it's very important—the first backing track has to have the attitude of being a keeper.

Do you ever record a guitar DI signal as a kind of insurance policy?

Very rarely. Trying to feed the signal through an amp afterwards never works. Forget that. When you record a band and they come in to hear the first playback of their first backing track, that is the moment when most producers shit themselves. That's the point at which the trust is established, whether they're going to trust you because you're giving them a great sound and you're going to trust them for their feedback. If they complain or if they don't say anything at all, you immediately know where you are, what their trust level is. So that moment of first playback is very important—you have to impress people with that first playback. You have to cover all your bases—you have to make sure that all the band members are pleased. All the sounds have to be right, as well as the arrangement, the key, the tempo, all those things. And it's usually at just that moment that the manager and the A&R man walk in. So it's got to be good. You can't apologize, you can't say, "Well, the guitar's DI'd, we're going to feed it into an amp later on, and the bass is out of tune so we're going to work on that afterwards, and the drums are still being sorted—but doesn't it sound great?" (laughs)

It's almost like that first playback has got to be the finished product. That's the school I come from: within half an hour of starting the session, you've got to have something to play that is good. If you go for a great thing happening at the very beginning, you can never take that away. You can do loads of overdubs and fuck it up, but you know that you can always strip it down and go back to that magic you had at the beginning. So it's important to capture something, even if in the heat of the moment something happens like a mic stops working or you have something misrouted. You don't start again, you work with it; the magic on the track is going to override any technical problems. And sometimes that magic is a little bit indefinable—you don't know quite where it's come from. You've always got to use something if it's got something special. And that's what producers and engineers should always go for—to let the artist create the magic.

Do you prefer analog recording to digital recording?

To be honest, I haven't done much digital recording, and I haven't been happy with the few experiences I've had. You can't beat tape, really. I prefer to work at 30 ips, no Dolby, but if I'm recording long performances, I'll work at 15 ips with Dolby SR.

It's interesting that you work exclusively on analog tape, yet you don't generally use tape saturation. For many people, that's the main reason for using tape.

Well, I would for an effect, but I don't see the point of doing it generally. I'm very careful when I'm recording snare and bass drum—particularly bass drum, because whatever level you record it at, it never comes back the way you put it down. I'm always trying to retain as much attack on the drums as possible, because you can always take the attack away, but you can't add it. To me, it's stupid to take away that attack by squashing it on tape, softening it. If you're disappointed with the bass drum sound, there's no way you can harden it up once it's been saturated on tape. So you've got to keep everything as hard as possible.

Some would argue, though, that tape saturation produces a qualitatively different effect than either tube or solid-state compression.

Yeah, but you don't have to overdo it. And again, you're not controlling it. You can simulate tape compression with a low ratio on a tube compressor. But for me, making that first recording on analog multitrack, you really want to keep things as strong and upfront as possible. Sure, you have to make a sound—you don't record everything flat; I'm a believer in lots of little bits of EQ. I might have two compressors on the bass—a tube and a solid-state—but always low ratios, long attacks, and fast delays. So it's just catching little things, not changing the dynamics too much. You've got to capture all the notes the bass player is playing, and if you squash it too much, it just turns into a low-end hum—it might as well be the low end of an organ or a synth bass. The whole idea of plucking strings—whether it's a guitar or a bass—is that it has attack, it has dynamic range, it has a shape. It's so easy to destroy all that with compression.

Do you mix to analog as well?

I usually mix to half-inch at 15 ips, with no Dolby as well as to DAT, preferably through Prism A/D converters. The 15 ips analog tape always sounds a bit bass-heavy; when you get to the mastering room, you usually have to knock a bit of low end out, put a filter on or something. So I usually choose the DAT, maybe 80 percent of the time.

Have you done much hard disk editing?

Not really. I do a bit at home—I don't shy away from it—but I'm very reluctant to switch on the Pro Tools, with all its possibilities, in the middle of a recording session. Because I know it's going to take months—and I don't mean weeks, of extra days. As soon as Pro Tools appears on one of my sessions, I book another month or two! (laughs)

I'm sorry, but the band's got other things to do with their time—they've got their career to do. If the band wants to fiddle around for a year with Pro Tools, they can, but maybe I'm not the man for the job. No manager should allow that—it's disaster. There are simply too many choices. Sure, there are people who are very creative with it, but I always just come back to tape and razor blade editing. I'm never frightened to edit the multitrack to get the best of each take. I know that people rave about hard disk recording keeping you from having to do that, but I do it as a matter of course—I've been editing two inch tapes for 30 years.

What order do you usually bring faders up when you start a mix?

I usually bring them all up. I work with as many faders up as possible, because what you're doing is making a balance of instruments. It's easy to spend six hours fiddling with the drums, but they may not work with the vocals and instruments. You've got to spend six, eight hours fiddling with things individually, then bring them in together, add in the vocal, decide it all sounds terrible, and then start all over again! (laughs)

One common problem, especially for novices, is getting a vocal to sit right with a backing track.

It's a funny thing, because there's this thing about having loud vocals, especially in the last few years here in Britain; everyone likes having the vocal shouted in your face. But I think everyone's starting to get a bit tired of that—I know I am. So I think we're going to see vocals mixed down a bit further. But there's an art to balancing the vocal within the music. The main thing is to limit or compress the voice, but without squashing the life out of it. Be careful of sibilance, but if you have to brighten the voice up, do it without making it sounding thin—keep the voice sounding warm. With a good singer, a vocal can usually go from recording to mix without any EQ.

In terms of vocal compression, sometimes I use the UREI 1176 full-on, with the needle pinning all the time, but always at low ratios. Always use the most expensive compressor you can get, because there's a reason why it's expensive. If you only have access to a cheap compressor, you're better off not using it at all on the vocal. It's worth hiring in a good compressor for vocals.

But the most useful tool for taming vocals is automated mixing. I can spend up to three, four hours manually riding each vocal line, making it sit, getting all the quiet bits louder so they don't disappear—but, again, without changing the performance. Because once you move that fader, the position of the singer changes, obviously, which means his attitude changes. The big question is where you put the vocal up against the snare drum, because the snare drum and vocal, in rock music, have to fit together. It's where each syllable hit goes with the snare drum— I guess that's what I do when I mix vocals. It's about making it sound like it's never been touched, even though the fader's going up and down. It's a great technique, because all the little secrets get revealed. At the ends of lines, a lot of singers will trail off, and if you lift the fader 10 dB right at the end of the line, there's lots of things you haven't heard before, and sometimes there's a lot of character in the breath when the singer finishes his line; suddenly there are new things happening in the song.

But the way to get a vocal to sit is to start with a great singer, use a great mic to record him— I tend to use a tube U 47, a great compressor, not overused, and automated mixing.

How important is the preamp relative to the mic itself?

Well, you always want to use a great mic on vocals. If the original source is good, it's always going to shine even if you don't have such a good preamp.

Do you tend to set up two or three generic reverbs and route multiple instruments into them, or do you use discrete reverbs for each instrument?

I tend to have two reverbs, one delay and special effects—flange or chorus. That's the basic setup I would use, and I'd send multiple instruments in. I never really use discrete effects; I don't know where that all came from, actually—perhaps it's something to do with the '80s when there was lots of equipment available for the first time.

In terms of effects, you're always searching for something that catches your ear, something that's going to enhance the song. It's that little bit of magic; sometimes you get a reverb or a setting that seems to be made for a voice, and suddenly it all fits. That's really what you're going for—one whole sound.

Getting back to the question of balancing a vocal within a track—everyone wants a loud vocal, but it depends how important the singer is. Sometimes, with a band, if you put the vocal way up high, it doesn't sound like a band anymore—it sounds like a solo singer with backing musicians. At the end of it, you really want the four instruments—vocal, guitar, bass, and drums—at equal level, so you can hear everything. That's why, very often, rough mixes are used on an album. The idea of a rough mix is simply to hear what you've got, so you make your balance so that you can hear everything. And, really, that's all you want out of a finished record— to hear everything. The worst thing is things getting obscured. People will turn the music off when they can't hear everything, when it's a strain to hear what's going on. It's like watching a film that's filmed in darkness so you can't see what the actors are doing.

Some bands come to me and they want no reverb on the vocals, and sometimes you can use effects to give the impression that there's even less reverb than no reverb! You can actually make something drier by adding something. For example, using the Lexicon 480 Small Room algorithm, or something with an early reflection, 40 ms or so. Anything that's short and a little bit dark kind of makes the sound a little bigger and a little drier as well. One thing I like to do— which is made much easier by automation—is to use a small room on something, and then, once the listener is aware of the sound, just cut it out, then bring it back in again. Whenever there's a little sibilance or a little something that ends in a sharp attack which sets the reverb off, just trim the effect send during the mix to where you can't hear it. You've still got the bigness, but it never sounds reverby.

You can't just say that the vocal either has reverb or no reverb, because there are all these things in between, like the short room and the little delay. I'm a big fan of using a tiny bit of rock and roll delay—250 msec, 400 msec. That delay came about from tape echo, and you either ran the machine at 15 ips or at 7 1/2 ips, and you made the delays dull so the sibilance didn't repeat. And just use that delay maybe once during the whole song; that gives it the mystery, that little bit of magic. Because when you hear the human voice, the mind instantly thinks of it singing in its place, and suddenly, halfway through the song, there's this little other place going on. Suddenly you're not so certain, suddenly you're thinking, maybe he's not there at all. Maybe that's what makes people want to listen to records again—"Hang on, let me hear that again. Where was that person? Where was he standing?" All those things—like in *Dark Side Of The Moon*— where you don't quite know where the vocal is, whether it's close to you or far away from you.

The whole idea of putting reverbs on records is interesting, because it depends on where you play it and also where you record it. Different control rooms in different studios will make the reverb sound different. For instance, if you listen in a really small, dead control room, you tend to add more reverb than you need. When you go to a more live mastering room, there may suddenly be too much reverb. Through experience, you learn those rooms. But the trend now seems to be towards bigger, more live control rooms, so we've got deader records. People aren't putting as much reverb on records simply because they're hearing the reverb in the room, so they don't think they need it. But when they take it away, it sounds dry.

That's a problem that can be even worse in project studios, where often the control rooms have minimal acoustic treatment.

That's right. But all acoustic treatment is rubbish, I think. I know it's difficult to build studios, but I don't think you *can* control an acoustic environment. You listen to records in a normal room, with carpeting and a sofa and curtains. You don't listen in a room with a hardwood floor, bass traps, and a funny-shaped ceiling. As soon as I walk into a typical live-end, dead-end control room with bare floors, I ask for some carpets on the floor. The studio manager inevitably asks me why, and my answer is simply that I listen to records in rooms with carpet on the floor. Usually, it sounds great, because the room gets deader, so you create a brighter mix. And when you take the mix away, it sounds better because it's brighter, more radio-friendly. So, with project studios, don't be frightened to deaden it down. All that thing in the '80s with creating live-end, dead-end control rooms, it's all bollocks, really. All you need is heavy velvet curtains. Or hang carpets on the wall, and put eggshell crates on the ceiling. It's much better than spending a fortune on bass traps and fancy acoustic treatment. Every day, before you start your session, play your favorite CD, and tune your room accordingly. It's just common sense, and it's what I do whenever I go into a strange control room anywhere in the world—I put my favorite CDs on, and I soon know exactly what the room is doing.

Selected Listening:
Radiohead: *The Bends*, Capitol, 1995
Dr. John: *Anutha Zone*, Virgin, 1998
Robyn Hitchcock: *Respect*, A&M, 1993
Stone Roses: *Turns Into Stone*, Silvertone, 1992
Mott The Hoople: *Mott*, Columbia, 1973
Pink Floyd: *Meddle*, Capitol, 1971

Alan Parsons

There are hit records, and then there are hit records. Pink Floyd's 1973 *Dark Side Of The Moon* was unquestionably the high-water mark in the band's career, both in terms of creative and commercial achievement. Occupying a staggering 14 *years* on the Billboard charts (an all-time record) and ultimately selling over 25 million copies, the success *Dark Side* enjoyed has been unparalleled in the history of recorded music. Though he has enjoyed a rich career in the years since, Alan Parsons will forever be known as the man behind the board for this incredible accomplishment.

Brought up through the ranks at London's famed Abbey Road studios, Parsons assisted for the likes of Geoff Emerick, Ken Scott, and Glyn Johns in the late '60s and early '70s—learning at the feet of the masters, as it were. By the mid-'70s, he made the transition to producer, overseeing hit records by Al Stewart, Pilot, Steve Harley and John Miles, as well as striking out on his own with the formation of the Alan Parsons Project, a group of musicians assembled to render Parsons' own musical vision.

On the day we meet at his beautiful Santa Barbara home, he is gamely enduring a long VH1 "Behind The Music" shoot, dealing with inane questions along the lines of, "So what's it like to hang out with Pink Floyd?" Upon the film crew's departure, Parsons makes the wise decision to retire to a nearby bar, where we spend an enjoyable couple of hours unwinding over a bottle of wine.

What are your thoughts about the rise of the home studio?

It would be shortsighted and unfair to say that you can't get good results that way, but I've always felt that there's no substitute for a band playing together, and you can't get that interaction between players in a bedroom. Having said that, there have been some great records made in bedrooms, and you can't take that away from people that have the talent—good luck to them.

But lo-fi has become hip these days; bad sound is often considered a good thing. As a professional engineer, does that bother you?

Well, you can't just sit back and say that the only way to engineer is the way that we used to do it in the '60s or '70s. You have to realize that life goes on and people will take new approaches to things.

Do you think there's a "British sound" versus an "American sound"? If so, what accounts for it?

I think American engineers are more into the sound of an individual piece of gear than British engineers are. The British will go for more of an overall feel or an overall atmosphere in their sound, whereas an American might be much more analytical. But why spend hours of grief possibly losing the spontaneity of the artist in order just to establish what sounds best? American engineers are just more into their equipment and less reliant on the performance and the performer's ability to get a good sound.

Do you find that there is more emphasis on mixing in the U.S. than in the UK?

Yes, and there is more emphasis on mastering, too. I'm perhaps a little old-fashioned in that respect; I don't see the point of going to a mastering room, expecting to transform the project from what you had in the studio. What I want to hear from the mastering engineer is, "I think it sounds fine; I don't want to do anything to it." If he has suggestions, I'll go with them; a mastering engineer listens to a whole lot more records than I do, so he knows what to expect. But I think some people wrongly go into the mastering room, thinking, "Oh, let's try a bit of compression; let's try a bit of drastic EQ." I think perhaps I got a reputation for making decisions quite quickly, and I've rarely gone back to remix. Generally, if I mix something, that's it; that's my feeling of what it should be. I actually dislike coming back to it; it's a drag.

> *"What I want to hear from the mastering engineer is, 'I think it sounds fine; I don't want to do anything to it.'"*

Did you receive any formal training when you were starting out at Abbey Road?

No formal training, but there were so many great engineers to study under. How could you have better teachers than the guys who made all those great records? Geoff Emerick, obviously, taught me a great deal about how to engineer.

You worked on both *Let It Be* and *Abbey Road*. How would you contrast the engineering styles of Glyn Johns and Geoff Emerick?

Glyn was very much, "I want to have a good relationship with the artist and the producer—I want them to like me, I want them to be impressed with what I do." He was more ready to socialize and that kind of thing. Geoff was much more, "Let's get the job done." But at the same time, he was always ready to come up with an incredibly new idea, like wrapping editing tape around the capstan to make the machine flutter and stuff like that. It was a crazy idea, but it worked. And, although I wasn't there at the time, I'm sure it was his idea to get that amazing vocal sound on *Tomorrow Never Knows*, putting the voice through a Leslie. Nobody's ever duplicated that exact sound—it was an incredible sound.

I gather that *Let It Be* was more in the mold of their first album.

Yes, as George Harrison once said, The Beatles' first album took a day, and their second album took even longer! (laughs) Like the first album, *Let It Be* was a live album. It was, push up the faders, get everything on tape—that was the plan. Of course, even on the first album, they would have overdubbed vocals—but the idea behind *Let It Be* was to have no overdubs, to just play live. There were endless performances of the same song over and over again, just looking for the great take, so George [Martin] didn't really have a lot to contribute. It was essentially, "Let's record the event—let's record everything on film, let's record everything on tape, and we'll sort it out in the editing room." Ultimately, of course, it got overdubbed to kingdom come, but at the time they didn't know that's the way it would happen.

Do you feel the biggest difference between the two albums was the band's attitude, the difference in engineers, or the fact that George Martin was present for one and not the other?

I think if Geoff had been there engineering *Let It Be*, it wouldn't have turned out so drastically different. It was just the vibe at the time, the equipment that was being used, the attitude between them. They weren't happy; *Let It Be* was actually an unhappy affair. None of them really wanted to be there making this record. Paul was there trying to inject some kind of enthusiasm into it; I think the other three didn't really feel that they could achieve the necessary quality.

George Martin has told me that the making of *Abbey Road* was much more relaxed, at least partially because there was an unspoken assumption that it was going to be their last album together.

I think maybe I sensed that as well. I saw the friction between the ladies, and I also saw the fact that the four bandmembers were never there together. It was very much a Paul McCartney, John Lennon, George Harrison, Ringo Starr album—it wasn't really The Beatles; it was very much an individual effort.

Let's move on to *Dark Side Of The Moon*. Clearly, your skill as an engineer had a lot to do with its enormous success...

Well, that's not for me to say...

—but was more care taken with that album then other recordings you've been involved with? Was there a lot of agonizing over every drum beat, every overdub, every edit?

Not really. At the beginning, when we were getting drum sounds for the first track, it became quite unpleasant, with Nick [Mason] saying, "No, it's not there yet; I haven't heard my drums sounding like drums yet." We would agonize through that, and then finally we would say, "Yes, we think it's OK now; let's do the track." Then, after that first period, they would just leave it to me; there would be no question of the drums not sounding good, because they must have just started trusting me. It was only during the first period where it became very painstaking and very unpleasant. But somehow everybody relaxed and got into it and started working as a team.

One of the hallmarks of that album were synchronized echoes, but those were the days before digital delays. How were you able to achieve synchronization so successfully?

Good question. It was quite extravagant to put a varispeed on a delay machine, but if it was considered important—if a delay needed to be in time—we would do it. But a lot of the guitar solo echoes were actually generated by Dave [Gilmour]'s own gear, on a Binson Echorec.

Were any of the basic tracks recorded to a click track?

They recorded to a metronome ticking away in another room. I daresay that electronic metronomes existed, but we didn't have one. Abbey Road had, in a cupboard somewhere, a [standard] metronome which could be booked out and used. But on *Money*, for instance, the tape loop became the click track.

It's probably the first instance of a loop being used as the rhythm track.

Probably. We started off trying to edit that loop sonically and found that there was just no way of getting it in time; the only way to do it was by physically measuring the length of one of the sounds and then duplicating that exact length—otherwise it just wouldn't work. It took

quite a bit of doing, and it was made more difficult by the fact that it was a 4-track loop on one-inch tape, because we wanted it to work in quadrophonic as well as in stereo.

When you were doing the backing tracks, was it the four guys playing together or was it just Nick Mason playing drums to a metronome?

While we were agonizing getting sounds, there would be two of them out in the studio and two in the control room listening. But in the end—by the time we reached the third or fourth tune—they were all out there playing, and I was in the control room by myself, along with my assistant.

Were most of the overdubs adding to what was on the basics, or were they replacing parts played during the basics?

I'd say the majority of what was played on the tracks remained. There were a few replacements here and there, but generally, the first rhythm guitar part, bass and drums [remained]. There might have been a few repairs, but more often than not, it was performed. And I felt that was a departure for them, to be playing as a band. In their previous work, they had been much more into doing each part separately. But they were playing as a band, and that was one of the strengths of the album.

Was the whole album written before they started recording, or were they finishing it in the studio?

No, it was pretty much written, though it was known as *Eclipse* in those days. They'd actually performed it live by the time we started recording; it had been tried and tested on the road. There were a few significant changes; I think *Money* had a different feel because the loop was different.

So the loop was used onstage as well.

Yes, after we'd recorded the album version, they did play to the loop. But it was very difficult for the band, because of the quad system that they had live—the speakers were so far apart, it was completely chaotic. And there were no stage monitors, so it was just guesswork.

Was *Dark Side Of The Moon* recorded in 16-track or 24?

16-track.

Were there any reductions?

There were. In fact, it was nearly all second-generation—non-Dolby on the first generation, Dolby on the second generation. And if they had their way, the first generation would have been Dolby as well; I was actually the one who was anti-Dolby. They kind of insisted, and it probably was sensible to Dolby on the second generation, but we got rid of so much noise with Kepex noise gates, which were the new thing at the time. Bass and drums were reduced down to two tracks a lot of the time. I'm still to this day praying that I get the opportunity to remix the album one day, so that we can sync up [and work off] the original multitrack tapes.

How much time was spent mixing *Dark Side Of The Moon*?

Between two and three weeks. We usually got a track a day done. Sometimes a track would go to two days, but it was generally pretty quick.

Were a lot of the effects recorded, or were they generally added in the mix?

I remember that we slaved for several hours trying to duplicate a reverb that I discovered on a rough mix for the roto-tom section. That took some experimentation, because I couldn't remember what I'd used! (laughs) Everyone was saying, "That's a great sound on the rough mix, just do what you did there," but I couldn't remember. It was just a straight EMT plate with a little bit of delay through a tape machine.

The recording of those roto-toms was also interesting, because I think Nick only had four actual drums. If you listen to it, there's at least nine or ten different pitches being played, so we had to retune them and punch in for each chord change. So the tape op had to be pretty on the ball, to get in and out on a machine with a fair gap between the record head and the playback head. (laughs) The tape op, by the way, was Peter James, who was incorrectly credited on early pressings as "Peter Jones." So if your album says "Peter Jones," it's probably a collector's item!

Your whole concept of the Alan Parsons Project is fascinating. You're the focus, even though you don't sing or necessarily even play an instrument on the albums—in fact, they sometimes even include songs that you didn't write or cowrite.

I certainly didn't cowrite all the songs, although I was credited as such. Eric Woolfson was very much a very important part of the team.

But it was your name that sold the records, at least initially.

I was sort of baffled by that, because I was still really a backroom boy. *Dark Side Of The Moon* was a really big album, yes, and people who read the papers might have been interested to know who the engineer was, but engineers were still the poor relation; they were still background people. Sure, if you mentioned Pink Floyd or *Dark Side Of The Moon*, people might know me. But if it had just been my name, it wouldn't have meant anything.

But you were probably the first engineer whose name was recognizable, perhaps even more so than Geoff Emerick or Norman Smith.

Yes, that's probably true. That was good marketing; Eric studied marketing. It was a good way of getting an engineer into the limelight.

But it also set a trend; today, many top engineers are fairly well-known.

Another first was that I think I was the first engineer to have a manager. (chuckles) Even producers didn't have managers in those days. Generally speaking, they worked for A & R departments in record companies; being an independent producer was quite unusual.

APP albums are distinguished by a lush production that is often reminiscent of Pink Floyd. Was that a conscious decision, or is it just your style of engineering?

I think it must be my style. I never went all out to try and duplicate *Dark Side Of The Moon*. I always worked on instinct; I never sat down and thought, "How can I make this album sound like that album?" I just followed my instincts, and to this day I'm amazed that people recognize that style.

Do you have one particular mic that you use for vocals most of the time?

No. (chuckles) Since the Audio-Technica 4033 came out, I favor that. But I'm happy with any good mic. [Neumann U] 47s, I've had a lot of luck with, but they're unreliable; FET 47s are usually fine. [Neumann U] 87s are rather boring as a choice; I've tended to avoid 87s as a vocal mic, just because it's what everybody else was using, though I've often got good results with them.

The vocals on your records have extremely good presence, but they're never even close to sibilant.

That's probably because I favor adding top during recording and de-essing afterwards. I have almost never recorded a vocal flat. I like to hear the sound at the back of the throat, and if it's at the expense of increased esses, then I'll take them off later. I boost 10 k shelving, as a general rule. But I don't like hard top on vocals; I always like the sort of breathy, airy top, so sometimes I might start at 12, even 14 k, and do more of it. With some voices, you can literally go as much as 6 [dB] at 14 [kHz], and it won't be at the expense of esses.

Do you ever roll out mids to create the smile curve?

Occasionally, but I'm more likely to do that on strings and electric guitars, where you're likely to get that hard, clangy top end. Especially if you're close-miking strings, you tend to get the undesirable 2, 3, 4 k nastiness. You just put a bit of airy top on and take a little 1 k, 2 k out—that usually sorts it out.

You tend to use reverbs and delays in a very creative way. How are they set up?

There's always delay on the send, and the send is nearly always mono. I think the predelay is the most important component of any reverb—it adds character—and it's the first button I reach for when I put on a reverb.

Do you typically EQ the sends or the returns?

I'd much rather EQ the sends than the returns. I'll roll lots of bottom out; occasionally I'll roll off top end as well. I'm quite happy for a very middly signal to be going into the reverb.

Do you use tape machines for the delays?

I don't possess any analog tape machines any more! (laughs) For the last several albums, I've been working with digital machines. And digital delay is fine; you can achieve most of the artifacts of tape if you want, just by rolling off a little bit of the top end on the send, it'll come back a little duller with each repeat. You can overdrive it, you can distort it.

But digital overdrive is qualitatively different from tape saturation.

It is, but you can emulate the tape generation distortion, which is mostly frequency response. You can emulate the weaknesses of the tape machine by rolling off a bit of top and making everything fuzzy and bassy.

Are you big on compression?

I hate compression with a vengeance. I avoid it. I'm a great believer in the dynamic range being preserved. I'll limit rather than compress a vocal in order to get it at the best dynamic range on tape, but I'll still be riding it [manually] on the mix. I never use compression on drums; I just hate that sucking sound. People often have surprised me by saying, "Let's get more punch out of the drums by compressing them." That seems like a contradiction in terms to me—if you're going to reduce the dynamic range, that's going to reduce the punch.

> **"I hate compression with a vengeance."**

In fact, even on *Dark Side Of The Moon*, I argued about compression with Chris Thomas, because he wanted to compress everything. I said, "Please, can we at least not compress the drums?" He agreed, on all except one track, though I can't remember which one.

Unless it was an effect, I would never want to hear a limiter or a compressor working. That said, there are classic examples of great compressed sounds on vocals; "Lady Madonna" is one of them. It's a great vocal sound, but it is a special effect.

When you record bass, do you take a DI signal or amp signal or both?

Always DI; I can't be bothered with an amplifier. They're noisy and they crackle and they hiss and they often don't represent the sound of what the bass player wants because they're turned up too loud. At least with the DI, you're hearing the instrument. You can emulate the sound of just about any amplifier with enough processing inside the control room. I haven't miked a bass amp for years.

Do you have a favorite DI box for bass?

Not particularly. I worked for years with the homemade Abbey Road ones, which were presumably some ghastly, very lossy transformer wired into these homemade boxes. But I always use passive DIs, not active ones. I remember doing an evaluation of DI boxes, and there were only subtle differences between the different models.

When you record electric guitar, do you use the standard miking technique of a 57 up against the grill?

(laughs) No, never. Every engineer I've ever come across—especially live engineers—has always had the mic touching the cloth, and the first thing I do is move it away literally a foot: Let's hear what the amplifier sounds like; not what the cabinet sounds like. I've always thought that most people mic guitar amps too closely. They supposedly make it up with an ambient mic, but I much prefer to find a mic position that works and process that, rather than mix in too much ambience.

What mic do you favor for electric guitars?

I like the Neumann 86 for guitars. I always use condenser mics on a guitar amp, never dynamics—they're too telephoney. That's an unfair expression for a very good dynamic mic, but by comparison to a condenser, you're not going to get the bottom end.

So you use a small-diaphragm condenser mic about a foot away from the amp?

Yeah. I might have it even further away if it's a very loud 4 x 12 cabinet—as much as four feet away. I think people can be overworried about the separation aspects of a guitar on a live tracking date. It's much more likely that the guitar is going to go elsewhere rather than anything else getting into the guitar mic. You can be four feet away from a guitar with a full band playing, and you're not going to hear very much of what else is going on; it's going to be the loudest thing in the room.

So are you a leakage fan or is that something you fight?

I don't worry about it. I use it if it's there; if it's a problem, I'll try and get some volumes adjusted. The worst case scenario is live drums and piano—that's always the nightmare—but the way around it is to move the piano as close as possible to the drums, which is contrary to what you'd think. Most people would say, "I've got to get this piano away from the drums because it's picking up so much." I would move it closer, because it's the time delay that's the problem, not the actual separation.

But if the piano were right next to the drums, wouldn't you get acoustic resonance from the kick drum through the piano mics?

It would be there, yes, but at least it would be happening at almost the same time [as the kick drum], not 100 milliseconds later. So whatever that sound is, at least it's going to sound like a smaller room, whereas if the piano is further away, it's going to sound like a bigger room.

Do you use room mics a lot?

I think that's a fashion thing. Room mics became very fashionable when the Phil Collins gated snare thing became trendy. They never really excited me hugely; I prefer the versatility of making those decisions after the event rather than with the event.

Do you always multi-mic drum kits?

Nearly always, but I try and steer away from using two mics on the snare. I prefer a good over-the-top snare sound, with perhaps a little more EQ than I'd like to get the brightness I need, because the high hat tends to creep in if you add too much top. I usually mic the toms over; I very rarely have any luck under-miking them, unless the bottom skin is off.

I always use a [Neumann] KM 84 on the snare; I could never get a sound I was happy with using any mic other than a KM 84. I'll use anything on the high hat, really; I'm not fussed about that. And I use dynamics on the toms—they're the only things I ever use dynamics for, apart from the kick drum, where I usually use a D112—that's the punchiest kick drum mic I've found.

Also, whenever I can, I put ribbon mics overhead, because I like to pick up a little bit of the room, and they're figure-of-eight. That was something Geoff Emerick taught me. I have a pair of Telefunken 4038s, and if I've got them with me, I'll use them for overheads.

How do you position the overheads?

Whatever looks right. If the guy's got lots of cymbals on one side, I'll try to compromise and position a little off center. I'm favoring cymbals because I know I've got a separate mic on the high hat, so I'm really trying to pick up cymbals and a little air.

Do you pan drums audience perspective or drummer's perspective?

I've always gone audience perspective. Often you've got so much EQ on the snare that you can't actually use the high hat mic, so you've got to use just a little bit of panning to shift the high hat slightly off center; if you pan it hard right, it's going to sound funny.

How will you EQ the drum kit?

On the snare drum, lots and lots of 10 k, shelving, to make it fizz—a close condenser mic on a snare always sounds kind of puffy. If I'm using the ribbons overhead, I'll put a bit of top end on those, because they're dull-sounding mics; if I'm using condensers overhead, I'll use them flat. High hat, because you're using so little of it, I would tend to make it flat as well. Toms, it depends what you want out of them, really. If you want a boomy tom, then you put a little bottom end in and take a bit of midrange out; if you want a hard, clicky tom, either leave them alone or add some mid.

Do you use the overheads for full-range signal, or do you filter out the low end?

I don't think I've ever found the need to filter them much. There's something about the general air that you create with the overheads; if I was filtering off the bottom too much, I'd feel that that wasn't being achieved.

So you're really creating the drum sound from the overheads, using the individual spot mics to fill in.

I'd say that. The single most important things in rock and roll—let's face it—are the kick and the snare. That's really what you need, and everything else is on top of that. I've always found it slightly difficult to get the toms to be in the same room as the kick and snare; that's something you have to sometimes fight a bit to get—to make it sound like it's coming from the same source. And that's where the overheads can help—the air around them can help make the drums sound like they're all in one room. Whereas if you have that very, very close sound of each drum, it can sound artificial.

How do you generally mic an acoustic piano?

I've always had a bit of frustration with piano; I just don't think I'm very good on piano sounds. (laughs) Some of it's because I've been unlucky enough to have to record piano with drums more often than I'd like to. Plus, great piano sounds are made with great pianos, and I don't think

I've worked with enough great pianos. They're either too clangy and hard and bright, or they're too dull and nasty. My idol for piano sound is Bruce Hornsby, but it's at least 75 percent in the playing. What a piano sound he gets! I went to a session he was doing with David Pack a couple of years back, and there it was—a pair of [AKG] C12s. Allen Sides was the engineer—I love his work, he's a bit of a hero. He knows what he's doing no matter what mics he uses.

Probably the hardest thing for the home recordist is to get the low end right—to get it tight without being flabby or woofy. What kind of tips can you pass along for achieving this?

The key is understatement; don't overdo the bass. A lot of records are so kick drum-driven; it becomes so much of a feature. You look at the meter and the kick's right up to zero and all the rest of the music is down there.

Are you saying it's more to do with level than EQ or compression?

It's mostly level. There are a lot of records I dislike where the bottom end is too dominant, where the producer has said, "I want a really fat, punchy kick drum." But it's not the most important part of the record, although there are notable exceptions: One of my favorite records of all time is "All Right Now" by Free, where the kick drum is just the star of the show. That record was very influential, particularly the sound of that kick drum.

But the emphasis today is on the kick drum—get it up there, to zero, compress it if necessary to hold it at zero all the time, then add everything else to it. I mix everything else first and then introduce the kick drum until it feels right.

So you'll mix with the kick drum out until the end?

I mix with all the drums out to start with; that's another Emerick trick.

He told me he mixes with the bass out.

I do that, too.

But you'll mix with both out.

Minus drums and bass, yeah. Because it's much easier to get all your stereo spreads without the bass and drums going on—to make sure that all your ADTs and all your double-tracks left and right are in perspective.

At what point do you bring in the vocals?

Instruments first, then bass and drums, then vocals. But I probably still listen to the vocals in there without the bass and drums as well, just to make sure all the echoes are balanced.

It can be difficult to get a vocal to sit correctly in a dense track. How do you go about doing that?

I seem to have an inbuilt sense for every line of vocal, and thank God for automation—it allows you to get every word, every line exactly right. Though I have to say a lot of the excitement has gone out of recording, with the coming of automation.

What advice do you have for the reader who wants to be the next Alan Parsons?

Give up now! (laughs) No, only kidding. Getting a job in a studio has always been the same: You have to know somebody, or you have to walk in the back door and you have to start as the assistant to the assistant, or whatever. But so much of the job is personality. Provided you're a likable person and you're determined enough, you can do it. I'm convinced that a great deal of my success is through my ability to communicate with people, not through any particular skill with knobs and buttons. Somehow I have the means to communicate the wishes of a musician or a producer through understanding them, not necessarily from understanding the technical aspects—just knowing what they're looking for.

The truth is that anyone can make a record now, because the equipment is so affordable. You can go out and make a serious quality record if you have a couple of good mics and some talent to go with it. It's all down to experience and determination. You know, anything goes. In fact, you can succeed through breaking the rules and doing nothing else. But don't expect to do it on your own—you need teams, threes and fours to make it happen. I don't think any single engineer, artist, or producer ever achieved anything by working on his own. You learn from other people, and you achieve great things by interacting with other people.

Selected Listening:
Pink Floyd: *Dark Side Of The Moon*, Capitol, 1973
Alan Parsons Project: *On Air*, River North, 1996; *Eye In The Sky* Arista, 1982; *I Robot*, Arista, 1977; *Tales Of Mystery And Imagination*, 20th Century, 1976
Al Stewart: *Year Of The Cat*, Janus, 1976; *Time Passages*, Arista, 1978
The Hollies: *Crazy Steal*, Epic, 1978
John Miles: *Rebel*, Decca/London, 1976
Ambrosia: *Somewhere I've Never Traveled*, 20th Century, 1976

Steve Churchyard

The Abbey Road lineage stretches a long ways, from Norman Smith to Geoff Emerick; from Ken Scott to Alan Parsons; from George Martin to Chris Thomas—all the way to Steve Churchyard. Churchyard's engineering career actually got its start in the early '70s at a dubious little demo studio called Orange Music, located near London's Tin Pan Alley, with the obligatory guitar shop overhead.

His ambition, though, was to work at George Martin's AIR studios, which was eventually realized, even though he had to take a step backwards from engineering to assisting in order to do so. As he recalls, after receiving their offer to start at the bottom and work his way up, he "thought about it for about five seconds and realized that doing Eurovision Song Contest demos was not the way I wanted to spend the rest of my career." This turned out to be a fortuitous decision, because within a short time he was assisting for Geoff Emerick on projects like Paul McCartney's *London Town* album before ultimately returning to the rank of engineer and working with The Pretenders and INXS. In the '90s, Churchyard relocated to Los Angeles, where he continues a busy career behind the board, crafting hits for artists such as Natalie Imbruglia, Sophie B. Hawkins, Celine Dion, and Ricky Martin. Soft-spoken and meticulous, yet with a quiet air of confidence, Churchyard's genteel English accent somehow meshes seamlessly with the laid-back L.A. studio scene.

Geoff Emerick has said that he didn't get any kind of formal training from Norman Smith. Did he provide you with any kind of formal training, or did he just expect you to observe and pick it up?

As you observed, you picked it up—you just assimilated anything and everything. Everything moves fast, and with Geoff, you just did everything. We were there hours before the session, we were there hours afterwards, and we just made sure everything was right. It was a great experience, and Geoff was just brilliant. He's got such a unique gift to make sounds work. As an assistant, you could put the drum mics *behind* the gobos and he'd make it work somehow.

Many producers maintain that moving a mic a fraction of an inch can make a world of difference, but Geoff doesn't really buy that.

Yeah. I'd sometimes ask him, "So what mic do you want on this, Geoff?" and he'd reply, "Put what you want on it." Which was great, because, rather than say, "Here's my drum mic list, do this," he would just let you try things out, though he'd certainly change it if it wasn't right. You could bet it would be dynamic mics on the drums with a pair of [STC] 4038s overhead. His drum sound, a lot of the time, was the 4038s, and that was pretty much it. Maybe there'd be one mic in the kick, and you'd spot mic other drums for extra presence. He just makes things work—the way he fits them together, it's masterful mixing.

In many ways, Chris Thomas was your mentor. What sort of things did you learn from him?

Chris was George Martin's assistant originally. He has a track record of the most incredible hit records across three decades. I think he's very transparent as a producer, and that's his great strength. If you listen to Roxy Music and Badfinger and Procul Harum and Pete Townsend and the Sex Pistols, all the records he's made —they're all very different. So what I learned was: here's the artist, here's the song, and the production just supports the whole thing. There are lots of producers that have a sound or a production technique that's even greater than the artist, which doesn't seem right to me.

But isn't that the producer's role when an artist isn't really sure what their sound is? Or does that mean they are not ready to be making a record?

I think there's a sound and there's a personality in everybody that can be nurtured and brought out. When I'm producing a record, it's not "my way or the highway"—it's, "What do you want in your record? What's your vision, what do you dream about?"

> "As a producer, it's my job to make the artist's dream a reality and actually make it better than the dream."

As a producer, it's my job to make that dream a reality and actually make it *better* than the dream. I've worked with many great producers where you're almost not aware that you're being produced. It's like having your pockets picked—it's a very subtle approach. And then I've worked with some that beat people to death, (laughs) and they just have a horrible experience, a huge clash of egos. I've left miserable sessions like that thinking, "You know what? Maybe I'll try landscape gardening instead."

But it's a fine line, because an artist may not have the experience or vision to realize when a record is finished or what a record needs. A producer's also supposed to be the person who knows that

I think every artist needs a producer. You need a guide to get through the forest of technology and to deal with the record companies so that as an artist you can just sit back and create.

But there are artists who don't necessarily realize what they need. Sometimes that's where the fights and the hassles come in, so a big part of the producer's role is being a diplomat and a psychologist.

Totally. You're a diplomat, you're a psychologist, you're their best friend. I think you only push so far, though, and sometimes you have to lead by example. OK, maybe that's the worst idea in the world, but do I have the right to say that it's terrible? Sometimes what seems like a bad direction might actually be quite interesting; it might lead to other things. When I'm producing, my attitude is, let's just try it. You want to sing while hanging upside down and swinging from a rope? OK. Just make sure you've got a video camera to document the process! (laughs)

PHOTO COURTESY OF STEVE CHURCHYARD

What about a worst case scenario where you know that an idea an artist has is really detrimental to the record. How do you handle a situation like that?

Well, if you dig your heels in and just say no, you're going to have a huge fight. So I think you have to compromise to a certain extent and try it. Maybe you're going to waste an hour or two, or a day, but I think that, at the end, they'll realize that it's not such a great idea. I'll tell them, "OK, I'll try your idea, but then you've got to try mine, too." It's a diplomatic process: Just try everybody's idea—within budget. (laughs)

When you're producing a record, do you usually engineer it as well?

Yeah. I always thought that at some point I'd just give it up and let somebody else do it, but I've always done it myself because it seems easier to me. If I have a sound in my head, I know instinctively how to get that sound. It's a lot easier than trying to tell somebody else.

So how do you start crafting sounds? What's the first step in that process?

I like to work very organically, towards a very natural sound—I want drums to sound like drums, guitars to sound like guitars. Drums are always my favorite. I'm a frustrated drummer, really.

So do you pan from the drummers perspective?

I always did it audience perspective, although I switched recently and I kind of enjoyed it, it was cool. The only time that gets confusing is if you're recording Phil Collins, because he's left-handed.

I really get into experimenting with drums. I tend to use a multimic technique. I've tried all the rest—I've tried the three or four mic technique, and if that's the sound you're going for, that's fine. But to me, at the end of the day you want a bit more clarity and a bit more punch in the drums, so a multimiked kit is definitely the way to go.

What are your favorite drum mics?

My standard arrangement would be a D112 or a D12 inside the kick and a FET 47 just out-side the kick. That FET 47 sitting outside the kick drum helps; it adds a lot more fullness and roundness to the sound. For snare drum, a 57 on the top. I'll put something underneath, but invariably I won't use it—it's there just so I can make the choice later. A [Neumann] KM 84 on the high hat, Sennheiser 421s on the toms—I use them just on the top. For overheads I use AKG C452s, and I almost always put something on the right cymbal, just for that extra presence—a KM 84, usually.

For room mics, almost anything: U 67s, M 50s, U 47s. I'll also usually put a 57 just in front of the whole kit—maybe about 7 or 8 feet away, at head height, maybe even pointing straight up—just to see what that does in the control room. That's the fun mic. I typically like to squash it with a Fairchild or gate it—I'll do something with it later, so I'll stick that on its own track.

Then I'll pan everything audience perspective and usually print everything discretely to separate tracks, including the two kick mics—put them on separate tracks, and then figure out a blend later. My usual rule is to listen to everything I record in the studio. That even applies to strings—I'll always go out there and listen to the sound and then weep because I know I'll never actually get that in the control room. (laughs) Don't tell anybody else that. If only microphones were like ears, you'd have a lot easier life!

I invariably start adding EQ to drums. Typically, I'm adding some low end—somewhere be-tween 60 and a 100—to the kick drum mics. Usually I put a Pultec on the kick drum and some-times on the snare, too. On the snare, I'll add some 10 k or higher, just to get some crack in the sound. And then I usually brighten up the toms—usually some low top, some 3 k, 5 k, just to generally brighten everything up, because when you use dynamic mics you want to help them out a bit. I'll go crazy with my fun mic—my 57. I'll crank some high end into it, some low end, compress it, maybe with a Fairchild or a Distressor, and just mix that back in with the kit.

Do you use compression while you're recording drums?

Typically not, except on my fun mic, or perhaps on the room mics, depending on the song.

Do you filter low frequencies out of the high hat or overhead mics?

No. The mic placement is really important for those guys. I'll usually use a spaced pair for the overheads, get those so it looks real symmetrical with the kit and experiment with the high hat mic for the best separation, so I'm not getting loads and loads of snare drum leakage.

The most important thing of all is phase. You've used a lot of mics at this point—you could be up to somewhere like 12, 14 microphones—so I'll spend quite a bit of time making sure the phase is just right between them. I mix a lot of other people's stuff and by far the most common problem with drum sounds—particularly when they're multi-miked—is phase. Typically, the overheads are out of phase with everything else, because they're hearing things later than the closer mics. So typically, I'll pop those out of phase with everything else, and usually all the sounds kind of come forward. When you've got things out of phase, it sounds like the snare's kind of sucked into the kit and the bottom end is gone; it's a strange thing.

That could be a problem between the two kick drum mics also, couldn't it?

Yes. But typically that distance is not quite as far as [the distance between] the snare drum and the overhead, so you can mess with the position of the 47 for the best phase. If you've got an assistant brave enough, give him a pair of headphones and let him move them around. I'd actually like to invent a little robot that goes in and moves a mic around.

Well, they had a motorized arm awhile back. I think it was a complete failure as a product, but it was an interesting idea.

Yeah. No, mine will have wheels on it.

Like the Mars Pathfinder.

Exactly. With a little D112 on it so you can scope it around inside the kick drum. (laughs) It's amazing how much the sound changes if you're completely on axis to the kick drum pedal beater rather than more off axis and to the side of the kick drum.

Something we used to do with Chris Thomas a lot was, we'd use a PA system as well. We always had a small PA system set behind the drummer, and we'd send stuff from the cue sends off the board into the PA and back out into the room, or we'd put effects through it. On the Pretenders' track "My City Was Gone," you can hear the delays, which were AMS delays on the snare and the toms put back through the PA. Plus, the PA has a tinny kind of sound that goes back into the room mics.

Did you do that during tracking?

Actually, yeah, during the tracking.

And it wouldn't throw the drummer off?

No, he loved it. It was kind of like his live monitors, so if we put the kick drum into the PA it kind of gave him a little push from behind. It becomes part of the sound. In those days, we would usually track with a Linn drum, and sometimes we'd have a pattern going in the PA as well. It would all get into the air and be part of the sound.

Do you usually print to tape, or do you record digitally?

Usually tape, although recently I've begun going straight into Pro Tools.

So do you saturate the tape for the snare and the bass?

No. Usually +6 over 185, and I'm not hitting it too hard. That's something I learned from Geoff. With Geoff, typically every VU meter is at -7 or -5, allowing the transient to show through rather than going to saturation. There are two schools of thought on that—some people will just pin it and that's great, but my training and my background is not to do that. Most of the AIR engineers never really subscribed to that "smash it on there" technique.

How do you typically record bass?

Bass is typically DI; that works well for me almost all of the time. If I use an amp at all, it will be an Ampeg B15. I'd use a FET 47 on the amp, but when I mix the DI and the amp together, sometimes the phasing really bugs me. It's like it's almost like a foggy negative—you're not quite sure where the sound is; it lacks a real center. It's fine if you use just the amp or the DI on its own, but when you combine the two, sometimes the phase is a problem. So to get more focus on the bass sound I'll typically just use a DI.

Do you compress the bass while you're recording it?

Yeah.

And then again during the mix?

Maybe

What compressors do you favor for bass?

The 1176 works best for me; I tend to use a 4:1 ratio.

What kind of EQ curves will you typically use for bass?

Usually I'll add some mid, some highs, and maybe some low end. On the DI, maybe some 10 k so I can hear some of the string a little better; 2.5 k maybe. Maybe a little bit at 100 Hz. I rarely filter anything out at this point; maybe later in the mix when I'm a little bit more focused on what's going on. But during recording, I always seem to be adding rather than subtracting.

What sort of recording techniques have you come up with for guitars?

Guitars are fun. I've recently been using this Royer ribbon microphone that I've had some good luck with. But more usually, two SM57s. If I'm using a 4 x 12 cabinet, I find two of the best sounding speakers, and I'll put a 57 right on axis and right on the cone of both of those guys. Then I'll mix them in the control room, combine the two together. It seems a little different than just using one mic. It's not twice as good, but it's just mixing the character of two different speakers.

Sometimes I might put a 67 or an 87 a little bit off the cabinet and mix them with the 57s. Again, you're going to have a little phase thing, so that's definitely the biggest thing to watch for—and when recording any instrument with multiple mics.

Guitars seem to take a long time for me, so I'll use a lot of different amps and cabinets. Sometimes I'll use two or three simultaneously. I've been getting a really nice effect by getting a great sound on, say, a Marshall amp, and then putting up an AC30 or a Soldano or something like that and then splitting the sound in stereo. It takes a bit of time to juggle the two sounds, but it works really well. You'll want a good A/B box so that you can split the guitar feed to the two amps and obviously use the shortest run. Ideally have the amps in the control room and run the longer leads to the speakers.

Will the speaker cabinets be in the same physical space, or will you have them in different iso rooms?

Usually in the same space, to make a sound in the room. I also pan the signals hard left and right in the control room; that's been working great for rhythm tracks, actually. Whereas before, sometimes I would double a part, now I'm just using the one guitar part.

What's your approach to recording acoustic guitar?

That can be really tricky. I usually try an AKG C451 somewhere about where the neck joins the body, not right by the sound hole—it's usually way too boomy there. Maybe 18 inches away from the fretboard, where it joins the body. The C451 is very bright, but I find that it helps the acoustic guitar to cut in the track, because you really want to hear the strings and the pick and that nice presence. If it's going to be just a solo acoustic guitar, I might try something more like a tube 47 or a 67; it's a richer sound—something that would be lost if the bass and the drums and the guitars were blaring away.

Do you typically compress acoustic guitars when you are recording them?

Yeah. Again, I usually use an 1176—my compressor of choice for most things.

Do you usually compress electric guitar signals?

Usually not, because it tends to take off some of the highs.

Do you enhance those highs with EQ?

Usually I'll get the sound that I want from changing mic placement and amplifier tone; I'll work on that first. If it's still not right, I'll add EQ.

So EQ is a last resort?

EQ is almost always a last resort for me. I'll try everything else first: different guitars, different amplifier.

So the goal is to get it down on tape flat and sort it out at the end.

I think so, yeah.

What's your approach to recording vocals?

I've worked with a lot of female singers in my career, and a FET 47 works very well for me, or a tube 47. My favorite mic is the U 67, but, again, in different studios, different environments, who knows what that particular mic's going to sound like? It's kind of like the '67 Mustang— was it taken good care of or was it thrashed? So typically, if I'm doing a vocal session, I'll see what the studio has, and I'll maybe put up six mics.

If I had to put my money down on any one particular mic working for me, though, a U 67 would be it, through something like a 1073 Neve module, flat, and an 1176. Sometimes I'll use two compressors—maybe a Fairchild—for the sound. So a little bit of compression before it gets to the Fairchild and then just a little bit of the Fairchild, more for the sound than for the compression.

I'll place the mic right on axis, and typically I'll use a pop filter and put it six to eight inches in front of the singer.

Is flat EQ also the goal when recording vocals?

Yeah, though I might try different mic preamps. The Neve 1073 is usually my favorite. Usually it will be flat but with maybe just a tiny bit of 10 k, depending on the singer. And I've been having some good results with Avalon preamps; they're very transparent sounding.

What's the craziest miking technique you've ever used that actually turned out to be effective?

One of the funniest things I did was using the microphones in a boom box to record drums. I came out of the earphone out and I used that as the mic, using the internal compression circuitry. I put the boom box on a chair in front of the drum kit, put the thing into record, came out of the earphone jack and used that signal. It was hugely compressed; the limiter inside there was just the worst quality imaginable. I mixed that back in with the actual mics; it made for a really interesting sound.

When you're mixing, what faders do you usually bring up first?

The first thing I do is I put all the faders up and just see what is going on. Then I'll focus on the drums and work on the sound of the drums and the bass. It's going to take me a little while to get that sound to mesh the way I would like it, usually by using a little EQ. If it's been recorded to analog, and I've been working on the tapes for awhile, I'm going to want to now add some more presence to the whole kit, and probably the bass. This might also be a good time to add some compression on the kick and the snare, in which case I might set up a send into a compressor—maybe a Fairchild or a Distressor, maybe an 1176, see what works best. I might recompress the bass also. I'll also invariably have a little bit of overall compression across the stereo bus—I'll always be listening through that. My favorite compressor is a Neve 33609, and that will be on the bus all the time, set at 2:1, though I don't really want to see it moving too much when the drums and the bass are in at this point.

I'll generally take a break before I start working on the vocal sound, because I'm usually listening to drums on the big speakers, getting a vibe going—I want to be excited by what I hear, and it's really hard getting excited on a pair of NS10s. Once I'm sure that the vocal is in a good spot, I'll balance around it. I'll do whatever I need to do with the guitars, pan stuff out, get them away from the vocal, and then start building everything else into the track. While I'm doing that, I'm writing down ideas of mutes that I want to try later, when I turn on the automation. Having a notepad helps, because my memory's getting bad!

Will the vocal typically be recompressed, or will you be riding faders?

Usually recompressed, but invariably there'll be some additional riding. The compression helps to tighten up the vocal, but it never seems to be enough that it'll just sit there. Invariably, it will have to be manipulated.

Are 1176s and Fairchilds the vocal compressors of choice during mixing?

Usually, the dbx 160 seems a little faster than 1176s or the Fairchilds, so if I need something with a faster attack time, then I'll use that instead. But I kind of grew up with 1176s—they're great, great compressors.

So it sounds like you use a fair mix of tube gear and solid-state gear.

Yeah, I love the sound of tube gear. When I started out at Orange, the board was all-tube, so I guess you get used to a certain sound, that analog sound. Digital is definitely an acquired taste, and the bad news is— it's not going away. It's here to stay, and you've got to embrace that technology. I love the facilities that Pro Tools offers, the flexibility and the editing capabilities; but at the same time, I still like the way analog tape sounds. And tape hiss doesn't bother me at all, never did. To me, tape hiss is like the air that you breathe; it's like the glue that holds the record together.

"Digital is definitely an acquired taste, and the bad news is—it's not going away."

It was part of that era too. One could make the case that times change, sounds change, ears change.

Times change, yeah. In the last two years, Pro Tools has been on every session I've done, somewhere or other. It's tough working with a hard disk system, because there's no time to sit back and rewind the tape and tell a joke! Also, when you start an analog tape, you can hear the comforting hiss to alert you that some music is going to come at you very shortly. Whereas with the hard disk, it's bam!, there it is. It's kind of unforgiving, actually.

So maybe there's hope for analog still. Maybe it's a great effect. Maybe you track in analog. I'm actually enjoying mixing in Pro Tools, because you're able to do more things. I know of people that actually get lost in it, tweaking forever, but I think judicious use of it is good.

The problem is knowing when to stop.

It's hard to know when to stop, because you end up fixing things that before you would never have bothered about. You didn't worry that the drums kind of picked up a little bit towards the chorus, maybe that was excitement, that was a little anticipation—but now, it's, "Let's fix that." And there's the danger of Auto-Tuning and pitch correcting. What do you then end up with? Something perfectly in time, something perfectly in tune— could be perfectly boring.

"Something perfectly in time, something perfectly in tune—could be perfectly boring."

Editing with a razor blade seems to have become a lost art.

I had to do that the other day, and it was really funny. We were in analog, and we had to do an edit. Pro Tools just wasn't around that day, and I said "OK, I'll cut the tape." And the look of horror on everyone's face—it was hilarious. I said, "This is easy, honestly." I said, "I'm gonna do it, I'm gonna cut the tape, but just don't tell anybody you saw me do it. This is called a destructive edit."

Actually, it's nondestructive; you can always take the splicing tape off.

Yeah, and hopefully not tear the tape. Once, when I was recording The Stranglers with Tony Visconti, we had a click on tape, and we were using an old MCI machine that didn't have a spot erase facility. So I'd left it on there, because it was too close to the program and I couldn't erase it. But Tony said, "Oh, I'll get rid of that." He cut a window in the tape! It was a 24-track tape, so he said, each track is 2.5 millimeters wide. He took a ruler and measured where the track was and he cut a little hole in the tape, put the tape back on, spun back, hit play, and it went through, no click. I was never so amazed—I just hoped it wouldn't rip, because of the hole in the middle of the tape. Now that's an *edit*.

Selected Listening:
Ricky Martin: *Vuelve*, Sony, 1998
Celine Dion: *Falling Into You*, Epic, 1996
The Pretenders: *Learning To Crawl*, Warner Bros., 1984
Sophie B. Hawkins: *Tongues and Tails*, Columbia, 1992
Duran Duran: *Thank You*, Capitol, 1995
INXS: *Listen Like Thieves*, Atlantic, 1985

Eddie Kramer

Heavy metal may owe its heart and soul to Hendrix and Led Zeppelin, but it owes its powerhouse sound to Eddie Kramer. The South African-born engineer/producer not only worked with both artists in their creative heyday but later went on to produce such second-generation metal mainstays as Kiss, Anthrax and Twisted Sister, as well as—surprise!—mainstream artists like Carly Simon, Santana, and Peter Frampton. Clearly, the guy's got a re-sume to kill for. More importantly, through the years he's developed a distinct sonic signature that has made him a true legend in record production.

Which is not to say the guy's a dinosaur—these days, he's as busy as ever, working with a variety of both new and established bands, as well as continuing to remix and remaster pre-viously unreleased Hendrix material. He's also making a point of passing on his considerable knowledge to the next generation of producer/engineers with an upcoming autobiography and with the active schedule of workshops he presents in recording school facilities around the world. Animated, intense, and focused, Kramer's droll sense of humor caught me off guard more than once, making our lively conversation as thoroughly entertaining as it was memorable.

Do you expend a lot of effort in getting sounds right during recording, or do you tend to "fix it in the mix"?

I'm a great believer in getting the sound right then and there. Put it on tape, and don't think about it anymore. I like to cut as naturally as possible, but at the same time if I hear a sound in my head, I'm going to go for it, I'm going to print it to tape. If I'm a little concerned about not being able to change it afterwards, I'll print the effects to spare tracks.

What's your basic drum miking setup?

I use a three-microphone technique on bass drum: a Shure SM52 and SM91 inside the bass drum and a [Neumann] U 47 FET outside the bass drum. By playing games with the various qualities of each, I get the sound I'm after. I'm a great believer in the sound quality of each microphone, and you don't have to use a lot of radical EQ to get great sounds if you choose mi-crophones for their particular qualities and put them in the right place. But I do like to com-mit to the sound in my head. If I know what kind of bass drum I want—for example, a thumpy bass drum with a lot of midrange—I'll carve out a sound for it, and I'll do whatever I need to do, whether it's gating, compression, EQ, whatever it is, to make that bass drum sound hap-pen, so I don't have to work so hard later. It's true that you could print each mic on a separate track and fiddle with it later, but that's bullshit, really; you'd be sitting there for hours. If I can't get a drum sound in twenty minutes, then I walk out. Boom, end of story.

With three mics on the kick drum alone, it sounds like you use a lot of mics on a complete kit.

I do use a lot of mics; however, it can be done with one or two mics. But they've got to be good quality mics—you can't use cheap ones. A bass drum mic and an overhead mic—that's all you need to get a great drum sound.

Where would you position the overhead mic in that kind of configuration?

You need to find the center, the "sweet spot" of the kit—but you need a damn good microphone, like a [Neumann] U 87 or U 47, or the new Shure KSM32, or an [AKG] C12, maybe. You need a really high-quality condenser mic; otherwise, you might as well just forget it, you're not going to get a great drum sound—I don't care what anybody says.

Is finding that sweet spot a matter of moving your head around and listening, or do you place the mic where the drummer's ears are?

If you listen to the drums carefully, you can position the mic over the center of the kit, generally. You also have to consider what the acoustics of the room are doing—are they helping you, or are they detracting from the sound? You want to pick a room that has good acoustics, because that's half the battle. A great microphone, a great-sounding kit, a great drummer, and great acoustics—and you can't go wrong. Listen to the stuff we did with Bonham—that's three mics on a kit, in a great-sounding room with a great drummer. He was certainly the greatest rock drummer that I ever had the privilege of recording.

Most people would agree with you, I'm sure. But a home studio environment is most often going to be a garage or a bedroom.

If it's a garage, where it's fairly live, you have a good chance of getting something halfway decent. See, my mic technique [for drums] is based on a classical recording technique, it's left-center-right overheads, it's close miking on the toms, multiple miking of the bass drum, the snare, the high hat.

Do you mic both over and under the snare?

All the time. And then I'll put multiple mics in the room: close room mics, distant room mics—it depends on the acoustics of the room. But if you're really looking for a great drum sound, my advice is: don't do it at home. Save up your money, get your drummer into a decent studio, cut the drum tracks there, then bring the tapes home and finish them at home. It's worth renting a decent studio for a day and cutting all your drum tracks. For the five hundred, seven hundred, thousand dollars, whatever it's going to cost you, it's worth every penny if you're serious about it and you don't have a decent place in your home studio to record

"If you're really looking for a great drum sound, my advice is: don't do it at home."

drums. Alternatively, if you've got a halfway-decent sounding room, go for it—just rent three high-quality condensers for the overheads and beg, borrow, or steal some good tube equalizers for them. Work at it, use what's at hand.

Can you record a whole band with [Shure] SM57s? Absolutely. It won't have the sparkly high end you'd get with condensers, but, hey, you can make it up with EQ. But if there's a choice, it's better to spend the money to go into a studio and cut the drum tracks there—you'll save on so many headaches in the long run.

What's the single most important piece of equipment in the home studio?
Your ears.

Okay, let's rephrase that. What's the single most important piece of equipment in the home studio you can buy with cold, hard cash?
You have to have a decent console. The board first, then the monitors, then the microphones. The quality of the board's mic pres are very important. I've done a lot of stuff on Mackie boards—their preamps are pretty decent, they're OK. You can make them work.

What are your favorite mics?
I like the range of Shure microphones for their flexibility. I use the SM98 mini-condensers on toms. The SM7 is a fabulous mic for bass amps; if you can't get a [Neumann] U 47 FET, which would be my first choice for bass amp or outside a bass drum, use an SM7; it's a great mic. It's a good vocal mic, too; it's very warm and fat. [Sennheiser] 421s are absolutely essential to the blend of what I do. If you can afford a ribbon mic, get one, too. To me, the best guitar mic is the Beyer M160, which I've used for 30 years on Hendrix, on Zeppelin, on everybody. I still use it.

If you can afford it, get a really good tube mic; a [Neumann] U 47 is a great way to go. There are lots of great tube mics available today at a reasonable price.

Let's talk about your approach to recording vocals.
Kill all singers. No, just kidding. It's really a question of, what are you looking for in the song? The song and the singer's tonality dictate the vocal approach. Some singers just sound terrible on SM57s, and you have to give them a high-quality mic like a [Neumann] U 87, U 47, or U 67. On the other hand, when we do Paul Rodgers' vocals, he uses a [Shure] SM57, handheld, in the control room. The band is kicking ass in the studio, and he's in the control room with me with the monitors blasting, and that's the final take—that's the keeper. Maybe we'll touch it up a little bit later...

Do you put the monitors out of phase?
No, he just stands right behind me and he sings. See ya, next. One, maybe two takes. But that's Paul Rodgers—he's a very gifted singer. If you get that great performance, who cares if there's a little leakage?

How do you position the mic for recording vocals?
Very few singers, unfortunately, know microphone technique enough that they don't need a pop screen, so I always use a nylon windscreen. I mic vocals dead-on. I always tell the singer to go like this (puts hand vertically in front of nose) and tell them, "If you get any closer than that, I'll kill you." (laughs) Quite often, I'll use an SM57 on a stand that they can hold on to [in addition to the "real" vocal mic], and I may or may not use it. Sometimes I have used it as part of the sound, because the singer may want to move off mic, though there can be phase problems when you mix it with the real vocal mic, especially if it gets off axis. But it sometimes gives a singer a feeling of comfort to hang on to that stand—something you can't do with a hanging condenser mic—and that sometimes works.

What's the best way to get a singer in the mood to deliver the optimum performance?

(deadpan) A two-by-four upside the head.

I hear that sometimes works well.

Depending on the song, depending on the vibe, I'll do things like put candles in the studio, dim the lights, make sure there's water on a barstool nearby. If it's a big room, I'll put a three-sided screen around them, put a low light on the music stand, carpet on the floor. Anything to make it intimate and warm and comfortable, so you feel like you're singing in a living room.

Do you ever experiment with ambient miking of vocals?

Yeah, sometimes on backing vocals. But what's the point of doing ambient lead vocals, unless it's for a special effect? I want to hear the person breathing, I want to hear the lyrics, I want to hear every nuance. I think it works great on backing vocals, but I'm not so sure about using it on a lead voice.

Do you ever experiment with different polar patterns?

No, not really. What's the point of using omni for a lead singer? I'll sometimes use figure-of-eight for two singers, put them on either side of the mic and let them balance themselves by moving in and out. We used to record symphony orchestras with just three microphones and let the conductor get the balance, so sometimes I just leave it to the musicians to get the balance.

Do you record vocals with limiting, or do you ride the faders?

I always record with multiple limiters patched in and sometimes compressors too. In the home studio market, dbx limiters are good, especially the 160—that's a great limiter. The JoeMeek is also a very nice limiter.

What sort of inexpensive room treatments can be used in the home studio?

Packing blankets! (laughs) Let me tell you, packing blankets have saved my ass in every situation you can think of. The best, cheapest thing for deadening down a room quick is packing blankets: gaffer-tape them to the wall, that's it. They're also great for making a tunnel for a bass drum, so you don't get any high end coming down the mic. They're wonderful, they're very, very effective, and I don't know a recording studio in the world that doesn't have 'em; that's part of the deal.

Also, you can buy four-by-eight foot sheets of one inch rigid fiberglass at a good hardware store and just wrap it with some nice fabric, pin it to the wall, and there you go. That'll run you about 20 bucks. RPG makes a really good diffusor—those are tough to make yourself—for just over a hundred dollars. Put a couple of those in the corners, throw up some rigid fiberglass, and you're set. If you have a budget of a thousand or fifteen hundred dollars, you can do wonders in treating the acoustics of a home studio. Get some nice wood, make a frame, hang a packing blanket within it, and put it on the wall, get some air behind it. There are all kinds of tricks you can get up to.

What if you've got the opposite problem—an overly dead room, like one that's got acoustic panels in the ceiling. How do you liven a room?

Well, that's a tough problem. Try lining the room with four-by-eight foot sheets of plywood, the walls, the floor, the ceiling, everything. You might as well rebuild the room if you're going to do that. It's much easier to go the other way around, so if you're building a room from scratch, build it live—you can always deaden it down.

You're one of the acknowledged masters of great electric guitar sounds. Any hints you can share with us?

You know what it is? It's the guitar player, it's not me. It's just correct miking and being able to define what the guitar player is hearing, and how can you get what's in his head and what's coming through his amp to relate to the same thing. Generally, most guitar players at a certain skill level have refined and tweaked their sound to the point where they know what they've got. They come in, they plug in, and you've pretty much got the sound. It's the guitar player and his or her ability to be able to play, number one, and, number two, to be able to have their sound already defined.

I'll find where the cool speakers are and stick one or two mics in the correct place to capture that sound. I use a three-mic technique: a [Shure] SM57, a [Sennheiser] 421, and a [Beyer] M160, all in a very tight pattern. Then I can pick and choose the tone quality, because each mic is totally different. I combine those together, and then I put a [Neumann] U 67 away from the amp to get the ambience. Then I go to town with different pieces of outboard gear. I'll process the sound in stereo—various kinds of limiting and EQ to make the guitar jump out of the track, to give it impact—and I do all this processing before the signal hits tape. This way, when it comes time to mix, I don't have to do anything—I just put the faders up, and it mixes itself. I can almost tell you where the faders are going to sit, because I know what that sound is.

I find that's a very English approach—get it right the first time and it mixes itself. Many American engineer/producers just aim to get the signal recorded as cleanly as possible so they have as much latitude as possible in the mixing stage.

Exactly. To me, it's stupid to try to mix it afterward. I don't want to spend 24 hours in the studio mixing. I want to get in there, get my sounds together, get all the moves, and print it to tape. Because it's agonizing being in there 12, 14, 16 hours a day mixing. What the hell for?

How long do you typically take to mix a track?

A long time. (laughs) But that's because the clients want to hear this, hear that, and fine tune it to the point of obsessiveness. And I think it's silly, I really do. My early rough mixes are usually better. However, I'm a great believer in putting stuff down on tape that, while it may not be the final sound, is damn close. Where it contains the instinctual ideas of the producer, the engineer, and the artist, on tape. If you delay the process to three, four, five days later, you'll be asking yourself, "What the hell was I thinking? What was the sound we were looking for?" Now you're EQing something that's already been recorded in an effort to recreate a sound that you can't quite remember. Unless you mix right away—which not a lot of people do—I don't believe in that philosophy at all; it's an anathema to me.

Do you always record guitars in stereo?

It depends. If you've got enough tracks, it's nice to be able to record guitars in stereo.

Do you always pan stereo guitar tracks hard left and right?

Again, it depends on what I'm doing. If I have two stereo guitars, probably not. Recording them in stereo gives me a lot of room to move the imagery around and to make a bigger space or a smaller space for the guitars. I can pan them out, pan them in. It makes for a nice sandwich.

Do you have any special techniques for recording acoustic guitars?

Ah, that's a whole different ball game. My favorite mics for recording acoustic guitars are a [Neumann] U 47 and an [AKG] 451. I like using condensers for acoustic guitars, and I always compress the signal. For me, when recording acoustic instruments, it's always important to have two mics, two equalizers, and two limiters. For drums, acoustic guitars, and piano, I prefer tube outboard gear—and tube mics, too, if they're available.

Let's talk about your overall approach to mixing.

The mixing process for me can be frustrating but it can also be very rewarding, because that's the one time where you really have an opportunity to expand the tone color palette. That's how I look at it. Mixing is the final stage of creating a piece of music that has been conceived by the artist, reinterpreted by me, put on tape, and tweaked and messed around with. It's a reading of a person's musical ability—their songs, their emotions, all the stuff is on tape and you've now got to sculpt it, shape it. It's important to have done your homework beforehand, to have done good preproduction, good early demos. This all helps the final mixing process, gives you all your options. I'll hear something in my head, it sets off a bell...

Do you tend to start with a drum mix and then add other instruments?

Yes. I start with the drums. I may pull other things up for just a minute or two to see where I'm going with the whole song, then I'll kill everything and start working on the drums. I really try to define the bass drum so that it has punch, it has midrange, it has low-end stuff. But then you have to tailor that low end to what the bass guitar is doing. If the bass drum pattern is busy, you don't want too much bottom end. If the pattern is such that there's a lot of air and space between each note, you can afford to put a little more woof into it. It's a constant game you're playing—if you do something here, then something else is going to change over there. So it's my last chance to really paint the final picture. I think in terms of stereo imagery, although there are mono pieces to it, like the voice and the bass drum and the bass guitar. But I like to paint out to the edges—while a guitar might be far left and far right, there might be bits and pieces that I'll be panning into the middle. And I like to leave a nice hole in the middle for the voice and the bass drum and bass guitar to sit. Then I'll start moving things around as I see fit. Not many people like to pan [dynamically], but I do it instinctively. I do it as the music is flowing. That's a trademark of mine. I started doing that 30 years ago, and I haven't stopped.

I have found that my approach to mixing has changed a little bit more in the last few years as the music has changed. The basic philosophy hasn't changed, but some of the sound qualities have changed. Obviously, the sound is much drier—I use maybe a quarter of the reverb I used to use. And if I am using reverb, it's of the short kind, in deference to today's sounds—one second, a half second, with short decay times, also two or three different kinds of very short delays. I still to this day use a slap delay into the plate, though I pick and choose my moments when to use it—you can't use it on everything, the way we used to use it.

Do you send each instrument into its own effect or do you just set up a couple of master effects for the entire track?

No, each instrument will have its own effect. I'll use eight or ten effects, multiple layers of reverbs. They're subtle, some of them are absolutely down in level, but usually very short now.

What are your thoughts about surround sound?

I think it's a lot of fun, but you have to be careful with some of that stuff. The thought of doing, say, a Hendrix record like *Are You Experienced?* in 5.1 is frightening, 'cause I don't think it will work. However, doing a Hendrix live album in surround—ooh, baby, that could be very nice. I think it works great live. I'm not that happy with some of the mixes people have been doing [remixing older albums in 5.1], because I think they're destroying the artist's original concept. Can you imagine *Are You Experienced?* in 5.1 without Jimi being there to say, "This is the way I want it"? Forget it. It's just messing with stuff that shouldn't be messed with. A live show, on the other hand, *will* work. You've got the band, left-center-right, in nice imagery across the stage, and maybe you hear someone moving around a little bit, you've got audience reaction behind you and the decay of the hall. That'll be terrific—go for it.

Any final thoughts for the reader out there who wants to be the next Eddie Kramer?

Just learn where to put the mic, how to work a console, how to get a reasonable facsimile of a decent sound mixing-wise, and what it takes to run a session. With the rise of digital recording and the home studio, there's a revolution afoot!

Selected Listening:
Jimi Hendrix: *Are You Experienced*, MCA, 1967; *Axis: Bold As Love*, MCA, 1967; *Electric Ladyland*, MCA, 1968; *Band Of Gypsys*, Capitol, 1970; *Cry Of Love*, Polydor/Reprise, 1971; *Rainbow Bridge*, Reprise, 1971
Led Zeppelin: *Led Zeppelin II*, Atlantic, 1969; *The Song Remains The Same*, Swan Song, 1976
The Beatles: "Baby You're A Rich Man" *(Magical Mystery Tour CD)*, Apple, 1968
Kiss: *Kiss Alive*, Casablanca, 1975; *Alive 2*, Casablanca, 1977
Peter Frampton: *Frampton Comes Alive*, A&M, 1976
Carly Simon: *Carly Simon*, Elektra, 1970

Andy Johns

Walk into any music store in any town on any Saturday afternoon, and within minutes you're guaranteed to hear the strains of "Stairway To Heaven" wafting from the electric guitar tryout area, as yet another teenage Jimmy Page-in-the-making resurrects the ultimate heavy metal *tour de force*. Andy Johns was the man behind the board on the day that classic record—and many others—was being made. The younger brother of the legendary Glyn Johns, Andy has always had big shoes to fill, but he's still active these days, nurturing new young bands from his base in L.A., while Glyn has retired to the English countryside. His staggering list of production and engineering credits include the sole *Blind Faith* album; the Stones' *Exile On Main Street* and *Goat's Head Soup*; Van Halen's *For Unlawful Carnal Knowledge* and *Live: Right Here, Right Now*; and, of course, *Led Zeppelin III* and *IV*, as well as seminal work with Jack Bruce, Jethro Tull, Traffic, Mott The Hoople, and Ten Years After. Effusive, emphatic, and somewhat larger than life, with a storehouse of—mostly unprintable—behind-the-scenes anecdotes that could fill a book (unfortunately, not this one), a chat with Andy Johns is every bit as lively as it is informative.

You've recorded so many guitar legends. Was there a standard guitar miking technique you used, or did you have to come up with a new one each time around?

The miking technique I used on electric guitars for years was two [Shure SM] 57s, one straight on and one at 45 degrees. Put 'em together, and it always works. But there aren't any rules. I have knowledge only because I have experience. If something isn't working, it doesn't frighten me anymore, because I know that it can be fixed.

These days people are doing in their bedrooms what 20 years ago you could only do in the top studios in the world.

Maybe 30 years ago.

Is this a good thing or is it a bad thing?

Nothing is bad. Some people can make things at home under very peculiar conditions that completely break all the rules. I did a record with a guy in his house—he was just renting this little house, and the guitar amp is in his wife's closet, and there's dresses and coats draped over it, and it's as dead as a doornail, and we've got one mic stuffed right in the speaker, and I'm going, "No, with years of training, one would know that just won't work." But it was a fucking gorgeous sound; it was lovely. He got a drum sound in his bedroom that would knock your socks off, and I'm at this point totally convinced that there is (posh voice) only one way to work and with a certain cubic capacity in these microphones and it might take me two hours to tune the kit and...(back to normal voice) Bam! It sounded great.

Whether it's healthy—well, it couldn't be unhealthy, because people are making *music*. People are using drum machines and programming, which is very convenient. You can write quickly with that, and I like the fact that, using Pro Tools, you can find out if your ideas work or not very quickly. But then you end up with each chorus being identical and relying on samples. For me, personally, the best way is to have some people in a room playing with each other, and hopefully there is a little bit of improvisation going on and they are bouncing ideas off of each other. Because then, as a listener, you can get inside their minds as individual musicians, as opposed to just this overall sound.

Are you getting a lot of tapes from home studios?

Yes, of course, and they get better and better all the time. A record company will send me tapes and say, "These are the demos, Andy." What... these are *demos*?? Jesus, I'm going to try to beat that? Pete Townsend had this studio, Eel Pie Island Studios, and he would bring these demos in which would petrify my brother, who would say, "How am I going to beat that?" How *do* you beat that?

I think when people are working just on their own, though, they can lose objectivity. Because the gear is there, you've got to keep going back and ditzing with it. Nobody can work on their own unless you're like Beethoven and you sit at home with the piano and you're a damn genius. I think that it takes more than one person. The more people that are playing at the same time, the better—as opposed to doing overdubs—and that's very difficult to do at home. So you tend to get more Lego-like sounds and a lot of Pro Tools and drum machines mostly. You might like it the first time you hear it, and maybe it will grow on you a bit more as you get more and more used to the song—but the depth in the song will disappear a little quicker. You might not listen to it for a year or two, and you come back and after the first couple of listens you'll think, "Yeah, that's great!" But after two or three listens: "It's going, it's going, it's going." Whereas a truly classic record, where you've got a lot of people playing at the same time and they're really knocking it down, you can listen to that over and over and over again.

What are the kind of common mistakes you are hearing on the tapes coming out of home studios?

I don't know if it's home recording or the way that people wish to make records now, even in a big studio, but they seem a little two-dimensional. Out of every 100 hours spent working, there's maybe 10 hours with other people, and that's a bit two-dimensional. But they don't do anything more at home than they would in a regular studio; it's the same gear. It's just that in a regular studio there might be more gear, and the mixing console is far more expensive, and there might be some big monitors. A lot of rooms I go to now, they don't really bother to tune the big monitors any more, because nobody uses them. But because I grew up with big monitors, it's important for me to have a big monitor setup that works, not only because I like to dance a little when it's loud, but I can tell what's happening in the bottom end more.

For the *Blind Faith* record, the console I had was poor quality as far as distortion and things went, and the EQs were like—well, there's some bottom. (laughs) And there was a midrange control; I think it worked at 1.5, maybe 3 k. The other frequencies were so narrow-banded, it was like a mosquito or something. But the mixes were fine. People in home studios have got far more output gear than we had. In those days, what were the effects? If you wanted a quick repeat, you put tape around the capstan. Or you had phasing, plates, or backwards, or delays, and that was it. So you've got all that at your fingertips, the same gear that you'd use in a regular studio where you pay. No, I've got no problems there; it's just I'd never have one at *my* house.

Why not?

Because when I go home, I go to listen, not to work. That's where I go to try and be objective, and I don't want a load of filthy, dirty, smelly, greasy, fucking musicians peeing on the lawn and my wife getting crazy! (laughs) No, it's not the same thing as going to another place where you're under a little bit of pressure and people are working for you and they will supply hopefully every need. There's something very nice about being in the same room for six, eight months a year because you've got it down and you're sure "it sounds like that to me in here." At that point you're not actually hearing what comes out of the speakers—you're hearing what you *know* comes out of the speakers. When you walk into a new room the first day, you hear this sound and you go, "Well, that sounds pretty good"—unless it's horrid. After you've been there two, three days you go, "Hello, there's a hole at 200 cycles." Maybe a month, two months later you start mixing, and you go, "There's very little depth on the top end, there's no transparency, how can I mix?" But you figure it out. And then at certain times, with taking tapes in and out, your brain starts letting you hear what is actually there. For example, if I'm mixing, I'll have the big guys, a pair of NS10s, and then I'll maybe take some JBLs and put them out in the room, and I'll check on all three systems. Then I'll get a DAT and I'll run up to my house. Even after 32 years of doing this, all my life, you go to your house and you go, "My God, when it goes to the B flat, the bass just disa-fucking-pears!" And you get back to the studio, and now, armed with this information, you hear the same thing on those three sets of speakers at the studio. Your brain's gone, ding, that's happening, and it's right. Your brain, psychosomatic or whatever it is, will figure it out.

> **"When I go home, I go to listen, not to work."**

Let's talk a bit about the overall approach you take to mixing.

You can do a mix where all the balances are perfect, but it means shit unless the overall sound—the bottom and the top—is going, "'allo!" If that ain't there, see you later, so you start with that. And the way I do that is you have to have something to compare it to, so I'll constantly be playing CDs.

What faders do you pull up first?

The drums, because, for me, that's where the fidelity comes from.

What sort of things are you listening for?

Air. Air and power and decay time. And then you bring in the rest of the rhythm section and make it start moving. From that point onwards, when I EQ I don't really solo things very much unless it's to find out if something's wrong. If you add, say, some 4 k to a guitar on its own, you might think, "Yes, that's nice," but when you put it back in with the other instruments—because they are covering up a lot of that frequency—it might get much more shrill. This is obvious, and what has always astounded me when I go into other people's rooms is that sometimes they'll listen to the drums for an hour. Now drums are going to sound fine on their own whatever you do. So then, it's, "Let's listen to the bass and we'll do this and we'll do that." They're going, "I think another half a dB there." And then they put it all together and then wonder why it isn't working.

Even if I've done a bazillion overdubs, it's supposed to sound like the best rehearsal the band ever did and you are standing about 12 feet back from the stage. It's supposed to sound like you're fucking there and they're playing for you. If you can get that, for me, that's how rock and roll is supposed to be. And it was just your fortune and privilege to be there that afternoon.

In home studios, many people have a lot of trouble knowing when to quit and go past that point. Instead, they polish and polish and polish.

You can do that just as easily in a place you are paying for; there's no difference.

But the difference is, because you're not paying, you just keep going. You don't have that pressure hanging over you.

You have to have the courage and relentlessness to not give up until you're dancing. You can sit there and go, (posh voice) "This is very good. I can hear everything, that sounds really super, yes, that's excellent," (back to normal voice) but you're not going, "Yeah!! Hoo hoo!!" If that's the case, something's wrong. You've got to be going, "Man!"

Ray Davies has written about the first attempt the Kinks had at recording _You Really Got Me_. The reason he demanded they go back in and redo it was, in his words, "it didn't make his girlfriend wet her knickers."

So the end of the story is, when he took the next mix home, she did.

Apparently so.

Did you wet yourself yet, my dear? (falsetto) "Yes!" (normal voice) It must be alright then! (laughs)

But I think you're talking about pretty much the same thing—you're talking about reacting on a visceral level, not just technical perfection.

Yeah, and there is a lot of intellect involved when you're mixing, 'cause you're checking. You put it up the first time, and it always sounds good. But halfway through, you're going, "This is useless, how am I going to make this work?" Then you get past that and, at the end, it's the details. And it's the details which are the difference, which make it something you are going to

> **"Your first responsibility is, have you made the artist happy?"**

want to listen to in 15 years and go, dammit, there's no guilt on my part. You just keep at those until there are no questions left in your mind. If you're mixing stone cold on your own, with no one else there, then you've got to be yourself, and you've also got to pretend to be each individual member of the band; what would they think? If the artist was sitting next to me now, or if he was listening at home, would he be going, "Great, that's what I want it to sound like!"? Your first responsibility is, have you made him happy? 'Cause he's given you this chance, you know, and you have a responsibility.

And there really aren't any nasty people that are musicians. I mean, I've met some difficult people and I've been a little tough myself to people, but on the whole, well, most people are nice, you know? And I think that most people that want to play music, God, there's something that's OK about them if they want to do that.

Selected Listening:
Led Zeppelin: *Led Zeppelin III*, Swan Song, 1970; *Led Zeppelin IV*, Swan Song, 1971
Rolling Stones: *Exile On Main Street*, Virgin, 1972; *Goat's Head Soup*, Virgin, 1973
Van Halen: *For Unlawful Carnal Knowledge*, Warner Bros., 1991; *Live: Right Here, Right Now*, Warner Bros., 1993
Television: *Marquee Moon*, Elektra, 1977
Jethro Tull: *Stand Up*, Chrysalis, 1969
Blind Faith: *Blind Faith*, RSO, 1969

Tony Visconti

They say lightning never strikes twice. But they're wrong, as Tony Visconti can attest. Imagine discovering and developing the career of an artist with the stature of a David Bowie, then finding another gifted (if enigmatic) young singer by the name of Marc Bolan, and going on to produce a string of hit albums for him, too.

Born in Brooklyn, Visconti made his fateful move to London in 1968, initially apprenticing with the legendary producer Denny Cordell. His musical and arranging talents soon made Visconti one of the most in-demand engineer/producers on that side of the Atlantic. In the nearly two decades he spent in England, he built his own studio (Good Earth) and helped craft dozens of important records, not only with Bowie and Bolan/T. Rex, but also with Procul Harum, the Moody Blues, and Joe Cocker, as well as numerous post-punk artists such as Iggy Pop, Adam Ant, Hazel O'Connor, Thin Lizzy, the Boomtown Rats, and Sparks. In 1989, Visconti returned to his native New York, where he maintains close contact with the listening public through his Website (www.tonyvisconti.com) and continues to nurture new talent in his state-of-the-art home studio.

As an American who learned your craft in England, do you think there's a distinct English "sound" versus an American "sound"? If so, how would you account for the difference?

By the time 8-track came along, Americans were superstitiously printing stuff to tape with no effects and waiting until the mix to do it all, whereas the British way was completely the opposite—if you had a great effect going, you printed it. I'd say that's the difference between British philosophy and American philosophy, and I think it still holds true. Brits are just wild men—anything goes. If you go through the rest of Europe, they are more conservative, like Americans are. In France, they don't print effects; the same goes for Germany.

But do you think there was a qualitative difference between the sound of the records being made there versus here?

There had to be, because, first of all, they didn't use the NAB [equalization curve]—they used the European EQ curve, which always seemed to me to be brighter. And, because they lived closer to the German manufacturers, they had more condenser microphones in the studio, so there's more of that high end you hear on British recordings. I used to record in America in the early '70s, and I wouldn't see an awful lot of condenser mics—I'd see a lot of dynamic mics and RCA mics and things that we wouldn't normally have in Britain. An SM57 was a vocal mic for stage in Britain, but in America it was a studio mic, like other dynamics.

You'd think that American studios would be so much better funded since it's a bigger industry. George Martin, for example, has talked about how the Abbey Road people were in awe of all the equipment that the big studios had in the U.S.

Well, I'm just talking about the microphones, because if you live in England, it probably will be cheaper to buy a German microphone there than it would be in America. Telefunken and Schoeps mics—there's loads of them in England. I'd say the percentage of condenser mics to dynamic mics is greater in England than I've seen in American studios.

But, you know, in the late '80s and '90s, everything leveled out. You could put me in a studio in England and blindfold me and I wouldn't know what country I was in, because it's the same in France, it's the same in Germany, it's the same in Japan. Especially when you see the ubiquitous SSL or the Neve flying fader board—you could be anywhere in the world then.

Do you feel that things are more homogenous now in terms of the sound of the recordings?

Yes, but there still is a philosophy in England. When Hugh Padgham came up with the gated Phil Collins drum sound, that was printed to tape—that wasn't a mix thing. You won't find Americans doing a thing like that; that could have only been invented in Britain. Nowadays you could simulate it, but that's a physical sound that Hugh Padgham had the foresight to think, "I'd better print this." That's really British thinking.

So is there less time spent on mixing over there as a result?

Probably. David Bowie and I have discussed this many times, that [having] less options in mixing is a positive thing. For instance, the snare drum on *Low* and *Heroes,* which is that harmonized dropped-off thing—I would always print that to tape, albeit on another track; it wouldn't be on the snare track. But every time we put the multitrack up, it would be there. And it would keep us going in that direction—we wouldn't deviate from that sound. We'd want the album to sound that way, ultimately. A lot of people wait till the mix to do those things; they have no idea what the texture of their album is until they get into the mixing room, and then they'll sometimes spend months mixing to find the album's sonic personality. Whereas in England, we used to just go for it. When I made a T. Rex record, I did certain things like print a lot of slapback to tape—it was a T. Rex characteristic—and sometimes it would be on the guitar track itself, so it could not be removed. Because it would always be there, that dictated the direction of the subsequent overdubs—we'd always tailor the new overdubs to the old sound. Of course, it was only 16-track, but I could probably mix as many as three songs in one day. We'd just book a week to mix the album, and that would be indulgent.

You're one of a small group of producers who were active in the '60s and '70s who have kept current with technology—for example, you've got your own Pro Tools rig. Do you feel that this is really a better way to make records than in the old days?

It's just another tool in my arsenal. I used analog tape this summer for a group called Rustic Overtones, and we flew some tracks into Pro Tools for digital editing. When we flew it back to analog, we found it actually improved the sound. Maybe because of phase shifting, there was more depth to the recording, there was kind of a more three-dimensional sound to it. It's undeniably the future, the way to go. I suppose, like Phil Ramone, I never stood still; I've invested a lot over the years in new technology.

You know, anything new will be viewed with suspicion, especially by people in this business. I fool a lot of people. They assume I'm an analog guy, and I play them my mixes, and they go, "Yeah, Tony, that fat sound is so analog," and I go, "Yeah, but that's Pro Tools, buddy!" It's not analog; it's not what you think it is.

How did your home studio evolve?

It started out six years ago as a 4-track cassette Portastudio™. I just wanted a writing studio, and then Annie Haslam came in and I bumped up to 8-track cassette. I already had an early version of Pro Tools called Sound Designer, so I flew her vocals in there and cleaned them up a little bit, took out some bad drop-ins. I found myself making a commercial record with that 8-track cassette recorder, and that was in my spare time. So my studio is my alter ego—it's where I have the most fun. When I have to make an official project, and they want to spend hundreds of thousands, I'll go and spend their money on all the analog gear and SSL boards that everyone feels that they need to make records. But my own studio is getting very serious now, to the point where I think I don't really want to go the other way. I'd like to just keep expanding what I have and have people come here, because it's a much happier environment, and it doesn't cost as much. It doesn't matter whether you're David Bowie or a new baby group that's coming up—the one thing you really do want is comfort and ease in a studio; you don't want a studio to impose its awesome official personality on you. So I'm thinking quite heavily now about investing a lot of money in this setup. This was my demo studio, and now I'm making commercial records in it, recording people like Bowie and other big label people. It's fun to discover baby bands and work with them, and I couldn't do that if I didn't have this facility.

> **"I've heard people make very bad records on expensive gear. The gear does not dictate the quality—it's how you use it."**

Your story is proof that it's not the quality of the gear—it's the knowledge of the person using the gear.

If I say that, it'll sound big-headed. (laughs)

No, I'm saying it.

I have to agree with you. A compressor is a compressor—it doesn't matter whether it's a $5,000 one or a $150 one. You have to know how compression works to use it, and I've heard people make very bad records on expensive gear. The gear does not dictate the quality—it's how you use it.

Clearly, having a home studio has really changed the way you work.

Well, I try to have fun, and when I'm spending $2,000 a day in a studio, it's more serious. Plus the commuting is great here—I just roll out of bed. Sometimes I can't sleep, and I'll come down here and work on a mix; I never had that luxury before.

Also, I don't have an A&R guy telling me that so-and-so wants it remixed a certain way. This is for me; this is what *I'm* doing. They either accept what I do, or they don't—that's the deal. This is the way I made records in the '70s. In fact, there was very little A&R interference in those days. We would just finish the album and deliver it, and the record company simply promot-

ed and marketed it—they never told you how to make the music. You have to do 18 different mixes now to please everybody— it's appalling, it's not the way we used to make records. When people say, "Wow, man, you made those great records in the '70s," I say, "Fine—let me make them that way!" (laughs)

A lot of today's recording schools are focusing on digital recording and editing in Pro Tools. Are those the best skills for people coming up to be learning? You started by cutting analog tape...

I started in the days of wax cylinders! (laughs) I think anyone starting out has to know everything. You can't just say, "I'm going to jump straight into hard disk recording," because the old technology is still going to be around for years. We'll still have analog recorders, and fifty years from now, there are some people who will wax lyrical about them. You can still buy 78s now, you can still buy the needles, the styluses for them—it will always be around, and it's good to know how these things work.

But a lot of today's records are being made from prerecord-ed samples as opposed to people making sounds from scratch. We seem to be moving away from the art of capturing a real sound in a room.

Well, mic technique is still very important. In fact, the key word in what you just said is "room." It's not so much that you're miking a guitar—you're miking a guitar in a room. I had a cellist

"It's not so much the instrument; the room is very much part of the sound."

in here recently, and I moved her until I got a good sound. Once I put her in one particular corner, her cello just sang—the room just filled up with the low end, and the sound exploded! A person who hasn't had years of experience might not have thought of doing that, but I could just tell there was something lacking when she was in the center of the room. That's mic technique. It's not so much the instrument; the room is very much part of the sound. You can go into an anechoic chamber and play the most beautiful Stradivarius in the world in there, and it will sound like crap, you know—the sound of the room is very important.

Take my drum room. It's an accident, but it's a controllable accident. It's live, and vocals in there have a nice body to them. Drums sound amazing in there, if a little on the live side. The room is probably 12 x 8, but it sounds much bigger than that. Instead of all these fancy foam squares that you can spend a lot of money on, I use moving blankets—they make the greatest deadening wall surfaces in the world.

You're committing the grievous acoustic sin here of having parallel walls, yet you're saying the room works—which makes the point that you don't have to follow the "rules"; you can be in a square room and it can still work.

Well, I'm working all nearfield; I wouldn't sit in the back of the room and analyze my mix. In nearfield, it will always work. But you have to be in that equilateral triangle to really understand what's happening inside your mix. I don't believe in perfectly acoustically treated [control] rooms, because no consumer will ever sit in an acoustically treated room. People listen in their cars, they listen in a living room, they listen on boom boxes—so I evaluate my mixes more on those things than I would in a perfectly treated room. Of course, it's very nice to go to a great mastering facility and put your mix on. If you've done it in a stupid room like this and it sounds great, then just pin a medal on your chest—but that's the beauty of nearfield monitoring. If I had in-wall monitoring, it would be a different story—I'd have to bring in an acoustic expert. That's a real kettle of worms.

You're a bass player, so I'm particularly interested in the approach you take towards recording bass.

I'll split the bass and record both DI and amp. If I'm in a big studio and I've got lots of tracks, I'll record them on separate tracks. Again, I come from the old school where if the sound is great, you can blend the two—just check the phasing, always check the phasing. I've got a nice Manley DI that I carry with me; it's got tube circuitry and it's quite expensive, it's one of my high end boxes. I've also got the ART preamp; I use that sometimes as a bass DI. If I'm playing bass, I don't usually like to play through an amp in the studio, so I'll just use the DI—I have enough gizmos here to make it sound fat.

When you are recording both amp and DI bass, do you tend to use one signal for low end and the other for attack?

Yeah, that would be the case. The DI's going to have more attack than the amp, so you might as well go for a fat amp sound—that's all it's really good for. You're not going to get clarity out of a bass amp.

Do you typically compress both signals as you are recording them?

Oh, yes.

Do you compress them again when you mix?

I'm a compressor freak. Compression is the sound of rock. At some stage, you have to compress a lot, especially low end. I don't really slam it when I go in, so it's actually quite nice in the mix. Sometimes I won't compress the bass on a mix, but I'll put it high in level, and I'll put compression over the stereo bus so the bass just kind of does its thing and interacts with the kick drum. Pumping is acceptable.

One problem that many people have when recording bass is getting a fat sound without it being woofy and flabby. How do you tighten up the low end?

Well, whenever I compress a bass, I do it through a stereo compressor and put the link in—that's one way of tightening up a bass sound. In other words, your DI might not hit the compressor as hard as the amp would, but the amp might hit it really hard and it'll bring the attack down appropriately. I'll do that on the mix as well.

So you're sending the DI through one side of the compressor and the amp through the other side, but linked.

Yes, so it's like treating it as a stereo source, which it really isn't, but the levels will always ride each other. So on those notes where the DI might be much louder than the amp, the compressor's controlling it. Sometimes after I do that, I might gang the two signals and send it to a third compressor to squash it even further.

How do you approach EQing the bass?

I don't do anything radical except that I look up the frequency of the key that the song is in. Say if it's in the key of F, I know that the low F on the bass string is something like 48 cycles. If that note's not loud enough, I'll pinpoint that frequency and boost it. In fact, you can often get more clarity—you can make the low end seem more apparent—if you boost it again an octave higher. So if I'm boosting it at 60 cycles, I'll also do a slight tweak at 120, and I might even go to 240. Even a bass sound has got harmonic overtones, and sometimes that's where the definition lies—it's not just only in the low end.

When I discovered this principle, I found that if you go a little higher up, you can actually hear the note itself—not just the warmth of the note, but the clarity of the note. This way, in the whole mix, you can actually hear the notes that the bass player's playing.

Do you have any favorite equalizers, or do you tend to use the board EQ?

Well, for these precise things I have to use a graphic. Any graphic that divides the octave in three or four will do, and parametrics will also do the job. I don't have any favorite equalizers; all these things are tools.

Do you find a different flavor between digital and analog EQ or compression? Do you favor one over the other?

I find digital plug-ins quite satisfying. They don't do exactly what their physical counterparts do, but they do it, and they do it in a different way, and you just have to play with it. I've invested a lot of time in trying to understand how they work, and I use my analog philosophies with them, but they don't work exactly [the same], so I would have to adapt. But when I work in the digital realm, I really don't use my analog gear at all. If I really want [an analog] sound, I'll have to think ahead and put the signal through my favorite EQ on its way into Pro Tools. I'm British trained, so I have to mess up the sound as it goes in—I have to screw it up and twist it and maul it—so I use my analog gear going in. My stuff is so treated by the time it hits the hard disk that I'm pretty happy with the sound, and the digital plug-ins will further that sound a lot; I don't have to do much after it's in there.

Do you use both analog compressors and digital compression?

In the mix I'll use only plug-ins, and in the recording I'll use only the analogs.

So you do your mixing in Pro Tools?

Oh, yeah, as much as possible. The first time I did that, I was amazed at the sound. It's clearer, fatter, and bigger than when I go through the analog outputs of my board to the analog inputs of my DAT.

What's your general approach towards recording electric guitar?

I'll have my tape op audition speakers for me; there's always one gem, and there's usually one very bad one. Once I find my happy speaker, I'll put something on there. Depending on the player, it might be a dynamic mic, or it might be a condenser mic.

Do you use the standard electric guitar miking of a 57 up against the grill?

Yeah, and that works most of the time. But I have put [U] 47s, I've put [U] 87s, and they all have a different sound. I'm very much a fan of the room sound, too. I always record it if it's a real heavy rock guitar with power chords and crunches and all. I'll go around the room and clap my hands and I say, "Put the mics *there*, that's it." Quite often, I'll turn the room mic towards the studio window, and you'll get a reflection of the guitar sound—not directly facing it, because you're looking for reflections. And, by the way, I'll use the same technique for hand claps. I find that often the sound of the hand clap coming off the glass into the microphone is much better than the direct sound.

I presume that you'll use a condenser mic for the room sound.

Yeah, my distant mic's a condenser—usually a couple of 87s. That's my favorite, my desert island mic—if I can only have one mic, that's it. I also love amp simulators; I've got the SansAmp and the Roland VG8 guitar. I'll put them up and give the guitarist a choice, and 75 percent of the time they prefer the VG8 or the SansAmp to their own rig. Sometimes you can blend the two and make an incredible wall of sound. Ten years ago, all these effects were very cheesy.But now they're so good, they sound so convincing. If you're going to solo it, you might smell a rat, but in a mix, who's going to know?

Have you had that same experience with sampled pianos versus acoustic pianos?

The acoustic piano is probably the hardest thing in the world to sample or to simulate. Kurzweil has a few good samples, though you can still hear it's a piano in a room, and it's not the way I would mic it—it's someone else's miking technique. There's also the Alesis NanoPiano—they have one great patch on it—the first patch, number one, which is an incredibly well-sampled Bosendorfer. I usually have to resort to using these samples, though if I were working with a very heavily based piano artist, I would have to take them elsewhere to record a real piano. But most of the time I'm working with a rock group that just needs a basic piano overdub. These sampled pianos are fine for that.

When you do record an acoustic piano, what's your general mic technique?

Again, that changes, but I'll open the top and do a crisscross kind of stereo thing with the two mics pointing towards each other like a pyramid. Two [U] 87s. Or [KM] 84s—Neumann 84s are my favorite for piano.

Positioned over the sound holes or over the strings?

Over the sound holes. I don't go right up to the hammers—I like to raise the mics a bit and let the sound wave form a bit. And occasionally I'll use a third mic if I'm not getting really good low end. I have this philosophy that a stereo piano can sometimes sound smaller than a mono piano. You can't record a piano that sounds as wide as a 20-foot stage—it's a psychoacoustic thing— so sometimes I'll record a piano in stereo and then on the mix I'll just mono it. But I'll record in stereo for insurance, so we've got that sound. If it's a great room, you've got to put room mics up and blend them in. So with piano, I might use up to five mics at once. Again, I use stereo compressors; I can't emphasize how important that is. If you put a mono compressor on each mic, you're going to have the worst sound balance in the world; you'll have a very lopsided piano.

Are you creating a stereo image out of the five mics and then feeding the stereo send to a stereo compressor?

No. It's usually a two mic technique—I'm using that 80 percent of the time—so my stereo mics will go through a stereo compressor. If I'm using stereo room mics, then I'll have a stereo compressor on those stereo room mics so at least both sides will go up and down. I might not use a compressor on the fifth mic at all, and maybe I'll stick it on another track. I don't usually use the low-end mic; in my whole life, I've done that maybe 5 percent of the time.

What sort of compression ratios do you use? Heavy compression or gentle?

I never use a quick attack on anything—that's ridiculous. It'll be around a 50 millisecond attack so the initial attack gets through, and then it kind of tapers off. The compression [ratio] will be maybe 3:1; usually no more than that. If it's really going to be rock and roll, maybe 4:1.

Are those the same kind of compression settings you'll use for bass and guitar?

You know, I'll use the same compression settings for any instrument. I kind of have this philosophy where I know how much compression I like to hear, and it almost applies to any instrument. On the mix, however, if it's a very uneven bass sound, I'll really hit it. I might hit it 10:1 on the mix. But basically the same thing applies—3:1 on the bass, 4:1 on recording. I don't think 2:1 is compression; you might as well turn it off.

In vocals, the same thing: I'll do gentle 3:1 compression on a vocal on the way in, but, again, if it's a vocalist who's really whispering and screaming the next minute, I'll have to hit that maybe 5:1 or 6:1 on the mix. If there is a whisper part, in Pro Tools I'll just slice it out and give it its own track and treat it differently from the scream part. It's ridiculous [to think] that one compression setting will cure all evils. Sometimes you just have to mult something out for different parts of the song.

What's your generic approach to miking drums?

First of all, when I get a good drum sound, I take photographs of the mic placement. I have a series of photos from over the years—they're like photographs of my drum sounds.

Generally, I try to use the minimum number of drum mics until I find a problem—then I'll start sneaking mics in. So I'll use one mic for the kick, one mic over the snare. For high hat, I like to get as close to the stick as possible. I have been known to tape an AKG 451 to the actual pole of the high hat, or even clip a lavalier mic to the pole, so as it goes up and down, so does the microphone— and it's always following the same signal.

And it's not picking up all the kind of woofing and wobble from the stand?

No, because when I record a high hat, I'll filter out all the low end so you won't get any air.

There's nothing on a high hat that is below 200 [Hz]—it's just junk, so I take it out. If I'm mixing someone else's track and they haven't done that, I'll do that during the mix.

Sometimes I'll take a second microphone stand and hang the cable on it so the mic dangles over the high hat like a marionette. Another way I like to record high hats is to take a 451 that has that screw-in elbow so the capsule can be bent at a 90 degree angle, like the Concorde jet. Then you can sneak the microphone right over the high hat and bend it downward. Again, I love to get as close to that stick hitting the metal as possible. For toms, I just like to sneak the mics over the rims, aimed at where the stick will hit.

What's your mic of choice for toms?

In England, [U] 87s; in America, [SM] 57s. I like 57s on toms; they sound really good.

In the kick drum, I'm not a big fan of the D12, and to this day I'm still putting different kick drum mics in there. If I use a D12 or the D112, I find it's hard to get the clarity, so sometimes I'll put in a second mic just for the high end; sometimes that might be an Electro-Voice RE20.

With both mics inside and up close?

Yeah, both inside and up close. I'll put the D12 right at the outside of a hole cut in the front skin. Just at the perimeter to get the maximum low end, to get the waveform a bit. But I'll sneak the RE20 right in there, a few inches away from the beater. I'll blend the two, and I'll send them both to one track. If I've got the sound really great, then I'll commit that to one track.

How about snare miking?

On the top I'll have my latest—a mutated 57 which I took apart and...I've got to show it to you! (brings out an SM57 which has been cut open and retaped together so the capsule is at a 90 degree angle to the body) You could sneak this over anything, you could sneak this over a tom; it sounds really great.

Do you also under-mic the snare?

If I'm not getting brightness, if it's a very dull snare, or something's wrong that day, or it's just not cracking—then I will put an under-mic in. But I will always gate it; I don't like it rattling around all the time.

You gate the under-mic as you are recording?

As I record. I want to clean that bugger up before it gets on tape. It's quite easy to set the threshold, because the only thing that's going on in there is the rattle. Toms don't seem to affect it, kick drum doesn't affect it, so it's quite easy to gate it.

Will the gated under-mic be recorded on a separate track?

I always put it on a separate track. And invariably it's out of phase with the top one. I have never ever had the good luck of having both mics in phase naturally—so if you do that trick, you must check it. Even though it's being gated, you'll hear a big difference if you just play with the phase button, and you'll find that the low end will disappear if it's out of phase.

What mic will you stick under there?

Whatever I have on top. It doesn't matter.

What do you use for drum overheads?

For overheads I like to use something really hi-fi like an AKG 414. And lately I've been using the [Audio-Technica] 3041—they're just amazing. They're too fat on the low end, but put in the low end cut and they work great.

Where do you position them?

I'll just position them until I find a good sound and I'm picking up the ride, with the crashes much louder than the ride cymbal. I try to not use a separate ride cymbal mic, but sometimes I have to if the ride cymbal is underneath one of the crash cymbals and it's just not picking up. I'll put the overheads fairly high up, at least a foot over the drummer's head. Sometimes I'll blend the overhead mics with the room mics and record them on the same track. In a small room, the room mics and the overhead mics could very well be one and the same.

What mics do you like to use for vocals?

The Neumann U 87 and the [Audio-Technica] 4050, which I like mainly for female vocalists; it seems just to open up their voice more. The 87 is a very masculine microphone; it's thick and it sounds really good. For really rock vocals, I'll use a 57 and a 58. And recently, [I've been using] the Telefunken ELAM 251, a very expensive tube microphone. I used it on Bowie's voice, and he just sounded beautiful on it because he's got low end in his voice, but the high end on that mic is brilliant, too, so the vocalist leaps out at you. That's a dream mic. I'm contemplating buying one—I'd use it all the time, on everything.

Do you ever record vocals with compression?

Yes, all the time, though I try not to let it go beyond 10 dB of compression at a 3:1 ratio. Beyond that, you're going to really hear the compression. But most of the stuff I do is rock, so that's acceptable. I will compress less on a singer like an Annie Haslam, but people like her have an even wider dynamic range. But, again, she's singing to a track that has a wide dynamic range too, so when her vocal goes down in level, so does the track, usually. She's one of those classy singers who has really good technique. It would be unfair to over-compress her, so I'll back off on a singer like that. I'll probably keep the same ratio—3:1—but I won't let it go beyond 6 dB of compression.

Will you compress it again when you're mixing, or will you do manual gain riding of the vocal tracks?

On a rock record, I'll let the compressor do the riding. It works—it's the sound you want—but then even on a lot of rock records you still have to do manual leveling for one word or for one syllable. With Pro Tools, I'll just go into the sound file, and I'll boost the words that are mumbled; I'll even put EQ on it just for those brief words so I can hear the t's and d's of a word. That's a whole new level of mixing—that's micro mixing.

When you're starting a mix, in what order do you bring faders up?

Kick drum first, snare drum second, and bass third. I try to get some kind of harmonious relationship between those three, then I'll build the drum kit around those three initial instruments.

How do you go about getting the relationship between those three components?

I was taught by Denny Cordell right from the beginning that the bass and kick drum have to interact—they have to be almost like one unit. You have to make sonic room for them—you have to hear the notes on the bass, yet the kick drum can't be anemic. You have to hear the low end, but you can't put too much low end, because then it'll obliterate the actual note that the bass player is playing. So I really work on that relationship for a long time. I can't tell you exactly how I do it, because it changes from player to player, but I know what I'm looking for; I'm looking for a sound where the kick drum and the bass are just pumping out, where they're actually taking up most of the energy of the mix. In the '70s, that sound would be about 80 percent of the mix; nowadays, guitars are brought way up to the front with a lot of low end, so the bass and kick drum have gone down percentage-wise—maybe now they are only 60 percent of the mix.

On certain snares, I like to pull out some middle and emphasize the high end and the low end to really get a wallop. I also like to *feel* the snare; I'm not a big fan of piccolo snares at all. I like to feel the snare almost as powerfully as I feel the kick drum, and at this initial stage of the mix I'm actually monitoring quite loud because I want to see if this is really going to move air , if this is really going to have an impact on you.

So you'll get that sound from the snare by rolling out middle frequencies?

Yeah, sometimes it's important to roll out a little bit out of 1 k.

You're not boosting the low end—you're just taking out the mids?

Yeah, take them out. I have an engineer friend—a guy called Bruce Tergesen who was trained by Tommy Dowd and Jerry Wexler. And they always emphasized that it's like a Chinese proverb: One cut is worth a thousand boosts. (laughs) Just find the offensive frequency, and remove it with some kind of notched filtering—do it very narrow. First emphasize it until you find it and it really sticks out like a sore thumb, then cut at that frequency, and you'll find that the result is a much more pleasing sound.

A little bit of compression also always helps on the kit. Sometimes, if it's a real in-your-face rock track, I'll bus the entire kit to a stereo compressor like a Distressor or a Behringer Composer.

I gather from what you're saying that it's the bass guitar that occupies the lowest frequencies?

It does quite often—especially now when you have five-string basses. You don't want a kick drum to go that low. When I boost my kick drum, my frequency is around 100 Hz.

Will you actually filter out the lowest frequencies in the kick drum?

It depends. Again, I'll find the octave of that sound and boost that to make it clear. Often, the bass drum might have a lot of 50 Hz, which you're not going to hear; in fact, it'll wreck most speakers —it'll rip a car speaker apart if you play with that frequency. So I'll find the octave of it—which will be 100 or 200, and then the kick drum is fat and it's clear . Then I'll also go up higher, around the 2 k range, and find where the beater is and just tweak a little bit there. I'll assign most of the low end to the bass guitar. Again, it depends; I haven't done a lot of hip-hop, and I think the reverse would apply there.

So you're saying, if the frequency you want to boost doesn't work because of other things in the mix, go an octave or two octaves higher, and that'll give you the same psychoacoustic effect. Does that work for all instruments?

Yeah, play with the octaves. In opera, a voice has its *tessatura*—its range where it sounds most pleasant. A singer might have a four-octave range, but there's maybe one octave that's golden, and you want to sing things in that register. The same thing with instruments. Technically, with its undertones, a guitar will go down to 40 Hz because that's an octave lower than the E string. But does it sound good down there? Do you really want to boost those frequencies, or do you want to go where the guitar sounds most pleasant, to the area it was built for? The same thing with a kick drum, the same thing with the bass; every instrument has got its range that's beautiful, and that's what you want to find. That's my philosophy, and that's what you want to draw out of a mix. And quite often you'll find a conflict, say with a guitar and a piano, because, in rock, they pretty much are playing around the same area, though a piano might be a little higher and a little lower.

So, OK, there's your trick for the day: How am I going to make these things work? Well, obviously, separate speakers is a good idea—put the piano on the right and the guitar on the left—but if they have to overlay, you have to find out where the piano's going to sound its best and the guitar is going to sound its best, and then they can live harmoniously. But you would never have them fight each other—that's ridiculous.

However, you'll have to decide which one of them is going to have priority. If it's the piano that's going to play second fiddle to the guitar, you should still find ways of making it sound attractive. Luckily, a piano has a lot of sound to play with. The harmonics on a piano go way high up, a lot higher up than on a guitar.

That's a wonderful practical application of the psychoacoustic theory which states that if you hear only overtones, your ear invents the fundamental.

That's right, your mind is filling in the rest. But what you're hearing is a clear piano, so you assume that you're hearing everything in it.

A common problem, especially for novice recordists, is getting a vocal to sit in a mix.

The vocal is probably the most important part of the mix. If the vocal is poorly placed in the mix, it's going to defeat the purpose, it's not going to sell the music. People will remember vocals more than they'll remember the guitar licks—most people buy a record because it's a great song. My way of doing that is, again, to see where the vocal lives sonically. See where it lives and play with the EQ until you find where the vocal is going to be really hot. An expert at this is George Massenburg— I just cream when I hear his vocal sounds; he really does that absolutely right. So if I can, I'll use a Massenburg EQ—he's found that thing that makes vocals sound great. It's kind of in the upper middle and the extreme highs, the sound from the back of the throat. Instead of just the tone, you hear all the physical things that make up the tone, too.

Compression will help, and don't ever be afraid of putting the vocal too high in the mix. Sure, there's a point where it's ridiculous—I've heard some people put it too high—but you've got to hear every word, and what you should do is ask someone not involved in the production if they can hear every word. That's really the acid test. That's a real pitfall—if you've been working on an album for three months, you know every word of every song, and psychoacoustically you think it's all there. Then a person comes in the room, and you say, "What do you think?" and they say, "Oh, it's very nice, but I couldn't understand one word the vocalist was saying." It's a shock—it's a jolt—when you hear that. It's happened to me many, many times, so if I don't have the benefit of a person like that, I will just leave the room for a half hour or an hour and come back in and listen to my mix and try to be that person and see if I can hear these words.

If a person has a real pretty voice, you have to show it off with compression and a lot of high end. I'm not a fan of microphones like the AKG C12 that boost the low end. Everyone raves about this mic, but to me it sounds like someone singing into a blanket, and it's a tough mic to really bring out in a mix; the high end isn't as prominent as the low end.

But it's also a fine line; it's easy to make a vocal too brittle and too high end. How can you tell when you're crossing that line?

You just have to use your ears. Of course, I'm a firm believer in de-essers, too, because you need to have a lot of brightness on a vocal track, but if you just start tweaking, the s's are going to rip your ears off—they'll give you permanent hearing damage. So what I'll do is, I'll take a feed directly off tape and hit the de-esser first; I put it before the EQ. Then I'll patch it into my channel, and I'll start tweaking the high end. That's a big mistake I made in the early days: I just didn't know how to control sibilance until I discovered the de-esser.

Frequency-specific compression is a difficult concept for the novice to grasp.

Yes, it is. I used a multiband compressor all the time in the '70s—the ADR Vocal Stressor; I loved it. When I sold my studio in London, I had to leave it there. It's horrific, you know—there's too many knobs on it. It even had an expander circuit. Again, that was another way of solving that bass guitar that had a G that wasn't as loud as everything. I'd just tune it in with the equalizer and the expander, and it would expand that note, it would level it out. Instead of compression, it would be a different way of approaching the same thing.

With effects, as you're mixing, do you assign discrete effects to each instrument, or do you set up two or three master effects and feed multiple instruments there?

Good question! I don't share the drum effects with any other instrument, but I might share the vocal effect if it's pretty generic and nonspecific. I use Rich Plate a lot with about 60 milliseconds of pre-delay; sometimes just a little splash of it will sound good on an acoustic guitar—it might sound good on strings, too. So sometimes I'll share, but I'll keep the drum effects just for the drums only. If it's in a big studio, I might be running about six effects; I don't really go crazy with a lot of reverbs. Though [especially] with all these nice digital things, you want to go a little crazy sometimes.

I'm still a fan of [mechanical] flanging. I'll still do it the old-fashioned way if I'm in a studio that has enough tape machines. You can't beat it. There's no box in existence that can go forward and backward in time, which is what you're doing when you do tape flanging—it's actually a time machine you've created on a little scale. When you pass the node and you go before the signal and then you go at that node, it's just the most attractive (sucking sound). It's quite complicated to set up, but I remember the formula! (laughs)

Selected Listening:
Any David Bowie recording from 1969–1984
Any T. Rex/Marc Bolan recording from 1968–1977
Thin Lizzy: *Bad Reputation*, Vertigo/Mercury, 1977; *Live And Dangerous*, Vertigo/Warner Bros., 1978
Iggy Pop: *The Idiot*, RCA, 1977
Hazel O'Connor: *Breaking Glass*, A&M, 1980
Sparks: *Indiscreet*, Island, 1975

Part Four

Back in the States

Jack Douglas

J ack Douglas is one of the genuine nice guys in the business, with an enthusiasm that is positively infectious. Though he's been crafting monster hits for mega-artists like Aerosmith and Cheap Trick for more than two decades, his face still lights up as he recalls memorable sessions and recounts his favorite miking and signal processing techniques. It's easy to see why no less a legend than John Lennon handpicked Douglas to preside over his landmark (yet sadly foreshortened) comeback album, *Double Fantasy*, back in 1980.

These days, Douglas is involved in setting up his own project studio in Manhattan, where we met him recently for a most enjoyable—and informative—chat about his unique approach to making records.

What sort of recording mistakes are people making in the project studio demos you're receiving?

The first mistake is to send me the tapes! (laughs) Seriously, people are sending me stuff that sounds so good, I don't want to have anything to do with it! It's like, what do they need me for? The awful stuff is over-distorted, over-compressed, unlistenable—some of the heavy metal stuff I get is really screwed up, with Marshalls buzzing away and a vocal buried somewhere. But for the most part what I get in the mail is just scary.

What's the secret to getting good sounds out of inexpensive recording gear?

Start by doing anything you can to find the right acoustic environment for the instruments you want to record, then get as straight a line from the mic to the recorder.

"Start by doing anything you can to find the right acoustic environment for the instruments you want to record, then get as straight a line from the mic to the recorder."

Also, think in terms of creative signal processing. I recently completed a live album that was recorded on [Tascam] DA-88s and the tracks sounded a little flat to me. My first idea was to bounce the tracks to 16-track analog machines and overload them a little bit to get some tape compression, then send them back to digital. The other thing you can do is to put a digital signal through tubes and then back to digital. Go to flea markets and find old radios, then take the amplifier section out. On one recent project, I put LA-3As in front of some old passive Altec filters to drive the signal, then I set every frequency at the neutral position. The filters then acted like active equalizers, and they sounded amazing—they were the best on guitars, the bottom end was unbelievable. On the live project, we ended up using an eight-channel tube processor called *Charisma*, made by Beyer—they're only available in Germany, but they sent me one here, and it was absolutely amazing.

Another trick is to route a signal to a reverb and add a little compression to both the source and reverb return channels. Then run the whole signal [both channels] through a tube to give it some hair. What will happen is that every time the signal dies, the compression is going to lift the reverb up a little bit and you'll get a real breathing sound.

What sort of reverb times are we talking about?

It depends on the instrument. I always go by the amount of sustain the instrument has, because you really don't hear much reverb until the instrument dies. If it's a vocal, I'd go for something in the 200 msec–1 second range.

Another cool thing to do is to try to find some kind of analog reverb in your house. Somewhere in your bathroom with the shower door closed, you're going to find a neat reverb. All you have to do is put a speaker in there and a mic—now you have a natural echo chamber. Just the characteristics of that will make it stand out in your mix simply because it's not going to sound like anything else.

Just finding strange places in your house can add to a recording. Most of the time you're going to be in a room that's pretty dead—that's necessary in a control room so you can at least mix. But if you go down to your garage and you set up in a corner that has cement walls, there's going to be a very interesting standing wave there. Any place that has a strange standing wave is a good place to do a vocal, 'cause it's going to color the vocal—it might make it sound nasally, for instance.

You know, a guy called me recently and said, "I've run into this thing called an Ursa Major delay. I can get it for $50—do you think I should buy it?" That's an old, horrible digital delay line—8 bits or something—so I said to him, "Well, do you have anything else like it in your system?" He said, "No, all my other stuff is pretty much consumer top end, but this thing looks so different." My response was, "By all means buy it, and I'll tell you why. Because when you put something in there and you get the thing to sound pretty good, it's not going to sound like anything else in

> *"Don't always use a microphone the way it's supposed to be used."*

your system. So if you put it on a vocal, for instance, it's going to make the vocal stand out because it has such a different sound. It may sound crummy and cheap on its own, but in the mix it just adds character."

Sometimes the weirdest things—like an old spring reverb—can sound really phenomenal in a mix. By itself, it's going to sound awful, like surf music. But use it right—color it a little bit, filter it, EQ it—and it's going to sound cool in your mix. Cheap stuff can be really good.

Do you ever use cheap microphones?

Sure, absolutely. I have a collection of pretty horrible microphones, most of them out of old tape recorders; I love 'em.

The other thing is: Don't always use a microphone the way it's supposed to be used. That's very important. I learned that more from John Lennon than anybody else. I used to listen to

Beatles records and wonder how George Martin got those vocal sounds. Now, George Martin is a genius, but when I got to work with John I noticed that he worked the mic in a very strange way. He would sometimes sing a word or two on the backside of the mic. Also, he'd never use a pop filter—he'd just flash his 'esses' by waving his hand in front of his face, just whisking them away. He was really good at that, and you'd never hear any sibilance on his vocals. But he'd also go to the back and the sides of the microphone. Learning how to use a microphone is critical.

For guitar overdubs, the best EQ in the world is the phase EQ, which you get by using multiple mics on a speaker. For example, take a [Shure SM] 57, a Sennheiser 421, and your favorite condenser, and set up a triangle with the two dynamics at an angle up against the grill, but off

> **"For guitar overdubs, the best EQ in the world is the phase EQ, which you get by using multiple mics on a speaker."**

axis. Then take your favorite condenser mic, put a 10 dB pad on it, and place it about a foot away, facing the speaker on axis. Bring up one mic at a time and get it to optimum level on your board. To check that they're all in phase, make sure the signal is adding and not subtracting as you add in the other mics. If not, use the phase switch on your board to reverse the phase [of the offending mic] or put something in-line to reverse the phase. Then start to put up each mic, one at a time. The signal from the 57 will probably be pretty bright, it's got some meat in it, a lot of 5 k. The Sennheiser's going to be all 3 k, not much bottom. Your condenser will sound good, full. Now bring up all three—the 57 at about -10 [VU], the Sennheiser at about -3, and the condenser at 0. As you move the faders back and forth, you'll hear the greatest EQ, because of the phase relationship. If you've got an automated console, you can even set it up to move the faders for you while you're recording. Then, if you flip the phase on one of the mics, you can really have some fun—it'll act like a filter.

You know, when you build a mix—I don't care if it's 4 tracks, 8 tracks, or 96—the real nightmare is when you put something up and the only way you can hear it is by blasting it. There's nothing worse than putting up something that you're excited about, and it's gone. If you do things like this [using multiple mics and altering their relative levels], I guarantee you that as soon as you put the sound in the mix, it will be there. Not only that, it won't wipe out everything else in the mix, because it will have such a separate and distinct character. The thing that will make it sit right with your mix is the use of some compression on the stereo bus and the use of some reverb that is common to all the elements. It really helps to get individual sounds that are different, especially when you're using samples.

How do you get problematic individual sounds to sit in a mix?

You know that picture of the old square peg in a round hole? That's often what happens—you've built a beautiful square peg, and there's a round hole that it's got to go in. So you've got to do one of two things: you've either got to make the square peg round, or you've got to make the round hole square. If you're so in love with that sound—if it's the key thing in your mix—then you've got to go to the rest of your mix and sculpt it, get things out of the way. You don't want to lose them, but you may have to make some instruments smaller by taking out the bottom and the top end—then you can slide them back into the mix.

The other thing to try is to tear down your mix completely and put this thing that you love into the mix *first*. It could be a guitar, it could be an oddball thing that you normally wouldn't

build on. Normally you build on drums—for me, it's drums, then I put the vocal in, then I put the bass in. But if there's something I love—let's say hypothetically it's the cello from "hello"— a cello that means *everything* to me. But when I put the guitars up, the cello disappears, and when the vocal's up, it makes the cello disappear even more. So I put the cello up first. Now I've got a cello right in my face and I start to build around it. I'm going to EQ the other tracks, compress them to get them out of the way of the cello, and I'm going to have these instruments now surround the cello. The cello's not going to be just a part of the mix any more, I've decided that it's the thing that's most important. Maybe its placement in the track will have to be considered—maybe it has to go slightly left or slightly right to be featured more than if it were in the center. Maybe I'm going to put the cello on the left and the lead vocal on the right instead of in the center so these two things have voices of their own.

You've got to remember that the stuff that's going to take up the most room in your mix is on the bottom end. If you just let the bass take up that space, you can get out a lot of the low stuff in the other tracks—up to around 160 Hz—and it will still sound massive. You might want to leave in some of the low stuff, but then compress it.

Do you generally assign the very lowest frequencies to the kick drum or the bass?

There's no rule on that one, but I like to use a subharmonic synthesizer because so many systems have subwoofers, you've gotta have stuff to feed that. It's funny, I'll come into a studio after there's been a rap session and these guys are using massive subwoofers and blowing things up, and it's always seemed to me that that's backwards. If you can get tons of bottom on a normal system, then you're going to have a really cool mix with tons of bottom. But if you put tons of bottom on really huge systems, the mix is going to end up bass light.

Do you record bass direct or mix it with an amp signal?

I always combine the direct signal with the amp signal. I like using [EV] RE20s, I like using Audio-Technica 4050s. I use the direct signal for a super-clean low end I can build on. But I like the speaker for all the raw power and crunch. I compress both signals together—in fact, I compress them *three* times. I'll compress each signal individually and then compress the both of them together. Then I'll make a separate bus of the bass drum and bass guitar and compress that, too. I always throw a Neve compressor across the stereo bus also. Just tons of compression—and the mastering engineer will often add even more of it! (laughs)

Another trick I'm doing these days is to spread out a bunch of powered subwoofers—maybe six of them—in the room. Then I'll put a contact mic on the bass drum and use that as a trigger so whenever the drummer hits his bass drum, everything from about 80 cycles down to 20 suddenly shakes the room. The subs fill the room with this low wave, which everything picks up—room mics, guitar mics, everything. That'd be pretty tough to do in a project studio, though.

I suppose you could take a kick drum sample and feed it into a subwoofer in the room.

Yeah, and then stick a mic in the room to pick it up. I guess everybody's putting their vocals through guitar amps and stuff these days. There are no more rules anymore, but, hey, there never were—at least, I never thought there were. As soon as we started sticking things into Leslies, that was the end of it.

I think George Martin and Brian Wilson were the ones who broke all the rules—before they came along, there *were* rules.

That's what woke us all up—we said, wow, there's an art called record production. In fact, listening to the *White Album* was what made me want to eventually change from being a musician to an engineer and then a producer. I said, hey, there's really something else going on here besides the Beatles' playing.

George Martin has observed that it is technical imperfection that often makes a sound interesting, citing the ADT developed at Abbey Road, where the tape capstans were constantly slipping. In fact, he told me that John Lennon called him from New York during the *Double Fantasy* sessions to complain that the ADT didn't sound as good.

That's the absolute truth. John used to scream about the ADT. I only used analog tape delay on those sessions—I had a machine running at 30 [ips] with a double-sized capstan and a heavy-duty motor so I could run it at 60 [ips]—it had gigantic hubs on it. It had a variable-speed oscillator so I could crank it up even higher if I had to, but usually it came down a little bit lower. That was as close as I could get to what he liked.

The machine was probably a little more stable than he was used to.

Yeah, it didn't move as much. But when we were doing *Imagine* back in '71—'cause John started screaming *then* about it—Paul Prestapino built a 4-track machine that could do live flanging and ADT. It had two sets of playback heads, right next to each other, and was running at 60 ips, so it was practically a doubler, it was running so fast. Then he had this kludge contraption on top of the machine. As you turned it, what looked like a tension bar came in and moved the tape into a groove between the two heads. The two heads were so close, what happened was the equivalent of a two-machine flange, and this thing was unbelievable—what a sound it made! It's all over the *Imagine* album, and it was used on a lot of records done at Record Plant.

John had this thing about his voice—he hated the sound of it, absolutely hated it. The only way he could deal with the sound of his voice was if it was processed heavily, and it always had to be doubled. He was the best in the world at doubling, just perfect. I remember when he sent me the demos he made for *Double Fantasy* while he was in Bermuda. Here were recordings made on a cheap boombox, and before he could send those to me, he got another boombox and sang over it while it was playing so it doubled his voice. So even on those rough demos, the vocals were doubled—it was amazing that he would do that.

But in the studio it was really neat to hear John unprocessed and raw, to hear what his voice really sounded like. It was the best rock and roll voice that ever lived.

Steven Tyler [of Aerosmith] has also got an unusual voice. How do you mic him?

Because he puts out such a tremendous amount of dirt and grit and grime, I find that a [U] 47 is way too warm for him; [U] 87s are just too real; [with] RCA-44s and 77s, the ribbons start to ripple a little bit. My favorite mic on Steven is a Sennheiser shotgun—we did tons of vocals on those even though they're a difficult mic to find. I'd put a [Shure SM] 57 in front of him so he'd have something to focus on, and have the Sennheiser shotgun about 5 feet away from him, pointing directly at his head. I'd record that on a separate track with just a ton of compression, so you could hear all his natural noise and distortion—practically singing harmony with himself.

Selected Listening:
Any Aerosmith recording from 1974 - 1982
Cheap Trick: *Cheap Trick*, Epic, 1977; *At The Budokan*, Epic, 1979; *Standing On The Edge*, Epic, 1985
John Lennon: *Double Fantasy*, Geffen, 1980
Alice Cooper: *Muscle Of Love*, Warner Bros., 1973
Patti Smith: *Radio Ethiopia*, Arista, 1976
Graham Parker: *Another Grey Area*, RCA, 1982

Thom Panunzio

Talk about being thrown in on the deep end: the very first session Thom Panunzio ever assisted on was a tracking date for John Lennon's *Walls And Bridges* album. That's the way it was when you hung out in New York's famed Record Plant studios in the mid-'70s. Scant months later, Panunzio was watching (and helping) history be made as a fledgling artist by the name of Bruce Springsteen prepared to take the world by storm with *Born To Run*.

Training under some of the top guns in the Big Apple— people like Jimmy Iovine, Shelly Yakus, Jack Douglas, and Bob Ezrin, to name a few—prepared Panunzio for his own stellar career as a producer and engineer. He soon became one of the leading experts in the vagaries of live recording, working with Link Wray on *Live From El Paradiso*, with U2 on *Rattle And Hum*, and, more recently, with Black Sabbath on their *Reunion* album and on the live Ozz-Fest releases. These days, Panunzio is based in the sunny climes of southern California, but his Yankee cap and Jersey accent belie his roots as a Noo Yawker, through and through.

As an East Coast guy who's now living in L.A., do you think there's an East Coast sound as distinct from a West Coast sound?

Sounds represent people's cultures, their neighborhoods, their environments, but right now I would say I see less difference [than before]. The world is more the same because of the Internet and computers—everybody in the Midwest knows what we're doing in California. When I first heard sounds from England when I was a kid, it was, "Wow!" Now everybody knows what's going on in England even before it's a hit.

But do producers in L.A. approach making a record differently than producers in New York?

I think it's pretty much the same thing. When the sound needed to get bigger in the '80s, the rooms got bigger in California and they got bigger in New York. When kids started making records—hip-hop records or things with drum machines—it seemed like they did that because it was a cheap way and the only way to express themselves. They didn't have the money to go get real drums and go into a real studio and do it, and it became universal once somebody figured out you could spend four thousand dollars instead of four hundred thousand dollars to make a record if you had these tools. It's the same thing now with computers and Pro Tools; there are Pro Tools rooms East Coast and West Coast. You can take your floppy disk or your hard drives and go from one room to another, from New York to L.A. In fact, you can *be* in L.A. and record in New York! The technology has advanced so much and everybody's using it to the utmost.

There are people making records just with Pro Tools, and they're doing it on the East Coast as well as on the West coast. Sometimes I'm in a studio and I'll say, "OK, I'm hungry." I'll think of something I want, and then I'll go, "Oh shit, that's L.A.! We're in New York!," or vice versa. Especially with no windows, you forget not just what room you're in, but what coast you're on! (laughs)

You recently produced a Deep Purple album—an English band recording in a New York studio with an L.A.-based producer—but it still has their sound. What does a producer bring to the table when working with an established band that's already got a well-defined sound?

Well, every record is different, but a lot of it is just capturing what they do. With Deep Purple, I had all the members up in Bearsville, and I had to deal with everybody on a daily basis. I felt more like a camp counselor—it took me five days to get them all in a room the first time! (laughs) I played soccer to be close with Ritchie Blackmore, and we would bond on the soccer field. I got the singer running every day with me, drinking fruit drinks and health shakes, and it was more just trying to get the thing to happen than it was being a creative producer.

In the studio, though, I had to be on my toes because Ritchie likes things real loud, but he has problems with his ears, and so we had to build walls so he could be loud but it wouldn't hurt him. Then you've got to deal with leakage, so you've got to be somewhat of a magician in the studio just to make it work. I find that my main job in any situation is to be able to get the best out of the band, whatever that takes. Knowing what it takes to make them feel secure and comfortable, even if that means going to Bearsville or out in the middle of nowhere. Environment is a very important thing; if the environment wasn't right for Ritchie, he wouldn't be able to create, and it's like that for a lot of guys. You have to figure all this out and make it work for them. It's like when you do vocals—some guys can walk into any room anywhere and do anything, but for most people, you've got to figure out what kind of vibe, what kind of environment's going to make them comfortable and be able to perform and get the most out of them.

How did you mic Ritchie Blackmore's amp?

Well, Ritchie is one of the greatest guitar players in rock history, so you don't want to change what he does—you want to capture it. I'm not going to tell Richie Blackmore what his guitar should sound like—*he's* going to tell *me*. So what I have to do first is make the environment work for him and then deal with the technical issues. Sometimes that's very difficult. Sometimes, for instance, a band doesn't want to use headphones—they want to monitor on speakers instead, but if that's going to get a performance out of them, you've got to work around that. It obviously makes my job much harder—having monitors blasting in a room rather than having a nice quiet isolated sound—but with Ritchie I just went in the studio and spent some time with his amp and made sure he was hearing it the way he wanted to. What I have to learn is what the amp sounds like to *him*. Once I know that, it's easy for me; it's just a process of elimination, going through different microphones, adding a little low end, adding a little midrange, whatever. If you're guessing and you don't know what it sounds like, then it's just a matter of opinion; there's no right or wrong. But I listened to records of his; I bought every Deep Purple record. Great people have a sound. Keith Richards has a sound; Jeff Beck has a sound; Ritchie Blackmore has a sound, and you just try to capture that.

It's very important to me to know what the band sounds like. It doesn't matter whether it's live or in the studio, it's all still live. I don't even like to mix a band without seeing them play live, and whenever I record a band live, I like to walk out in the audience and listen to what that band sounds like in the room with the audience because that's what the record should sound like.

Anyway, we put Ritchie's amps up in a loft, and we built a wall around it to close the sound off. It wasn't really an isolated sound, but it wasn't like I was miking a big room. I put up a few different microphones—a [Neumann] U 87, a [Shure] SM57, and a Beyer [M] 160, and I mixed the 57 and the 160 together, put a little light limiting on them, and moved the 87 back about two feet. I don't like just miking an amp tight; I like to hear what it sounds like a couple of feet away because that's usually where the guitar player stands.

Is the distance mic placed at ear level?

It doesn't have to be at ear level; it can be in line with the speakers, because if the microphone is up there, that doesn't mean it's hearing things the way your ear is hearing them. It's just got to be in line with the sound.

Were the 57 and the 160 up close against the grill?

Yes, though I move them around, because you have to make sure all the mics are in phase. You also need to find a good speaker, because you can really waste your time just sticking mics anywhere.

What about Jon Lord's organ miking? He's the other member of the band that has a really identifiable sound.

He runs his B3 through a Marshall as well as a Leslie—that's his sound. Again, you want to capture the sound, and it was almost like miking a guitar—a couple of tight mics, a mic off one of the cabinets to get a little bit of the room sound. We put three mics on the Leslie—two 87s on the top and a 57 on the bottom. I'd usually end up with four tracks of organ—two Leslie and two amp—and combine that down to two later.

Would you limit the organ as well?

Oh, yeah, especially the low [Leslie] mic; I wouldn't limit the high mics that much. I like to use something that doesn't change the sound, a tube limiter like an LA2A.

Did you use Roger Glover's bass amp, or was it all DI?

No, he played through an amp. I used a combination of the two.

Do you tend to use the amp for the low end and the DI for the attack, or vice versa?

It all depends on the player and the song, the part he's playing, and if he's playing with a pick. Sometimes the direct is lower than the amp, but usually you're going to get more of the low end from the amp and more of the attack and the clean sound from the DI. Sometimes, though, the sound that comes out of the amp is more like a guitar coming out of an amp; it sometimes has effects, it's a much more aggressive sound. But you can do more with a direct signal— maybe put it through an equalizer and punch a lot of 100 [Hz] and 63 [Hz] to get some bottom. It can be hard to get a good solid bottom out of an aggressive guitar-like part, especially if it's got a lot of effects on it coming out of the amp.

That's one of the hardest things for the novice: getting sufficient low end but getting it tight enough so it's not flabby and woofy. What techniques have you come up with for achieving that?

A lot of times, you can't do it with just a bass guitar—you've got to put some kind of low

PHOTO COURTESY OF THOM PANUNZIO

synth in with it, or you need to add a subsonic booster from a piece of outboard gear. On rap records and stuff, that's how they get that low end; that's not bass guitar—they've got toys that are adding all kinds of low end, and they use a lot of low-end synthesizer. That's the way industrial music or any of the new real aggressive hip-hop music is made. The bottom is still there, like on other rap records, but you also have the other aggression on top of it. Basically, you've got to add stuff with the bass guitar.

Do you compress bass during recording and again during mixing?

Yeah, I like to limit bass a little bit on both. You just hear it better; it makes it punchier, and it's easier to mix up a little louder.

What sort of compressors do you use?

If I want something fast, I'll use a dbx 160—that always worked for me. But if I want a great big bass sound, I'll use old Neve limiters on both the direct and the mic.

What compression ratios do you use?

It depends so much on what the guy's playing, so I don't have any standard settings. If I have that many Fairchilds that I can have a Fairchild on the bass, I would obviously set it differently than if it was a 160. I also work in Jackson Browne's studio when I can get in—it's one of my favorite studios—and they have a lot of the old original Record Plant gear. Their old Raytheon limiter really works well on the bass—it's big and ballsy yet clean—but you don't see those in too many places.

Do you prefer analog tape to digital recording? Tube to solid-state?

I like to combine both worlds, but when I'm recording I like to get big, nice warm sounds, and it seems like the old tube gear works really well for that. I love working on SSLs; I think it's the best tool ever made, and I love the sound of them, but I like to combine the old and the new. If I can, I'll record at least the basic tracks on16-track tape; I'll then take that tape and I'll make a B reel onto a 48-track digital, and I'll put the 16-track tape away so it won't get used at all until it's time to mix. Then you take it out and you rock! Your digital tape—which has been run a few thousand times through the machine—is still as good as the first day because it's digital, so that's a perfect example of using both analog and digital. I like to mix to half inch analog; to me, nothing sounds better. I'll also run DATs as backup and occasionally, when you get into mastering, you might find for whatever reason it sounds better on the DAT. What you hear coming off tape or analog gear isn't *really* what it is—the equipment is adding to the sound. Sometimes tape is compressing, and it's adding warmth; it's got a sound. But with digital, it is what it is. All I know is that I'm not hearing what I hear on tape, which is what I like. I like what I hear when I hit the tape really hard and I hear it compressing and distorting a little bit; I like having that as another tool to use.

The same thing with Pro Tools. You make a record in Pro Tools and people say it's got a sound or it's digital, but what you're actually hearing are the converters. What it really comes down to is people buying the song and the singer. All the rest of it is just creating an atmosphere and a vibe around that, but that's what people are really buying. So a lot of times you get in and, especially in this profession, you spend days, hours, weeks to make the tiniest difference in the sound quality. We'll travel halfway around the world spending thousands and thousands of dollars just to make it that much better. You should always strive for that, but sometimes people get a little caught up in that. But if it works—if it sounds right—hey, that's what it's about, however you get there.

> ## "What it really comes down to is people buying the song and the singer."

How do you reconcile disagreements you might have with an artist—for example, if you're convinced a vocal is not right but the artist is equally convinced that it's perfect?

You don't always see eye to eye, but I have two rules about this. One is that, at the end of the day, I never do anything that the artist doesn't want to do. It's not about me, it's not about all these electrons, it's about *them. They're* writing the songs, it's their face on the cover, they are going to live or die by the records—you are going to go on to do others.

My second rule is that you always do what's best for the record. That rule is second because sometimes it contradicts the first rule, (laughs) but I'll lobby heavily for what I think is right. I like to work with people that have the same vision I do, where we're going for the same thing. So you're not talking about apples and the other guy's talking about oranges—you're probably talking about something that's very minor, something that most people aren't even going to hear. What I like to do in a situation like that is, I say, "Look, at the end of the day, it's your call, it's your record, whatever you want—but let me have a version like this, let me do a mix of it like this or a piece of it like this. Just keep an open mind to it and at least try it." I'm not a Nazi. I'm not coming in to try to reinvent what the band's about. I want to try to capture them and have the same vision they have. OK, people can differ because there is no real right or wrong—sometimes it's just a matter of opinion: is blue a better color than green? There's no right or wrong to that. Sometimes it's obvious that somebody's flat or one vocal's better than the other, but usually the guy's going to hear that. And usually, at the end of the day, what's right stands out and most people agree. It takes two minutes to do alternates with anything, whether it's a drum take, a vocal or whatever. Just lay it down both ways and live with it, then decide later.

But, as the producer, your role—at least in theory—is to be the objective pair of ears, whereas the artist is the subjective pair of ears. That's sometimes the source of conflict.

Sometimes it's that way. But I'm not saying you do this with every little word. I'm saying you do this if it's a big issue.

For example, when you're recording a live record, the artist knows how he felt as he was giving the performance, but you're the guy who was out in front of the house who actually received it. He may think he gave the greatest performance in the world, but you're sitting in the audience knowing that he did better last night, that you should use last night's take instead.

Well, picking takes of a live performance isn't something as intimate as just being with one guy in the studio and deciding if that word is right or that vocal take is right. Usually there are other people that are going to put their two cents in—other members of the band, the manager, the record company.

Producing a live record is very different from producing a studio record. Does your role become more of a facilitator, as opposed to actually working on arrangements and conceptualizing how things are going to be presented?

It's not very different. My point of view is that my job on *every* record is to do anything I can to make it work. Is it talking to this guy before the show and making him feel good? Is it scratching a microphone so somebody sitting there in the truck tells me it works? Is it trying to track down a bad cable? Is it listening to another record by the band before they go on to decide on a drum sound? It's whatever it takes to make it work.

> **"My job on every record is to do anything I can to make it work."**

Doing a live record is almost like being in the army and going into battle, because you only get the one chance—and that's the only real difference between live and studio recording. With U2, doing *Rattle and Hum*, there were two remote trucks, a film crew every night, helicopters with cameras, cranes, railroad tracks around the stage. If you didn't get the sound, all that's wasted.

So in both kinds of records, you do anything and everything you can do to make it work. In the studio, if it means running out and getting a glass of water to the guy, or if it means blowing up balloons and burning incense and having candles, or if it means clearing the whole studio out and being the bad guy—whatever it takes to make the session work. Same thing for the live record, except, as I said, with live recording, you only get one shot, so you've got to have it together.

What do you think is the essence of a great live record?

My favorite live records aren't necessarily the best sounding ones or even the ones with the best performance. Sometimes, they're the ones with the loudest audience, because I think the most important thing about a live record is feeling like you're there. That's what I try to do when I mix a live record—I like to close my eyes and feel like I'm right there in front of the band live like I was that night.

What are your favorite live records?

I love [U2] *Rattle and Hum,* which I was a part of. Not because I was a part of it, but because it was a great record. Also, the Ozz-Fest records, because there's such a mix of different artists, from baby bands to the top metal groups. Plus, I love Ozzy!

Maybe we can move on now to your approach to mixing. Do you put more of the work into the tracking and just sort of let the mix come together, or do you tend to just kind of get the tracks down and then "fix it in the mix"?

It seems that these days the mix has become such a crucial thing; people even wonder who's right for a particular mix. I think there's been a lot too much emphasis put on the mix. There are some great mixes out there, and there are guys who can really make a difference in a record—you don't get the right mix and you can blow a record, you get the right mix and it can make a difference—but to me, if you don't have it on tape, you don't have it. A lot of remixers are really *remaking* the records, especially in the R&B world. That's different—that's additional production, that's rearranging, that's re-producing. That's different from just mixing. Years ago, mixing was not as big a deal because you didn't have the options you have now. These days, you can change the whole record, and record companies know it's their last chance.

You can still only do so much in mastering. Mastering hasn't changed as much because it's all digital. Every mastering room has Pro Tools or Sonic Solutions or something to do digital editing, but basically what you're doing to the mix hasn't changed that much. You're com-

"You've always got to be thinking down the line; if you don't, then you get into trouble."

pressing a little bit, you're adding a little high end, a little low end. Unless the guy wants to edit it or rearrange it, but to me that's not mastering—that's digital editing or additional production. Especially with live records, it's such a great tool to get the applause at the right level and to make it all sound like it's a live record and take things out or move things around. For example, if the artist says something you don't want on the record—if he mentions a city and it's not universal—you just pop it out. But the mix can only be as good as what's on tape.

As you are tracking, are you constantly thinking ahead to the mix?

Always. For instance, if I have an effect that's really working and the band is playing to it, I'll always print it. I'll print it on another track so I'm not locked into it, but I'll print it because maybe I won't be able to get it like that in the mix, or I won't remember what it really sounded like. But you're thinking about not just the mixing, but the overdubbing stage. You've always got to be thinking down the line; if you don't, then you get into trouble.

How long do you typically spend on a mix?

A day is what I feel is appropriate. What's ideal for me is to set up a mix and work all day on it, then take it home and live with it in the car on the drive home and on the drive back. Then I come in the next morning and tweak it and then move on to the next one.

In what order do you usually bring the faders up?

I usually start with the drums and then add the bass, guitar, and keyboards. I usually bring the vocals in last. If I find that I don't get a good balance right away, I don't have a problem with working on the mix for a day and then pulling it down and starting over. I don't think I would work on a mix for a day if I didn't think the mix was right. My initial balance is usually what's good. I'm not the kind of guy who sits there for days tweaking things—I don't have that much patience. My rough mixes are sometimes better than my real ones!

Perhaps the toughest thing for the person starting out in their own studio is knowing when to stop.

Yeah, that's tough for a lot of people.

What do you use as a guideline?

Well, a lot of times, it's the budget! (laughs)

But if you're in a home studio, you're not concerned with budget.

It depends on whether you're experimenting or whether you have something in mind. That's why I like to have a vision beforehand. If you've seen a band live, or if you've heard them rehearse, or spent enough time talking about what the record should sound like, you have a vision. So you work until you reach that vision. Some guys create in the studio, and if you're just creating, you can go on forever. But a lot of times you know what you want it to sound like, and maybe that'll take five minutes to get, or maybe it'll take five days to get. It all depends on how important it is and what your timeframe is.

Which is perhaps the most important reason for having a producer —somebody who knows when enough is enough and when it's done and not overdone.

Yeah, but a lot of times producers *don't* know. A lot of producers will mix and mix and mix because it's not on tape. They didn't capture it, but they think they can in the mix. Then, when they don't get it in the mix, they think the mix is wrong. That happens a lot—A&R guys do that, producers do that. But you can't polish a turd, as they say. A lot of times if something doesn't sound good, you can mess it up and it will work, rather than trying to make it sound good. For instance, if a guy isn't singing well and you can't get a better vocal out of him, rather than giving him a pristine, crystal clear vocal sound, you put it through a little Marshall or Pignose amp to disguise it.

A very typical problem in mixing is getting a vocal to sit in the track correctly. What sort of tricks or techniques have you come up with for getting a vocal to lay in there just right?

There are a lot of different ways to do it. Sometimes, if you have a big snare drum, you need to pan it off to the side a little bit. Or maybe you need to take a little of one frequency out and let the vocal pop through. Sometimes you've got to make the vocal a little bit louder than you'd normally make it but then put something on it to give it some dimension so it doesn't sound like it's going to fall off the front of the speaker. If you have lots of things in the middle, you've got to put them to the sides; sometimes just the effect can make a big difference.

One thing I used to do—and I still do it occasionally if I can find one – is, I'll take a Dolby 2-track and I'll hook it up backwards and put the vocal through it so I have a fader with the vocal unDolbied and noisy, since it's encoded but not decoded—similar to the Aphex effect. Then you mix that in a little bit. A lot of times I'll take a mult of the vocal, and I'll run it through a 1176 and limit it a lot, bring that up on another fader—I do that a lot, maybe EQ that one a little differently, too, or maybe that won't have an effect on it, or maybe it will have more of an effect on it. Or put the signal in the room through a Marshall amp and just mix a little bit of it in, not so it sounds like the devil, but so it gives it an edge. That's always fun.

Presumably you need to check carefully for phase.

Sure, anything and everything should always be checked for phase. I go through every microphone cable and piece of outboard gear; I check the bass drum phase with the overheads, I check the snare with the overheads, I check the toms with the bass drum, I check the toms with the snare—you've just got to go through all that. Same thing with guitar mics—if you can't get a good guitar sound, chances are half of them are out of phase. All you've got to do is just hit the [phase reverse] button on the console and see if it sounds better in or out of phase. It's very simple; you just go down the line and check it. It takes no time—if it took an hour, it would be well worth it for the trouble it saves you later. If something is really out of phase, and it's a problem later, that's a nightmare.

Who are the producers you really admire?

Well, I'd have to say that, when he was producing records, Jimmy Iovine, who I worked with quite a lot and learned quite a lot from. Because he really knows how to deal with artists and he knows how to make a vibe. He knows a hit song, he knows how to make a hit record, and he doesn't stop until it's right. He knows how to put people together, and he knows how to make things happen. And because he's *real*—no bullshit goes by him.

I also learned a lot from Jon Landau. Jon taught me that you always do everything you can to make it as good as you can do it. You don't want anything out there except the best—everybody should always hear everything at its best.

Those are words to live by: No compromises.

Yeah, no compromises. You're talking about two guys at the top of their fields, and that's why.

How do you see your career progressing as you get older?

I like working with real bands and making real records, making a whole record rather than just a song—I still enjoy doing that. There are a lot of great bands out there and a lot of great records still being made. It's still fun, it's still exciting.

Selected Listening:
Deep Purple: *The Battle Rages On*, Giant, 1992
U2: *Rattle And Hum*, Island, 1988
Black Sabbath: *Reunion*, Sony, 1998
Various Artists: *Ozz-Fest Live*, Red Ant, 1997
Stevie Nicks: *Street Angel*, Modern, 1993
Jeff Healey Band: *Cover To Cover*, Arista, 1995; *See The Light*, Arista, 1988

George Massenburg

George Massenburg is, without a doubt, one of the most influential, knowledgeable, and respected producer/engineers on the planet. His recordings, with artists such as Little Feat, Toto, Linda Ronstadt, Lyle Lovett, Carly Simon, Aaron Neville, and Emmylou Harris, are a sonic treat—meticulously crafted, with rare definition and spaciousness. He's also a technical pioneer: inventor of the parametric equalizer and, through his company, Massenburg DesignWorks, prime architect of the highly regarded line of GML outboard processors and console automation products. These days, Massenburg continues to blaze trails, working on means to improve the quality of digital audio (he's long ago left the world of analog recording) and turning out some of the best surround sound mixes ever heard.

All of this also makes Massenburg one of the *busiest* people on the planet, which in turn makes interviewing him a tough assignment indeed. Our trail of phone messages and e-mails could probably stretch from New York to L.A. and back, several times. But, as you'll read below, it was worth it. Sometimes terse, often witty, and *always* sharply opinionated, Massenburg's comments may occasionally be slightly tongue in cheek but are nonetheless insightful.

What do you see as being the essential difference between a producer and an engineer?

This varies widely, but in my opinion, the engineer has the freedom to zero in on detail and then get lost in his or her right (spatial) brain searching out a "context." The producer absolutely has to listen to artists and musicians whine about the most inconsequential details—everything from music stand lights to credits.

The technological advances of the past twenty years have proven to be a double-edged sword. On one hand, they have enabled more people than ever before to make music. Others can argue, though, that they have also enabled more bad recordings to be made, and more bad music to glut the marketplace.

The "average" quality of recording has certainly risen. Unfortunately, the overwhelming majority of the contemporary recordings released are far less than superb. But wouldn't you have to say that more "good" music reaches more people? And the John Stuart Mill test of this being, overall, for the good, is fulfilled, isn't it? Under these circumstances, mightn't that make it more likely that some genius out there can take the technology and make a benchmark recording? And, anyway, if we *didn't* like what was happening, what would we do? Reverse the technological advances? O.K., haven't the tube-only guys done that? You know, the Steve Albini look-alikes (and I really respect Steve's work) who only use old U 47s, tube mic preamps and 8-tracks? And has this really given us the music of the '60s back? Nah.

Why are you so opposed to tube gear?

I feel that the majority of the "tube-sound" guys are babies who want everything to sound the same way: puffy and smooth. I like clarity and transparency, and I've found it's infinitely harder to hear—and to balance, timbrally and dynamically—and to sell to A&R departments. But it's better in the long (i.e., 20 year) run.

Do you think that a great recording can be made on less-than-great equipment?

I don't know what "great" equipment is, independently of what it does for great music. Conversely, there have been many benchmark recorded performances made on what might be considered as compromised gear.

In a truly timeless recording, you can hear a lot of music, unfettered, all of it seemingly in rhyme; you would certainly have ambiguities sufficient to have that performance reveal itself in many different, though subtle, ways over its lifetime.

But most importantly, I wouldn't want to focus in at all. That would be the wrong way to go. You wouldn't be listening, then. You don't *want* to focus on the details of the music, but rather have the music set in motion thoughts and emotions to bring you closer to some sense of connection with a "truth." No less than Henry James thought that music was utterly worthless unless it could raise the fortune of the noblelady's carriageman standing outside the opera house in the hard, cold rain.

What are your thoughts on analog vs. digital recording?

I only record digitally, and I think it's important to improve that technology as much as possible.

Do you use analog tape for anything these days?

I do not use analog tape for anything.

What do you listen for in a demo when you're deciding whether or not to work with a particular artist?

Genius. Flexibility. Commitment. Not in that order.

Genius is when a piece takes you somewhere, and you have no idea how you got there. Flexibility is when the artist takes the twists and turns of the schedule and other circumstances and makes the most of them. Commitment is when the artist carries on with his mind's ear's direction after yet another idiot A&R man has completely missed the point of the artist's work.

How do you generally approach a new project with an artist you haven't worked with before? What steps do you take to put them at ease?

I'm doing that right now. I try to put them at ease and in touch with their better angels. This includes picking the best, and I mean best, musicians—whatever that takes.

Which is more important: a great performance or a technically perfect recording?

Doug Sax asks this of all of the newcomers to The Mastering Lab. The answer is, and always has been, "a great performance."

What's the best way to achieve maximum separation between instruments?

A well-organized musical arrangement.

One of the hardest things for the home recordist is to get the bass under control. Do you have any tips or techniques for accomplishing this?

"There's a reason mixing seems so simple: it is simple."

The first step here is establishing a good reference listening system and environment; if you can hear the flaws, you can control them. I'd spend whatever it takes to get a good pair of speakers that I can relate to, and put them in a room with controlled floor to ceiling resonances, not to mention a space where all of the resonant surfaces (and there are many indeed) have been treated or at least understood.

You're renowned for your vocal sounds. What are the key elements to recording vocals successfully?

As in everything else, listen and listen hard. Do everything possible to remove technical issues from the situation. Earn an artist's trust. Feed the artist good food. Don't spoil the artist too soon.

Another often difficult task is getting a lead vocal to sit right in a dense backing track. How can this be best accomplished?

There's no automatic answer here, that's for sure. Your production work should have left room for the lead vocal by the time you mix; almost all of the answers come back to musical decisions. I'd have to say that my problem is more often getting the vocal loud enough.

What are the most common mistakes that you hear people making in their home recordings?

One mistake really stands out, and that is thinking their first efforts are great. I wish guys would pick up several of the top one hundred CDs—the ones that they're trying to emulate—and *listen* to them compared with their work. And then, tell themselves that their ears are *not* deceiving them.

What advice do you have for the reader who wants to be the next George Massenburg?

Learn how to do something useful; learn how to write. Learn how to do electronic CAD, and give me a call. I've got a thousand applications from second engineers. I don't need second engineers.

Get a clue. There's a reason mixing seems so simple: it *is* simple. Can you say "steep learning curve?" Everything else is hard, especially dealing with girl singers.

Selected Listening:
Little Feat: *Feats Don't Fail Me Now*, Warner Bros., 1974; *Hoy-Hoy*, Warner Bros., 1981; *Let It Roll*, Warner Bros., 1988; *Shake Me Up*, Morgan Creek, 1991
Linda Ronstadt: *Mas Canciones*, Elektra, 1991; *Frenesi*, Asylum, 1992; *Feels Like Home*, Asylum, 1995; *Dedicated To The One I Love*, Elektra, 1996; *We Ran*, Elektra, 1998
Lyle Lovett: *Joshua Judges Ruth*, MCA, 1992
Bonnie Raitt: *Nine Lives*, Warner Bros., 1986
Toto: *The Seventh One*, Columbia, 1988
Aaron Neville: *Warm Your Heart*, A&M, 1991

Nile Rodgers

We may not have much to thank the dreary '70s for—it was, after all, a time that was musically dominated by the polar opposites of disco and punk—but one of the few highlights of the era was the ultra-tight, ultra-polished R&B sound of a band called Chic. Cofounded by guitarist Nile Rodgers and bassist Bernard Edwards, Chic dominated the charts for several years with a string of carefully crafted songs, including "Le Freak" and "Good Times." Before long, other artists were turning to Rodgers and Edwards for their production, arranging, and songwriting skills, resulting in massive hits like Sister Sledge's "We Are Family." In 1979, Rodgers brought his magic touch to David Bowie's milestone album *Let's Dance*, and a few years later, he hit solid gold, producing Madonna's landmark singles "Like A Virgin" and "Material Girl." Work with a diverse crop of artists followed, including Jeff Beck, Eric Clapton, Mick Jagger, Duran Duran, the B-52s, David Lee Roth, INXS, Grace Jones, Al Jarreau, and the Thompson Twins.

Today, Rodgers heads up his own label and production company, as well as Sumthing Distribution, a national record distribution company. As one of the most in-demand producers and session players in New York, his time is understandably limited, but he was nonetheless kind enough to invite me to his Connecticut home, where he shared his unique perspective and philosophy on the art of making records.

You got into production from a musical background, as opposed to an engineering background. How do you think that changes the approach to making a record?

I'm not sure, because it's the only approach I know. My concept is songs, song structure, and groove. I've always been into that primal concept of a song—that if it moves you in its rawest form, then you have a foundation on which you can build. You write songs from the base up, almost the same way that you record. So the bass and the bass drum are an integral part of the foundation of my compositions and my arrangements. The stronger that foundation, the more artistic freedom you have. If the bottom is strong—if the foundation is solid—it will support a larger structure, so it's almost like a law of physics. If the foundation is weak, the stuff that goes on top of it can't be too heavy, although that doesn't mean you can't have a good song or a successful house—as long as you don't have too much wind or any earthquakes or too many elemental variables that are going to tear it down.

It's like when I did [Madonna's] "Like a Virgin." That was a very simple record. If you look at the track sheet, you'll see that there aren't very many tracks used—it's just bass, drum kit, one guitar, keyboard pad, one keyboard overdub and Madonna's vocal, plus one other vocal track with Madonna, to double herself in the chorus only—and that's it. So to me, the foundation of this record isn't the kind of foundation where you need to put a lot of stuff on top of it. It's a *nice* structure, [but] it's like a bamboo house. That record wasn't made to be some gigantic club record, to be sampled and to put all sorts of other grooves on it. It lives for what it is, it does what it's supposed to do. It's a building that lives in the confines of its environment.

So you're saying that a solid foundation doesn't have to be a dense foundation.

Not necessarily. What goes on top of a record like that is light and fluffy, very easy to support. But if I had put depth and density and stuff like that on top, it would have collapsed. It would overpower the foundation; there's not enough substance to support it, it wouldn't sound right.

It's the same thing in cooking—you've got to balance the ingredients or else it doesn't work right. The base of your soup needs to support the other elements that are going to go on top of it or else it's going to make a person frown and go, "Ugh!"

Is it the song that determines how heavy or how light the structure needs to be?

It's everything. It's the song, it's the artist, and it's the audience. Ultimately, I try and make a record for the entire world, but I know that can't be possible. When I went to see the film *Pulp Fiction*, I thought it was genius, yet I saw people getting up and walking out—they were offended and pissed off. That shows you right there that you can't make everything for everybody. So when I'm making a record, I have to be very aware of who I *really* am making it for: my artist. If the record doesn't reflect that artist and their personality and their fan base, it doesn't make sense; it's almost a non-record. It's like when you go to a restaurant and you see a children's menu. That menu presupposes that there are a whole bunch of kids that are going to like franks and beans and fried chicken and pizza and spaghetti— you don't try and get the kids to eat caviar. All of these life lessons govern me and define the limits of what I'm trying to do.

Now, the interesting thing is that, because I come from a jazz background, the rules and the boundaries are there to be broken—if you're clever enough to break them without tearing the house down. And I use all these other examples—like food and buildings and things like that—so that a person can get a picture, because I deal with music the exact same way. To me, a song is something that has substance and dimension; it has form, and it has weight. When I say, "Man, I'm cutting a heavy song" or a heavy band, I *mean* that. I wouldn't say, "Oh man, I'm cutting this really heavy record and it goes..." (sings fluffy pop lyric in a soft la-de-da voice) I mean, that ain't heavy, you know—that's light. And that's really how I think. I think of weight and substance, and I understand flavors and ingredients and textures and how to work with sweet and sour, hot and cold, funky and smooth.

It seems that you're really talking about dynamics.

Absolutely. Man, I'll never forget the first time I heard the Nirvana record, "Feels Like Teen Spirit." It just blew me away—I thought, damn, this is how we used to use dynamics in the old days! R&B was like that, with the verse dead silent and the chorus exploding. When we were playing "Le Freak" live, you could hear a pin drop over the verse.

A good sense of dynamics is one of the things that seems to separate a mature professional artist from a novice; it seems to be one of the hardest skills to master.

It's funny, but I see it all the time. I go see bands playing live shows and I think, man, they don't get it, they don't understand how to break down in the verse and to keep it smokin', to be able to play with intensity even though you're not loud. That's so much a part of a music. And when you think about classical pieces, the dynamics are so much a part of the composition, it's unbelievable. You know, I would sit there and listen to Stravinsky. You'd have your little Koss headphones on and the next thing you know, bam!

"A great artist makes a song better; a great producer makes an artist better; and a great artist makes a producer better."

Is that something you look for when you're considering working with a new artist?

Not necessarily, because I believe that I can teach them how to bring that level of artistry to their performance. What I'm really listening for is sincerity and their interpretive abilities. A great artist makes a song better; a great producer makes an artist better; and a great artist makes a producer better—we all complement each other. Great equipment makes my stuff sound better; a great instrumentalist makes his instrument sound better. Sure, you can own a Stradivarius, but if you can't play, big deal! I'm sure that Itzhak Perlman would sound great on any old cheap school violin.

Do you think that every artist benefits from having a producer?

Every artist *could* benefit from having a producer, if the producer were in tune with that artist. But I don't think that every producer is good enough to make every artist better—absolutely not. I'm a perfect example. When I first started, we couldn't find a producer who could make Chic sound good, let alone better. They couldn't make us sound good on a record, because they didn't understand what we were all about. And I always have to remember that, as simple as it was for me to understand Chic—because it was my band and my music—these top shelf guys couldn't get it, and we wound up having to produce it ourselves. I have to remember that I always have the ability to miss it with another artist.

And I don't believe that I've gotten it right every time. Sometimes I think I'm in tune with somebody—I'm sitting there digging them—and I realize that this person wants to walk out. Every marriage is not made in heaven. On the other hand, I can think of some records I've done where I *didn't* think that I was going to be in tune with the person, and I was so in tune it was absolute magic. A case in point was *Let's Dance* with Bowie. Even though David and I aren't the best of friends or anything like that, I never was more in tune with an artist than I was on that record. It was almost as if God put us together and said, "Make this record."

Did that synergy come about through discussions, or was it an intuitive thing?

It was discussion, it was talking, it was respect, it was clarity, it was our powers of improvisation, it was our depth of musical knowledge and our depth of artistic knowledge about the world, it was our ability to be open-minded. All those things, everything a great record is supposed to do, we went through on that record. Everything—angst, tension, fear and jubilation, it was just unbelievable. That's one of the most perfect records of my life. To think that the whole thing was done in twenty-one days, start to finish—even mixed. Twenty-one days! It was actually really nineteen, 'cause the last two days I didn't show up! (laughs) I was too drunk, I was celebrating, I was so up, I was saying, "This is a smash!" I didn't even want to hear about remakes, it was *done*.

Since you're a guitarist, I'm guessing you've come up with some great techniques for recording guitar, other than the old 57 up against the grille.

(laughs) You know, the thing is, the SM57 up against the grille is pretty damn good! Or a 421 or all sorts of little things.

I gather in the days of Chic you did a lot of DI guitar.

Yeah, and I still do to this day. Nowadays, technology has come so far, and the quality of outboard gear is so great, that I find myself using something like [Line 6] Amp Farm. Man, that's ridiculous! We can do so much now that we used to have to toil over in the old days, and now I can't really tell the difference, especially spiritually.

But I've done things like put different amplifiers in series up a staircase and place microphones all up and down the staircase to see which sounded best...all sorts of nutty stuff. Taking the sound out of the back of an amplifier that's not supposed to really be miked in the back, just to see what it sounds like. The old Pignose amps sounded so great to us, we were going to cover them in fur and call it Le Pignose and sell it for ten times as much! (laughs)

The thing is that beauty is truly in the eye of the beholder, and [using] the right tool for the right job is all that I'm into. I remember Stevie Ray Vaughn telling me that he never sounded better than when I recorded him. I would think to myself, well, it's Bob Clearmountain and David Bowie and Nile Rodgers in the Power Station—what a really great day, brother! With a great band and a great song and a great vibe—hey Stevie, I think that had a lot to do with it! Yeah, maybe it sounded better than some of his other stuff, I don't know. But it was a hit, and hits always sounded good.

I don't mean to downplay the technical aspects of it because, yeah, it did sound great and it had a great vibe, but Bob Clearmountain is fabulous. Some of my best records have been done with Bob. I started with Bob—my first record was done with him—and a person knows who you are, and in turn you hook up again and you do something really great, based on your growth and their growth and where you are at that time. And nothing is too wacky—you'll try anything: "Hey, wow, you see those room mics that are up on the ceiling? Let's see what happens when we put them halfway down the room and we put the amps face down or..." You try anything to get the right sound and the right vibe for the record.

It's funny that, as I've gotten older and have done so many different things to make records, I find now that my depth of knowledge is sometimes stifling. You know so much that you go, "Wow, what weird thing do we do now?" Are we doing it for the sake of weirdness or so we can have a cool article in EQ magazine? Or are we doing it because we think it's the right thing to do? After having made hundreds, if not thousands, of records, every now and then I realize how cool the simplest little thing sounds.

So these days to record guitar, you're generally taking the direct signal and then using Amp Farm?

I hate to say it, but that's generally what I'm doing now.

More often than actually re-amping the signal?

Yeah, that's really the deal now. And the thing that I really love about that is, when I take it direct, I really hear the character of the guitar. Then, after I've done a performance that I think is the right performance, I can sit back and say, *now* let's try different amplifiers. That's an amazing sense of freedom to me. In the old days we used to do some of that —we would record pretty much direct, and then re-amp it, send it out into the room into amps. But I find that, in today's world, some of the other stuff that I'm picking up along the way, I'm not so thrilled about. Just the fact that I'm sending my signal along a journey before it gets back to my ears, there may be things that I don't particularly want. And when I'm fooling around with plug-ins, I find that it's a *new* set of sympathetic stuff that comes along with each device now. There's some new bull that we have to deal with.

Only now it's a *model* of sympathetic stuff.

(laughs) Yeah! But I'm quite impressed with a lot of the gear that I've been using lately. Right now, you've just caught me at a point in time where I'm really discovering the quality of my instruments, pure, without amplifiers. What's great for me is that I can now interpret the music based on it being a very clean sound, which also makes me do more with my hands. Whereas a lot of times, when an amplifier is doing its thing, you play based on what the amp is doing— you can't help it. Say you plug into a stack of Marshalls. You're going to start playing "Foxy Lady" and you start dive bombing, doing an Eddy Van Halen solo or playing "Stairway To Heaven." You know, you can't help it! Me, I'm always playing "Ramble On" or something. But when I'm playing clean, I'll find that more of what I'm doing artistically is here. (gestures with hands) Then I can amplify that and go, "Wow, go check that out." So that's just a phase I'm in right now.

What's your usual signal path for DIing guitar?

It all depends on the record and on the song and the guitar. I have a million DIs that I've been using from the beginning, but now that I'm recording to hard disk, I use a little Neve sidecar that adds just enough warmth to take the edge off the digital converters.

I still have an old Countryman DI that I love, and it sounds great. I also have a custom-made one from the Power Station that's unbelievable; it sounds like what my Strat sounds like to me.

Do you find that different DI boxes complement different guitars?

Absolutely. And they complement different songs. We pull them all day long and check them out. I come from the school where, even if the band uses one drum kit for the whole record, I want it tuned right for each song. We'll change the heads or tune it differently, all that kind of stuff, in order to create a different vibe. Sometimes we change the beaters—all sorts of stuff. It all depends on how those frequencies are responding to the key of the music, to the pulse of the music. Every record is different, every song is different, every tape is different. If I think about how many times I've recorded a song and it felt fantastic and I ran in and listened to it, only to go, "Ahh, man, the bass drum is detuned, now we've got to do it again." Now, with modern technology, we'll just go, "Forget it—we'll just key another one."

When you're recording a backing track, do you like to get as many musicians in the room as possible, or do you just record bass and drums?

I never just do bass and drums. Usually, if it's a band, I'll try and record the entire band— everybody plays at the same time, only knowing in my head that all I care about is the drummer. But I want the feel and the vibe of everyone. I want the drummer playing to his people, his comrades being inspired the same way that they'd be inspired on stage.

Will you have a guide vocal set up during the recording of the backing tracks?

Yeah, absolutely.

Do you ever end up using the guide vocal?

Not a lot, but sometimes, because every now and then they'll do something amazing. But I don't set up to believe that I'm going to use the guide vocals. So sometimes I almost try and paint myself into a corner and let spillover come into the booth and stuff like that. But lately, I treat every piece of information as if it were gold. These days, our methods of transference and preservation are so advanced that if something happens that's amazing, we don't have to worry about it—we can move it from here to there, and preserve the quality.

You know, I never thought that this would be part of my world, but I even sometimes try and degrade signals, because we can get stuff sounding *too* good now. Who would have ever thought this would be a problem? It's unbelievable!

You were one of the early pioneers of digital recording back in the days when it really was in its infancy, and I'm assuming you're still a digital guy.

I'm a digital guy.

Do you use tape for anything these days?

Yeah, sure. For storage, for archiving. I like tape, I just don't like touching it. I'm always going to love the way tape sounds, and I can't help it—it sounds better to me. I don't think that there are many people that would disagree with me. Tape sounds amazing, and mag sounds even better to me. I recently heard some old Elvis Presley stuff recorded to mag, and it was unbelievable.

Do you mix to half inch analog more often than you mix digitally?

More often now, yeah. Sometimes you'll say to yourself, "Why am I recording this to half inch when it's going to wind up on a damn CD anyway?" But we like to preserve as much fidelity as possible; we technically go after the best sounding record we can make. I really wish that everything came out 24 bit, 96 k—I'll love it when we start recording direct to DVD. Sixteen bit is what it is, but people make hit records on it, too. That goes back to my philosophy of the quality of the materials that go into your building: If the stuff is good and strong and is happening and is the right thing for the right job, then regardless of the format that it winds up in, it's still going to be cool. I remember the first time I heard a CD of *Let's Dance*; I thought it sounded amazing. It didn't sound as good as the [vinyl] record, but it was pretty damn good. And the cassette rocks my world, too.

Everything's relative, I suppose.

I'm not really an audiophile. I would love to sit around and just listen to records all day, but that's not my world.

The common thread through all of your productions is they're all remarkably clean and high-fidelity, so there's got to be that sensibility there.

Yeah. Well, if it doesn't sound good, Nile does not dig it. And I've been very, very fortunate that I always have top-flight engineers—whether they are stars, whether the rest of the world knows that they are top-flight, doesn't mean anything. I know they are and they wind up being big stars—almost every engineer who's worked with me has gone on to become huge superstars in the business. Maybe there are one or two engineers that I've worked with over the last 20 years that *haven't* won a Grammy for Best Engineer, but almost all of my guys have.

Is that because you gravitate to them, or is it because they pick up things from you? Or is it a combination of both?

It's both. It's mutual in that they appreciate my history. They dig working with me, and I dig working with them.

Are you very hands-on when it comes to the mix, or is that something you leave to the engineer?

Well, the way I do it is, the engineer takes it to a certain level, and then he calls me in and says, "I think this is good," Then I listen and either go, "Yes, you're right, but let's do this or that," or not. I work with engineers who are very, very competent and have their own opinions about music, and I like what they bring to the party. So I let them do it, but I've got to like it. I never let a mix go down that I don't think is right, but I still remain open-minded to see if I can be swayed.

One of the hardest things for people working in project studios is knowing when the record's done, knowing either when enough is enough or when they haven't done enough to complete it.

That really is an art in and of itself. I've been very, very fortunate in that, more often than not, I know when a record is done. Even when I get pressure from a record company, if I really feel that it's done in my heart, I won't succumb to the pressure; I'll just say, "No, I think it's done. Why don't you go test it and see what the people think?"

"Like A Virgin" is a case in point. It was very simple, and it really wasn't any more fleshed out than a demo might be, yet you knew it was done.

Well, there was a little bit of a fight there, but we stuck to our guns and ultimately won, and won big time. That Madonna album is a very simple album. You know, it took me a long time before I got to 48 tracks. I was able to do everything on 24 tracks for a long, long, *long* time, and the records still sounded full. I did the Madonna album in 24-track, and on "Like A Virgin," I didn't even fill it up, so it wasn't like I didn't have enough tracks—I had more than enough for that song. The same thing with "Material Girl." Everything on that album was very sparse. But it doesn't sound like it's not enough—it's done. Same with the Chic records.

I actually miss those types of records, having to figure out how to get all that music on those limited number of tracks and having to do a great performance right now because you won't get a chance to fix it later on —it's got to be brilliant, and it's got to be in the pocket, and it's got to groove. And when one person makes a mistake, you go, "I guess we've got to keep it because the rest of it works—oh, leave it in there." I love the [Bill Haley] record "Rock Around The Clock." The saxophone player goes through the riff before the rest of the band and, to me, it's so clearly a mistake, but they left it because the rest of the record is swinging.

For all the technological advances of the last 20 years, do you think records today *sound* better than they did 20 years ago?

No, absolutely not. Because for whatever we've gained in technical superiority, it makes us not necessarily work as hard. And unless you're really into the music business, it's hard for people to see it. We could use film as a great example. With all of the technological advances that they've made in the optical world, does the latest *Star Wars* look better than *The 39 Steps*? I'm not so sure about that. The fact was that we had to overcome all of those problems that the equipment gave us, and the net benefit of overcoming all of those variables was an artistic statement in and of itself. In the old days, we all used to play together in the same room, and I realize after going back and listening to some of these records, that there was a blend and a vibe going on in that room that, to me, translated into that record.

The old restrictions in technology forced us to do things right. It forced us to have to make decisions. It forced us to spiritually be so in tune with the other people that magic had to happen. It made you step up to the plate, whereas now, when I go to play on someone's record I feel uncomfortably free—and I almost hate that. I can actually play on a record all day long and do ten different solos and take all these different approaches to the rhythm and all this kind of stuff. And then the producer has to look at all this work like a film—they have to go back and edit and figure out which bits they want to use. Whereas in the old days, when a person hired me to work on a record, I had to get it right, right there. You had to play great, you had to be smokin', and there was no way that they could fix it and make it better.

When I played on Michael Jackson's last record, I knew what they were going to do, so I just said, "Hey, Michael, here's like a billion ideas. I'm going to play all this cool shit, and you guys go off and do it." So I didn't have to write it, so to speak. I didn't have to give them *the* definitive, perfect, guitar part; I gave them *lots* of definitive, perfect guitar parts, and they decided which ones to use. That's weird to me. Once you're unlimited, you'll never play that same way—you'll just go on and on and on and on. It's like the ultimate jazz person's fantasy: "You mean to tell me I'm going to solo for the rest of my life, and you guys will think it's great?"

Having infinite options also means you don't have the pressure on you...

It's pressureless.

—which means that you won't necessarily work as hard as you would if you knew you had just two takes in 20 minutes to get it right.

You can't help it. You see, I grew up in the days of, time is money—as Madonna would say, "Time is money, and the money is mine." And I like that, I love that.

You had a limitation of tracks, too. You were lucky if you had two tracks and you could do an alternative take.

You know what people do now when they want me to overdub on a record? They'll send me an album with a mix, and I have like 22 open tracks of guitars I can put down. So now you guys are going to figure out what my part is.

Presumably you're hearing a lot of tapes that are coming out of project studios. What common mistakes do you think people are making working on their own?

So many of the times when people send stuff that they want me to overdub on them, I end up fixing their grooves. (laughs) I think that they don't resolve it to the beats properly. It's because I'm a human guy and I understand the concept of a groove. I play with musicians who are known for being able to interpret feel. So, if a person tells me to play in the pocket but play on top, I know how to adjust my feel to do that.

We never recorded Chic records with a metronome, and we were a dance band! I never heard of such a thing. It took me years and years and years before I ever played with a click track— years and years and years before I ever played with a drum machine in a recording studio. And then I did it for an artistic statement. I didn't do it because I needed that groove—

I did it because of those weird drum sounds on the Linn Drum. I certainly wasn't doing it for timing or anything like that.

I remember the first time I recorded a band that had never recorded without a drum machine. They asked me, "Nile, have you ever made a record with a drum machine?" I looked at them and said, "Have you ever made one *without* a drum machine?" (laughs) I realized that I had now crossed over into a new period of time. So now I don't make any records without drum machines—or at least without using a click—because I know that we're going to do so much editing later on.

So you're saying that a common mistake is not getting that groove right before you start overdubbing.

See, even though I record to click and drum machine, I still feel the groove the way that I would feel the groove as if I were just playing free. It's not like some of these new bands where everybody gets hooked up to a click and it's samples and loops going on. To me, a live show is a live show—it doesn't have to sound like a record.

More often than not, the type of production I'm going to make is going to sound like a band. Therefore, I don't like the way some people resolve clicks; I don't like the way some sequencing programs resolve their samples to a beat, because I'm trying to look for the ultimate feel in a groove. When I'm playing with a musician, and he's laying into the groove a certain way, I can tell that he's convinced that his part is working. So now it's up to me to come up with another part that complements what he's doing—I have to start to adjust my feel and groove and interpretation to make that better.

When people send me records and they say, "Nile, we want you to overdub to this," I'll call them and say, "Hey, man, can I fix your groove and make it the way I think it should sound?" I believe in that stuff, I believe in groove templates—that there's a certain thing in the interaction between this person and that person and then that together makes the groove. *I* don't make the groove and *you* don't make the groove—*we* make the groove.

And that's a real problem if somebody's working on their own.

Right. Those records feel different to me, and I strive to make those type of records feel like group records, even if it's Madonna as a solo artist. The difference between my record with Madonna and her other records is, you can tell that that's Madonna singing with a band. And that's why you only need twelve tracks—because we got our parts worked out right. It's filling up the room and we're movin' a lot of air, and at that point we could be Tom Petty or the Rolling Stones or Herbie Hancock. So you just take Madonna, stick her in your band and, bang! Now you have that record. It's a very different record than every other record she's ever done. So, yes, she's a solo artist, but she's in my band when I'm making a record with her, or I'm in her band—whatever way you want to look at it. It's not like I'm preparing some tracks and she's going to go on top of it. She's singing, we're playing, and that's the record.

What advice would you give to the reader out there whose goal is to be the next Nile Rodgers?

I really think that my experience is based on my life. That means I come from being in a band, a cooperative collective of individuals that come together to do one thing. And, unfortunately or fortunately, that colors my records. That's the filter through which my musical ideas pass. And I look at the world like that—to me, that's what you've got to do.

That's not to say that other people who aren't from bands—people who are engineers or tech heads or even just solo players—don't make valid and great records and even better records than mine. That's fine—that's a person's opinion—but that's why my records have a sort of organic feel, if you will. Because it's based on a salad—it's based on a meal; it's definitely not based on one thing. You've got to mix it all up together, or else it doesn't taste right.

You know, certain people in any band are always better technically than others in the band, so that means that the people who aren't as proficient on their instruments have to support the better technical people. You've got to blanket around them so that the technical people can shine. That's what a band does, and if you have a spectacular drummer, then everybody's got to lay off. And if everybody is super technically proficient, then you get one of those really cool bands that do great stuff. You get an Earth, Wind & Fire, you get a Return To Forever—a band that makes hits but is interesting to the ears technically.

So you're saying, get as many different musical experiences under your belt as possible.

That's exactly what I'm saying. The more you know, the greater the palette of colors you have to choose from. You have to study the information and equipment and songs that have come before us, because each one of those is a project in and of itself. When Bowie and I did *Let's Dance,* we got a pile of records and we sat down and studied them. They were from all different areas of music: We listened to the Pink Panther, and we listened to Cab Calloway; we listened to the Beach Boys, and we listened to the Beatles. We just took licks from all over the place and stuck them in. It wasn't samples—it was ideas, it was licks, it was stuff. We were superimposing all different parts of pop music and culture. David would say obscure things like, "Let's not listen to anything that's been played in the last 20 years; let's act as if the blues had never been invented." (laughs)

I had never done that before. People had told me stories about them doing that with my records, but I never did that with anyone else's records. Up until *Let's Dance,* every musical idea came from my memory. I never studied other people's stuff before I made my records. And now that I'm getting ready to make my next crop of records, I think I might try that whole *Let's Dance* philosophy again—listen to a bunch of different things and see if that inspires me to write riffs and play differently. Sometimes it's good to look back in order to get the inspiration to go forward.

Selected Listening:
Any Chic recording (coproduced with Bernard Edwards)
Sister Sledge: *We Are Family* (coproduced with Bernard Edwards), Cotillion, 1979
Madonna: *Like A Virgin,* Sire, 1985; *You Can Dance,* Sire, 1987; *Royal Box,* Sire, 1990
David Bowie: *Let's Dance,* RCA, 1983; *Changesbowie,* Rykodisc, 1984; *Black Tie, White Noise,* Savage/BMG, 1993
Duran Duran: *Arena,* Capitol, 1984; *Notorious,* Capitol, 1987
INXS: *The Swing,* Atco, 1984

Keith Olsen

K eith Olsen is fighting a heavy cold on the day I brave the forces of El Niño and visit his L.A.-based studio. But it takes more than a hacking cough and low-grade fever to stop this veteran producer, best-known for his ground-breaking work with '80s megastars Fleetwood Mac, Pat Benatar, Jefferson Starship, Foreigner, Heart, and many others.

After issuing a warm greeting and dosing himself with some industrial-strength decongestant, he plays me some tracks that he's mixing for an as-yet unnamed band out of Nashville. They may not have a name or a record company-manufactured image yet, but there's no mistaking the trademark Keith Olsen sound that permeates the track—slick, humongous, with whomping guitars and hooks galore. Olsen is also a master at keeping things loose in the studio—with a gleam in his eye, he confides that the secret to his success is actually...an aerosol can labeled "Bass Remover." Legend has it that one gullible visitor actually began spraying it on a master tape—nearly ruining it in the process—before an alert engineer intervened!

Is it possible to make a great record in a modest home studio?

Sure. But a bunch of phrases come to mind—you can't polish a turd, garbage in, garbage out. The bottom line is that all the gear in the world, all the techies in the world, aren't going to make a bad song good. Start with a great song, you can record it on an old boom box with one mic in the room, and it'll still be a great song.

How do you go about getting that famous Keith Olsen guitar sound?

A guitar sounds only as good as what's coming out the speaker at the guitar amp. If you have a great-sounding guitar and a great-sounding amp, all you need is a piece of wire and a mic in front of the speaker, somehow, somewhere. It's just personal preference as to how many mics to use and where to place them. But I've found that one mic on a good-sounding amp sounds twice as good as five mics all over the place—in a big room, turned up to twenty. Just a great-sounding amp and a great-sounding guitar, and a wonderful guitar part, and everything's going your way. It doesn't matter if the amp and guitar sound great if the part's terrible—it'll basically sound terrible. It's all down to the song and how you treat that song—the arrangement—that's where your taste and your creativity come in.

It sounds like what you're saying is that a great guitar and a great guitar amp with an average mic will give you better results than an average guitar and amp with a great mic.

Yes, but I'm going to add one thing—it's got to be a great part played by a really great player.

Where should the most money be spent in a home studio?

I would make sure that I had an adequate console, one that sounds pretty much the same on the output as it sounds on the input. Less is usually more when it comes to a console; you usually don't need to get all that extravagant. Mackie, for example, makes wonderful-sounding gear that's really simple and easy to use. Get one good mic, and a couple of other mics. And make sure that you don't use the one mic for everything, everywhere, so you have the coloration of that mic on everything. That's the key that unlocks the door between masters and demos a lot. I hear a lot of demos where somebody put it together one track at a time, using the same mic. There's the same coloration on absolutely every instrument. It may be interesting, but it ain't a master. Get a couple of Audio-Technica mics and a Mackie mixer, and you've really kind of got it. You'll need a good compressor and one or two good effects units, and you can probably do everything you need to do.

Are effects usually overdone or underdone on the demos you hear?

They're usually overdone; less is more when it comes to effects, too. When you have a limited number of tracks and a limited number of pieces of gear, the tendency is to print them when you're recording. And as you do that, the tendency is to start using them a little too much, and at the end you wish you had things a little drier—but you can't go backwards.

The other important thing to have is a great-sounding headphone. Because what you hear in your cans when you're singing is going to be directly proportional to how you're singing—the feel and the emotion that you drive into your vocal. Personally, I think the AKG K141 is the most amazing headphone known to man. It's loud, it's studio-tough, and you can hear just enough acoustically around you so you're not relying 100 percent on foldback— you can hear yourself pitch correctly without having to wear the headphones halfway off your ears, which kind of limits you.

So it all comes back to the importance of getting a great performance.

Oh, yeah. See, there are three things that make a record and three things that get you noticed: song first, performance second, then sound. And sound is last, definitely last. A lot of artists may confuse that issue, but if you think of the acts that are out today that actually have a shot at being around tomorrow, you can see that they are all song- and performance-based. Every single one of them, without a doubt. Look at the phenomenon of Alanis Morrisette—great songs, performed really well, with good arrangements.

> *"There are three things that make a record and three things that get you noticed: song first, performance second, then sound. And sound is last, definitely last."*

And most of it was recorded in a home studio on ADATs.

Exactly. It doesn't matter, it really doesn't matter. She was right. She had the right songs and the right attitude at the right time. There's the three Rs: right, right, and right.

What do you see as the dividing line between a demo and a master? Parts of *Jagged Little Pill* could almost be construed as demos.

No, it actually doesn't sound like her demos. Even though a lot of it was cut at home, what was done to it made it a master. She went in to cut it as if they were masters, not songwriter demos. Demos are a different kind of animal. There is a time in your life when you have to de-

cide, OK, I'm going to be an artist now, I'm going to cut my demos and try to get a deal. In the home studio, you're afforded an infinite amount of time. You can either get your stuff down on tape in a timely manner and get it out to the record companies to see if you have a shot at being an artist, or you can spend an infinite amount of time at home developing your art in a demo state, where you almost never get it out to the record companies. Or, two years after you start, you finish it, and you think, gee, it used to be timely when I started it, but musical styles have changed! (laughs)

It should take you a couple of days a song. If you're going to do a five-song demo, then spend ten days at home. Does it pay to have a home studio if you're only going to use it for ten or fifteen days? No it doesn't, it absolutely doesn't. There's too many other little demo studios out in the world that you can get for $250 a day. But as a writing and developmental tool, it's really great. People have always wanted to have something in their home where they could work on developing their sound, their art.

But when does a great demo change into a great record?

I don't know. I've heard great demos that have gotten bands signed, and the masters that have come out afterwards have been real good—and I've heard it the other way, too.

Often the masters are not as good as the original demos.

Sometimes there's a certain amount of magic that happens when you're doing a demo at home quickly and you don't care, you don't pull everything apart. Then when you get in the studio, you say, "I don't want that mistake in here, let's do it again." Then you do it again until it's sterilized—that happens. It's up to the producer to make sure that doesn't happen.

What are some of your favorite miking techniques?

Every mic has its own characteristic, just like every speaker has its own characteristic. Listen to the same CD on ten or twelve different speakers, and you'll be amazed how different it sounds—just make sure you turn the balance control so you listen to just one side at a time because there are coloration differences from left to right.

Do you find yourself frequently breaking mic selection and placement "rules?"

Well, there are no rules—after all, there are only twelve notes. At any one time, you're only a couple of steps off from being on. But, yes, you would think that doing a vocal with a cardioid instead of an omni is definitely the way to go. But there again, you have a proximity effect with the cardioid that you don't have with an omni. A microphone is not like our ears—it cannot differentiate between a wanted and an unwanted sound, like our ears can. So you just have to think about what the microphone is going to hear, and use your head. If you put an amplifier/speaker on the floor and put a microphone a foot away, do the geometry—you have the direct versus the reflective sound. And so you have time delays. If you want to get real technical about it, you can calculate what frequencies are going to be out of phase by measuring the distance from the speaker to the microphone directly, and then the angle down to the floor—angle of incidence, angle of reflection—and then see how much longer one is than the other, figuring the speed of sound on a standard day. Do the calculations—you can find out where you're going to have problems.

> *"There are no rules; after all, there are only twelve notes. At any one time, you're only a couple of steps off from being on."*

Is that something you actually do when deciding how to position a mic?

(Laughs) Of course not. But you can, that's the point. And that's the stuff that happens, so you have to think about it when you're setting up an amp. Leo Fender put those legs on the sides of the Fender Twin, and he did that so the guy in the orchestra could actually hear it when he was playing soft. But the other reason is that when you put a mic up against an amp tilted that way, the angle of incidence changes and you don't get phase cancellation problems off the floor and wall.

Let's take it one step farther. Let's lift that speaker cabinet off the floor and put it up on something that is stable enough to be able to give the speakers a platform to work from, but where the difference is so great when you mic it up close at an angle, the reflected sound is going to be so far down in volume to the direct, it's of no real consequence. And where the angle is so drastic that it's of no consequence. All of these things start adding together into mic technique, stuff that you learn over the years. Take tom-toms. Here's this thing called a drum kit, and, yes, it's easy to make each of the individual drums sound good. But then you turn on all of the mics together, and it's a mess because there's some constructive and some destructive interference, caused by the different angles of all the microphones. So the ambient sound has all these glitches in it and all these peaks and valleys. You learn to start worrying about phase instead of worrying so much about cardioid versus omni. But there are instances when the mic pattern is important. Acoustic guitar, for example, sounds terrible with a cardioid mic too close to it—you get boom and click. Take an omni and get in there, and you're OK.

Do you typically use single mics for instruments?

It depends on what the instrument is. On multispeaker guitar amps, I like to use two mics, both close. I'll pick a couple of speakers that sound good, and I'll mic them closely. Doing that will actually make the coloration of the speakers combined so that you get more of the sound of the guitar instead of the sound of each individual speaker. Ambience can be your friend, and it can be your enemy.

A lot, I guess, depends on the room you're working.

Yeah, I've heard a lot of home recordings that were done all in a garage. And there's a lot of what we think is deadening, because it takes out the top end. That might save the neighbors from calling the cops, but the bottom end and midrange is still real ambient, it bounces all around the room, and you get phase destruction. I hear lots of vocals cut in closets that sound like they were cut in closets.

Is there any way of getting a big sound out of a little room?

Sure. Just make sure you don't have parallel walls and don't put a lot of soundproofing in—just put in enough to stop reflections. Don't do all the walls and the ceiling—do alternating surfaces. Get a really good windscreen and sing up close to the mic and all of a sudden the room means nothing. An omni would be a good idea, unless you want to have that real rich sound—then use a cardioid, and use the proximity effect to best advantage. Always keep the proximity effect in mind, also the ratio of wanted to unwanted sound. The closer you get to the mic, the less the room has to do with it. The farther away, the more the room has to do with it. If you have one room and you want room sound on everything, then you've basically got to put every sound in its own box and then start stacking boxes on top of each other in the mix. If you can, keep stuff dry and free of ambience. That way the room doesn't come into play, and it affords you more choices later.

Do you prefer analog to digital recording?

A great song can be recorded on a cassette, on analog tape, on a 48-track digital multitrack—it doesn't matter. Digital machines today, there's good ones and there's bad ones. I use Sony DASH a lot, with Apogee filters on the inputs and the outputs, and it does not sound harsh. Analog can sound real good if it's recorded correctly, or it can sound real clamped, 'cause a lot of people start hammering the tape. As soon as you get any transient above +14 [VU], it's 100 percent distortion, period, so there is a ceiling. And remember that transients are typically 10 dB above your VU program meter. Plus, some digital machines just shut down when you overload them, they just say, screw you, we won't put out what you put in. That's a particularly hideous form of distortion, because it flattens out the wave. But look at the harmonic distortion that happens on analog: analog sounds great at 0 output, but at +14 it sounds hideous, because it's

100 percent distortion—what you put in is not what you get out. Another thing is that you cannot record a square wave on analog. So if you have a synth part that is a square wave, remember that when it goes into an analog machine, the state has to always be changing for magnetic tape to work, so it will be distorted. If you record conservatively to analog, it can sound great, too. I don't particularly like the head bumps in some machines at different frequencies; it screws with your bottom end. But I also don't particularly like the way some digital machines get harsh in the top end. It's always a trade-off. Basically, your storage medium is your tool, so you've got to have something that will sound the same today, tomorrow, and a month from now as it did the day you started. Digital's better for that. You know, you pull out these analog tapes from ten years ago, and you've got to bake 'em, and then they don't sound as good.

Do you prefer tube gear to solid-state?

Tubes have a definitive message. So does Class A solid-state, so do ICs. They all have their places in the chain. If you think you're going to get rid of ICs by using a tube mic and tube pre-amp, forget it—as soon as you go down to your tape machine, you're going down 30 IC stages, so screw it. There are some incredible all-tube devices out there, but the prices are out of hand, totally out of the question for the home studio. A tube has a very soft knee when it comes to distortion—that's why, most of the time, tube guitar amps sound good and solid-state guitar amps don't. The distortion curve of a tube is exactly the same as the distortion curve of the human ear. A tube is a wonderful device, but remember that anything you do with a tube today, it's gonna sound a little different tomorrow when you turn on that power supply. And six months from now it's going to sound way different. Turn a tube guitar amp on and off forty times and play the same E chord each time, and there will be quite a difference from beginning to end. So unless you're an absolute purist, most of these little consoles are just fine.

What are your recommendations for signal processors?

For a home studio, the Alesis Midiverb is really good; the Yamaha SPX90 sounds great. Hopefully you're not going to use that many effects. Turn up the drums, turn up the bass, turn up the guitar, check for phase, and you're there.

Let's talk about drums. What can be done to improve the sound of a drum machine?

Get a really good programmer. You've got to think like a drummer—subtleties, nuances. If you're playing eighth notes on a ride cymbal, are every one of those 'tings' going to be at the same volume? Or the same waveshape or the same pitch?

They're not going to be perfect eighth notes, either.

There you go.

Sounds like you're not big on drum machines.

Oh, no, I love 'em, especially when you put in the nuances. There's that fine line of absolute feel and absolute tempo.

Any tips for recording bass?

A, a good bass; B, a good D.I.; C, a good compressor.

Do you usually compress bass both on the way in (to tape) and on the way out?

It depends if it needs it. If going on the way in is enough, that'll be fine, but you do want to compress on the way in. Use ratios of no greater than 3:1; even 1.5:1 will work well, with no more than 8 dB of gain reduction. A lot depends on the player. If he's using his fingers, you'll probably need more compression than if he's using a pick. There are a couple of pretty darn good inexpensive compressors out there: the Behringer Composer—what a good dual compressor, for $200–250 a channel.

Do you recommend putting the final mix through a stereo compressor?

Gee, that's never been done before! (laughs). In every mastering room, they've spent all this money on these fancy compressors so they can compress left-right. So, sure, why not? It depends on how it sounds.

Some inexpensive compressors can't handle full-range material, though.

A lot of them can. There is a piece of gear that everybody with home studios should know about: the TC Electronic Finalizer. It's great—just a phenomenal piece of gear. It's one piece of gear that you can just take left and right signal, run it through it using one of their presets, and it almost always sounds better coming out the output. Just let it do its thing—don't try to get too creative with it by changing the presets. It sounds really good.

> *"One thing for every musician to remember is that this is their life's work, if they're serious about it."*

Any final advice for the reader who wants to be the next Keith Olsen?

One thing for every musician to remember is that this is their life's work, if they're serious about it. And there's no such thing as an overnight success, 'cause an overnight success is six, seven years developing your art, two years learning how to market your art, and then, all of a sudden, you're an overnight success!

Selected Listening:
Fleetwood Mac: *Fleetwood Mac*, Reprise, 1975
Pat Benatar: *Crimes Of Passion*, Chrysalis, 1980; *Precious Time*, Chrysalis, 1981; *All Fired Up*, Chrysalis, 1995
Heart: *Passion Works*, Epic, 1983
Jefferson Starship: *No Protection*, RCA, 1987
Grateful Dead: *Terrapin Station*, Arista, 1977
Whitesnake: *Whitesnake*, Geffen, 1987; *Slip Of The Tongue*, Geffen, 1989

Frank Filipetti

On the day we visited Frank Filipetti in early 1998, he was, in his own words, "jazzed." And who wouldn't be, after winning two Grammys (Pop Album of the Year and Best Engineered Album of the Year) for an endeavor—James Taylor's *Hourglass*—that was recorded largely on project studio equipment and started life as preproduction rehearsal tapes. Either the guy is very, very lucky or he's very, very good—and insiders know that the latter is the case. It's no coincidence that his resume includes not only Taylor but Carly Simon, Barbra Streisand, Mariah Carey, and many other pop icons.

Ever-present cigar in hand, Filipetti grabbed some time between sessions at New York's famed Right Track Studios to chat with us about the making of *Hourglass* and to share his unique approach towards, and philosophy about, recording. Talking rapid-fire, with barely a pause between thoughts and with an unbridled enthusiasm that is positively contagious, one thing is absolutely clear: the man loves his work.

I gather that *Hourglass* was an unusual record to make.

James Taylor called and said, "I'd like you to come up to Martha's Vineyard to record," so I said, "Okay, I'll put together a package." I called Neve and asked if we could get a baby Capricorn [digital console] up there, and I spec'd out a bunch of mics and preamps. Then I called James and told him what I had assembled. His reaction was, "No, wait a minute. There's gonna be a lot of woodshedding, a lot of rehearsal work putting things together. I don't want to be worrying about the technology—I just want something really simple. If we get something, great—and if we don't, so what."

We had some good people on this project—notably, Jill Dell'Abate, our associate producer who got everything organized, and John Morrison, who was our tech guy. But, you know, people have asked me, what A/Ds did you use? What preamps did you use? Nothing. I went up there with only a Yamaha 02R, three Tascam DA-88s, and some of my own microphones. The only things we rented were some cables and mic stands. The concept was, we're going to record a preproduction rehearsal of the band and see what happens. We started setup the first day at ten in the morning; by two in the afternoon, we were tracking. Here we are in Martha's Vineyard, and I'm looking out a big picture window at the ocean with a big fireplace over here and James Taylor singing over there, and I'm thinking, this is *too* cool!

Then, when we finally got the stuff back to New York and listened to it, we said, "Jeez, this really sounds good, this is a record!" We went to L.A. to do the backing vocal overdubs and came back to New York to mix and add our guest lineup—Yo-Yo Ma and Stevie Wonder. Those overdubs were done here at Right Track, but all the tracking—drums, guitars, James's vocals—were done on the 02R and the three DA-88s.

So I gather you're a big fan of home recording.

I have to say that this is probably *the* most exciting period for a musician that I can ever remember. You have keyboards that will let you emulate any sound under the sun, and you've got home recording equipment that is the equal of anything you'd find in any studio in the world five years ago. I can remember sitting in my basement with a TEAC 3340-S [analog quarter inch, 4-track tape recorder] and getting really good sounds but knowing it was never going to be as good as what I could get on a Neve with an AKG C12 [mic]. Now, even great microphones are available to the home studio. There are $700 tube mics out there now that are damn close to the top-level mics. So for a very small investment, the best gear is now available to everybody.

There used to be a time when recording in a professional studio and recording in a home studio were quite different, because of the storage devices involved and the consoles. Nowadays, what you have in the home is almost equal to pro studio equipment, so you can use most of the same techniques. I think [*Hourglass*] proves that. I went in there with no particular expertise in the small project studio environment. We weren't in a recording studio, we were in a home. We did the same things that you would do in any home studio. The very first thing we did— and something that is of major importance—is to deal with the sound of the environment. You're in a room somewhere, and I don't care how tight you mic—sooner or later, aspects of the room sound are going to become apparent. So you need to decide what you're going to use in that room and what you don't want to use and get rid of—reflections or what have you. In our case, there was a bedroom off the foyer with sliding glass doors, and that became a perfect vocal booth.

What sort of acoustic treatment did you do in there?

You've got to be careful that the sound of the vocal booth doesn't color things too much. You're looking to create a tight but warm environment, not brittle, not hard, and not totally dead. Also, in James's case, because he plays acoustic guitar at the same time he's singing, you don't want too many reflections off the walls, since you're trying to get most of the guitar out of the vocal mic, and most of the vocal out of the guitar mic. In the end, we just put some blankets and curtains up on the walls.

James Taylor's acoustic guitar playing is such a big part of his records. How did you mic it on *Hourglass*?

We've tried a variety of things with James over the years, and other engineers have as well. People have built little boxes, little cages for his guitar, but things tend to get in the way. It's a problem with a singing guitarist—especially when the lyrics aren't always there [during tracking]. You may want to keep the guitar alone, or vice versa. Also, because James is a performer, the guitar is always moving around. So I started with our typical miking—a Schoeps up around the third or fourth fret from the sound hole, as close as I could get it without being in the way. But he'd move too much, especially from one take to the next, so it just wasn't working. So I ended up taking an ATM35—small condenser mics which I usually use on tom-toms—and I clipped it on to a popsicle stick and taped the stick to James's guitar. So now we had a microphone that moved with his guitar, which allowed me to have a consistent guitar sound.

Where was the popsicle stick fastened?

It was sticking out from the body a few inches, pointing in again at about the third or fourth fret from the soundhole. We moved it around a little bit until it sounded the best.

Which brings me to the second point: Always be prepared to improvise, to say, "Nah, that's not working out, let's try something else." Ascertain what it is you're trying to accomplish and try to think of the simplest way to do it. I could have gotten really complex and started making all these boxes and stuff, but I just said, "Look, let's just tape the microphone to the guitar so it doesn't move." Much like what a contact mic does, but it's a real microphone positioned in a good spot.

> *"Always be prepared to improvise, to say, 'Nah, that's not working out, let's try something else.'"*

How do you deal with keeping vocals out of the guitar mic, and vice versa?

We tried doing an out-of-phase thing, but for some reason it didn't work. So I simply miked as close as I could, and I also took a direct feed out of James's guitar [from its built-in contact mic]. During the mix, anytime there was too much leakage, I would just switch to the direct for that phrase and would then go back to the mic sound as soon as possible. I'm not a fan of the sound of the direct, but if you start out the song with the miked sound and then just pop the direct sound in for short periods when it's underneath the lyrics and the band playing, you really don't notice it. If I tell you now where those bits are, you can hear it—but if you're not listening for it, you won't be aware of the shifts in sound. The ear tends to go with what's going on at the moment, so as long as you're careful about where the switch is and how it's done, you can get away with all kinds of things.

We had a real problem with the song "Up Er Mei." We did four or five takes, but the very first take was the one that we liked—it had a great band improvisation. But, of course, it had to be on this particular take that the guitar mic started cutting out—I think James inadvertently kicked the power supply, which was sitting on the floor. So there's all this clicking and massive change in level. We tried porting the track into a hard disk editor to remove the clicks and even it out, but in the end I had to use 90 percent of the direct sound in that section. I sent it through some effects to mask it a bit, but it's still not quite the guitar sound I would have liked. But the section was so good, we had to use it. It's always about the performance; if I got a great performance with a sound that's not so good, in the end I have to go with the performance. It's like watching a great live gig. There's a spontaneity about it when things are really working, an immediacy—it covers a multitude of sins. In the end, it's the emotional content that's important. I'm fastidious in that I want everything to sound great, but you've still got to go with the great performance over the great sound.

What kind of fairy-dust can you sprinkle over a great performance that doesn't sound so good?

Well, you obviously want to try using effects. I'm a fan of the Eventide H3500; it's got some great guitar programs. A good reverb is also important. If there are big changes in level, you can ride the fader and then print the result to another track of the tape.

What sort of room treatments did you do up in Martha's Vineyard for recording the drums?

Because the drums were in an open living room area, we had to put up a fake wall. We made two four-by-eight foot wood frames that held soundboard (3/4 inch drywall) covered with Sonex. Then we put a four-by-eight foot Plexiglas sheet on top so Carlos [Vega, the drummer on *Hourglass*] could see out and hung a blanket between the frames for a makeshift doorway. We used tape so it didn't ruin the walls or floors, and it only took about two hours to put it up. Keys and bass were recorded direct, and I sat in the hallway between the drums and James's bedroom/vocal booth and monitored at low level on near-field Genelec speakers—I didn't use headphones. Put it all together, and you had a makeshift recording studio. Sure, if you listened to James's vocal mic, you heard some drums—but you do in big studios, too. The main thing was knowing ahead of time what we were looking for.

Clearly, you're a big fan of digital recording. What are the main things to be aware of when you're recording those ones and zeroes?

The main thing with recording digitally is that everything has to be recorded as hot as possible—otherwise, you're only using some, and not all of the available bits. This may not be so critical on a 20- or 24-bit system, but it is particularly important when you're using a 16-bit system. If you're recording at –10 [VU], you're down to 12 bits. Way too often, I get tapes to mix where the tracks have been recorded much too softly. Don't be afraid of those red lights. If it sounds okay, then it's fine. If it's distorted, then obviously you're recording too hot. But you can record a transient sound like a drum hit much hotter than you can record a steady-state tone like a vocal, and it will sound fine, no matter what the lights tell you. You need to understand the medium that you're working with.

You also need to have a good enough knowledge of your microphones to have an idea of what each mic is best at and how to set it up accordingly. We didn't have a great selection of mics for *Hourglass*. I do have a vocal mic for James, which we've been using for years—a Neumann 269. But there are a lot of good vocal mics out there at a reasonable price, like the Audio-Technica 4050, or a lot of the new under-$1,000 tube microphones. It's worth investing in at least one really good microphone. But for a lot of the other stuff, [Shure] SM57s really work. They're still ubiquitous in every studio in the world, they're used on everything from tom-toms to guitars to pianos. They're overall great workman mics, and they're only 80 bucks each. With a couple of 57s, you can do amazing stuff.

How important are mic preamps?

You know, if the song is there and your artist is great, 90 percent of your battle is won. I used the 02Rs onboard preamps for *Hourglass*. If I had used a Massenburg or Avalon preamp instead, would anybody have noticed a major difference? I don't think so. If you have a sound in your head and you know what it is, you can get it. You may have to work harder on lower quality gear, but you can get it. When I plugged James's microphone into the 02R preamp and heard it on my Genelec speakers, it was the sound I wanted to hear. So much of what we do is about the way things work with each other. What we heard sounded great to us, and I saw no need to try to improve on it. What was the point? The be-all and end-all of all of this is, use your ears. Does it sound good? If not, find another way.

But how does a novice develop the sense of knowing what it is they want to hear?

The best way to do that is to work extensively on a limited system like a 4-track, then experiment with bouncing tracks together so you have a good sense of how sounds interact with one another. Learning how what you do here affects the process much later on. You start to get to know certain things—for example, you can't always fix things later.

I think the solo button is the worst button you can use. There is no point to listening to a sound by itself, other than for some technical reason. I know engineers who do all their EQing with the solo on, all their reverbs with the solo on, they're putting all their effects with the solo on. What in the hell is that supposed to mean? I have no idea what that means. Granted, I started out doing that 18 years ago when I started engineering, but very quickly I started to realize that it has nothing to do with my song. One of the first lessons I learned was that if you start mixing by just working on the drums, yeah you can get this incredible drum sound—on its own. But as you start adding everything else, you realize the drums don't sound good at all. They're great on their own, but they sound like hell in context, because they have nothing to do with everything else. So now when I'm cutting tracks, I start with all mics on and set all the faders at 0 [dB]. I listen to the whole band as a band as they're running the song down, and I start tweaking the preamps.

When you're mixing, which faders do you bring up first?

> *"I think the solo button is the worst button you can use."*

I start with all monitor faders at 0, then I put the bass drum, snare drum, and bass about 2 dB higher, and then I put guitars, synthesizers, and any sweetening about 2 dB down. That works as a good starting point. Once I have that pattern on the console, I can almost set the preamps by listening to them. When the meters are right, my balance is pretty much there. And I also know that nothing is going to seriously overload; I may be a dB or two hot, but everything's going to be at pretty much maximum level when it needs to be, and I don't have to start messing with faders.

The key is to get this initial balance and to hearing everybody together. Once I have the sounds overall as an item working together, then I'll solo things and just tweak them, making sure there's no noise on the track, maybe adding a touch more of this or that.

For me, it's all about the vocal; the drums work around the vocal, not vice versa. I started out as a drummer and, like most drummers, I was very egocentric about the drum sound. But now I think people spend way too much time on the drums. In fact, I have found that with a great band, balance, and vocal sound, the drums sound a lot better. The Beatles records are an amazing testament to this synergy concept; the individual instruments may not sound terrific on their own, but together they have a sound that goes far beyond. To me, that's what recording is all about: the way things sound together. It's got nothing to do with an individual guitar sound or a snare sound.

Speaking of drums, for me, the drum sound is in the overhead mics. The snare sound is in the snare mic *and* the overheads; I like that air that comes around the snare. So when I set up drums, the first thing I do is to get the overheads up, so I can hear what the kit sounds like from the overhead mics. I place them near where the drummer's ears are, so we get the basic sound the way the drummer hears it.

When I start a mix, I begin by setting up a rough mix—usually dry—then I start adding what I think is the vocal space. Then I start bringing the other instruments around it. This may take maybe a half hour or an hour. Then I'll focus on the individual instruments and do my tweaking, but always listening to them in relation to the overall mix. So if you were to boil down the essence of everything I do to one word, it would be *synergy*. Everything has to work with everything else; none of these things sit in a vacuum.

Emotional content is everything; there are lots of records that sound like shit, but they move me. Yes, I can dissect a sound and say, "Jeez, I wish this were better, I wish that were better," but in the end, if the band captured the essence of the music and the singer captured the emotional impact, it just doesn't matter. In the end, the performance is the thing. There are very few people who will buy a record because of the sound of it; nobody walks out of a record store humming the drum sound! Ninety-nine percent of the public buys a record because it does something to them, it moves them, there's an emotional impact, it moves their mind, it moves their body, it does something to them. It's really just people in the trade who can get into the sonic beauty of a record. And even if you have a great-sounding record, if the performance isn't any good, nobody's going to hear it, 'cause nobody's going to buy it!

I'm absolutely charged about the ability of almost anyone to be able to record in their home. But, on the other hand, the danger is there are a lot of people who think that all they need to do is come up with a drum machine pattern, put down some chords and do this generic kind of melodic stuff, and suddenly they've got a record.

The other danger is people thinking that great-sounding equipment by itself will give them a good sound, that they don't have to put in the hours of training time.

In the end, your ears, your mind, and your musical abilities are what it's all about. Put a George Massenburg, a Hugh Padgham, a Kevin Killen together with *any* kind of gear, and you'll get a great-sounding record. Because they have not only the musicality, not only the knowledge, not only the attention to detail—they have the love of it. They enjoy what they do, and they take pride in what they do—as I do. Years ago, you *had* to have that to make it work. Now, you can get lucky because the gear is so good, so well thought-out. Fifteen years ago, to do an album in somebody's house took some real doing. Today, as long as you have good ears and the patience to do it right, you can come up with some great stuff.

Do you ever record with dynamics processing?

When I used to record on analog consoles, I would occasionally record with compression—not often—because I wanted to get a certain level to tape, but I would be very careful about how much I used. I would never use a gate when recording. You don't want to take that control over the mixing engineer. For example, many times a drummer will do roughs or stick drags between beats, and with a gate you lose all that.

Now, because I work on digital consoles, if I want any analog compression at all, I do it when recording, because my thinking is that once I'm in the digital domain, I really don't ever want to go back to analog again. The most difficult part of the process is the conversion from analog to digital and digital to analog; that's when you lose most of your information. So once I make that jump to a digital format, it's the last time I want to do a conversion. The next time it should go back to analog is in your home, when you listen to the digital CD through your analog speakers.

The same is true if I want to use some kind of great-sounding analog EQ; I'll do it in the recording process, before I go to tape. But I'm finding such great flexibility in the new digital equipment that I'll reserve anything else for the mix stage. Unless I really want a certain analog sound on something, I'll just record most tracks flat.

Also, with digital you want to get maximum level, so if you're going to do a significant amount of compression, you want to do that before you go to tape. Because the more compression you do, the more level you get to tape, which means the more bits you're recording. For this reason, I do a lot more dynamics processing to tape than I used to. But on *Hourglass*, because it was an experiment, I actually was a little freer—I used the EQ and compressors and limiters on the 02R while we were recording, just to see what they sounded like. But generally speaking, I prefer less processing than more during the recording process. That gives me more freedom when mixing.

When recording vocals, do you ride the fader, or do you use a limiter?

I tend to ride the fader, because it doesn't color the sound in any way. There are singers like Barbra Streisand who get so unbelievably soft, and can then get so unbelievably loud. You don't want to use a compressor there, because the whole quality of her voice would be gone. So I just learn the song, knowing where the soft and loud parts are, and ride the fader. I'll always have my hand on the vocal fader, both in recording and in mixing.

Do you typically double-compress bass, using it both on the way in and on the way out?

A lot of it has to do with the bass sound you're looking for and the bass player's own technique. With a guy like Jimmy Johnson [bass player on *Hourglass*], he does all the compression he needs with his fingers. Sometimes during mixing, I may feel the need to do a little something with the bass, but I can tell you that on *Hourglass*, there's no bass compression at all. Jimmy played the bass the way it's supposed to be heard. Someone like a Lee Sklar—I wouldn't touch his bass! Everything he does, he does with his fingers.

There are occasions when you really want the *sound* of compression, you actually want to hear the bass linger, you want to hear that pumping. But I can't make that decision going in. Like I said before, it's synergy, it's how everything works with everything else. The first thing I need to hear is how the bass player himself is hearing it with everybody else. It doesn't make any sense to just have an automatic bass compression setting.

What's your approach to recording electronic instruments like keyboards?

It's amazing; when you have a real acoustic guitar and real drums in an acoustic environment, they are providing a sense of life, so that when you put a digital piano in there, you have this sense that he's there playing a real one, whether you think it's a well-recorded one or not. So many things depend on so many other things. That's why Beatles records are so instructional. Many times, McCartney's bass on its own would sound so weird, so huge or so tiny, and yet it made everything work. It's about how things work as a package; it's never about "the drum sound" or "the guitar sound."

Mixing is all about those exciting little moments, and they can carry through in an entire song. In the song "GAIA" [on *Hourglass*], people talk about the tom-tom sound, where they come in about three-quarters of the way through the song. They weren't recorded in any special way, but we did something interesting in that we experimented by recording them both played with brushes and played with sticks. I liked the sound of the two of them together, so I used them both. But in the mix, I not only took out the drums altogether during the sax solo [immediately preceding the tom entrance], but I dropped the entire level of the track 2 dB. Then I bumped it back up again at the tom hit, so there's a real impact. You know, after about five or six seconds, the ear becomes accustomed to the new level, and starts to sit with it. So suddenly now, when the tom comes in—even if it's at the same level it was earlier—it's this huge thing, because you've become accustomed to the lower level. Again, everything works with everything else; nothing exists in a vacuum.

Paul Samwell-Smith—truly one of the most unique individuals in music—was the person who first got me to hear things differently. One of the things he used to do was, rather than hitting a drum or a gong hard, he'd hit it really soft. If you bring up the gain on the microphone, it sounds incredible. When a drummer really slaps a tom, the force of that stick actually deadens some of the sound. Take that stick and just let it lightly drop, and the skin rings forever. If you then boost the gain of your mic preamp enough to make it sound like a loud tom, the result is amazing. It sounds almost bigger than the huge hit.

What do you feel are the most important advancements in audio technology over the past twenty years?

Well, mix automation is a wonderful thing. Before, when you mixed an album, you used to have to mix individual tracks, one at a time, and you didn't move on to the next track until you finished the previous one, 'cause it took so damn long to set up the board for each mix, and it never came back precisely the same. I am now mixing *albums*. I'll come in and get a rough mix on eight songs in a single day, get a vibe on the entire album. Then, the next day, I come in, recall those mixes, and, one after another, tweak them and refine them. Not only am I refining the songs as I go along, I'm also hearing the album as a whole—I'm hearing one song after another, instead of just being tuned into one track. I'm now not only hearing the drums in relation to the bass and the vocal, I'm hearing song A in relation to song B to song C. That's another reason I think *Hourglass* works so well as a whole. And you can do this in your home now!

Digital is truly a revolution for everybody. At the time that it came out, it wasn't ready. Now it's ready. And it's going to make it possible for anybody who ever picked up a guitar to put their dream down on tape.

Selected Listening:
James Taylor: *Hourglass*, Columbia, 1997; *Live At The Beacon Theatre*, Columbia, 1998
Carly Simon: *Film Noir*, Arista, 1997; *Letters Never Sent*, Arista, 1994; *My Romance*, Arista, 1990; *Cross The River*, Arista, 2000
Elton John: *Aida*, Polygram, 1999
Dave Grusin: *West Side Story*, N2K, 1998
Barbra Streisand: *Higher Ground*, Columbia, 1998; *A Love Like Ours*, Sony, 1999
Original Cast Albums: *Annie Get Your Gun*, Angel, 1999; *A Funny Thing Happened On The Way To The Forum*, Angel, 1996; *Passion*, Angel, 1994
Luciano Pavarotti: *Pavarotti And Friends*, Decca, 2000, 1999, 1997, 1995

Mitchell Froom

Mitchell Froom is one record producer who marches to the beat of a different drummer. Working with engineer Tchad Blake and a diverse crop of artists that includes Sheryl Crow, The Pretenders, Los Lobos, Del Fuegos, and wife Suzanne Vega, he is the man behind some of the most individualistic, off-kilter recordings of the '80s and '90s—records that seamlessly merge the musical traditions of the past with modern technology. We recently visited with him in his project studio in the middle of the meat packing district (really!) on Manhattan's West Side. Surrounded by his incredible collection of vintage keyboard and percussion instruments, Froom talked earnestly and insightfully about his philosophy and approach towards making records.

These days, so many demos sound like masters—and vice versa. Where do you see the demarcation between the two?

Interestingly, one of the most popular records I ever worked on was a 4-track demo cassette that was badly aligned. But [the music] was so beautiful, there was no way I could suggest that it be rerecorded. This was the first Latin Playboys CD (*Latin Playboys*, Slash/Warner Bros., 1994), with David Hidalgo recording a bunch of music at home, in his kitchen at night, just using guitars, spoons, drum machines, stomp boxes, whatever. But the result was probably the most interesting tape I've ever heard. It didn't have any singing on it, so we decided to bounce the 4-track to 24-track and overdub on it. The thing about 4-track cassettes that's wonderful is that they have a very cool sound. They have a fantastic low end, they have a lot of character—the tape hiss, the slight warbly quality. It's instant atmosphere, built into the machine. Even if you're thinking in terms of releasing your own record, I'd still use a 4-track cassette, and something else—I happen to like hard disk products for their editing capabilities. You can record onto the 4-track and bounce that to the hard disk to edit, maybe record clearer vocals on the hard disk system. You can make a fantastic record for almost no money if you have the time and the knowledge and the desire.

And these days, lo-fi is hip again.

I think for awhile it became *too* hip. I find it disappointing when people say, "That's slick, so it stinks; this is cool 'cause it's so rough." You know, the "I'm so cool because I use cheap equipment" school of thought. In many cases, things sound rough because the artist is really unaccomplished—because the person's not ready to be making records. It makes me long for the jazz days, where musicians would jam in clubs after hours. If you didn't cut it, you'd get thrown off the stage. You'd have to go home, figure out what you did wrong, practice, then come back. So before you ever got to record, you were at a certain level. You had to develop yourself, you couldn't just strum a chord, sing badly, and think it's cool because it's rough. That doesn't mean anything in the real world.

What *is* the point at which someone is ready to make a record?

It's the point at which you have something to offer with a distinct personality. For the singer/songwriter, it's when he starts to come into his own. You know when you're hearing a true individual. For a band, it's the way that you play together—there has to be something unique about it, something that makes you stand out from the crowd.

One of the great myths of the music business is, if you have a great song and a great performance, it doesn't matter how well it's recorded.

It's a huge myth. As a producer, I want to be involved with the definitive recording of any song that I work on—I want to make the hit record of the song. And making a hit record is very deceptive, it's not an easy thing. It's not just getting good sounds and getting a strong performance. A hit record is the mystery of it, discovering something, having something that's surprising, that cuts through the airwaves and makes people want to hear it again.

So where does one start in pursuit of this Holy Grail?

A lot depends on the kind of artist you are. What I look for [in an artist] is their eccentricities and strengths, and sometimes that's difficult for someone to see in themselves. If what you're about is words—say you're not a great singer or a great guitar player—you want to make sure that the lyrics come off in the strongest possible way. So perhaps you'd do things as sparse as possible. Vocally, you want to make sure that the song is written within a range where you can be convincing. Learn about mic techniques, find out how you can record your voice in a way that's

> *"The key is to search for what makes you different and accentuate it."*

attractive. When Tchad [Blake] and I work in the studio, 99 times out of 100, there's only one effect that we ever use on a vocal, and that's a little analog slap—just a little stomp box pedal analog delay, to different degrees, different widths, or whatever. That's all you need to fit a vocal into an environment. If it sounds great dry, leave it dry. The key is to search for what makes you different and accentuate it.

One thread that runs through most of your productions is an intimacy in the sound. Your records tend not to be bigger than life—it always feels like there's a bunch of musicians hanging out in the room with the listener. How do you achieve this?

Well, you start by putting everybody in a room together! (laughs) Popular music at its best, if it's going to be artistic, is a form of a folk art. Bombastic pop music is about the most ridiculous-sounding thing to my ears that I can imagine; you have people singing love songs and they're singing from the top of a mountain, which is the least convincing way of conveying an emotion. Somebody screaming at you that they love you—you're gonna want to run away from them! So we don't place music on a big stage—it's not Beethoven, it's not Tchaikovsky. To me, the word "big" conveys big tones that are almost confrontational.

Do you use a lot of close miking?

Some. The drums are usually in a very small space, and Tchad will use some fairly wild compressors to get a sense of ambience and power, though he doesn't use very many microphones. Often we'll have the drummer not play too loud. It's important that the drummer put together a kit that's right for the song. But we don't go for the classic, modern punchy drum sound with everything perfectly separated. We look at drums more like the way they used to be viewed, that they are part of the group. We try to get at least two or three people playing at the same time, if not in the same room together, at least able to see each other. Sometimes it will just be a drummer and a guitar player, sometimes with bass, live singing, and keyboards.

Even your final mixes sound very much like it must have sounded during live tracking.

But the whole thing is still like entering a kind of fantasy world. We're trying to express emotion—we're not trying to make it sound authentically like you're in a club and you're watching a band. There's no way you can approach the experience of watching people play live in a club—there's not the dynamic range, you don't have the music bouncing off the walls, there's nothing to look at. You have to embrace the studio to create an emotion from sound.

As a keyboardist, you have an obvious predilection for older, analog instruments. Do you use a lot of older analog recording gear as well?

Anything that's characterful. We don't necessarily use the latest microphones. I'm very happy to use a piece of modern gear, though. Sometimes we'll do a rough mix to DAT, and it will sound better than an analog mix. I don't necessarily love the fact that something's analog—in fact, I sometimes curse the fact, because analog gear takes up so much room. I wish that the 800 sounds in today's keyboards were all great, 'cause that would make my life much easier!

What's the most important piece of gear in the project studio?

The most important thing is to have good instruments. If you've been playing one guitar for your whole life, just keep playing that guitar—don't think you have to change to a different one just because it's more fashionable. That guitar you have probably sounds better in your hands than a brand-new model will. I'd also spend money on little stomp boxes, things that might do radical things. You might want to get a 4-track cassette and some kind of digital recorder, so you can move between lower and higher fidelity in an easy way. Get a few mics that you like the sound of, that function well in a number of ways.

Any mics that are personal favorites?

Well, I like really rotten mics, like the little square things that used to come with old reel-to-reel machines. They distort and have a limited dynamic range, but they have a really cool sound. I would always pick up a cheap mic and see if it sounds good on something by chance. On the other extreme, the only microphone I personally own is a Telefunken 251. It's an incredible microphone, but I don't use it much anymore. I used to use it almost exclusively on vocals and acoustic guitars—it's beautiful, very big, with a very natural high end.

Any favorite signal processors?

One piece of gear I'd definitely recommend is a compressor called the [Empirical Labs] Distressor. It's really great for just about everything, and if you had to use just one compressor, you could probably get away with just using that.

Any tips for recording keyboards?

I don't usually use amps for recording keyboards—I almost always go direct—but if I want an amp sound, I use the SansAmp Classic. It provides a lot of variables, so you can get an amp-like sound without the problems of having an extra amp in the room. Sometimes I'll run stuff through a Leslie—I do that quite a bit. And I use a lot of stomp boxes, anything I can find. I just plug it in and see if something happens. Sometimes the buzz [from the stomp boxes] is a big feature! It's the glue that holds it together, something that we usually find really attractive. I don't worry about buzz and hiss—you have to trust the moment when something sounds great to you.

How do you record bass?

We always record DI and usually also a SansAmp track. So we don't use an amp, but we get that growl, that midrange kind of thing, sometimes with just enough distortion to make it pop out better.

Do you record with effects?

I often do, if it's possible to keep them on separate tracks. But things like the reverb coming from a guitar amplifier, you always want to record with that, because it sounds completely different than the reverb an outboard processor would add later. The processor's reverb will have all these high frequencies that don't exist in the guitar amp reverb. The reverb sound from the amp is much more attractive simply because it's coming through a guitar speaker—it's a better sound for a guitar.

Do you have any mixing tips to pass along?

If you view a recording as living in a kind of fantasy world, you can make your music more emotional if you are prepared to pan things in a radical way. Don't put one guitar just a little bit to the left and another one just a little bit to the right—go all the way! Use far left, far right, center, and don't mess very much with those areas in the middle. Panning something hard left or right can also allow you to hear the character of the playing more. Sometimes a guitar wants to live right where the vocal is, sometimes you can put a bass out on the side. Sometimes it's a matter of putting together little groups; maybe the groove is coming from a guy strumming guitar and the drums, so you'd want to put those two things together. It's good to try to be bold with panning.

Is there an order in which you bring instruments into the mix?

No, I don't fuss and fret over a mix—if we're doing an album, I'll usually do two or three mixes a day. There's almost a degree of improvisation to what Tchad and I do; we don't feel bound by any rules. We try to get into where the groove is and how to project the song in a straight-ahead way. Also, we're very attracted to things being slightly out of balance. You want to push that threshold, because if something's "too loud," it oftentimes sets the groove off in a whole different way. A lot of Sly Stone records are like that—there's just this great feeling going on, although it's completely askew. Oftentimes it ends up that the rough mixes are the final mixes. There's no big problem in that. It's a tough thing to explain to artists, because they want the most for the music, and they feel that they have to go to the absolute limit, but that's not true. You just have to get it really good.

Many people go past the point of diminishing returns, and they end up sabotaging themselves.

Yeah, it starts getting smoother around the edges and losing everything that's vital. If you can't get it going really fast, go to a different song, do something else. I made this mistake a lot when I first started, just tucking it in, getting it more and more precise, and the results were absolutely terrible. I would work that hard if the result was better, but I've never heard a three- or four-day mix that sounded any good.

"I've never heard a three- or four-day mix that sounded any good."

How do you feel about the trend towards people recording themselves in their own studios?

It's a very good way to start and to learn. But because so much is written about it, there's all this common information out there, so you don't get as many distinctly characterful recordings. You used to have to go to Memphis to get one kind of sound, to a different place to get something else. Now you get the same sound everywhere [because] everybody's got the same equipment. These days, I couldn't tell you where anything is recorded. My deepest wish is that when somebody hears one of my records, they say, "Where was *that* done? Siberia??"

Selected Listening:
Latin Playboys: *Latin Playboys*, Slash/Warner Bros., 1994
Los Lobos: *La Bamba*, Slash/Warner Bros., 1987; *Kiko*, Slash/Warner Bros., 1992; *Just Another Band From East L.A.*, Slash/Warner Bros., 1993; *Colossal Head*, Warner Bros., 1996
Del Fuegos: *The Longest Day*, Warner Bros., 1984; *Boston, Mass.*, Slash/Warner Bros., 1985; *Stand Up*, Slash/Warner Bros., 1987
Sheryl Crow: *Sheryl Crow*, A&M, 1996
Suzanne Vega: *99.9 F°*, A&M, 1992
Crowded House: *Crowded House*, Capitol, 1987; *Temple Of Low Men*, Capitol, 1988; *Woodface*, Gold Rush, 1991; *Instinct*, Capitol, 1996

Ed Cherney

Ed Cherney is one of the most popular engineer/producers in the industry, and it's easy to see why. Loose, relaxed, and witty, he's got exactly the kind of laid-back personality required to put even the most neurotic artist at ease—but make no mistake: when that red light goes on, the man is all business.

Cherney began his career in the mid-1970s, assisting for legendary recordist Bruce Swedien. Before long, he was working with the likes of Barbra Streisand, Ry Cooder, the B-52s, and Bob Dylan. In the mid-'90s, his career took off like a shot. His work on Bonnie Raitt's *Longing In Their Hearts* netted him the 1994 Grammy for Best Engineered Album; shortly thereafter, the Rolling Stones hired him to man the desk for their *Stripped* and *No Security* live albums as well as their *Bridges To Babylon* studio release. Somehow, he still found the time to become one of the founding directors of the Music Producers Guild of America (now the NARAS Producers and Engineers Wing). Cherney recently chatted with us at Ecstasy Studios in L.A., where he and coproducer Mark Goldenberg were putting the finishing touches on a new Jann Arden release.

What are the common mistakes you're hearing in the recordings that people are making in their home studios?

Bad songs. You can tell when a song is amateur hour, but anything goes with recording. Look at what people are buying—you've got stuff that sounds like a tin cup on a string, and you've got things that just fill the speakers. Certainly, we're living in a scratchy time for music (laughs), but nonetheless, it's still music. Unless you're listening to the symphony or something, it's not important, it's not an issue.

If it doesn't matter, what's the justification for working in a professional studio?

Primarily, the service. There will be equipment in a professional studio that you won't find in a home studio, and some equipment is tailored for the artist. For some artists, only a Neve 8078 will do them justice; others can create their tracks on a laptop in a garage, and it will be fine.

How do you approach working with an artist that may have talent and good songs but doesn't have a clear concept, technically, of what they want to do?

I don't know if I'm necessarily qualified to work with an artist like that. Typically, I work with an artist that has a vision, and it's my job to deliver that, hopefully make it palatable to the record company. But it's not my responsibility to provide the vision. I generally work with artists that have an idea of who they are and are expressing themselves rather than manufacturing a teen idol or something like that.

What approach do you generally take to recording guitars?

I've been using these new Royer ribbon microphones, kind of all around the room, and that's been working really well. Typically, the kind of guitar players I record come in with their own rig and their own sound, and it doesn't call for much except for the usual miking down the hall, finding a good corner of the room and blending microphones together. The guitar player will have messed around a lot at home, and they know what they expect to get out of their amp, and usually what they give me is pretty darn close [to the final sound].

So you're talking about simply capturing the sound that they craft at the amp.

Yeah, I'm a pretty straight-ahead guy in terms of that, though I'll go chase some things around. With Ry Cooder, we hung an old ghetto blaster, an old SuperScope that had a microphone that was really limited, and we took a line feed out of that. I've recorded guitars out of those kinds of things to get a certain "bing!" kind of sound.

Do you often double guitars?

It depends on the music, but usually not. If I do it, I'll usually use different instruments for different textures. It can be nice to double an acoustic guitar that's strung normally with another one that's strung differently or capoed up. That adds some harmonics to the sound, which works well. The kind of records I'm making these days tend to have a bunch of individuals playing as opposed to a big wall of sound, so you can pick out each musician; each has his own character, and you're trying to invent a new sound each time in order to develop that character. But you're typically stumbling across it—there's not a whole lot of premeditation involved. Making records is different every time—there's really no "typical" way of doing things.

One of the biggest problems facing home recordists is getting the bottom end right—big but tight and not woofy or flabby.

There's a couple of things working against guys in home studios. One is that they're probably not working in a space that's acoustically beneficial to getting a good, tight low end. There's typically parallel walls and standing waves, so they don't know what the heck they're getting, and they may be listening through speakers that aren't maybe that great, so they can't turn them up to shake the low end. And it takes years to learn how to use your EQ correctly. What I see most people at home doing a lot is just boosting frequencies. They give it a boost at the kick drum fundamental—at 30 Hz, with maybe shelving, so it starts to go all the way up and begins to fill up the sound at 250, 300 [Hz], where it starts to murk up your record. Then you've got no place to put the bass. So people need to know how to use their EQ—learning how to dip some frequencies and move the fader up instead of boosting all the time. It can take ten or fifteen years to learn how to do that. That's the biggest mistake that rookies make—they just reach down and boost the EQ and say, "That's better because it's louder now," but they're not necessarily listening to how the sound is being shaped. But that's just experience, and that's one of

> "Somebody who knows what they're doing can make a great record with a two-by-four, and somebody who doesn't is going to get a poor result regardless of how good the gear is that they use."

From Left to Right: Ed Cherney, Bette Midler, Don Was

the hardest things to learn. It's very difficult to shift your thinking that way.

A lot of home recordists also have trouble dealing with dynamics processing.

Well, the thing is that guys like me and a lot of my contemporaries served apprenticeships in studios. We worked under engineers that started in the '40s and '50s and built the gear that they used and went from big bands to symphonies to rockabilly and country, then eventually to rock and roll; guys who saw the technology evolve. Sitting behind the Bruce Swediens, the Phil Ramones, the Al Schmitts—we learned how to listen. We learned what worked and what didn't and how to use that stuff, more than just reading the manual. But when you're at home, you're on your own—you usually don't have a mentor, and you never really sit behind somebody who's been there, done that, has 30 or 40 years experience, and knows how to make great records.

Like they say, it's the nut behind the wheel. Somebody who knows what they're doing can make a great record with a two-by-four, and somebody who doesn't is going to get a poor result regardless of how good the gear is that they use.

When you're recording bass, do you take an amp signal as well as DI?

I do, to shape it. The truth is, with a great player that has the touch, you can stand his bass anywhere near a recording machine, and it's going to sound great. A great musician is real easy to record.

What mic will you typically put on the bass amp?

I've had a lot of experience with FET 47s; they work really well if you're careful to pad them down and are aware of what the proximity effect is doing so you find the sweet place to put them. But I always listen to a good direct box first, just to see what's coming out of the bass. Then you go out into the studio and listen to the speaker; it's fairly simple.

Do you use the amp signal for the low end or for the bite?

Most signals will only take so much EQ, so I'll use the amp as filler for the low end, and I'll use the direct more for the string noise and finger-popping, for the attack. Then, without using a lot of EQ, you can make it brighter or duller or fuller just by moving one fader up and down against the other. You can fill it in that way rather than ruin the phase of the thing by twisting EQ knobs.

Do you compress both signals as you are recording?

Typically, I'll put just a little compression on the direct signal as I'm recording it and leave the amp compression-free and EQ-free if I can. I don't want to lock myself into something that I can't undo or change later. But with a great bass player that has the touch, you don't need a compressor, because he makes the instrument speak. Certainly, having a compressor with variable attack and release times is important. That's a lot of the big trick about compressing bass: using the right attack time so you can get the attack of the thing and using the right release time so it's not pumping—unless you want it to pump, of course. Basically, you're trying to get all of the notes to speak evenly so there are no holes, nothing sticking out.

What sort of compression ratios would you use on bass?

4:1. But you might go 12:1 or even 20:1—whatever it takes. It's going to be dependent on the way the guy plays it and what the music is calling for.

Do you typically compress the bass again when you mix?

Lately, I've been adding a little bit of compression just on one of the tracks; sometimes I'll compress it two or three or even four times.

Home recordings often lack "ear candy"—the little, almost subliminal elements that seem to make a record a record. How is the decision made to add a little percussion here, a little sound effect there?

If we've got an open track, let's put something on it! (laughs) You just lead with your heart. Your instinct tells you what needs to be there and when to leave something alone. You listen to stuff over and over again, and you may find yourself thinking, we need a little action over here, something to set this part up a little bit better. You just go for what the song asks for, so you try it, you put it on, and if it doesn't work, you get rid of it. When you come to a fork in the road, take it!

"When you come to a fork in the road, take it!"

Which leads to the next question: How can you tell when something's done, as opposed to not yet complete or overdone?

You just know; it comes from the heart. There's nothing quantitative about being an artist or making a record. That's why not everybody is rich and famous! (laughs) I think it's down to hearing every individual musician somewhere in the soundscape, somewhere in the band, rather than necessarily having every color, every space, filled in.

That's probably the hardest thing for the home recordist working on their own—knowing when to stop.

Yeah, but for people at home who are just doing music for the enjoyment of it, that's the whole point of it—to just keep sitting there working on it, messing around and trying stuff. If it's not going to find its way onto a rack at Tower Records—if it's just going to find its way into cyberspace, maybe that's the point of the thing, to just keep working on it, to keep it as a work in progress. But if you have a deadline and there are record executives counting on you to fill in the numbers on their quarterly reports, you're certainly dealing with a different set of problems.

Some artists, it seems, are never satisfied with their work; others can let it go after the record has been released.

Well, yeah, and I know both kinds of people, though I can't name names while they're still alive! (laughs) What happens, too, is that a lot of times an artist records a song before they have a chance to perform it before a lot of people, and as you perform it dozens and dozens of times, there's a certain life, a certain texture that you discover. You don't get that if you're making a record and you just do a few takes.

That's a good point, and it probably accounts for the sophomore curse of a lot of second albums.

Very true.

What can you as a producer do when it's clear to you that a song just isn't ready to be recorded?

You have to say so—in the nicest way, of course. If you're working with artists that write for themselves, you have to inspire them to write by playing them lots of songs, perhaps pointing out examples of what you're talking about. But you have to do it in a very decent, very kind way. These days, though, there will be a lot of people listening to the songs, and there will usually be a consensus of opinion.

Producing by committee, almost.

Yeah, there's a lot of that, unless you have an artist that contractually has the right to have things done their way.

How long do you typically spend on a mix?

As long as it takes. I have a reputation for being really slow and driving everyone crazy.

Is that because you're a perfectionist?

No, it's definitely not that—I'm really a slob! (laughs) But you delve into a mix and you get led down different paths—you want an opportunity to explore: Where's the groove, where's the pocket, where's it at? Having said that, if the stuff's really well-recorded, it's largely a matter of putting the faders up and figuring out how to pan it, where to put a stunt here and there, get the vocals sounding right and balanced, and you go from there.

Which faders do you bring up first?

All of them. I start out by pushing everything up and get a feel for what's on tape, where everything is. I rarely solo stuff unless I'm looking for a problem. I balance from the perspective of looking at it as a whole instead of looking at each sound individually.

Once you've got all the faders up, what do you do next?

At that point, you can make arrangement decisions—maybe you don't need the four trombones in the verses, and maybe we can empty this out or use that part to build the chorus. But the shaping of the sounds is done with all the faders up. That's the best way to do it, though it takes discipline—you've got to concentrate and listen inside the music instead of using your solo button and listening to one thing at a time.

"Listening inside the music" is an interesting concept...

Well, I'm talking about things like finding that guitar line that's inside and then finding its counter-line—being able to isolate and identify the different things that are happening in the context of the entire spectrum.

Are you talking about achieving maximum separation?

Not necessarily. It depends on what is called for—it might be achieving a perfect mess! (laughs) You have to listen with your heart and do what's called for. That's what makes some people great artists and some people not. Some people can throw the ball and some people can't; some people can run and some people can't.

Any tips for getting a vocal or a solo to sit right in the track?

It's a major pain in the ass. You just have to keep wrestling with it. Vocals are usually the trickiest thing, especially in country records, where everybody wants to be able to hear every single word. In modern rock or other genres, you can get away with things like burying it or moving it to the side. I usually start by putting the vocal up dry and see if I can shape it around the music. If it doesn't sit right—if you have to make it too hard to get up over the music—I might try cooling out some of the music around it by cutting some of the upper mid range. It's all about creating a space; you only have so much 2, 3, 4 kHz that you can fit on a record before curling everybody's eyebrows. So instead of stacking it up, I'll try to dip some out and see if I can fit it in there, frequency-wise. A lot of people who haven't been doing this a long time, the first thing they'll do is start reaching for delays and reverbs and all that kind of stuff, but that's missing the point. You want to shape it so the music is sitting around it and the vocal is telling the story like it should, so it's in the right place. And then if you want to add something to it to put it in a space, go ahead, but you have to shape it first.

Do you typically use one or two reverbs for all the instruments, or do you favor using discrete effects for each instrument?

From experience, I know that I'm going to want something that's short and bright—a room reverb set to a second, second-and-a-half, kind of thing—and I know I'm going to want something a bit longer than that, maybe 2.5, 2.6 seconds. I'm going to have effects for maybe three acoustic spaces: something short and bright, something medium, and then maybe a long hall with a long predelay. I'll definitely start with those, and those will be off echo sends. Then I'll have an eighth note or quarter note delay, and I'll have some Harmonizer™ left/right stuff. But I won't send much stuff to it at first; I try to balance the music dry and then use the echo sends to put it in an interesting space. I just like to have the options, and then I turn things up and down and mess with it until I stumble upon the truth.

But you'll send multiple instruments to each of these effects?

Sure. You're putting together a cocktail, so some things will go into others—it can be quite an extravagance. Usually you don't have enough echo sends.

When you talk about setting up "stunts" in the mix, what kinds of things are you talking about?

It could be little lo-fi things, stuff like that. Different vocal treatments in the chorus, any kind of event that will add excitement. Changes that will catch your ear a little bit, up the ante. That's the kind of musical world we live in now—you have all these digital and analog tools, workstations, all this different stuff—and that's what's making it fun, combining all the different elements and using all the different tools. It's a broad palette.

What's your typical vocal chain?

I have some Class A [Neve] 1073 mic pres in my rack, and I've got a very nice Mastering Lab tube mic pre that I use. As far as compressors, it could be an 1176 or a GML; for some kinds of singers, a dbx 160 works really well if you just want to protect the tape.

Do you ride the fader as you're recording vocals?

Not really. Basically, when I'm recording, I'm just trying to fill the meter and get it fat on tape. Then we've got plenty of room to trim it up later.

Will you use EQ while you're recording vocals?

Yeah. If there's some rumble in the room, I might roll some rumble out of there. Maybe add a little top, but I'll do the very minimum to get the sound right. Then you've got plenty of time to screw it up later! (laughs) Plus, a lot of times when you're doing vocals, you're in a hurry—the singer is out there and they're ready to go. They're not going to sing for a half hour while you're trying to get a vocal sound. Also, you may get good stuff out of a guide vocal during tracking, even though it's the last thing you're thinking of while there's five or six or seven other musicians out there with instruments. But you may get a great performance, so you'll be locked into that kind of sound during overdubs and fixes, at least for the rest of the song. So a lot of times you're moving fast; you don't have a lot of time with most singers—there's a window of time, maybe an hour or two that they can sing in—and you've got to hit the red button and go get 'em.

How would you sum up the audio state of the art in the year 2000?

In a lot of ways, it's the worst of times and it's the best of times—in terms of the way a lot of records sound now. It's a fairly graceless age—especially 16 bit, 44.1—but it's also a time when everyone can be an artist and make music. And why not? Even if 90 percent of it is crappy, there's always that other 10 percent. I'm waiting for the time—and it could happen any day—when somebody at home is going to make some sort of record and put it on the Internet and a hundred million people are going to download it. When they figure out a way to get paid for it, it's going to sweep the world, and it's going to shake things up about the way people do things. It could happen anytime, and I want to be there for that—it's an exciting prospect. Just to reach so many people and do it independently, which would open a lot of doors for a lot of people that may be perceived as being old or out of the mainstream.

What are your thoughts about the impact of MP3?

Well, it doesn't sound too good right now, but it will get better. It shows that people are still more interested in the content and the flavor than in audiophile records. As professionals, you always want to make each record sound as compelling as you can, but it's about the message and not the medium. It's the message—the art and the tale and the melody—that people move to.

Selected Listening:

Bonnie Raitt: *Nick Of Time*, Capitol, 1989; *Luck Of The Draw*, Capitol, 1991; *Longing In Their Hearts*, 1994; *Road Tested*, Capitol, 1995

Jann Arden: *Time For Mercy*, A&M, 1993; *Living Under June*, A&M, 1995; *Happy?*, A&M, 1998

Rolling Stones: *Stripped*, Virgin, 1995; *Bridges To Babylon*, Virgin, 1997; *No Security*, Virgin, 1998

Bob Dylan: *Under The Red Sky*, Columbia, 1990

Ry Cooder: *Get Rhythm*, Warner Bros., 1987

Mike Clink

If you bumped into Mike Clink on the street, you'd never guess his occupation. Soft-spoken and thoughtful—even (dare we say) clean-cut, he looks more like your local shopkeeper than the man behind the powerhouse sound of heavy metal stalwarts Guns N' Roses, Whitesnake, Triumph, Megadeth, and Sammy Hagar. A self-described frustrated guitarist, Clink paid his dues assisting and engineering at L.A.'s Record Plant in the '80s for pop artists like Jefferson Starship, Eddie Money, and Heart—"experience" he says, "that helped me to be able to add some musicality into the hard rock bands I now work with." Today he is a popular and well-respected producer, and after talking with him it's easy to see why.

You've established your reputation producing hard rock bands like Guns N' Roses, yet you're such a laid-back, mild-mannered guy! Is it a case of opposites attracting, or are you really a wild man when you get into the studio?

If I was as wild as some of the bands I've worked with, nothing would ever get done! I don't know about opposites attracting, but they actually work really well together. When people are going crazy, I'm the center, I'm the hub. I can keep it together when everyone is scattered and moving in different directions. I think that's one of my strengths.

Did your experience as a guitarist help you when working with people like Slash, people who are very fussy about their guitar sounds?

It definitely helped, because I really was able to understand what he wanted, and I understood the little nuances that guitar players can add into their playing. Because of that, I know when someone can do it better, and I know when they can't do it better. It also helped in getting sounds, in knowing what worked and what didn't. In the case of the very first Guns N' Roses record, we were developing the sound. They didn't have any gear. I think Duff may have had a bass and a cabinet with no head. With Slash, we went through 40-some amplifiers trying to get the right sound for him. We actually went through that same process on the second album also, because he didn't have the amp that we used on that first project.

Some producers view their role as simply capturing a band's sound. Yet you're saying that, at least with Guns N' Roses, they really didn't have a sound, and you had to work with them to craft one.

Well, they had a sound—they just didn't have the means to accomplish it. Guns N' Roses were who they are and that never changed, but we worked on getting the right sound for Slash and Duff. It was very deliberate—and when we got it, it was amazing. For the drums, Steven [Adler] didn't own a kit, so I rented a kit that I thought would be appropriate. That became the sound that we used on the first record. I would say it's 50/50 as far as bands having their own sound; I did another band called Pushmonkey, and they definitely had their own sound. They had integrated a lot of effects into their guitars, and it wasn't so much me changing their sound as it was stepping it up a little bit and maybe changing the songs a little and making it work together.

But with Guns N' Roses you a had a very definitive idea in mind before you started and you worked towards that.

I think we all wanted to make a classic record, and I knew what that entailed. So we worked together to make sure that the sounds were not contrived, that they were real, and we worked towards that end. I knew there were certain amplifiers that weren't going to cut it, and I knew the kind of guitars to use. When I first started working with Slash in rehearsals, he had a Jackson guitar, and it just wasn't right for what we were trying to accomplish, so I said, "How about a Les Paul?" We got him this Les Paul, and he fell in love with it, and that's the guitar he still uses.

After the record was made then, the band had to set about replicating the studio sound on stage.

They could do that—they definitely had that sound, once we went through that process. That's the beauty of being able to do this—once you develop the sound, you incorporate it, and it becomes your sound. When they went onstage after the record was done, that was their sound. It wasn't that they had to grow into it—they had to grow into some of the performances, but they didn't have to grow into the sound, because it was there. We had taken it and developed it, and when they hit the stage and Duff plugged into his bass cabinet, that was it—it sounded like the record.

Do you have a tried-and-true formula that you use when recording electric guitar?

My basic approach on electric guitars is to use a [Shure SM] 57. I'll point it exactly dead on, though I might move it an inch or two to get the right sound. I'll also listen to each individual speaker; any time there are multiple speakers, I'll move the microphone to hear which is the most pleasing of the speakers. But I'm also open to suggestions if a band has recorded something on their own and used a microphone that they like and that may be exactly what you're talking about, part of their sound. I won't say no, I'll listen to it, and if it's better than what I'm doing, then we'll go that route or else maybe use a combination of the two. And I change microphones on acoustic guitars. My tried-and-true mic is an [AKG] 452. When I recorded all those acoustic numbers with Guns, that's what I used; I used a ton of them. But I just did a record with Sister Hazel, and Ross Hogarth was one of the engineers that worked with me on that project. He brought in some B&Ks that he owned and, oh my goodness, the sound that we got from those was completely unique and crystal clear. It may not work for every single artist, but in this case it was perfect—the shoe fit. So everything is not etched in stone. But you have to have a starting point, you have to start somewhere. You take a left, you take a right, and sometimes you go back to the starting point because that's the thing that works out. But that's my philosophy: have a place to start, and then experiment.

What's the craziest guitar miking technique you've ever used on a record?

I think it was probably with UFO. Michael Shenker was playing through a Marshall stack

and we had that miked in a traditional way with 57s, but then we also put a Pignose in the room and put one of the Anvil cases over the top of it and dialed in a sound and put a microphone on that. It kind of picked up the rumble in the room, and we got a nice blend between the Marshall and the Pignose.

Do you typically use room mics when you do guitar overdubs?

No, I use close miking. You know, years ago, room miking was *the* thing to do. But with the advent of better reverbs and better sounding delays, close miking has come back. We were limited as to sonically how good a delay would sound with those old Eventides. They were good but they weren't great, and they had a particular sound, but you knew you could get a better sound by moving the mic away from the cabinet. With the advent of better gear, I found that I didn't necessarily need to do that, because you could add all these different effects and you weren't limited by how far away the microphone was. By changing the different parameters of the outboard gear, you can get a multitude of sounds and get it just right for the track.

Do you typically use limiting when you record a guitar?

Yes. I'm a big fan of dbx 160s, the old style original ones with the VU meters.

What sort of ratios do you use?

4:1. Maybe we'll have a gain reduction hit, just tap it, maybe 2, 3 [dB], something like that. I don't want to take away anything from the sound, I don't want the guitar player not to be able to feel exactly what he's doing. Used sparingly, I find that it does add to the sound.

Do you ever mic the strings of an electric guitar?

Yeah. On the Fuzz Bubble record, I miked the strings on the electric in the intro and outro to one of the songs. It's just an electric guitar with a faint amp sound, and most of it is the actual strings of the guitar. But it's got to sound good acoustically, so you've got to have the right guitar and the right guitarist. In that instance we used a [Gibson] 330; it had a really nice sound to it, and so it worked. For the microphone, I probably used a 452, or I may have used a [Neumann] U 47 tube.

What other acoustic guitar tricks have you come up with?

I think that the biggest issue with acoustic guitars is the guitar itself, making sure that you have the right one. Some guitars sound great for picking, some sound good for strumming. Then the next process I go through is selecting the pick. The pick determines quite a bit of the sound when someone's playing, so I'll experiment with a soft, medium, and heavy pick, and make that choice. You can even tape two picks together around a dime or a nickel so you actually get two plucks on a string— that's kind of a neat effect. Another thing that I've used on guitars instead of a pick is Q-tips—those long swabs they use in the studio to clean the heads on the machines. I use them to tap on the strings. It gives a neat little sound, almost like a dulcimer kind of effect.

What about mic selection and placement on acoustic guitars?

My tried and true is the [AKG] 452, and I'll also try a tube mic like a 47 or a [Sony] C24 or C12 or Telefunken—or, after working on that Sister Hazel record, the B&Ks. Because every guitar sounds different, and everybody plays the guitar differently, I move my head around to see where the best sound source is. Before I ever place a mic on an acoustic guitar, I've got my ear moving around a radius trying to find out where the right sound is coming from. Sometimes I'll use multiple microphones, a blend, using one to get more of the strings and one that will get more of the whole experience.

Do you tend to use bass amps in the studio or just the DI signal?

I always use an amp, with the choice of amp determined by the sound of the band. There are so many great new bass amps. I've used the SWR system quite a bit on the last couple of records I've done; I really like those amps. The Trace Eliots are great, too. I think you can get so much more out of an amp—you can get a bit more grind out of it, a bit more dirt out of it— than you can from just plugging a bass in directly. Even trying to use pedals doesn't accomplish what an amp is doing, it doesn't move the air. But with an amp, you can really tap into the strings and into the low bottom.

Will you ever use it to the exclusion of the DI or always both together?

I favor the amp. A lot of people will do a rough mix for me, and I'll see that the DI fader is louder than the amp fader, and the first thing I do is switch it. I just like the sound of bass amps.

The hardest thing for many engineers is getting a tight low end, getting it punchy instead of flabby. How do you accomplish this?

I'll always listen to how the bass sounds with the drums. I never go for a great bass sound on its own, because that doesn't work. It's got to be able to work within the constraints of what you have drum-wise and, to some degree, guitar-wise—but especially that relationship between the bass and kick drum. That goes for almost everything you're working with—you can't just get a great guitar sound and expect it to work in a track. You've got to listen to everything around it to see how it's going to work. I think that's one of the keys.

When you line the faders up [to do a rough mix], you should actually be able to hear the bass. If you have to push the bass up high, then you know that the sonics of what you are trying to accomplish are not quite there. Not that everything should be in a perfect straight line, but when one instrument's fader level is so much higher than the others, you know that something is out of whack, that the sonics of it are not able to compete with what's going on in the track. I'll listen to multiple speakers. I'll listen to see how it works with the NS10s, to see if they fold if you push the bass signal up. That's telling you that you've got too much low sub on it; you'll have to filter that and get a little string sound in there to get it to cut a bit.

Do you typically compress the bass as you are recording it and then again as you are mixing it?

Yes, though I never recompress everything through the same set of compressors. I always record with my [dbx] 160s—I have quite a few of them, because I find that they are fast and quiet—so when I'm mixing, I'll put the signal through a different compressor like a [UREI] 1176 for guitars or bass or an LA-2A for the bass.

Why do you use a different set of compressors?

Because it's almost like adding a different EQ. When I mix, I rarely run [a signal] through the same EQ that I recorded it with because each circuit has its own sound quality, so it adds a little different flavor.

So the concept is that you use one set of equalizers and compressors on the way in and a different set on the way out.

Exactly. One of the compressors and EQs that I've fallen in love with is the Avalon 737. Brilliant piece of gear, really nice. It sounds clean, it's punchy, and the EQs on it are amazing. So I'm starting to use more of the Avalon stuff now, even though I have Pultecs and Langs in my rig.

I gather from this equipment list that you are very much an analog person.

I'm an analog in kind of person, but as far as the actual storage medium goes, I'm kind of changing my thinking. The fact that everybody uses Pro Tools now raises the standard on the playing field a bit. Whereas you used to have drums that would move around a little here and there, now what you do is you throw them into Pro Tools and tighten them up. I like the sound of drums to tape, but the logistics of going from tape to Pro Tools and then back to tape gets a bit complicated with sync issues, so it gets a little more time-consuming. I'm still grappling with the exact way that I'm going to do things, but I'm thinking that probably what I will do is go into Pro Tools, and once I get everything chopped and cut and edited, then put it back to tape so I have that sound. I love the sound of analog; people use tape like a piece of outboard gear. I think that you get less fatigued listening to analog all day than when you listen to digital. Digital won't play anything until it's processed all the numbers, while tape kind of has a gentle slide as it starts and it doesn't just hit you. I've noticed when I'm working on digital all day, it's like taking a pounding.

It's like the difference between working under fluorescent lights versus incandescent lights.

Right, that's a pretty good analogy. So, yeah, I'm an analog guy, but I see the beauty of Pro Tools and digital editing systems. I have a little Pro Tools rig in my office that I use to edit things.

What do you think of digital compression and equalization?

I like my [analog] EQs, and I like my compressors; I haven't found any great compressors or EQs in Pro Tools yet. I do like some of the plug-in effects they have, like Amp Farm, being able to take the drums and put them through Amp Farm to make it sound a little smaller. It's funny, because in the old days we'd try to make the drums sound bigger; nowadays, we try to make the drum sound smaller. There are a lot of bonuses to going into digital editing systems; they can do things that you just physically cannot do in analog, or if you can do it in the analog world, it takes forever. The downside is that I get frustrated when a musician comes to me and says, "Well, you fix it." My attitude is, "I know I can fix it, but I know you can play it too, so if you can't get it now, practice it overnight and come back and we'll do it." Because your job as a musician is to be proficient in your playing and to write songs. So by at least not trying you are selling yourself short. If you can't get it right the second or third time, I'll use the technology to enhance it, but I want everybody to at least try to get it on their own first.

Also, there is a lot to be said for vibe. On basic tracks, do you prefer getting all the musicians in a room and playing off of each other?

That's how I start; I'll get everybody in a room playing together. If there's a problem with someone nailing a part, or if one person's kind of pushing a track or dragging it, I'll eliminate that element or put it down in the headphone mix so much that it's not really a consideration. People play differently when they're playing together; I've proved that point time and time again. When someone comes in and says, "I don't want to hear any of the other guys—I want to play on my own, and then you can add in the other guys," I'll have him play the track by himself, and then I'll have him play it with the band. Then I'll play it back and 10 out of 10 times they'll like the track that they are playing with the other guys. One of the things that still keeps me excited about recording is that I love a great performance. I love it when the hair on my arms stands up on end—it's magical. It's happening less and less now, but when it happens, it's wonderful

Perhaps the single most important role of the producer is to be the one person who can identify when something is nailed and it's time to stop. Often the artists themselves don't even know it; I've heard many stories of magical takes when people in the control room are blown away but the band is saying, "Let's do another one." What sort of criteria do you use to determine that?

That's why people hire a producer—that's their job, to be that outside influence. I'm convinced that bands working on their own always want to outdo the last take. They're always grasping for that carrot, always thinking, "The next one's gonna be better than the one I just did." I think artists go past that point many times, so your job as a producer is to know when to say no. And in order to be a good producer, you need to be able to know when that happens. That's something that starts to happen all the way back in rehearsals. You kind of walk around the room, and you learn what the strengths and weaknesses of the band are. It becomes even more apparent when you start cutting your first tracks. So it doesn't take me more than a day to figure out how hard to push each musician. At the point where I feel that it's a great performance and it's not going to get any better, I'll make the decision to stop. If the artist wants to try another one, I'll definitely try it, but I'm not going to lose what I have, because I'm usually right.

Having to erase tracks is pretty much a thing of the past, unless you're working with analog tape under severe budget restrictions.

Right. With digital you save everything, and that's a problem too. I've learned that, in the Pro Tools world, less is better. You don't need ten performances of a drum track in order to edit it. You just make notes and say, "OK, this is good, that's good, the verse is good, the chorus is good," and that's how you assemble it. You don't need track after track after track to put it together; that just makes things worse.

What psychological gambits have you come up with for eliciting the best performance from a singer?

The number one pointer that I can give is to visualize what you're trying to say. When I'm sitting in the control room during vocal takes, I always have the lyrics in front of me. If I close my eyes, I'm trying to see in my mind if the singer is telling me the same story as what he's written down lyrically. If you can do that, that's the biggest hurdle to overcome. A vocal can't just lay there in a linear manner; it's got to take you up and down, depending on what the lyrics are trying to say. If it's sad, you want it to bring tears to your eyes, to make you a little misty. If it's "Fuck you," you want to hear that energy and emotion. If you can do that— if you can look at your lyrics and listen to your vocals and say, "It's telling the story, and it's taking me on a journey"—then you've accomplished a great performance. If I'm not feeling it from a vocalist, I'll tell them so. I'll get them to draw from within, to tell that story. There has to be emotion behind the words, no matter what you're saying—I think that's the key.

How do you get a problematic vocal track to sit in a mix?

I try to get it to sit right as I record it. It gets back to my thinking that, if you have to push the bass up too high, it tells you there's something wrong with the track. The same thing goes for vocals. When you're actually recording them, there are certain warning signs that tell you, previous to mixing, that something's not right. You either don't have the right microphone, or your compression ratio is incorrect, and you need to rethink what you're doing in that respect. Or you don't have enough gain going into the compressor, or too much gain. These are all the tell-tale signs of what makes a vocal track work. I think one problem with home recording is that people tend to get a sound and just leave it—they think it's going to work for every song. And it doesn't, because in a ballad where you're projecting a lot less, you're going to have to crank things to hear all those deep breaths. It's all about being able to work the microphone, your proximity to the microphone, the air that you're pushing, the settings of the mic pre, how much you're sending to the compressor.

I also ride the faders as I'm recording; when the guy is singing the vocal, I don't just sit there and listen to him. I'm feeling the emotions in my fingers, so to speak. When he's down, I'm pushing him up so I can hear every single syllable. It's kind of a performance. As you do multiple takes, you actually learn the moves as you're recording it. And I'm following where he's going as far as how much he's projecting. So by the time I get to the mix, I've done a lot of that fader riding. My chain is usually a [dbx] 160 when I record the vocal and an 1176 when I mix it, because it adds that bit of brightness, and it almost makes a vocal sound a little more alive.

Do you typically record vocals with EQ, or do you record flat?

It depends on the microphones that are available and on the vocalist himself. I might add a little bit of EQ just to bring out some presence, maybe around 7 k, or maybe even some top at around 12 k to add a little sparkle and clarity. But I don't over-EQ on the record side; I tend to add more EQ when I'm mixing.

So your advice is to do the work as you're actually recording it.

Exactly. When your rough mixes are sounding amazing, you know that you're onto something. If your rough mixes aren't sounding good, something's not right. So before you get to that process of mixing and trying to figure out where the vocal is going to fit in, you should know ahead of time—yeah, that's right, this is good.

How long do you typically spend on a mix?

I tend to start around noon. By maybe 10 o'clock at night, I'll have it done. But we'll leave it up overnight so we can listen to it with fresh ears and fix anything that needs doing in the morning. Hopefully, it will only need minor changes, and we'll move on pretty quickly.

How do you usually build your mix?

If we're in the analog world, it's important to get things as quiet as possible, so I start by doing the mutes. Then I'll start working on the drums first and then the bass, but I'll always bring things in and out to hear the song because I get bored listening to just one instrument on its own. So I'll be working on the drums, and then I'll put the guitars up, and I'll try to see how they're working with the EQ that I've put on the drums. Same thing with the bass: I'll put it in next to see how it's working and then bring in the guitars and vocals to see how that's sounding. I know there are people that start with the vocal and then bring everything else around it, but I just don't know that technique; I don't have a clue how to do it like that. So I start with the rhythm section and then bring the vocals in.

How do you set up effects during a mix?

I usually start with a couple different standard reverb and effects settings, though I'll change the parameters if they're wrong. First thing I'll do is change the delay times to match the tempo of the song. Sometimes I'll change reverb lengths, again depending on the tempo of the song. But I tend to use less and less effects and reverbs as it goes. I think we only used one or two reverbs on the whole [Guns N' Roses] *Appetite For Destruction* record. A lot of times people add so many different reverbs that they compete with each other, and it sounds incongruous; it doesn't seem to jell together. I think the reverb has to be the glue that makes everything sound like it was recorded in one setting, so I'll feed multiple instruments into one or two reverbs.

Do you think there's too much emphasis placed on technical skills these days?

You know, whenever I record a project, I make a book. In it I write down every single thing I do, down to the microphones used, the compression amounts, everything. I give it to the band when we're done—I don't want it, because I do things differently each single time. Inevitably, they'll call me up a year later when they decide to do their next record on their own and say, "Hey, this doesn't work even though we're doing everything like the book says." That's because it's all about subtleties. If something doesn't sound right, I'll go out to the studio and move the mic an inch, and that can make all the difference in the world.

Selected Listening:
Guns N' Roses: *Appetite For Destruction*, Geffen, 1988; *Use Your Illusion*, Geffen, 1991; *The Spaghetti Incident*, Geffen, 1993
Sammy Hagar: *Unboxed*, Geffen, 1994; *Marching To Mars*, Track Factory, 1997
Survivor: Eye Of The Tiger (Rocky theme song), Scotti Bros., 1982
Megadeth: *Rust In Peace*, Capitol, 1990
Triumph: *The Sport Of Kings*, MCA, 1986
Whitesnake: *Slip Of The Tongue*, Geffen, 1989

Part Five

Across the Pond Again

Craig Leon

One of the maxims of the music business is that it can make for strange bedfellows. Who would have thought that a classically trained musician with finely honed composition, harmony and arrangement skills would be the primary architect of the second-wave New York punk movement of the mid-1970s?

The man we're talking about is Craig Leon. Not only did he discover the original thrash-rock band—the Ramones—and go on to produce their groundbreaking first album, but he proceeded to bring many other denizens of CBGBs and Max's Kansas City to the listening public—bands such as Blondie, Richard Hell and the Voidoids, and Suicide. Eventually abandoning the Big Apple for the lure of L.A., Leon's eclectic career took a decidedly country twist—working with singers Rodney Crowell and Dwight Tilley—before he relocated to London, his present base of operations. In 1999, Leon reunited with Blondie for their critically acclaimed comeback album *No Exit*, and today he finds himself returning to his classical roots as he explores new ways of assimilating modern recording technology with conventional orchestra performance. To say that he has a singular perspective on the past, present, and future of record production would be an understatement.

How do you feel your classical background has enhanced your ability to make pop records?

I taught myself how to engineer in the '70s because I was flying by the seat of my pants and nobody would engineer the way I wanted to. I originally came from an arranging background —orchestration, composition, and piano—and a lot of that ended up in my method of production. I would actually attack each recording as you would a composition—lay it out in blocks, like you would with normal orchestration. So I would do a lot of things in the arrangement that ultimately affected how the record sounded. Not on something like the Ramones, where everything was just a big wall of sound, but that approach is more evident on something like Blondie—music that has a lot of countermelodies in it. Even something which sounds radical, like the Suicide records, were really thought out in terms of sonics—which frequencies people were going to be playing —rather than trying to EQ it. It's about, "Let's change the register where that bass is," going through that type of preproduction to create a hole for the vocal. So, consequently, on a lot of those old punk records—and even up to the new Blondie record—I don't use a lot of EQ, and I don't use a lot of effects; the arrangement is what shapes the sound of the record.

Which is not a million miles away from what we were doing with classical records. Doing things with harmonies and different chord changes, and not necessarily playing the root all the time in the bass, changes the way a record sounds more radically than anything you can do electronically. The sound of a record has much more to do with what the musicians are playing and singing than it does mic placement.

"The sound of a record has much more to do with what the musicians are playing and singing than it does mic placement."

Conversely, how has your experience as a pop record producer influenced the work you're doing now in the classical genre?

Actually, what I'm trying to do is to *not* do core classical recording. I'm doing more modern things—something that's very early music, but modernized. I'm trying to incorporate some of the techniques of pop in classical recording, like using multitrack—even though they are live orchestral performances—and doing things with sequences. Sometimes, there are live instruments sequenced [through digital editing] and then overdubbed with more live instruments. So it's actually making very radical recordings in the classical world—I guess I can't ever quit making radical recordings of one kind or another! (laughs) There's not a lot radical you can do in pop right now; it's pretty much established.

In 1900, they said that everything that was ever going to be invented had already been invented, so that's a dangerous point of view.

Well, I'm not quite saying that. Someone could come out in the next year and make the killer record of all time that nobody's ever heard before—please, somebody do it! But I'd like to do a straight core classical record in a modern way, where you do something multitracked and use different EQs and different echoes to change the shape of the music a little bit. That's one thing I'm really interested in right now.

You said earlier that you learned engineering because nobody was around who could engineer the way you wanted.

Well, you've got to realize that it wasn't that far away from the '60s when we were starting to do Blondie and the Ramones. When you'd go [into the studio], you'd have people that were still unaccustomed to live, loud music. They were still trying to dampen things down, even in 1973 and 1974, when I started doing some of the preliminary work on the things that came out in '75, '76, '77. So you'd get very conventional engineering, very flat-sounding compared to what I wanted to hear. I wanted to hear the impact of a Ronettes record without having 300 things playing. (laughs) That was the goal; I wanted to hear the band sound like that. But wanting to get that larger than life sound involved a lot of things that were different in those days.

The way we did the new Blondie album is pretty much the same way we did the old Blondie stuff, which for then was really radical but now is the standard way to make a record. It was using a lot of room mics with leakage. On the early Ramones and Blondie stuff, there's hardly any processing, and there's very little reverb. Even though it sounds really roomy, that's actually the sound of a huge studio. Then, that was really radical—you didn't do that. Instead, you put an amplifier in a little cage, and you put the drums in a little booth with styrofoam all around it. So I'd have a lot of trouble with engineers wanting to do that.

A couple of guys really got it. I worked with Shelly Yakus on a couple of things back then, and he really had it down. But because of the low budget nature of a lot of the records I was making, I couldn't get him all the time. So I'd have to go and do it with whoever was in the studio. I'd just put the mic wherever my ear was, and hopefully it would sound right. Nobody taught me that—it was just a matter of moving things around until they sounded right. You know, "What's this? A limiter? Well, let's put it across everything and see what happens." In those days, nobody was limiting the mix before it would go to mastering, or putting the whole drum kit through a stereo limiter. Everybody was saying, "This is technically incorrect," especially when it's a pair of API limiters that crunch the hell out of it! (laughs) So we were trying a lot of things like that, and I had to do it myself because there was no method for doing it. We were still having people that were very used to recording close-miked jazz sessions and stuff, which was really cool also, but it just wasn't what I was after, not with those bands. Later on, when I did Rodney Crowell and people like that, we did a mixture of both—a very conventional close miking combined with a bunch of room sounds and having the drummer play in the bathroom and things like that.

So you are definitely from the "leakage is good" school of thought.

Oh, yeah. That, and getting as much of the live performance as you can possible get on the record. Even today, when you're hearing things sequenced, get as much live as you can get. I never really separated things a lot, not even to this day.

But, with the exception of the Ramones recordings, there *is* good separation. You clearly carved out spaces for the individual instruments within this broader brush of the big sound.

That's because there are a lot of overdubs, but the basic core of it is one big sound. We did a lot of the new Blondie record in the basement of Chris Stein's house, in his rehearsal room—a home environment, albeit with a lot of the equipment from my sophisticated studio. But still, the basic feel of the album was the bass, drums, two guitars, and keyboards recorded live at Electric Lady for a couple of days. We then took that away and stripped things down and built on top of that, so you still have the live core of what the band was sounding like, even though there later is a bunch of separation from the overdubs.

Generally, you can get a very good picture of things—even within the mass—by panning instruments hard left and right. That comes from me listening to old Beatles records, where, by necessity, the whole band is on one side and then a guitar solo and a tambourine is coming out of the other side. (laughs) I thought that was really the way they were supposed to be! Because I grew up in America, I didn't know that the band and George Martin disowned all of that stuff.

Yeah, they were never actually meant to be heard that way.

Hey, sorry guys, you made people do a lot of things in weird stereo! (laughs)

Do you tend to use fairly standard drum miking in addition to the extensive room miking?

It's pretty much a close-miked kit plus a stereo overhead of one kind or another. Sometimes there's added emphasis on a cymbal or two if it's not being picked up, but it depends on the drummer. How you mic something and how you EQ it—in fact, everything that you do—is actually driven by the way the instrument is being played. If it's a guy that has a really heavy foot, you would use a different mic on the bass drum than the guy who has a very light foot. You would judge where the room mics and where your overheads are placed more by that than anything else. How the drummer is playing determines your mic setup, so there isn't a standard setup that works; no one thing works all the time. I'll even change mics within a session. [Blondie drummer] Clem [Burke] is pretty consistent in the style that he plays, but within different styles of music, we use different setups; sometimes the room mics and the overheads will be way overhead, and sometimes they will be really close, depending on how hard he's playing the cymbals.

> **"How you mic something and how you EQ it—in fact, everything that you do—is actually driven by the way the instrument is being played."**

Do you experiment with placing the drums in different areas of the room?

Yes, or even in different rooms. If you're going to throw a whole bunch of digital reverb on it later, it wouldn't really matter, but if you're trying to get an organic sound, the room means so much more than which specific mic you're using.

For example, we did some overdubs on that first Ramones album in a huge room—again, there's that connection between punk and classical music, because it was Arturo Toscanini's old rehearsal hall with the NBC symphony above Radio City Music Hall. So we were in this room that was about 65 by 100 and 30 feet tall, and we had room mics all over the place. We wanted the sound of an explosion on one song, so I ran around and had people climbing up ladders and putting room mics all over the place while Tommy [Ramone] hit a tom-tom. For all that, it just didn't sound roomy enough. No matter what we did, it sounded like someone hitting a piece of paper—even if it was 50 feet away and cranked up and run through API limiters. So we just took a pair of grand pianos and put them around Tommy's kit and put bricks on their sustain pedals. Then we put up a pair of 87s in a normal pattern over the drums, cranked them up, limited them to death, had him do one hit, and it sounds like cannons exploding.

That's not just an isolated incident, either; something like that seems to happen on almost every session. For example, on the latest Blondie album, Debbie [Harry] didn't want to have as resonant a sound as she usually did, so we got different pieces of foam to put up above her head and we'd lower them or raise them to get more or less resonance on her voice. There were even a couple of songs where she wanted to do something *really* deadpan, so she'd actually put the foam on top of her head and wear it like a little hat! (laughs) Maybe that sounds like 1920s recording techniques—you know, move farther away from the horn—but it works. We'd have people, within the course of a track, moving in and off mic on things. We'd move mics—do half of a guitar solo with close mics and then do another take with different miking, maybe putting the two mics out of phase—and then combine the two in the middle of the solo. As much as I want a live base, I do stuff like that a lot.

One of my favorite records of all times for recording technique is *Sketches of Spain* by Miles Davis. In the stereo version—maybe even in the mono version—he basically has guys walking around the room to make castanets get louder and softer. That's like the old jazz technique of stepping in for solos or stepping back, depending on what's in the score. I've been doing some classical things that way, too, and it's been blowing people's minds. For example, I'll have the bassoons lean forward on one note and back on another note so they're all choreographed. But it works—it's not just bullshit. They were doing that in *Sketches of Spain* for a reason. That's why it sounds the way it does—even though it was done in 1960 without multitrack, without mixing, without effects, without anything. You can literally hear a change in the psychoacoustics of the castanets within one single roll. They were doing something right, even if they did it accidentally.

And that appeals to me, still. Even with modern technique, even with digital equipment, I like to record in natural environments where people are happy to play, which again is something that's done all the time in classical music.

Every incident that I'm describing is not an over-the-top trick; it's something that worked because the guy really thought about the way the piece of music was meant to sound, about what the composer intended or what the artist wanted out of his guitar solo. You want to do what emphasizes that and not just do it for the hell of it. And when it's done right, you really get that bit of magic that makes the record something special. You want to use whatever devices you have at your disposal to any extreme in order to make the record sound right.

What is the dividing line between a demo and a master?

These days, there is none. I start off making a record these days. I haven't done demos in years, and when anybody says, "Do you want to demo something?" I don't know what they're talking about, because if you put all the effort into making a demo, it might as well be a master. Generally, the demos that I get now are really treated as a demo. For example, the Blondie song "Maria." The demo of that is Jimmy Destri singing over a phone into a cassette recorder that I had at the other end, singing Debbie's voice in a falsetto voice. It wasn't remotely what ended up becoming the record, but the hook line and everything was there. That's a demo.

I was in record mode from the first day we started the new Blondie project, even while we were routing songs, and we used some of the guitars that were being played in those rundowns. I just taped everything, or, rather, hard disked everything on the Radar. I also taped those things that I wanted to tape to analog at the same time, because there's no law that says something should be all-digital or all-analog, all-Dolbied or all non-Dolbied. I've used bits of analog and bits of digital all on the same project, and it doesn't matter to me—nothing is written in stone.

What's behind the decision-making process? How will you decide to record a particular instrument on analog versus digital?

I'll use analog if I want to hear tape saturation, and that wouldn't necessarily be on the instruments you would think you'd want saturation on. I've done acoustic cello on a classical recording with tape saturation and heavy, heavy compression. Why not? It's almost like a little homage to George Martin.

So the only reason you'd go to analog would be for tape saturation?

Well, there's a theoretical "warmth" factor, which really isn't the right word. It's just that, because we grew up listening to analog, it sounds right to us. And the more I've been working in digital, the more analog is sounding older and older to me. That's more in my past than my present, but when the transition to digital was happening in the '80s, I'd always have in the back of my mind that it doesn't sound right until it's analog. Now, because we're ending up in a different medium—because we're not going to vinyl anymore—I don't know how valid that is. But there are certain things where I'll go for analog, maybe more from worshipping some sound that I heard in my youth than any other reason. Maybe I'm wrong, but I have a feeling that, as the years go by, I'm going to be less dependent on hearing that old "warm" sound.

> **"The more I've been working in digital, the more analog is sounding older and older to me."**

That's kind of the tube versus solid state argument, also.

It's the same thing. When I started doing some of these classical things, I had access to the mic cabinet of both Decca records—which is unbelievable—and the mic cabinet of Abbey Road, which has everything, you name it. I would be able to set up fifty M 49s if I wanted to, but what ended up sounding right to me was a modified transformerless M 50. On the other hand, I'll use valve [tube] mics on certain instruments, because they sound a bit more midrangy and brighter to me in an odd kind of way. You'd think the opposite—that they'd sound round and warm and velvety, but they don't. Nowadays, especially when you're recording to digital, the criteria for not using a valve mic is generally noise. When you're doing very, very low level recording of something, they just won't work. But I tend to use valve mics more in pop stuff than in classical, because it's masked, and it gives you a different kind of a punch—kind of a midrange, lower octave punch. I also like to use valve mics as overheads on drums—a C24 instead of a pair of 414s or something like that.

The flavor of tube equipment on tape is also different than tube to digital.

Which is why I'll do things simultaneously. On the Blondie album, there are a lot of things that I ran to analog and to digital simultaneously—bounce some bits over from the analog, edit some bits on the digital. There are times when I've actually used the analog drum take for the verses and the digital drum take for the choruses. It's all subtle stuff, but it builds up over the course of many instruments on a record. I wouldn't say that that's going to miraculously change anything, except in your own mind when you're doing it. But if you apply that philosophy to many different elements of a recording, then it can all of a sudden open up in the choruses as opposed to being really intimate in the verses.

Do you generally mix to both domains as well?

Not anymore, because we're in the CD medium, and you might as well get it sounding good in that medium as soon as possible. I'll use outboard analog, but I usually mix to digital.

As an American producer living and working in England, do you think there's an "English sound" versus an "American sound"? If so, what accounts for it?

I do. There's a different approach and a different mentality. I think it's because the control rooms in England are drawn up more by the seat of their pants. You're working on speakers that are extraordinary, but they're not positioned using any kind of scientific method; they're placed according to what sounds good to the people that are working in the room, so it's done by ear. Whereas in America, I think it's done a little bit more technically by the book, and that creates a different sound.

I find that I actually push myself a little more in English studios, because the environments are a bit unnatural. One of my favorite rooms to work in here was the old AIR studios. The control room had big floor-to-ceiling windows overlooking Oxford Street. That was how the room was designed, yet George Martin would sit there and get the most incredible sounding things out of there, and I got really good results as well.

All of which proves that the sound doesn't come from the equipment, but from the way you hear things in the room. The most important criteria, more than anything outboard, desk choice or anything, is how you hear something coming through the speakers.

But will a number one British pop record and a number one American pop record have qualitatively different sounds?

These days, it's really odd, because chances are both of them were recorded all over the place, the vocals were done on an ISDN line, and they were mixed by some guy in Sweden. That's another thing that's becoming great: the ability to work on things in many places. As a result, the sound of records has become more universal now.

What advice do you have for the reader who wants to be the next Craig Leon?

That makes me feel old, because at one time I wanted to be the next George Martin! I guess my advice would be—have a hell of a lot of fun, and don't let anybody tell you anything is wrong. Just do what you think sounds right. If you like the records I do and you send me a record for criticism and I say, "Well, that sucks," don't let that influence you—hey, I'm an old fart. (laughs) Go do what you feel, regardless of what anybody tells you. Use any means necessary to get the best performance out of the artist. Sublimate your ego and focus on whatever techniques you can use to get the artist's vision on the record in the best possible way. That way, you'll be the next you, rather than the next anybody else.

Suggested Listening:
Ramones: *Ramones*, Sire, 1976; *Ramones Mania*, Sire, 1989
Blondie: *No Exit*, Beyond, 1999
Suicide: *Suicide*, Red Star, 1977
Richard Hell and the Voidoids: *Blank Generation*, Stiff, 1976
Rodney Crowell: *But What Will The Neighbors Think?*, Warner Bros., 1980
Izzy: *Libera me*, Decca, 1999

Mick Glossop

For more than 30 years, Mick Glossop has been lending his considerable talents to top-flight recordings, including a long-term collaboration with Van Morrison and work with Queen, Mott The Hoople, Frank Zappa, Renaissance, Tangerine Dream, Waterboys, and John Lee Hooker. Glossop is unique in that he's served as staff engineer at some of London's finest studios, including Wessex, Townhouse, The Manor, and Nova. This long apprenticeship gave him the opportunity to study and absorb numerous different production techniques—invaluable experience that has undoubtedly aided him in his own illustrious career.

On the rainy London afternoon we sit down to talk (what other kind is there?), we were plagued with a power outage, resulting in the interview being conducted by candlelight while frantic staffers in his office ran around trying to conduct business by battery power. None of this seemed to have any perceptible impact on Glossop's powers of concentration, however; for more than two hours, he remained focused on the task at hand, giving thoughtful, insightful answers that reflected his intensive training and singular dedication to the craft of making records. At one point, having just asked him a particularly challenging question (and before hearing his answer), I had to run out of the room in order to feed the meter—an inescapable fact of life for those foolhardy enough to take a car into central London. During the five minutes or so it took me to complete my task, I inadvertently left the tape running (honest, Mick, I didn't do it on purpose), and when I later came to transcribe it, I simply heard silence during that period. While most others would take advantage of the break to stretch or make a phone call, Mick Glossop was instead *thinking* about his answer. In retrospect, I can't say I was surprised.

What do you think have been the most important changes in audio technology during the past 30 years?

One of the most radical changes was the development from 8-track to 16-track. That's a really massive jump because 16-track was the first time you could really put instruments on separate tracks. In particular, the drum sound is instrumental in determining the sound of a record, and with 16-track you could have kick and snare on separate tracks. So it was the first time you could really change the drum sound afterwards, and the first time that mixing as a concept really came into its own, as well as the idea that you could leave major decisions about the sound until later.

Then, of course, we started seeing more boxes that enabled us to do things with sound.

George Martin, in talking about making Beatles records, would often say, "We had to make our own sounds in those days," and I think that was a very important thing because it produced a greater sense of originality in records. There were no presets—there were hardly any synthesizers, really—and there was nothing you could dial in. You had to create everything from scratch, and if you had any ingenuity then you were driven to that, anyway; you liked the idea of doing things differently. That's part of your stamp as an engineer or as a producer. The other part has to do with relationships, how you get on with people.

Are you saying there's less room for originality today?

Well, I'm not necessarily one of those people who yearns for the old days, because today we have more freedom. I tend to be a bit cynical when people say that the magic of a *Sgt. Pepper* came from limited choice. Undoubtedly, it had an effect on the way the record came out, but I'm sure there were times when they were frustrated as hell about things they wanted to do and couldn't.

> *"It's all about decisiveness and having the confidence to move forward."*

It's all about decisiveness and having the confidence to move forward; to me, that's the essential thing. It can be frustrating to work with an artist who's indecisive and isn't confident enough to say, "Yes, that's great." It makes the job easier if you can say, "Well, we can't do it any other way. You have to accept that because we have to move forward, and that's the only way to do it." It helps you get the thing done, whereas if you've got all this choice, then you can't use that argument.

These days, though, it seems like there's almost too much choice, at least for the novice. Someone who is experienced will know in advance that certain options won't work, whereas the novice has to wade through all of them.

Yes, it is tricky. I'm in favor of restriction of choice from a creative point of view. One case in point is the third Peter Gabriel album, the one that had no cymbals and the big Townhouse drum sound. The room wasn't designed in any sense whatsoever—it was more or less accidental. It's live, with a stone slabbed floor, which was done at least 50 percent for aesthetic reasons. Given the context of the day, it was very, *very* live. If you hit a snare drum in the room, it was so loud, it was incredible. We were contemplating changing the acoustics in there because we felt it was a bit uncontrollable, but it went on to become the vehicle for a classic drum sound!

How did that happen?

Peter had decided before he even went in the studio that he wanted to restrict the choice of percussion sounds inasmuch as he didn't want any cymbals on the album —he didn't want any crashes, rides or high hats. So the rhythmic components that were traditionally played on high hats and rides had to be played on floor toms and that kind of thing.

On the Townhouse SSL, there was a talkback system that used a mic rigged up in the ceiling, connected to a really vicious compressor. So vicious that if somebody hit a drum, the volume of that drum was the same as the level of their voice, which is exactly what you want [in a talkback system]. It was probably Phil Collins who was playing the drums at the time; they were talking about something, and he started playing, and in the control room they suddenly heard this amazingly compressed drum sound. Peter Gabriel heard it and said, "Wow, that's fantastic! Put it on the record!" And I don't think that they were working towards that. So [engineer] Hugh [Padgham] then set about using the SSL channel compressors to reproduce the sound of the talkback compressor. In the course of that, he was playing around with the gate, and again Peter responded, because Phil hit the snare and the gate chopped off the reverb—which is the classic sound that has become legendary. It was really Peter who insisted that the sound be used, though it came about by accident.

But the point is, if they had been using cymbals with that kit, they wouldn't have been able to use that sound, because the gating would have chopped off all the cymbal decays in a very haphazard way, which would have messed up the sound. The sound is basically the sound of a drum being hit and the ambience compressed and then, as the ambience tails off, it chops off sharply because the gate's got a short release. It just doesn't work if you play cymbals as part of the rhythm. So it was only possible to get that drum sound—which then went on to be the drum sound of Phil Collins "In the Air Tonight"—without using cymbals. That's an example of a massive sonic creative effect being made possible only by a restriction of choice.

And a series of accidents.

And a series of accidents, yeah, especially if you think about the room design not being planned. So good things can come about if you say, "Right, we're not going to use that piece of equipment"—whatever that equipment is, a musical instrument or whatever.

So you're suggesting giving yourself some restrictions beforehand in order to find a way to accomplish what you want with limited options.

Absolutely. Instead of yearning after all the gear, choose wisely and think what the essential things are—just make sure that they are the right individual bits of equipment. Given the kind of recording technology we have now, with hard disk recording, etc., you can create fantastic results with very little musical equipment, with one keyboard that has a selection of tones, one guitar; you don't even need a bass guitar, really. If you're working on your own in a project studio, you can create bass parts with either the keyboard or the guitar, using octave dividers. You can speed the tape up and play a bass part on the bottom strings of the guitar, use that sort of thinking. If you get into that kind of boy scout mentality of making it work with a piece of string and a pen knife—seeing what you can do with not much equipment—that will bring an originality to your work, and it's fun as well! You just have to work a little harder mentally, rather than just calling up preset 25.

> **"Sound is not a separate thing from the music; the two are totally interlinked."**

The thing about sound is that it's not a separate thing from the music; the two are totally interlinked. When you're creating effects on records—not in an effects box sense but in a musical, sonic sense—the two are the same. So choose two or three bits of equipment with care and then set about doing what you've got to do with those.

If you're putting together a project studio from scratch, what's the most important piece of gear?

It depends on what you want to achieve with your studio. I suppose you could divide equipment up into the stuff that you are creative with and the medium upon which you record—the tape machine or hard disk recorder. I think it's worth getting quality for the medium, because that directly affects the reproduction quality of what it is you are creating. You can buy a computer-based system with a PCI card, but use the best converters you can, so at least you can do transfers with the best quality; it's quite important, and you can't really bypass that. I suppose the next thing on from that would be to make sure that your listening environment—by that I include the speakers and the amplifier—is as good as it can be. That doesn't mean you have to have a big massive system with 18 inch bass drivers. You can get very good results using a pair of Yamaha NS10s. A tremendous number of producers and engineers work for maybe three quarters of their major projects on NS10s.

Is that what you do?

Yeah, most of the time when I'm mixing, I'm listening to a pair of NS10s. I check it on the big speakers and I use Auratones as well, which takes that idea even further. Even if you are going to use, for example, a pair of NS10s and a Quad 405 amp—which is the standard combination a lot of English engineers use—try and make sure the room isn't adversely affecting the sound too much. I know I'm being very general about that because there's a tremendous amount you can do, but you don't need to spend a lot of money on acoustic treatment.

What sort of treatments come to mind that will help?

If you want to split the frequency of the spectrum into three bands, there's the high-frequency stuff, there's a midrange band—which is a very wide range—and there's low frequency. The bands are kind of inversely related to the amount of money you need to spend [to control them]. Controlling very low frequencies costs more money because it's big movements of air, and you need mass and big trapping systems to do that. So you'd be lucky if you can do that without spending a lot of money. High frequency, it's just soft material. Midrange is more complicated because it's a wide range anyway, and to a certain extent it depends how much absorption and how much diffusion you want; there's a balance between those.

It's weird talking about acoustic design, because you can get complicated equipment in, but it comes down to what you want to hear. You kind of mess around, really. Normal domestic furniture plays a big part in the way a studio is going to sound, so don't be frightened off by the mystique of acoustic design. It's worth just getting stuck in and putting stuff in the room and listening to CDs that you know the sound of and see what your monitors sound like. If it sounds a bit muddy, then get some books on the wall and see what that does. Try the old test of making a recording in the room and then playing the tape elsewhere and seeing what it sounds like on different systems. If it's bass light, then there's too much bass in the room, so you need to absorb a bit of that. I think the listening environment and the quality of the recording medium are the two most important things, really, because what you hear obviously determines what you do.

Is the quality of the mic preamps more important than the quality of the mics?

There are companies like Mackie which are making desks that have mic preamps which are great. This is very subjective, of course, but as far as I am concerned, they are better in some respects than SSL E-series mic amps, and we made a lot of records in the '80s on SSL E-series consoles with E-series mic amps. So in terms of mic amps, if the budget's restrictive, then get a Mackie. Not just Mackie—there are other cheap consoles with reasonable mic amps, like the Soundcraft ones. And rather than just one mic, it's good to have a choice of mics—at least one dynamic and at least one condenser mic for different things, because they sound different.

Do you experiment much with different polar patterns?

I don't spend a lot of time doing that, but it's something that I keep meaning to do. I might go for omni if there's a particular ambience in the studio that I want to capture. There's a bi-directional mic technique which is quite useful for a singer with an acoustic guitar who's singing at the same time—it's a classic problem, trying to keep the voice out of the guitar and the guitar out of the voice, but particularly the voice out of the guitar. If you use a bi-directional mic on a guitar such that the dead sides are pointing up and down rather than side to side, then you get more rejection of the vocal than if you use a cardioid mic, which doesn't really have as good side rejection; it has good back rejection. If you use an [AKG] C414 bidirectional and have it sideways, it picks up less vocal. So I might experiment with polar patterns from a rejection point of view, though generally I use cardioid for most things. But it's an area that's valid; it's a question of the way that the sound gets into the mic. It's as valid as what happens when you put it in an effects box.

Do you tend to use a lot of room mics?

Yeah, when it's appropriate. I particularly like Steve Albini's approach to drums, which uses lots [of room mics] all over the place. You don't have to use them all, but it's good to record them. It's good to have them set up and to use them collectively.

Do you ever process room mics differently?

Oh, yeah. I use delay sometimes. One trick I've read about that interested me was that Abba would close mic the drums when they did the drum track, and then they'd double-track the drums but only record the room mics, put them on a separate track. I thought that was neat. I like double-tracking and changing the sound of the double-track in some way. I do that with guitars a lot, where you double-track with a different guitar, or you've got the same guitar with a different amp or a different mic.

One trick from the old analog days was doing a slight varispeed for the double-track.

Yeah, and it's not the same as using a Harmonizer; it's not static. Analog tape machine speed changes all the time, so even though there's an LFO kind of effect on the Harmonizer, it's a constant sweep; with tape, it's a random thing.

Random, that's an interesting concept—a very Brian Eno kind of thing—but it's something I've been getting into recently, trying to get modulation on things that's done in a random way rather than a sweep. You can create it in different ways. If you have several effects that each have their own LFO modulations, then if you combine them, since they're not locked together, you'll get some interesting combinations. But also deliberate random modulation, which you can do on some old analog synths—you can run the noise through a sample-and-hold circuit to create a random variation of modulation signals so that the pitch is just shivering away in a weird bubbly way, which is quite nice. I think that's a much more natural thing—if that's what you're going for—than a constant sweep.

Is there a basic drum miking setup that you tend to begin with?

I try to avoid that as much as possible. I used to do that, and it's something I have to force myself to avoid because, if you've got something that works and you've got a job to do, you think, "Well, I've got so much time to do this, and that'll work, so I'll do it." But if you use the same mics in the same positions every time, you're led down a certain road of creating a sound. Sometimes you'll find yourself using the same EQ without actually listening—you're going, OK, I need to take 700 Hz out of the snare, I need to add 5 k, and I need to add a bit of 12 k, and maybe put in a 75 Hz filter to get rid of the kick. Yes, that's a snare sound, but it's also what you did on ten other recordings.

Although perhaps people have hired you because that's the sound they want.
Maybe. It's difficult to know that.

Do you go into the room and listen to the kit acoustically and start deciding from there?
It depends on the project.

But how do you make the decisions?
The question of what the record is going to sound like is the main thing. You've got to start somewhere, so you have to get a concept, to use a grand word, for the sound of the record, which will come about when I first listen to demos of a band; they'll give me an idea of what their direction is. From the demos, I'll form an idea of where I think I need to make changes musically and sonically, but also I start to get an idea of how I think the record could sound, but not too specifically at that point. Then I meet the band. We talk about the sound, the sort of things they like, the sort of records they want to make—and that sort of crystallizes that idea of what sort of sound the record's going to have. That's the reference for virtually all the decisions that are made, notwithstanding the fact that you are going to have some experimentation and some surprises along the way.

One extreme will be that the record is going to be a very fidelity, acoustic reproduction kind of sound, where, for example, the drummer has a sound that has to do with the kind of kit he has and the way he tunes it and plays it. [In that case], you put that drummer in a room which will enhance the presentation of that sound, and you set about choosing and placing mics in such a way that what comes out of the speakers is a representation of his sound. So you're not talking about processing in order to change anything; it's reproduction in a classic hi-fi jazz sense, I suppose.

That's one extreme, but the other extreme is where the idea is to create a sound which is conceived in the collective imaginations of the artist and the producer and the engineer. That sound is conceived in theory first, then you set about creating it by whatever means are necessary. Both [approaches] are interesting, but the second one is, in a way, more interesting— because there's more imagination, there's more creativity. That's where you get into concepts of originality—when you want to make the record sound like a record that hasn't been made before. And quite often you'll end up with different sounds on different songs as well—different drum sounds for each song. Then you start talking about the percussion content of the record; it doesn't have to be drums, it could be combinations of classic drums and classic percussion. But then you start to talk about sequencing and sampling and creating different sounds using distortion, changing a high hat into something else, into a shaker sound or into something that just sounds like distorted white noise—the whole thing is wide open. In those circumstances, you might still put the drums in the room, and the band might still have a drummer who physically plays, and you're still dealing with acoustic material, but it's going to be transformed into something else. So you don't necessarily walk into the studio and listen to the way the drums sound in the studio; you might actually avoid doing that! You might even just tell the assistant to use whatever mics he wants.

Have you done that?

Occasionally, yeah. One of the things you have to do when you make your record is choose your vocal mic for a particular lead singer. Assuming you're going to pick one mic and use it for the whole thing, you need to choose a mic which is best for that voice. Again, you can fall into the trap of saying, well, I think a 414 or a U 87 will sound good on that, so you put those up and choose between the two. But you are letting yourself open to all your pre-formed ideas about what a 414 or a U 87 should sound like. So I might give the assistant a list of mics and ask him to add a couple to them, set them up in the studio and plug them into channels one to eight, but not tell me which is which. I might ask him to switch on the appropriate phantom switches so I know which are the condenser mics and which are the dynamic mics, but I'd rather just push the fader up and just see what they sound like. It's quite fun to discover that the Tandy Radio Shack PZM mic actually sounds better than the M 147 or something like that. I don't know if it's a perverse sense of humor on my part, but I quite like that idea of getting a great vocal sound with the mic you would least expect, as a sort of discovery, I suppose.

It's funny, actually, because when PZM mics came out, we did experiment by unscrewing the plates, just clipping the mics on. Although the low-frequency response wasn't all that great, I thought the high-frequency quality was really special. I guess it's because the electret capsule is very small so it doesn't interfere with the high frequencies in a physical sense so much. The top end was fantastic.

Do you take the same approach in miking guitars?

Oh, yeah. Everything, really—just trying to do things differently, trying to get a different sound that hasn't been done before. I think everybody's blazing a trail to a certain extent; you want to add your stamp to things.

What's the oddest idea you tried that actually ended up being used and really worked?

Hmmm. Let me think about that. (pause) In one recent session that was rather rushed, I had a snare mic on the top and another mic on the bottom, [routed to] separate tracks. When I listened to the track back later, I found that the preamp must have been too high on the bottom mic, because it was distorted all the way through. Not tremendously, but certainly distorted. And that actually created an effect which I think is part of the sound. It was a kind of compression thing that beneficially affected the sound of that mic.

I also remember recording an elecric guitar once, and I had two or three mics set up, and I chose an AKG C28, which is a valve [tube] mic. About three hours later, I was wandering around the studio, and I found the assistant had set up the mics in an odd way. The C28 has a pencil mic kind of shape, and you're supposed to point it at things, but it has a grille that extended 'round the side of the mic. The assistant engineer thought it was the kind of mic you sang into from the side and that was the way he pointed it at the amp, so it was pointing up in the air. But it actually sounded better than the other mics that were positioned in the correct fashion. That was an interesting discovery.

So it's worth trying to face your mic in different directions.

It's definitely worth doing that. It's a combination of knowing the "official" way to do things and using those techniques when they sound good, but also not being afraid to break the rules. I think that's very much in the tradition of English engineering—breaking the rules, being a maverick, doing stuff wrong. Mind you, a lot of engineers have done things wrong because they actually didn't know what was the right thing in the first place, but that doesn't matter. It's the end result that counts.

What do you listen for when you make a decision to work with an artist? What can they do to get your attention?

There are classic things, like the songs. That's a major, major thing. The style, the writing. Originality is very important. I think it's almost more important for a singer to have something about them which is identifiable than it is for them to be a technically good performer. Certainly, originality is more important than being technically good. Originality in terms of the vocal performance and originality in terms of the musical concept—the instrumentation, the way you've chosen to arrange the songs, the way you play the instruments or program the instruments. There's so much stuff out there that you've got to compete somehow.

Do you prefer to hear a fairly finished demo?

Oh, no, no.

So a simple piano/vocal demo will work for you.

Sure, because that's the song. Again, that's a classic thing: a good song will stand up if it's played with very basic accompaniment: vocal/acoustic guitar, vocal/piano.

But that's a song demo as opposed to an artist demo.

Yes, except that you still have the voice. If somebody sends me demos of vocal and guitar or vocal and piano, that will tell me half of it, I guess. From my point of view, I prefer to hear some kind of musical realization on their part because I find it more difficult working with an artist who doesn't have a clear idea of how they want their musical identity to emerge. The artist needs to have some idea of the sort of record they want to make, the sort of things they want their musicians to play. I feel a little uncomfortable when I'm working with solo artists who expect the producer to create that. I guess that's because I'm not a writer myself, although I dabbled in it a bit. But even if I was a writer, that's a collaboration; that's not really a producer working with an artist. So I like working with artists who are pretty clear on what they like and what they want, with some scope for movement. I like working with artists who are pretty strong about what they want as well.

A lot of producers would not say that.

No, they wouldn't. I've never believed in the producer's record; I don't really like that idea. I don't think I have a particular sound; it's just not appropriate for me. My job is to realize the musical vision that the artist has. You work with the artist, and the artist says—and they may not verbalize this, but it may come out in the way they perform—these are the songs I write, this is the way I like to perform, this is the way I think I'm going to get it across to people, and this is the kind of musical environment I want to create. Then it's the producer's and engineer's job to realize that, to show them how to do it.

Do you tend to engineer your own records?

It varies. It's something I decide as I go along in preproduction. It depends on the kind of record, the way that we are going to go about it. Generally, I prefer to do it all myself because you get there quicker. However, one of the advantages of having an engineer for the recording is that you can sit back and get a bit more distant with the way you're hearing things. Also, if you're working with an engineer who has something to contribute, then you've got another source of good ideas. Mixing I always do myself because it is instant—I just go ahead and do it. It's very frustrating for me personally to describe what we need to do to the snare. I suppose I could work with an engineer and let him do that and be very, very overall in terms of comments, but I don't think I'd enjoy that very much. I like to actually be doing it; I like it to be *my* mix. Maybe that's an ego thing, but I enjoy doing it, so why not?

What is the essential difference between the role of the engineer and that of the producer?

The roles are becoming very blurred. Coming up as a staff engineer, I worked with a lot of producers who were completely and totally in control; the engineer was there to realize what he wanted, and it was his production. But I also worked with a lot of producers where I was getting into that realm; I was half producing the record. That happens a lot, as everybody knows. All we've got is a record or CD with the credits that say produced by Joe and mixed and engineered by Fred, but nobody really knows who did what. It might have been the keyboard player in the band—who is going to be a producer in two years time— who actually contributed more to the production than either the producer or the engineer. We don't have enough words to describe what people do when we talk about the way records are made.

But if you're an experienced engineer, then you've got that direct experience of what mics sound like, what you can do with a combination of a mic and a compressor. You're just that much more familiar with how you can get a particular sound from a particular instrument, so you can get it much more quickly. Again, in the sense that the sound cannot be divorced from the music, you're tapping into what's going to happen to that musical part directly. A producer who is musical but doesn't have that link to the sound has got to rely on his engineer to do that.

"We don't have enough words to describe what people do when we talk about the way records are made."

What are the common mistakes you are hearing in tapes that are coming out of project studios?

It's difficult to answer that, because they're not really mistakes. It's just to do with skill, and again to a large extent it comes out of experience for which there's no substitute. Things like not being able to use a compressor in the right way, not knowing whether something is too compressed or not compressed enough, over-equalization.

I've listened to a few records recently—finished CDs which have been recorded digitally—and the reason I haven't liked the sound of these records is because there's something about the transients which are excessive, particularly in cymbals and drums. There's an aspect of digital recording which results in transients being too present, for me, anyway. The hit of the stick on the cymbal is too clear, too apparent. It's something which needs controlling.

It's very difficult to describe, but one of the benefits of analog is that those transients are controlled, and they enable a blend of the instruments which is very appropriate and very pleasing to me. A lot of digitally recorded releases are made on low budgets, and that's usually the reason for it: lack of expertise and cheaper digital formats where those transients aren't being controlled. As a result, the instruments aren't blending properly, and a cymbal crash, for example, is sticking out too much and dominating the listening experience. It's inappropriate because it distracts your attention from the main event, which is the vocalist. That sense of how to deal with what's happening in a digital recording is something that you need to have an awareness of. So I think a pitfall that's being fallen into is the allure of those transients.

When you put a microphone up and you start getting a drum sound, the fact that digital recording preserves and in some ways actually accentuates those transients is something which initially can be appealing. You think, oh wow, that sounds like quality. It's like sometimes when you add high frequencies to a sound, it immediately makes it shine more and you think, oh, that's better. But it isn't necessarily better. It's just that you're being kind of drawn into that; it's seductive, I suppose. I suspect that some engineers and studios are perhaps being attracted to that in an inappropriate way, so that those transients are just too dominant in the recording.

What techniques can you use to tame those transients?

One of the things that I've really only learned in the past three or four years is that, if you're going to record on a digital medium, you can't expect to use the same mics you've used for analog. There's an upper midrange quality that can be accentuated by digital, [a quality] which was always smoothed off by analog. So you could use a mic that had a spike—an upper mid boost to it—on an electric guitar or a cymbal, something that maybe had a tendency to be a bit harsh. Because the signal was going to analog tape, it would be dealt with. When you record on digital, it's going to be enhanced, so you need to choose a mic which has got less of that upper mid. Choose an Audio Technica or a B & K or an Earthworks—there are several mics which have been developed in the past five or ten years which have a smooth top end and nice, smooth low-frequency response but not much midrange enhancement. Those kind of mics are a bit more appropriate for recording spiky sounds or transient sounds. So that's one thing: use a different mic.

Distortion? There's lots of different kinds of distortion. Distortion can be viewed as a kind of compressor in a sense. There's a squaring off of the signal that prevents it from going beyond a certain point, which is what a compressor does. But distortion—I don't mean a kind of fuzz necessarily, although you can experiment with that as well—is a way of controlling the transients. It can be very mild. When people talk about what valves [tubes] do to warm the sound, it's a kind of distortion

So one idea is to put it through some kind of tube before it's in the digital domain.

Yeah, or anything. You could use a distortion pedal—you don't have to set it to full-on—or even put it through just a line amp that's not a terribly high-fidelity line amp. I got something in a junk shop the other day which was designed as a kind of PA amplifier—I think you're supposed to connect speakers to the back of it, and if you're in an office and you want to talk to the factory floor, you press a button and you talk into a built-in electret mic, and the sound of your voice comes out of a speaker the other side of the hall. It was cheap, so I bought it on a lark, thinking it might have a good sound. It's this hideous orange plastic box, and it's got built-in distortion, but it's quite a mild distortion that might be quite useful. So there are lots of devices that aren't really distortion boxes; they're just amplifiers that aren't that good. You can use them subtly to tame those things. Compression with a very fast attack—you need to have a fast attack to really cut the front off sounds—a lot of compressors have attack controls that go right down, so that's something worth looking at.

Do you tend to record everything on analog tape or just drum tracks?

It depends on the project. My philosophy is that, if possible, everything should go through one analog generation somewhere along the line, even if it's the half-inch mix. It's better, though, if it's before that because it helps to blend the instruments. I find it more difficult to get instruments to blend together when they've all been recorded in a digital format. If you're leaving the analog process to the end, then you're not going to hear it until you play back the analog tape, so it's a bit limiting. The analog process is perhaps not essential for vocals, but I think it helps drums. But that doesn't mean you have to record on analog first; I've done a lot of projects where I've used Pro Tools as a tape machine and then copied it to analog at some later date. A lot of people work like that with ADAT, for example. Again, you're not hearing the effect until after you've done the recording, so it involves a certain amount of experience to know to record onto the ADAT and to listen into the future. You've got to think, well, it sounds like this at the moment, but I know that when it comes back off the two inch [analog tape], it's gonna be smoothed off a bit.

Analog tape does have a beneficial effect on a lot of instruments straight off the bat. There are different ways you can achieve that. If you're working with hard disk, and you've got an analog quarter-inch machine sitting in the corner, you can come out of the hard disk through the quarter-inch machine back to hard disk, and then slide the track back into place to compensate for the delay. It's easy to do that—you know what a tape time delay is, so you just match that. So you can use the analog tape machine as a processor, working that way.

When you're mixing, in what order do you bring faders up? What are you listening for, and what are you thinking about?

I start off with an initial mental picture of how the song is supposed to sound—a general kind of personality for the mix. If it's something I've recorded, then I know what's on the tape, and I would have been recording with the mix in mind anyway, so I'm halfway there. Then it's a matter of just trimming, because I've done so many monitor mixes in between time, and I know how things can blend. The panning positions are probably already worked out, and most of the compression will have been done. If it's a track that I'm not that familiar with, then I'd listen to everything up and get some kind of a rough balance.

If it's a rhythm section oriented thing, then I'd probably work from the drums up, but I wouldn't listen in solo to the drums. I generally mix on an SSL, and I generally tend to assign each group of instruments to its own VCA master fader. So I'll have the drums on one, the bass on two, the guitars on three, acoustic guitars on four, keyboards on five, etc. I'll pull all the faders down to about -15 [dB] except for the drums, and I'll leave those up so I can work on the drum sound while listening to the other instruments at a reduced volume. That way, you're still listening in context. It's very easy to solo the snare or solo the highhat and spend half an hour working on the highhat sound, only to find that it doesn't work with the rest of the kit, let alone with the rest of the instruments.

Are vocals the last thing that you work on?

Well, you kind of move them around. All the midrange instruments have to be related in terms of their frequency band and the musical harmonic aspect. The vocals have to relate to the guitars and keyboards; generally, the vocals are in that midrange, so there's no point in getting a bunch of guitar sounds that leave no space for the vocals. So I'll work on the guitars for a bit while listening to the vocal. Whilst you are doing that, you are kind of with another ear listening to the sort of problems there are in the vocal sound that need to be dealt with. For example, if it's a song which has a quiet verse and a loud chorus, then it's very common for a singer's voice to develop a hard edge when he's singing loudly, which doesn't happen when he's singing quietly. So while you are doing the drums and guitar, you might be thinking, well, perhaps I'm going to have two channels for the vocals—one for the quiet parts and one for the loud parts.

An alternative to that may be using a frequency band compressor where you control that particular hardness factor in the vocals. The problem with using static EQ to get rid of the hardness is that it might solve the problem of the vocal in the chorus, but when the quiet verse is being performed, it will lack some presence because you've taken out some 4 or 5 k. So you could use a frequency band compressor to control that band. I use a BSS DPR901, which is four band; it's a really, really good device for controlling that kind of thing. It has a sidechain [listen function] so you can tune one band to that problem area. I use it a lot, particularly in vocals.

Another thing I do is that I have an AudioDesign Scamp rack, and I have a couple of modules which are frequency splitters designed for band compression for radio use. You put a signal in, and it's got four outputs for low, low/mid, high/mid, and high, so you can split the frequency signal up into four components. But then it has four inputs which combine those four components back to the original, so if you take the four feeds out and put them straight back in again, there's no difference in sonic quality because it's designed to have no phase shift; if the gains of those bands were changing and there was a phase shift between the bands, you'd get a swooshing effect. So it means you can take just one band of the signal, compress it and do whatever you want with it—pan it, whatever—but if you process it in a mono way, you can feed it back in with the other bands. You can compress just one band, and it works really, really well—it's fantastic. I use it in conjunction with four dbx 160 compressors—one on each band. The nice thing about those compressors is that each one has an output level control, so you can do the compressing and then balance up the four bands as they are mixed back together

So in effect you're equalizing as well.

It's dynamic equalization, but you can have a different compressor on each band. You don't have to recombine them through its combining network; you can bring those four signals up on the desk, and you can use different effects on the different bands of the vocals. You can put them through four auto panners and have them moving around in different frequency bands in the vocals, which is quite a nice effect. You can add a digital delay just to the upper mid, you can pan the high frequency just on one side and have the lower mid on the other hand side, things like that.

And presumably you've done all these things.

(laughs) Oh, sure. I simply realized when I started messing around with these boxes that you can split the signal up into these bands with a hi-fi respect for the quality. It's quite transparent; it doesn't compromise the sound in any way. It just splits and recombines if you want to. But once you've got those four components, you can do all kinds of things; you can use a phaser on just the high frequency. Again, vocals are one of those things that changes its character quite a lot, and so quite often you need to control narrow bands. So it's very good for that.

You could probably do that very easily with digital devices, but this way you have the benefit of working in the analog domain, so things are being smoothed out.

Exactly.

Do you have any general advice for the reader who wants to be the next Mick Glossop?

Just don't be afraid to experiment. That's very important. Most of what we do comes down to experience, and there's no substitute for that. So just spend a lot of time on it and mess around and experiment. Do crazy things, break the rules. And if you like the sound of it, then that's great. Have confidence in your own subjectivity; if it appeals to you, and you think it fits with what you are doing, then do it. You don't have to be purist about things. If it sounds good, then it doesn't matter how you got that sound.

Selected Listening:
Van Morrison: *Too Long In Exile*, Polydor, 1993; *Hymns To The Silence*, Polydor, 1991; *Enlightment*, Mercury, 1990; *Poetic Champions Compose*, Mercury, 1987; *No Guru, No Method, No Teacher*, Mercury, 1986; *Inarticulate Speech Of The Heart*, Warner Bros., 1983; *Into The Music*, Warner Bros., 1979; *Wavelength*, Warner Bros., 1978
Frank Zappa: *Shut Up 'N Play Yer Guitar*, Rykodisc, 1981; *Joe's Garage*, Rykodisc, 1979
John Lee Hooker: *Don't Look Back*, Virgin, 1997
Lloyd Cole: *Love Story*, Fontana, 1995

Mike Hedges

P roducer Mike Hedges started as an engineer in the late 1970s, at the height of punk mania. Since then he has gone on to work with an eclectic group of artists that includes Manic Street Preachers, The Cure, The English Beat, Marc Almond, Alex Harvey, and Siouxsie And The Banshees. His studio in France boasts a unique unusual acoustic design—which he described in this interview in detail—as well as the legendary mixing console used for the Beatles' *Abbey Road* album. Though tall—even imposing—in stature, Hedges is soft-spoken and introspective, the kind of producer you imagine would act as a sea of calm in even the most volatile studio situations.

What does it take for a new artist to catch your ear? What are the ingredients you listen for in a demo?

Voice, first. The vocals and the vocalist are very, very important. It doesn't have to be a great singer; it needs to be a great vocalist. There's a big difference between the two. It's something to do with performance, something to do with attitude in the vocal. Someone who can sing a song perfectly in tune and perfectly in time doesn't necessarily have what it takes to be a great singer or a great vocalist. The second thing is, if one of the songs is fantastic and the vocals are nearly there, again, that would be very interesting to me.

> **"Someone who can sing a song perfectly in tune and perfectly in time doesn't necessarily have what it takes to be a great vocalist."**

But even if one of the songs is great, if the vocals are nowhere near, I wouldn't touch it. These days, you can go into the studio and use Pro Tools and Auto-Tune and things like that, but if you're in the position where you can actually get the vocal 95 percent of the way there even before you start sticking it in Pro Tools, that's the way to go. Why spend a week retuning and retiming vocals? It does happen, though—there are artists who look fantastic and have a certain persona, but they can't sing a note. You can make them sound great-ish but not great.

How do you generally approach the start of a new recording project?

It depends on the band. Some bands can play live; others don't have the ability to play as a live band and have it great. The ones that sound good play together; they basically go straight into the studio, recording and rearranging as necessary. The ones that don't sound good, they have a choice of two things. One is to really rehearse in preproduction and spend several days

per song, rehearsing it and rehearsing it and rehearsing it till they get it to a certain stage and then go into the studio and do it. Then there are the bands that are never going to be able to play it, and then you have to say, "Well, let's get someone else in to play this particular instrument." The reason for that is I really like to put down a pretty good approximation of the finished track straight away as a backing track. It's important for the atmosphere and the feel and the vibe. It's important to get it as early as possible. You know that you've rehearsed enough when you actually put it down on the second or third take. I don't like having to do 7, 10, or 15 takes—I think that's killing it, really.

When you're going for this live feel, do you use a lot of mic leakage, or are you looking for optimum isolation?

It depends on the feel of the backing track I want. In the studio I have in France, the bass amp will go in a cupboard with sound-proofed doors. If you close the doors, you don't hear it; you open the door a crack and you hear a bit of it. So if you have a bass player playing with the drums, you just open the doors until you get the right amount of spill, if you want spill. It's exactly the same thing with the guitars—all the guitar amps are inside cupboards of their own, so you have complete spill or no spill.

My whole studio was built around this concept of having a big live room for the drums, where the whole band can stand around the drum kit and have no spill. Or you can open things out, and the whole thing is bleeding onto everything else. I'm not sure I should say this until I get a patent! (laughs) It really works well; it's an incredibly good way of recording.

Because of this, the headphone balance is the one absolutely crucial thing when it comes to doing backing tracks. The hardest part is to get everybody hearing themselves comfortably so they can concentrate on getting their part right. For awhile, there was this thing where everyone had their own headphone balance, but it wasn't a great way of doing things because people tend to have too much of themselves and don't play with the rest of the band. Using headphones and bleed, you can get it so people can all play in the same room and actually hear each other and hear themselves at the same time. One of the hardest things about that original backing track recording is the communication between yourself and the band, and between the band and themselves.

Some producers will actually put together a fairly complete semi-master in the headphone mix. They'll put effects in, they'll even strap a limiter across the bus to make it sound like a record.

Again, it depends on the band. Some bands don't like it to sound too good in the headphones; they like it crunchy and mono and right at the front. With others, you do exactly that—you add different effects to different instruments, almost like a mix. I sometimes strap a limiter and an EQ across the headphones so I can add a bit more bass to the overall headphone mix, taking a little bit of the top out if necessary so it's pumping the limiter a bit more.

I don't use too many effects on the headphones because, for me, the ideal on the backing track is to have no effects. You want to get a backing track of a band playing live that sounds great, vibey, punchy, even though you've done nothing to it—no overdubs, virtually no EQing. If you can get it to sound really good really early on, then you're halfway there. Then, as soon as you start glossing it up, you're three quarters of the way there.

That approach can also inspire the players to work that bit harder when they're doing overdubs.

Definitely. Also, you get an atmosphere from the track early on, so that when you start re-placing guitars and basses and things, you can always go back to that and say, "Hang on, are we losing something here? The bass sounds better, sure, but has it got what that live take had?" And if it hasn't got what that live take had, then you Pro Tools off the live take and fix the bit that's wrong: That bit's late, pull it a tiny bit earlier. Use it to analyze which are the best bits and keep those.

Do you tend to use a lot of mics on drums or do you take a more basic approach?

Both. Sometimes we use two [mics]—bass drum and overhead—or even just one overhead in mono, compressed up. And sometimes we can have twelve, fourteen mics on the kit. It really depends on the song, the band, the drum kit. A fantastic sounding drum kit hit right and hit in the right places can sound good with two or three mics. We often use two mics—one over-head and one on the bass drum—and then move the overhead mic to get the sweet spot. You tend to use quite a lot of compression when you do that, so you have that sort of beefy, roomy, John Bonham sound.

How do you search for that sweet spot with the one overhead mic?

You do it with your ears. You walk around the drum kit, listen to where you hear the power of the bass drum, and put the bass drum mic there. Then you listen upstairs and move the overhead an inch, two inches, five inches, until you get it right. It's as simple as that.

Would the bass drum mic be very close in or would it be a foot or two back?

Not very close in; you generally have the bass drum mic nearly as far away as the snare mic would be. So you have it out in front of the bass drum, and if you want a bit more crack on the sound, you'll actually be moving it in. There are so many ways of miking up a drum kit. When I was engineering, I was taught what we used to call the Glyn Johns way, which was three mics on a kit—bass drum and two overheads—both two and a half stick's length from the snare. One is over the floor tom, looking towards the snare, and the other one's directly over the center of the snare. Then you have to adjust one of them for phase. And the bass drum mic is just in front of the bass drum, not in it. After awhile, we started getting quite radical and started putting the bass drum mic in the bass drum, next to the skin. Also, at the same time, I was working with engineers that adopted the '70s way of having top and bottom mics on every single drum.

> **"The Glyn Johns way was three mics on a kit—bass drum and two overheads—both two and a half stick's length from the snare. One is over the floor tom, looking towards the snare, and the other one's directly over the center of the snare."**

The same thing with guitars—I almost always put a 57 right in close to the speakers. Depending where you have it—outer speaker or inner speaker—you get the difference in tone from the edge of the speaker and the center of the cone. I use a Sennheiser MKH 40 the same way—use it in close with the 57, or back it up for a bit more room. Because the guitars are in boxes—they aren't just cupboards, they're designed so you don't get too much phase problems and things like that—you can't really get the furthest mic more than two or three feet away from the speaker while recording backing tracks. I tend to use two amps as well. If it's a clean sound you're after, you can set up one amp with the clean sound you want and then overdrive another amp in a cupboard with the doors closed, and record that as well. Sometimes we even use three amps, depending on the song. When you record that, you've got to multi-track so you've got two or three tracks of guitar: one clean, one medium—say, half-driven—and then one really driven. As the song progresses, you might use the nice clean track during the verse; as you are coming to the bridge you fade in the heavier guitar sound, then back it off a bit; into the chorus with everything full on, then back to the next verse and drop it all out. It's all done on one guitar track so it doesn't sound like you've done ten guitar overdubs. It has a different quality; it sounds like a live performance, but you've got real dynamics in the sounds. It's a very effective technique.

You can take the same approach with drum kits. If you're using close mics as well as room mics on the drum kit, you don't have to have both in all the time. If you're coming to the chorus, you can fade the ambience into your drums at the same time you're fading the crunch into the guitars. The effect is like you're just swooping up into the chorus, with real power, and filling out. Then you just cut them both at the end of it, when it goes back to the next verse, and it goes voom! You've suddenly got this wall of sound cut into a vacuum.

Do you typically record a bass amp track or do you just use the DI?

I always use both, full range. The advantage of having both the bass DI and amp is that it gives you a lot of control over the space the bass is occupying, where it fits into the song. Obviously, the DI's got no life to it—it's a dead, close-up, quite Motown-y sound, which is pleasant. It's one of my favorite sort of sounds, but if you have the amp as well, you have two distinct sounds that you can phase against each other. If you put the DI out of phase, for example, and EQ all the middle into it and take all the bass and top out, and then fade that in, out of phase with the amp, you've got a completely different bass sound. Or you can do it the other way round. It's amazing—when you have a bass amp track that's a bit woofy, and it's taking up too much space, try EQing the DI against it, put it out of phase and slide it in again; it will actually take parts of the sound out. So I'll always have a bass amp as well as a DI.

So you're nulling out certain frequencies between the two; in effect you're equalizing by phase cancellation.

Yes, phase against EQ.

Do you typically compress or limit while you're recording the bass?

We compress *everything* a bit going to tape. A lot of the equipment in my studio came from Abbey Road, including the TG console—a very, very famous console which has 44 built-in compressors, though it's got very simple EQ, so most of the work we have to do in getting a sound is mic placement and microphones themselves. The board does have plenty of bass controls: one that's just bass plus and minus, and then there's a very accurate multichoice bass frequency. There's just one other EQ, which is presence. It goes from 800 Hz up to 10 k, but very broad, so it's not really 10 k—it's more 5 to 15 k.

Our main recording machines are two 16-tracks, which also came from Abbey Road. They were originally one inch 8-track, but we put in two inch head blocks—one is the old hard head block, which I much prefer the sound of. I run the multitracks at 15 ips because the sound is so much superior to 30, and I use Dolby A —I don't like the sound of SR. The backing tracks are recorded on one or two 16-track machines, depending on how many tracks we use. I then usually transfer into a 24-bit Pro Tools system to cut together the final take, and then put it back to analog for the overdubs. Sometimes, though, the backing track is complete, and I just start working on it.

Usually, I copy the 16-track master so it can be put away and not played until the final mix. On the copy, I'll do stereo drums, mono bass, stereo guitars, and end up with however many tracks are left for overdubs. I'll overdub on that 16-track, get the masters of the guitars, the vocals, whatever, compile them in Pro Tools, and put them back to a fresh 16-track, which also doesn't get played until the mix. The disadvantage of going in and out of Pro Tools is far outweighed by the advantage of the editing control you have over the individual sounds.

What's your mix format of choice?

I mix to half inch analog 80 percent of the time, but I mix to Pro Tools the other 20 percent of the time, simply because it's multitrack; you put down your backing track, you put down your vocals in stereo, you put down your backing vocals in stereo. You can split it and end up with a submix master.

I know the mix is important, but in an ideal world it's just a formality. I always want the rough mixes we've done up to the mixing stage to sound pretty good. Sometimes on the way to Pro Tools or when putting it back to tape, I've put signal through the desk and re-EQd it, so I've ended up with it at least partly submixed. So you should be able to throw up all the faders, and in five minutes it should sound good.

> *"I know the mix is important, but in an ideal world it's just a formality."*

Presumably you're hearing a fair number of tapes that are coming out of project studios. What are the common mistakes that people are making in their recordings?

I don't think they're making mistakes at all. A lot of the project studio stuff I'm hearing is fantastic. It's been harder and harder for me now because I hear a demo that somebody's done and I think, well, what would I do to this? OK, I can take it into the studio and rerecord it, but I would like to keep the vocals they've done because they're really good. And I really like that guitar effect; let's try and keep that. It's not uncommon now to start with that demo and work on it.

The main disadvantage in demos is drum sounds. Project studios often don't have live rooms, they haven't got loads of mics. On some songs, that can work, but it's touch and go, really, because you're so limited by what you can do. You've got to record your drums on 12 or 14 tracks so you can sweep your overheads in for the second bridge and back out again.

But I think in the future most recording will be done at home; I really see it going that way. People will just go into studios to take something that 10 percent further that you can't possibly do in a home studio. Where you've got 50 or 60 microphones to choose from, you've got large ambient spaces, you've got the big multitrack facilities where you can actually listen comfortably to 60 tracks at a time if you want to. I think more and more album tracks will be done at home, and then people will tend to polish up some of the tracks in the bigger studios.

Selected Listening:
Siouxsie And The Banshees: *A Kiss In The Dreamhouse*, Geffen, 1982; *Nocturne*, Geffen, 1983; *Hyaena*, Geffen, 1984; *Through The Looking Glass*, Geffen, 1987; *Peep Show*, Geffen, 1988.
Manic Street Preachers: *Everything Must Go*, Epic, 1996
The Cure: *Three Imaginary Boys*, Fiction, 1979; *Seventeen Seconds*, Elektra, 1980; *Faith*, Elektra, 1981; *Happily Ever After*, A&M, 1981
Marc Almond: *Stories Of Johnny*, Virgin, 1985; *A Woman's Story*, Some Bizarre, 1986
The Beautiful South: *Welcome To The Beautiful South*, Elektra, 1989; *Choke*, Elektra, 1990

Stephen Hague

With one foot in England and the other in his native U.S., Stephen Hague has a unique perspective on the art of making records. Keyboardist and cofounder (with Jules Shear) of the short-lived, late-'80s cult band Jules And The Polar Bears, Hague soon forged an alternative career as one of the most prolific alternative music producers, crafting hits for Erasure and Orchestral Manoeuvres In The Dark, as well as collaborating with the Sex Pistols' infamous manager Malcolm McLaren, and equally infamous lead singer, Johnny Rotten, on several of his post-Pistols Public Image Limited offerings. Work with other new wave/next wave artists followed, including Jane Wiedlin, Pere Ubu, New Order, Siouxsie And The Banshees, and, more recently, with English chart-toppers Blur, Manic Street Preachers, and Marc Almond. In between, he's even found time for a few mainstream projects, including a string of albums with teen-idol Pet Shop Boys, as well as Robbie Robertson's 1991 offering, *Storyville*.

We spoke with Hague shortly before he was to leave his home studio in Woodstock, New York and begin yet another six-month journey to England. Despite what had to have been a hectic time, he calmly shared his views about the art of making hit records on both sides of the Atlantic.

You came into production from a musical background as opposed to an engineering background. How do you think that changes the approach to making records?

I've been on sessions as a player when the producer was primarily an engineer, and I always found the lines of communication to be easily confused. Often you wouldn't know exactly what the guy was getting at—he'd be after more of a sensation than dealing with the specifics of musical arrangements or things like bar structure. Whereas when you're on a session with a producer that comes from a musical background, you're talking the same language right from the word go. As a producer, I've worked with several excellent engineers who've struggled with things like, "Can you take it from bar three of the chorus?" and things like that. I always feel for them because they have to feel a bit outside the thing. And then I've worked with other engineers who had quite a straight-up musical background—one in particular was David Jacob; he was able to relate to string players on a level that I couldn't.

I think that a producer who has a background as a musician has a sympathetic view of the players and the comfort levels of the session, and also has a better grasp on the line of communications. I find I tend to be more sensitive musically overall. I'm not saying that they can't be great producers, but when you look at a lot of engineer/producers, they often end up coproducing with a quite strong-willed artist. Someone like that can be quite successful, but generally only if they team up with someone who provides a strong musical presence in the studio.

Do you think every artist needs a producer?

It's case by case. One of my favorite records last year was by a new artist who produced his own album, and I was thinking of getting in touch with him with an eye towards working together. But he did such a great job, I think I would just fuck it up! (laughs) As far as somebody starting out and making their first record and producing themselves, it's a tough call. It really depends on their personality. Some people can get completely lost in it and get side-tracked onto all the wrong issues and lose oversight, or they can do something that no producer could ever do because they have the kind of hyper-vision that only they can have.

But the producer is supposed to be the guy with the objective ears. Can an artist ever have enough objectivity to really be able to see their work better than a third party could?

No, not in my opinion. But then that's not necessarily the end-all and be-all of what makes for a great record. Todd Rundgren makes fabulous records producing himself, and they still sound very cool to me today.

But another issue is the involvement of the record company in making records, which I think has changed a lot. I'm talking about the way people try and push things around; how they feel it's part of their job. And perhaps it *is* really part of their job—it's become a lot more cut-throat as far as how long an act is developed and how many records they're able to put out. In the '60s, all those great records were being made, and all the record companies were doing was kind of saying— it's done, cool, we'll put it out. It was made by the kids for the kids, aside from a couple of key music guys. A lot of the companies, particularly the smaller ones, were run by radio people, and it was just a side business. They weren't putting their fingers into all the product going out, but now it's really, really different—I see a lot of records get lost that way.

One common thread that seems to run through a lot of your records is that the artists always sounds very relaxed; they always sound like they're enjoying being there, and as a result they give a great performance. What kind of techniques have you come up with through the years to elicit the best performance out of artists?

Well, there's always a vibe in the studio, although I'm not one of those kind of guys who does a lot of scene-setting. One really important thing in the studio environment is that everything works, because there's nothing worse than starting to get someplace and have a piece of equipment go down. But beyond that, just try and keep it relaxed and not make it too precious or pressurized. There are situations where the schedule has you under the gun, and things have a different dynamic. But in general, particularly with vocalists, I always stress the fact that the singing can take place any time they want, for the most part, and at all different points across the running of the project. I've always found it dangerous to set aside a week where you have to do all the backing vocals or all the vocals, because that's when the vocalists tend to get sick. (laughs) I'll also do a lot of takes with the vocalist so as not make them feel like, if they blow something, then they can't go on. I don't like that process where you keep singing the first verse over and over again and you keep dropping in and you grab a line here and there. I like to do linear takes, and as many as they've got in them. People usually peak after a few takes, and then you might do a couple more where you might catch a few things. Afterwards, I'll sit down and I'll do a comp of the vocals to one track and then listen to it with the artist. At that point, we may find that we got some of it but not all of it, so I'll often do another round of vocals, but usually at a later date. It's all designed to make it so they are never really on the spot. That's actually the opposite way that a lot of great records were made in the '60s, when they would go in for three hours and come out with something that we still listen to today. But it's just a way of doing vocals that works for me.

What do you listen for in terms of a great vocal take? When do you know it's nailed?

That's one of those quite abstract things, like so many times during this process. It's very, very subjective and very much a matter of taste. Sometimes I'll hear records where I will just be sure that that singer could have delivered something more, but they might be very successful records. So it's sort of organic on one level, where what's right for the track is not necessarily the most blazing over-the-top vocal performance. It's not always the one where you're singing your guts out all the time, which I think can be a problem for a few artists out there right now. I don't really know how to answer that question, because it's a very subjective thing and it has to do with the nature of the song and the session and the singer.

Some of the work I did in the mid '80s was with some English acts where the singers weren't really singers per se. There was a really charming English thing—you know, that kind of "pretty boy who can't quite sing" thing—and I would often work really hard to get those sounding confident and upfront from somebody who's not actually confident or upfront. That's a case where you do lots of vocal takes and not worry about pitch and all that stuff, because I could alter the pitch later on in certain lines when the moment was there but the pitch wasn't. Having gone through that process with me—after I see them through it—then their confidence level can go up because they can see, "Well, I *can* sound good." That makes a difference to the session, particularly if you're doing an album. I always make a point with somebody who's not a great singer to try and get a couple of really good vocals together early on, whatever it takes, just so they have those under their belt and they feel better about themselves.

Well, what does it take? What means have you come up with to elicit that great performance?

Well, I don't like to over-analyze things as we're working. I'll say really simple things, like, "I think you should hit the chorus a little harder," or "I don't think you're getting the most out of that line." I'll make really simple suggestions—not particularly artistic suggestions as much as practical nuts and bolts kinds of things like louder, softer. Just to get somebody in the right ballpark and then often, when they're settled into the right basic way of singing it, that's when the multiple takes will start to pay off. Then you can always choose the best part.

Will you do the comps with the singer in the room with you?

I don't like people in there; I just like to pore through it myself. I also don't like for singers to hear those moments when they're really sounding rough. On the other hand, I'm doing a record right now with a new artist, and I've been doing the early comps with her—it was a good way to get to know her better and get to know her tastes better. Then later, I was able to do the comps on my own, and more to her liking. But in general, I like to do it myself, just as a taste thing. It's a way that I can set the tone and determine what's working best and also honestly discover what isn't working best.

But what if you and the singer don't see eye to eye on something?

It happens. I worked with one artist a couple of years ago who regarded it as interference when I would say, "That was a good take." (laughs) So, yeah, there have been a couple of tricky ones over the years. Some people get really wound up when they are doing vocals. They don't like to do it, and that kind of casts a bit of a pall on the session—there's this tension as they walk up to the mic. But that's not usually the case. Most people are there because they want to be there, and their insecurities aren't quite so rampant that they hold them back.

Do you go out in the studio and listen to the voice before recording it? Do you audition different mics, or do you leave that up to the engineer?

I certainly approve the mic selection as we go along. Of course, some singers sound better on some mics than others. With Chrissie Hynde, I actually used a Shure Beta 88, which is a hand-held mic, a stagey sort of thing, but there was something about it. It wasn't very detailed, but she has so much character in her voice that I didn't miss that part of it at all. Other people really only come to life on a really expensive Telefunken. Often with an album project that's just beginning, we'll set up five or six mics and just run through a couple of things while switching between them. You can usually tell pretty quickly. It's rare that we'll be in the middle of doing vocal takes and I'll change the mic.

At times, I've even used vocals or parts of vocals off low-quality demos, and you can almost always get things to match up if you really need to. I'm not downplaying the importance of mic selection, but on another level, what they're putting out is the most important thing. As long as, technically, it's not getting in your way, like major p's popping or sibilance. With some singers, the sibilance thing can be a factor in certain mics that you'd want to avoid.

Do you record vocals with compression?

Very, very light compression. For the past couple of years, I've usually been recording vocals to a Focusrite Red as the preamp. I usually bypass the mixing desk for most things—with drums, of course, you can't really avoid it.

So I just use a little bit of compression. That's one thing to really watch out for, because if you record something with too much compression, you can never get rid of it. Whereas if you just record it in such a way that you are not peaking out in your recording format, then you can add as much as you want at any point later in the process. But you can never, never get rid of that thing when someone sounds like they've got their face pressed up against a plate of glass; it's not always a pretty sight. On some things, it's perfect, and some singers that I've worked with like to hear a lot of compression in their phones while they're singing, but that's something that you just set up on a sidechain so that when they are getting their foldback it can be heavily compressed or really bright. Whatever they like to hear that gets them to do it, that's what I always try to give them.

I've talked to some producers that actually strap stereo compressors or limiters across the whole headphone mix so it sounds more like a record.

Yeah, I do that sometimes, too. I have a rack-mount SSL compressor, and I use that on foldback quite a lot. Or I'll set up things like a chain of one mono compressor strapped across the vocal into a stereo compressor strapped across the backing track. That way, whenever the vocals hit, the backing track will drop in level. They do that a lot on radio broadcast compressors, where whatever's loudest will force everything back down a bit.

Anyway, my tip for the kids is—don't record with too much compression, or you can really compress yourself into a corner.

Is there an "American sound" versus a "British sound"? If so, what's the difference?

> **"Don't record with too much compression, or you can really compress yourself into a corner."**

I find there to be quite a big difference. What finds its way onto radio in England—particularly national radio like BBC1—tends to be a bit more freewheeling than in the States. It can be a real big cross section of things—there's everything from Cliff Richard's Christmas prayer to French dance acts, which can be side by side on the charts—and that would be an extremely unusual situation in the U.S. Because it's such a free-for-all, it encourages a lot more different people to get involved.

Another area where it's different is that kids growing up in England are often encouraged by their folks to become pop musicians; in the States, that's either rare or definitely not as common as it is over there, where it's regarded as being a viable career alternative to working at the chip shop or something. In the U.S., parents will tend to say, "It's the last thing you want to do," or "Maybe after college."

Another area that I think makes a difference is the dole situation, where a kid can leave school after 16 or 17 and go straight onto the dole and have some source of income. I think if you were to survey a lot of kids who have hit it young in England or have really got something cool going in a young band, it's because they had that extra bit of latitude. That also encourages more of a personal approach to playing and handling instruments and things like home recording. In the U.S., if you leave school, the only way a musician can make a living, practically, is by learning how to play other people's music; going out and playing clubs and weddings and whatever you can get, in whatever kind of configuration you can arrange. People become very proficient on their instruments by starting out young playing clubs and bar bands and all that sort of stuff. At the same time, they're cutting their teeth, learning other people's songs and copying their guitar licks and solos and vocal styles. So they become a great conduit for other people's stuff, but they don't necessarily develop a sound of their own. Whereas in England that's the first question that gets asked—what do you sound like? And here's 90 pounds a week so you can find out.

Those are really more cultural differences. Do you think there are any technical differences between the sound of English records and the sound of American records?

I think what I've just been describing plays into that, particularly the self-taught aspect and how it's reflected in people having home studios. I do think that there is a cultural side to this question that has to do with people's attitudes: English musicians don't want to sound like somebody else, and they never had to experience themselves sounding like somebody else. That actually translates to the sound of the records. And also the English record companies, particularly in this day and age, figure into it in a slightly different way than the American companies do. There are still a lot of musical, "do the right thing by the artist" label people over there—in my experience, more so than in America.

Plus, engineers in England are less "by the book." If you have a mentor, oftentimes in the States, the protégé will carry on the tradition, whereas in England, the protégé can't wait until they can prove that they can do it better or cooler than the guy who taught him! (laughs) In the States, there's that thing about things being "tasteful" or "tasty"—you know, "that's a tasty lick"; you never hear that kind of talk in England. (laughs) Bands over there—especially when they are starting out—want to cause a lot of fuss and do it their way. Once again, I think it's somewhat cultural. Take American punk versus English punk: it was a whole different ball game. And the way that those records sounded, that was definitely a kind of socio-political event as well. Although there were some really good technical people involved in punk, like Chris Thomas producing the Sex Pistols.

A lot of punk musicians really could play; they were just dumbing themselves down for the market.

That still happens. A lot of people aren't always maxing out. It's like the guy who can play Steely Dan solos but instead he kind of pedals away on a couple of notes and that seems to be the perfect thing for a given solo on a given record.

You're primarily a keyboard player. How do you approach recording keyboards?

I have my setup configured in such a way that, when I'm looking for sounds, I take a signal out of the master MIDI controller into all my gear and then start auditioning with everything playing. Sometimes that can speed things up: instead of going through the libraries of one machine, I'll occasionally stumble on combinations that work. I'll often go through amps or effects pedals; I've got a [Line 6] Pod and I've been using that quite a lot for keyboards. I also use the Roland G3 Leslie simulator. It has an overdrive function that's not like any distortion box I've ever heard. I generally use it to emulate the sound of a rotary speaker being driven, but I often stop the rotary effect and just use the overdrive. I also went though a period where I was buying lots of those little tiny toy amps—the little plastic Marshalls and things like that—and overdriving those and putting a mic on them, sticking them in back of a room under a blanket. But everybody's doing all those kinds of tricks now—environmental things like putting an amp and a speaker out in a stairwell or in a chimney or something. If you're working in a home studio, you can try experiments like putting a Pignose in the shower and that sort of thing.

How do you typically record acoustic piano?

It depends on whether the piano is carrying the track. If that's the case, I'd often want to get the big professional well-miked sound. But I also like mono piano signals. I find the right place to place a relatively nondynamic mic and then compress it. I also record quite a lot of not particularly good pianos, spinets and uprights and stuff like that. Instead of struggling to get them to sound like a Steinway with four mics and loads of great outboard, I'll just put up a mic in a sympathetic spot around it somewhere.

Also, sample-wise, piano is getting a lot better now. The [Nemesys] Gigasampler has a stunning piano sample in it that's 3 gigs or something, so all that's getting pretty sophisticated.

Are you doing a lot of digital recording, or are you an analog guy?

I've been digital since 1984. I was one of the first guys over in England that was using the Sony 3324s—I had two of them, although I don't use them anymore. I never actually owned their 48-track, but I use it a lot, particularly when I get to the mixing stage. The Sonys can get a little crunchy up top, but that just became part of what I liked about them after awhile. But for the past three years, I've been using [Otari] Radars. They can get a little cranky sometimes, but I love them—they're really good machines. For a lot of guys moving over from analog, I would say the Radar is the closest—it does a bit of that thing that analog does.

I think analog is one of the great over-mystified formats. People couldn't wait to get away from acetate when tape came along, so now I wonder why everyone's struggling with letting go of analog. People know what it does to the signal—I use analog tape machines basically as a piece of outboard gear. I'll set up a Studer really, really hot to smash it onto the analog and then bring it back into digital.

Do you use tube gear the same way?

Not too much, no. When it comes to mix time, then lots of different outboard gear comes into play, but in the recording process, I like to use the Focusrite stuff—I've got their stereo mic preamps and compressors, plus some API things—and I think that sounds really good. I like to go through that kind of gear for the tape path.

Do you mix to analog?

I mix to DAT and half inch analog at the same time, and, while I often use the half inch, certain kinds of program material just sound better off the DAT.

So you'll multi-track digitally and then mix in the analog domain.

Yeah, that's the general rule, though I sometimes use the DAT mixes. I will use an analog console and analog outboard gear during the mix; I mix on an SSL, more or less exclusively.

Is the mix something you leave to your engineer, or are you very hands-on?

I'm very hands-on, though I don't like to set the mix up. There are two or three people that I like working with; we kind of know what to expect from each other. I really like someone to go in initially without me being there. Sometimes I'll go in when we're starting, just to say I have this or that in mind—so we don't have to backtrack later on—but as far as getting the bass drum sound together and establishing the spatial aspect, I know how to do it, but I just don't enjoy it. I think there is quite a valuable moment when I walk in and hear the mix the way they've set it up—it allows me to immediately spot the things that are not working for me. In the case of these guys who I work with regularly, there is almost always something that I wouldn't have heard quite like that—I wouldn't have set it up that way myself—but then I'll really like it. You can always put it back the way *you* would have had it, but you wouldn't get that moment where someone else contributed.

> *"People couldn't wait to get away from acetate when tape came along, so now I wonder why everyone's struggling with letting go of analog."*

I do all my own [fader] riding, though. Once the mix is set up, I sit down for a few hours and I establish all the final relationships. It's like everything else in this process—it's just a matter of taste. I certainly leave it to the engineer as to whether something is going to actually hit the mix tape OK as far as levels and signal to noise ratio and all that sort of stuff. Sometimes

I'll consult someone and say, "Is this going to be OK in the cut, compared to the high hat brightness?" and those kind of technical questions, but other than that it's really just a taste thing; I try to make it sound like I was always hoping it would sound.

What advice do you have for the reader who wants to be the next Stephen Hague?

Study the records that you love; that's what I did. Just listen, listen, listen. Also, you shouldn't listen to anyone who tries to tell you that you're doing something wrong—unless it's some obvious thing like making something stupendously noisy. It's good to have that signal-to-noise thing worked out—that just makes home recording more of a pleasure. But there really are no rules. Or at least there shouldn't be any.

Suggested Listening:
Jules And The Polar Bears: *Got No Breeding*, Columbia, 1978; *Fenetics*, Columbia, 1979; *Bad For Business*, Columbia, 1980
Orchestral Manoeuvres In The Dark: *Crush*, Virgin, 1985; *The Pacific Age*, Virgin, 1986
Blur: *Parklife*, SBK, 1994
Erasure: *The Innocents*, Sire/Reprise, 1988
Siouxsie And The Banshees: *Superstition*, Geffen, 1991
Pet Shop Boys: *Disco*, EMI America, 1985; *Please*, EMI America, 1986; *Very*, EMI, 1993; *Disco 2*, EMI, 1995

Steve Levine

Steve Levine is the rare professional producer who is also a home recording enthusiast. The miniscule studio in his London home is literally no bigger than a moderately sized walk-in closet, crammed from floor to ceiling with equipment. The vestibule outside serves as a makeshift vocal booth/overdub area, with the added advantage of glass doors leading to a small English garden.

Best-known for his work with Boy George and Culture Club—including their massive international hit, "Do You Really Want To Hurt Me?," Levine has kept up an active career that has seen him work with a broad range of artists, from rock guitarist Gary Moore to chanteuse Deniece Williams to the legendary Beach Boys. On the soggy afternoon when we meet, we're both under severe time constraints, but Levine nonetheless was gracious enough to share some of his perspectives on the art of home recording.

Tell me about your home studio—I've never seen so much equipment packed into such a small space!

I just did a track with Culture Club here, for their new album. I haven't worked with them for years, and it was really interesting for me, because that's the first time I've worked with them in this tiny little room. It's interesting the way these things happen. Originally, when I first moved to this house, I thought, I'll just set up a little editing/copying room, just to do the donkey [menial] work. But I was working with one particular act in a professional studio—we'd tracked the drums and everything, but we'd run out of time with the budget we had. I'd recorded onto ADATs—I've used them pretty much since they first came out. Anyway, the singer said, "Look, why don't we just try it back at your place?" So we did the vocals here, and when the A&R guy heard the tracks, he said, "Those are great vocals!" I think it's just down to the fact that the singer felt really relaxed.

From that moment, I started doing more and more work here. I had already been doing the programming and routing here, establishing things like keys, tempos, and song sections. But once you get something going, you just want to add more and more stuff to it and finish it off. Normally, I do recording here and mix outside, but I have done some mixing here, including that Culture Club track I was telling you about.

It's incredible that you can mix in here.

That's because the speakers [PMCs] are fantastic. They're phenomenally accurate within

this one small area, and their bass response is extraordinary. There's no room treatment, either, other than the fact that there's so much gear packed in here that there are no parallel surfaces anywhere! (laughs)

Most of the time I'm doing vocal work, so I'm on headphones. That's where this works incredibly well, because a large proportion of the time spent on records is now spent on the vocals, backgrounds as well as lead. It gives you the opportunity to develop a great relationship with the singers. Plus, you've got time on your side, so they can really listen to what they're doing. Very often you have to do a comp in order for them to hear how it needs to go, and then they come back and do it within one or two takes. Sometimes people experiment with things on the run-through takes; they may not necessarily hit the right note, but they're going in the right direction.

"When you're working on a vocal, you need the artist in peak condition."

As soon as they hear it back in context, it's much easier for them to get a picture of what needs to be done. Sometimes they'll take the tape home, go away for the weekend, come back on Monday and they're ready to sing.

Socially, working in the house is good, too. You eat well—you stop, and you have proper food. There are also hygiene issues—you tend to get ill less, because the cups go in the dishwasher and they're clean, things like that. When you're working in a commercial studio, you often get a cold or a sore throat because you're mixing with a lot of people. And when you're working on a vocal, you need the artist in peak condition. Those are small things that help towards that; it's clean, it's healthy, it's a good environment, and it's relaxed. In the summer, they can go out in the garden and get some sun; in the winter, the room is warm and cozy. If it's a nice, relaxed atmosphere, everybody feels at ease, and you get the best creative results.

One of the things that's revolutionized recording is the Line 6 amp; it's just made recording a breeze here. I'll even mic it up if it's being played at a reasonable level, and the guitar sounds I've been getting have been great. I've also recorded percussion overdubs here. The congas I've done here sound better than when I do them in the studio, because it's a very tight, controlled sound. Plus, I work with good players, so they bridge that gap between sampled and played; you can't really tell where the line begins and ends, which is how I think it should be.

There's home recording, and there are home studios. This is a home studio, and I make professional recordings here, whereas there are other people that do home recording, doing demos or works in progress, that kind of thing. The difference is that I use the finest mics, going into the finest mic preamps, through the finest cable, and into the finest converters; I've also got separate power in this part of the house.

How do you check the validity of your mixes?

Generally, I burn a CD and go play it in my car, drive around the block a few times. But if it sounds good on these speakers, it generally sounds good everywhere else. It's when you have speakers that are tricking you that you run into problems. Normally, it's the bass end that lets people down—you end up with not enough or too much because of a problem in the room. Nowadays, most speakers are manufactured to pretty good standards, so it's normally other factors that cause problems. I knew there might be problems in this room, so I chose speakers specifically for this room, auditioned lots of different ones right here.

What sort of things do you listen for on a demo that really make you want to work with any artist? What sort of things turn you off?

The song is always the most important thing. I've learned my lesson over the years—if you don't have a great song, it doesn't matter how good the production is. But the word "song" is quite broad; it can also mean a good idea for a song. For example, take "Bohemian Rhapsody." That's not a normal, traditional song—God knows what the demo of that sounded like!—but sometimes I can hear the concept in a demo that I'm sent, I can hear what they intend to do. So it doesn't have to be a traditional three-minute song, but it's got to be a good idea or concept for a song.

> **"If you don't have a great song, it doesn't matter how good the production is."**

For me, a demo needs to be as bare as possible. The more work that's done on the demo, the harder it is for me, because people are set in their ways; they can't see the forest for the trees.

What sort of common mistakes are people making in their home recordings?

Spending too long on things, and using things like Finalizers and squeezing the daylights out of the music. I don't mean to be derogatory—they are fabulous products, but they need to be used in the right hands. Still, so many people don't know what compression is, or don't know how to use it properly. By "properly," I mean either intentionally abusing the compression to get the snare drum to kind of smack you around the head, or using it for subtle gain riding, where you want to control the vocal properly. I have no problem with abusing equipment if you're specifically using it as an effect.

A lot of musicians now are expecting to become producers and engineers as well as musicians, and I don't think you can be good at all of them. I consider myself to be a good engineer and producer, a pretty good programmer, but a crap musician. I can get by for what I need to do, but I generally employ musicians, so I don't need to be good. I don't think it's important to be that good, because then you end up playing it yourself and you become less tolerant of other people who aren't as good as you. This way, I can work with musicians in bands that are terrible, and there's no intimidation because we're all at the same level! (laughs)

My strength is that, if an artist tells me, "This is what I want," I can try and fathom out what the hell they're talking about and try and apply it. You always need outside help.

A producer is a bit like an orchestra conductor in that you need to know how to do many different things. What's the most important skill to master?

Being a diplomat and having a good working relationship with artists. That will rise above everything else.

That's more important than having great ears or strong musical sensibilities?

Absolutely. When I was an engineer, I worked with lots of producers who knew absolutely nothing about making a record in the normal sense. They would spend their time taking the artist to lunch, doing those sort of things. But invariably they got good vocal performances because the artist felt so comfortable around them. They were almost like maitre d's. I have no problem with that at all, because if that's the strength that producer has, then fine.

When you're making a record, do you normally have a vision of the end product in mind? Are you always working towards a clearly defined end goal?

Absolutely, yeah. You never achieve 100 percent of it; I never have in my entire life. Sometimes you go down a road that meanders, but you do need to have a picture of the end result because you do need to work to a goal. But I'm totally flexible with regard to how I get there. Sometimes you'll do something, sometimes you'll make a mistake with a part, and all those lucky mistakes sometimes do things in the best sense.

Overproducing is a common problem. How do you know when to stop? What criteria do you use for deciding when a track is done?

It's like sawing legs off a table, particularly when you start manipulating too much stuff in hard disk recording. You start moving one thing, then that shows off the ugliness of something else, so you move another thing. I guess you just know when it's done. Experience, feel, vibe, you just know. And if you do put the odd extra thing on, you can always take it off in the mix.

Nowadays, making a record is almost like making a film, where the director shoots far more than he actually uses. The singers and musicians are kind of like the actors, the producer is kind of like the director, and you just over-record stuff and see what works. I'm all for trying out guitar parts—they can play as many passes as they want, and I'm happy to go through it later and sift through for the nuggets. When you come back to it in the cold light of day, sometimes the bit that you didn't even think was important suddenly becomes the hook. It's a hard thing; you just have to use your experience.

That's also an area where it's important to have an objective pair of ears.

That's why it's great when you work with an artist that brings something to the table. When you have a great relationship between artist and producer—like Alanis Morissette has with Glen Ballard—that's worth everything. On paper, you wouldn't think that that would be the natural choice of two people to work with each other, but you can't dispute that it's worked. Those relationships are really important.

How do you tend to approach mixing?

You've got to get a balance up really quickly. You've got to look at the big picture, so I find it easier to get a rough balance and then solo things and pull them back in. Especially with digital desks, you have to listen as you EQ—you can't just dial in certain frequencies because you know they've worked before. Sometimes you're selecting the most bizarre frequencies. They happen to work really well in the mix because digital EQs behave in a very different way. With analog EQs, you can often dial in EQs almost without thinking, without even listening, because you know they have a certain color. But with digital EQ, you really have to listen.

When we were recording on analog all those years ago, certain things would be bounced many generations down, so they would attain, by default, a different sound. Therefore, things sat in the track differently, because, for example, the top had gone off of it, or because the backing vocals had been EQd and bounced, EQd and bounced so many times, they ended up being a very processed sound. These days, we have open tracks for everything and nothing is second generation, so everything is full range. You can't easily find a hole in the track, so now it's more important than ever before to put a few things—not everything, or you're back to square one again—through a valve [tube] compressor. You have to mix and match, filter a few things, put a few things through a synth, use different EQs just for the sake of it, run signals through different pieces of outboard gear in bypass mode, just to change the way it sits in the track.

That would also serve to change the phase relationships.

Sure, changing the phase relationships can make a huge difference. Putting the drum overheads through outboard boxes can help separate the drum kit, even if you don't add much EQ.

Do you tend to use a lot of compression?

Over the top if I specifically want that. Sometimes on bass or vocal, I'll go completely over the top, but for an effect. There are other things I record completely flat, from the mic through the preamp and straight to tape. Very often, tube preamps and DIs can add a color on the way in. Some mics or preamps can enhance the top end, almost like a fake EQ. But I work to get a different tone in each track, just to get each one to sit a little differently in the mix. The big problem with overusing all this stuff is that you end up with demos that are just flat, with no life to them, no emotion.

Selected Listening:
Culture Club: *Don't Mind If I Do*, EMI, 1999; *Kissing To Be Clever*, Virgin, 1982; *Colour By Numbers*, Virgin, 1983; *Waking Up With The House On Fire*, Virgin, 1984
Beach Boys: *The Beach Boys*, Caribou, 1985
Deniece Williams: *Water Under The Bridge*, Columbia, 1987
Gary Moore: *Corridors Of Power*, Mirage, 1982

Part Six

Young Guns

Walter Afanasieff

Walter Afanasieff is, by his own admission, a perfectionist. He's also one of the top record producers on the planet. Coincidence? I think not. For more than a decade, he has almost single-handedly crafted a rich pop sound that has resonated with millions of listeners around the world.

A talented multi-instrumentalist (keyboards, bass, drums) and self-confessed fan of technology, Afanasieff takes a complete hands-on approach to his productions, often writing (or, with the artist, cowriting) the songs, devising the arrangements, and even playing most if not all the parts himself, presenting the artist with a complete backing track to add their voice to. After working with producer/drummer Narada Michael Walden for several years, Afanasieff set out on his own in 1989 and almost immediately struck gold, working with a then-unknown new artist by the name of Mariah Carey. As her career exploded, he soon found himself working with an incredible roster of internationally renowned artists, including Whitney Houston, Celine Dion, Barbra Streisand, Michael Bolton, Kenny G, Peabo Bryson, Luther Vandross, Ricky Martin, and Marc Anthony, as well as producing the band Savage Garden (*Affirmation*) and creating music for the soundtracks of major motion pictures such as *Beauty And The Beast, The Bodyguard, Hurricane*, and *A License To Kill.*

I spoke with Afanasieff just days after he won the ultimate acknowledgement from his peers—the 1999 Grammy for Producer of the Year. Soft-spoken and somewhat shy, he shared his views about making records and also gave us an in-depth analysis of the famed Afanasieff sound. If you could bottle it and sell it, you'd make a fortune!

Congratulations on winning the Grammy—it had to have been an incredible moment in your life.

It was one of the greatest feelings I've ever had. I've only been producing for a little over ten years, so this was very special.

I seriously thought that Matt Serletic was going to get it this year because he produced the

song "Smooth." It just got so many Grammys that night—the whole Santana thing—so why wouldn't it cross over into the Producer of the Year category?

But finally, for some reason, someone said, "You know what? Let's just give it to Afanasieff." (laughs)

In some ways, you're a throwback to the old school of production, where you do all the arranging and a lot of the writing, often creating entire backing tracks by yourself even before the artist sets foot in the studio. Obviously, not every producer can provide that kind of "full service" approach; especially with the Pro Tools style of recording, a lot of producers today are more technicians than musicians.

But no matter what day or year you're in, music is music. We're talking about songs, and a record is only as good as the song. Sure, you can go and Pro Tool anything to death, but if you don't have a good song and a good performance from the beginning, you're going to get into trouble. You may get away with it once or twice, but you can't always get away with it. So my philosophy has always been, I'm a musician, this is a really good song, and let's just take it from there. We can either go into a studio with a live band, or we can go into a studio and sit at Pro Tools all day long. Without question, you can do *anything* in the studio today. But I guarantee you that, without a good song, you're not going to have a good production.

> *"A record is only as good as the song."*

I gather that arranging is something you take great pride in doing.

There are different ways to produce records. The approach depends on the song and the circumstances. Producers nowadays can be simply overseers in the studio of how a song is going to be finished, without taking any responsibility for the creation of the music and the arrangement. I, on the other hand, am involved in every single nuance of the musical performance, from every single guitar lick that's going to be played to every single vocal lick that's going to be put on. I'm sitting there, and I'm actually either singing the part or I'm making sure that the part the musician created is the right part. That's just the way I do it. Other producers may not go that far, that deep, or do that much.

So you're really hands-on in every aspect.

Not just hands-on; I pretty much play every part, especially if it's a song done on a sequencer. If I have to go into the studio and do an orchestral overdub, I'm responsible for sitting with the arranger and creating the arrangement with them. And then if there are guitar players or background vocals or anything else to do in the live domain, I'm pretty much there, creating those parts. I don't see how I can be any less hands-on than I am. Though sometimes, it's down to the guys you have around you; if you have great programmers and great musicians and great everything, you can actually just hang out in the back and talk on the phone! (laughs)

But I imagine the total hands-on approach can limit the scope of artists that you might work with, simply because there are some artists that wouldn't be willing to give up that degree of control.

That's true, but other artists actually would flock to something like that. A lot of artists like the way I do things because they trust me. They just give it all up to me, and they say, "You know what? When you do your music, I'll come in and I'll sing my song, and then I'm going to leave a happy person." You have to differentiate between the two types of artist. There's the Mariah Carey, and then there's the Celine Dion, and those two are very, very different artists. Mariah writes, coproduces, is there from every step, she's there, no question. Celine Dion—she doesn't write, she doesn't produce, and she simply picks the songs that she likes to sing and trusts her producers to come up with the right track, and she walks into the studio, does her vocals, and then leaves. Which doesn't make her any less of a talent, of course.

Do you think there's a "Walter Afanasieff sound?"

Yeah! I know there's a sound, because I repetitively used certain tastes that I have. I have a sound because I like certain textures to go with other textures: I like big drums; I like really big background vocals; I like huge rock guitars—even if it's a really light R&B song, I'll put really big rock guitars on it. And I like big orchestras. I like to go really big where it needs to be big and really small where it needs to be small. And I think that a lot of the last ten years, specifically in pop ballads, I sort of came up with the tympani roll that goes into the big bridge, power chords coming in, cymbal swells—little things that make it my niche.

> *"I like to go really big where it needs to be big and really small where it needs to be small."*

And, very often, it's the little things that make a record—it's all in the details.

I totally agree. When you listen to a Babyface record, you know it's a Babyface record. He has an electric Rhodes piano sound that he loves to use, he has an identifiable drum groove and drum sound, and he has that unmistakable wall of Babyface vocals that he puts down in every one of his songs. So he definitely has his sound. When you listen to a David Foster production, you have this signature big-time Chicago-sounding thing. And I think that, similarly, when you listen to my productions—when you listen to "My All," or you listen to "Hero," or you listen to "My Heart Will Go On"—you kind of know that, well, yeah, there's that tympani roll, there's that cymbal swell, there's that big power chord, and there's that big wall of backgrounds. I'm flattered that other guys out there are now trying to sound like me, whereas for a few years I was maybe trying to sound like someone else! So we sort of pass the baton back and forth. It's kind of good but it's kind of bad, and I know that I've been guilty of doing it. I've had records where I've tried to sound like Babyface, and I've had records where I've tried to sound like David Foster, and so forth.

Just as, when you started in the '80s, everybody was chasing that classic big stadium sound.

Absolutely. We all have our bible, of sorts. In my bible are my favorite recordings. My ultimate bible, and my ultimate guru of music, period, is George Martin. I can't tell you how much influence he had on me. Anybody who needs to get anything out of music, go listen to all The Beatles records. It's all there for me. For some people, their bible piece of music is the Beach Boys' *Pet Sounds*. To me, it's not; I don't go there when I want to refer or refresh or inspire my soul to create music. I go to other places—mostly, I go to classical music. I can put on a Chopin piano, and I get inspired to play the piano parts on my next project. Or I listen to Rachmaninoff for some beautiful orchestral ideas that I want to put down. It's things like that, very personal things.

What are the most inspirational Beatles tracks for you?

When I moved to America, I was four or five years old, and I didn't even speak English. I'll never forget this AM radio my parents bought—it had a white dial, and it was really old. I was thumbing through the stations and The Beatles were playing "She Loves You." And that was it—that was exactly the moment in time that I knew that I was going to be in music for the rest of my life, all because of this song I was hearing. And when *Sgt. Pepper* came out—to me, that was the most significant recording of all time. For George Martin to create that piece of work on four tracks—that's history. In my opinion, nothing else has been done that's greater than that. I think nowadays when we look at our studios and our Pro Tools and our 96 tracks over here and hundreds of tracks over there flying around—I mean, come on! So for this guy to do a *Sgt. Pepper* in four tracks?

Both George Martin and Geoff Emerick have said that if *Sgt. Pepper* had been recorded on 24-track, it wouldn't have turned out as well because the limitations of 4-track forced them to make decisions and not put them off. Do you find that artistic restrictions of choice can help the creative process?

I'm sure they're correct—we have too much choice today. We have so much freedom, so much room for error, that at the end of the day it's not about aesthetics, it's that we didn't do it right—we went too far, we did too much. There are times when I wish I had the same circumstances George had during *Sgt. Pepper*. I wish that the singers didn't come into the room and say, "I want to do 12 more tracks, I'm not happy with this." OK, you can do 12 more tracks, and I'll spend six hours comping the 12 more tracks you just did, but I know that we already have what we need. "No, just let me do 12 more." Then after that, they'll decide to do 12 *more*. I've had that with artists, and I've ended up with literally 70 tracks of vocals! That's absurd—to have a singer do 70 tracks of vocals because they're insecure in the way they sing and they're not letting you, the producer, take it and go with it in the way you believe it should be done. Then it becomes pandemonium, and, at the end of the day, I wish there were just a 4-track machine sitting in the corner and you just needed to do one track, and I would have punched in what I didn't like, and you would have gone home.

When an artist is doing 70 takes, is it because they're trying to achieve technical perfection? Surely it can't be to capture an emotion, because with so much repetition, the feel has got to start evaporating.

It can happen when the producer is seeking to get something that he just cannot get out of the singer. Personally, the only time I've had to do that is because a singer really just wasn't giving me what I felt was good enough. We're talking about a situation where the inability of the singer comes through and it's up to me, as producer, to say, "You're just not giving it to me yet." That, in combination with their own insecurity: "I can do it better, please let me do it better." But you're so free to make decisions now because you have the technology to support you—whatever you want to do, it's there; it's never a situation where you don't have any more tracks available. That doesn't exist anymore.

When you're doing an arrangement on a song, is it typically done with input from the singer, or do you do it by yourself beforehand and then just present it as a done deal?

There's two ways. If I'm cowriting with the singer, they know what the arrangement is, because that's how we wrote it. Then it's up to me to give them tracks, and it's up to them to say, "This is great" or "No, it's not good enough" or whatever. But usually, I like to do everything all by myself and give it to the singer, and usually I believe in what I do enough to know that it's going to work at the end of the day, that they're going to love it. Sometimes there's an element of surprise that doesn't work in my favor—sometimes the artist will say, "I like it so much that I want it twice as long," or "Do you think we can change keys at the end?" Then it's a matter of going back to the computers and rearranging things. But for the most part I like to have everything pretty much done before the singer sets foot in the studio.

What sort of tricks have you come up with for eliciting the best performance from a singer?

It's quite a bit to do with their space. They're very insecure, very gentle creatures, these singers. (laughs) You pretty much have to be able to be their doctor, their spiritual advisor, their psychologist, their bartender. You have to be all these personalities, and you have to stroke their egos just enough for their security, and you have to be able to solve problems that they're coming up with—even problems that may not truly exist. I've been in situations before where there really was no problem, where the singer was creating a problem out of their own pandemonium or insecurity. Then it's simply the way that you solve it—by saying, for instance, "Well, let's try a different pair of headphones," or "Let's try a different microphone; maybe this one will

> *"They're very insecure, very gentle creatures, these singers."*

be better for you," even though there really isn't anything wrong. So you do this little thing where you just kind of keep stroking them, you've just got to keep taking care of them and pampering them.

Not that all singers are these types of people; most singers are completely professional, dedicated hard-working people that walk into a studio and say, "Tell me what to do; I'm here for you, man." Other times, well, it just isn't coming out right. And when they hear that it's not coming out right, there's nothing bigger or deeper than that singer getting into a funk. (laughs) But when you're dealing with musicians, you're dealing with gentle souls. We're all from the same tribe; we're all trying to do something that's art. We're doing it to please someone else; we're all here for that one reason. Maybe your form of pleasing someone is to get a number one record, or maybe you just want to get that pat on the back from your fellow musicians who say, "Man, that's some great shit." This is what I live for. I don't live for my position on the chart or how many copies have sold, how much money I've made. My reason for doing it is to get that musician guy to say, "That sounds really good, man"—I love that. But we're all here to do that, so if it's not coming around, we feel like shit, we want to go run back home. So you've got to be able to anticipate it and know how to handle it.

What do you do when you and the artist are seeing something in completely opposite ways?

If I feel that what we have is there and we don't need to do another take, but the singer feels that they can do it much better, my answer is, "Well, please, go out and try it." In my mind, I'm thinking, let them do it, and then I'll A/B it for them, and pretty much the argument is won over what's right. And sometimes they go out there and nail it *better* than I would have liked!

But if the singer thinks they've given it their best and I still feel we need to do more, that's a different kind of problem. At the risk of sounding a bit graphic, if someone thinks they've shot their wad, you can't just go out there a minute later and say, "Can you shoot it again?" (laughs) So that becomes a problem—how can you ask this giant superstar person to do it all over again? That can be a bit difficult, but usually it's me knowing what they've done is so phenomenal [and them wanting to try another take].

Do you engineer most of your own productions?

Only when it comes to the mixes. It's not engineering in the sense that I don't know anything about the mathematics and science of limiters and compressors and gates and miking techniques and EQ and all that. I'm not that kind of person, but I do know that certain parts of mixes require a real hands-on approach, just to ride those keyboards or bring up that orchestra in that perfect way or to make those drum fills a little bit more the way I hear them. Other than that, I completely trust the engineers that I work with. My main engineer is Humberto Gatica. Over his career, he's developed such a profound, interesting sound, and for live recording, there's no one better than Humberto. He's just the purest, most knowledgeable gentleman in the studio, and he's full-on. There are no pretenses; he really knows what he's doing.

The second person I've been working very closely with, who is a masterful, masterful engineer, is Dave Reitzas. Dave has gone inside of that computer, he's gone inside of that 3348 digital multitrack machine, he's gone inside of that SSL console, and he knows every single thing about these pieces of equipment to the point where there's not a second wasted of him trying to figure out how to make something work. And he's a wonderful musician. He knows music to the point where he anticipates what you're going to say—he's already there, unlike any other engineer I've worked with. He knows how to read your mind, because he's a super musician and a super technician and a super engineer.

And Mick Guzauski is pretty much the only guy that I would ever let mix a record for me with me not in the studio with him.

That's quite a compliment.

I'm so into mixers right now. To me, Chris Lord-Alge is an incredible mixer; Dave Way, who mixed the last Savage Garden album for me—he's a wonderful mixer. One of the more up-and-coming guys who works in my studio is Dave Gleeson, who's just wonderful. And then there are other people I adore who I just haven't gotten a chance to work with yet—for example, I really, really want to work with Al Schmitt.

One of the hardest things to accomplish in a mix—especially when there's a dense backing track—is getting the lead vocal to sit right. A number of engineers have given me technical solutions to that problem, but have you come up with any arrangement ideas that can accomplish the same thing?

There used to be a lot of truth in the statement that you could "fix it in the mix," but that's obsolete; you really can't say that anymore. It's got to pretty much be there at the time we're doing a vocal. If it's the right microphone, the right EQ, the right reverb, then you're safe. Then, when the mix comes, it's just a matter of riding the vocal. To me, it's not a matter of changing it afterwards in the mix; if it's not done right during the recording, then I don't know what you can do.

Are there ever times when you'll change the arrangement afterwards because the vocal didn't seem to be sitting well in the framework that you originally created?

Not too many times. I think that the only problem we've ever had is if there were a bareness to the track when the vocal was actually done. Where it sounded pretty good at the time, but then when you started filling up the whole thing with backgrounds and orchestras and guitars, we'd get into a situation where the vocal needed to sound bigger and stronger. Then you have to start making the engineer do a little more work. Sometimes it becomes a little dangerous there because you start having to take away certain musical things that you've done since the vocal was done. But pretty much the rule of thumb is, it's got to sound like it's supposed to sound when you're actually cutting the vocals.

At what point do you lay the vocal down? What instrumentation will have been recorded beforehand, and what goes on afterwards?

Sometimes it's actually the whole track; sometimes it's just the basics; sometimes it's just the basics with a good background section there to support the singer so the singer can go off and improvise, doing licks during the out choruses. I record background vocals before the lead vocal because I'm confident that the singer is going to love them, but it's kind of a hit-or-miss thing. Background vocal sessions are really, really expensive. I don't know why that is, but it is. I've yet to determine why a background singer can come in and sing for five minutes, and just because the song is a certain length and because you used a certain amount of tracks on it—damn, these people make a lot of money! (laughs)

But we pretty much commit—and it's a very expensive commitment—to putting the backgrounds down before the singer comes in to do their vocals. That's kind of a dangerous move, because if they don't like the backgrounds, or if they want to do the backgrounds themselves, or if the backgrounds aren't right, you've got to go in and do them again, and it's usually a big deal, because it's a lot of money. But if it works, it works great, because now the singer doesn't have to sing where he thinks he has to sing; now the singer can do a lick up here or a harmony over there. It becomes more fun and more creative.

Do you tend to use the same backing singers for every project?

I do. I have two groups of singers that I use—the San Francisco group and the Los Angeles group—though it usually is the San Francisco group that I use. I have created what I consider to be a masterpiece sound and technique with my background vocals. I have two guys and two girls, and we usually have the four of them sing a particular part in unison, and then I usually double, and then I go and I add a harmony that they sing in unison and then double. Sometimes I just have the guys sing, and sometimes just the girls. This technique and this sound—in my room with my microphones—is really pleasing to me. Listen to the end title song in the movie *Hurricane*: it sounds like a 100-piece gospel choir, but it's just the three or four people that I use. So I'm kind of married to that; I always want to do it, and I always depend on it.

But I've [also] been realizing that there's so much in the artists themselves singing their own backgrounds. On the Savage Garden album, Darren [Hayes] sang every single part—it was like walls of background.

A lot has to do with how the backing singers blend with the lead singer's voice.

The blend, absolutely. Though not every lead vocalist can do their own backgrounds. There are some people out there who sound horrible singing their own backgrounds; I don't think Michael Bolton is known for singing any of his backgrounds, because he just doesn't sound good doing it. Luther Vandross never sings any kind of a background. They'll do harmonies with their own leads, but that's just a perspective that lead singers do. With Darren in Savage Garden, it just sounded so great. Doubling, tripling, backgrounds, harmonies, everything—it's just all Darren. Other singers just really need to have that really good background action, those background vocals.

So on each take, you have the group of four backing singers sing a unison note?

Pretty much, unless they physically can't go that low or that high. When you hear the total, though, there's a lot of harmonies going on. In the old school, you have your baritone, your tenor, your alto, your soprano voices in there—be it three or four voices—and they're all singing their parts. And you would never ask a baritone to sing a soprano part, and you would never ask a soprano to sing an alto or baritone part—it's just never done. But why not? I'll ask that baritone guy to sing in falsetto, to sing the soprano part. So the guys are all singing falsetto, and the girls are all singing down low, and it's just a really good way to get different textures and tones in your background vocals. Plus, the singers really have fun doing it!

So the way you build up your chords is that each track has a different note.

I've done songs where all four singers do one unison part, then we double that, we triple it, and we quadruple it. So one line, one part, all unison, now becomes sixteen voices singing the one note. Same thing with the next harmony up: all the same four voices sing the same harmony note, four tracks of that. So that's another 16 voices doing that harmony. And then we do another harmony, and then we do a lower harmony, and then just the guys—because the girls can't sing that low—give me some really low notes.

Part of the reason for this, simply put, is that my level of perfection is unlike anyone else's. I just don't like the human error; I don't like the human part of it as much as I like the real, nailed, in-tune, perfectly executed part. I would love sometimes to put *everything* through a computer and Auto-Tune and clean it up and quantize it and fly it around left and right, because I really like that very clean, very precise style of recording. So to have three or four singers out there with each one singing different parts, they'd have to be the greatest singers in the world to me, because sometimes, somebody's going to be a little flat while the other three are perfect—and then you've got to do it again. And I just don't have the patience for that. (laughs)

Based on your records, I would have guessed that you were a perfectionist in the studio. There's a real polish, and there's no question that what you're hearing is a production, as opposed to a capturing of a live performance.

Well, when you start doing things on your own, you get into thinking of ways of doing things perfectly. You're in that school, and that's where I found my training. My school days were when I was in the studio with Narada Michael Walden, sitting with my computer or my [Akai] MPC60 or my Fairlight or Synclavier. We were already being taught to be perfect, because that computer was making it perfect; that keyboard is already in tune perfectly, and we were all doing things pretty much with perfection in mind. Then, when you finally get out there in the main professional workplace, you don't really like to hear something that's out of tune; you don't really like to hear something that's out of time, because you've been taught not to do it that way.

On the other hand, a lot of people have been brought up in the live band domain. Recently, I've been working with this group Train. There are five guys in the group, and all five of them are live musicians, and there's forgiveness, there's compromise, there's all these human allowances. They're not all playing in tune, and they're not all playing in time—they're not all doing it completely like my computers have always been doing it. So now I need to go, "Wait a minute—are they doing it wrong, or am I hearing it wrong?" (laughs) Do I make them do it again and make them do it so good and so clean and so polished that it takes away from their live thing, or do I have to do it so I allow for their own human mistakes to sort of be what their sound is? If you listen to Crosby, Stills, Nash & Young, they're not singing completely in tune, and that's the reason they sound the way they do. But sometimes you do hear live recordings and it's like, man, they're singing perfectly and playing perfectly. Is it because Mutt Lange sat there for months and months and months making AC/DC or Def Leppard do it again and again and again until it's completely right and in tune and in time? I don't know. My training, my school, has come from listening to perfect recordings and then trying to create them on computers. Technology sort of prevails in my life. I appreciate the philosophy that, if you're doing your job right, then you're going to do it perfectly. If you've learned to sing correctly, you're going to sing in tune; if you've learned to be a masterful musician, you're going to play in time.

If the performance is there—if it's evoking the correct emotional response, making you smile or cry—but it has technical imperfections, will you have the artist do it again?

No, no, no, no. On Savage Garden's record, there's a song called "Two Beds And A Coffee Machine." The song is a profound ballad—it's a really moving piece of music, and it's a very emotional subject. It's very poignant and very dramatic—it's about spousal abuse. And none of us were actually ready for Darren to sing the song—we were just doing the music recording, I was in the middle of doing piano. He said, "Let me just put down this guide vocal so everyone can build on top of it," and I said, OK. So we just ran out there into the room and put up any old microphone, and there were no baffles, and it was really not done in the way you would normally do a vocal in any sense of the word. In fact, I can't even remember if there was an engineer in the room! Anyway, he went out there, and he sang the song, and everyone in the studio was just moved to tears—we were just sobbing. At the end of the day, that was it—that was the vocal that was on the record because he could never ever do that again. It was the first time out of his body, the first time into our ears, the first emotion, the virgin part. If a plane crashed in the room, I would have kept it! (laughs)

So you strive for technical perfection, but if you get that magical performance, you go with it anyway, even if it's not perfect.

I think what I'm saying is that everyone should really learn their craft so that when you do need that magic performance, it would be done masterfully.

But there's a very fine line between chasing perfection and polishing the life out of a track.

Yeah, there's no question that you can make an orchestra play so many takes that the soul is completely taken out of it, because you're striving for a better intonation. They're just going to be rolling their eyes and playing you something that's very in tune—the intonation's there, but the soul has been taken out of it. That goes without saying for everything; it's just a matter of being able to rightfully compromise and juggle all the human and technical aspects and not make it a stale thing. Again, if it's a good song, it's in the song. At the end of the day, I really just believe in the song.

But not every song is a great song, and every album is going to contain some songs that are B-list and some that are A-list.

Of course, but that whole argument of what's an A-side and what's a B-side is just record company language—B-sides are just as important to me. I don't know why and how it was mandated that [to be played] on the radio, a record needs to be this type of song and only a certain length, that whole thing. I still remember a world where we were all driving around and "Stairway To Heaven" came on the radio. Or "American Pie," or "Inna Gadda Da Vida," or "Freebird." Come on, those are all seven, ten, twelve-minute songs. These days, if you go past three minutes, thirty seconds, forget it.

And all of those songs you mentioned have great feel but are technically lacking.

All of them are completely technically lacking. That's what I'm saying—it's just the song. You can't play those songs any better because it's the song.

Any advice you'd like to pass on to the reader who wants to be the next Walter Afanasieff?

Well, I'm just a musician who likes to talk a little bit about what I do and maybe set people into being a little more forgiving and believing. That's the thing: Just believe in yourself. Just really know that there's a place for everyone and everything here.

Selected Listening:

Mariah Carey: *Butterfly*, Columbia, 1997; *Daydream*, Columbia, 1995; *Music Box*, Columbia, 1993; *Emotions*, Columbia, 1991

Michael Bolton: *All That Matters*, Columbia, 1997; *This Is The Time*, Columbia, 1996; *The One Thing*, Columbia, 1993; *Time, Love And Tenderness*, Columbia, 1991

Kenny G: *Classics In The Key Of G*, Arista, 1999; *The Moment*, Arista, 1997; *Miracles*, Arista, 1994; *Breathless*, Arista, 1992

Celine Dion: *Let's Talk About Love*, Sony, 1997; *Celine Dion*, Epic, 1992

Barbra Streisand: *Higher Ground*, Columbia, 1998

Savage Garden: *Affirmation*, Sony, 1999

Chuck Ainlay

From his earliest childhood, Chuck Ainlay knew that he wanted to be a recording engineer. He had an uncle—a magician/banjo player/ventriloquist and audio enthusiast, who, in the late '50s, built a modest studio near Ainlay's northern Indiana home town, equipped with a single RCA microphone, an old Ampex mono tape machine and a homebuilt cutting lathe. Young Ainlay was a frequent visitor, and so, when college beckoned, he moved to Nashville to study recording at Belmont College. Before long, he was working in a "tourist studio"—one of those curiosities of Music City, where busloads of people would come in and do a handclap overdub to a prerecorded track, get a quick tour of the control room, and be herded out the door. After a spell assisting at Quad studios, he built a remote truck using equipment donated by a studio that had just gone out of business, recording notable bands that passed through town. Eventually, Ainlay became chief engineer at The Castle, where he came to the attention of famed producers Jimmy Bowen and Tony Brown. He hasn't looked back since.

Today, Ainlay is one of the most in-demand engineers and mixers in Nashville. He's worked with a veritable who's-who of modern country music, including Vince Gill, George Strait, Wynonna, The Dixie Chicks, Trisha Yearwood, Lyle Lovett, Nanci Griffith, and Mark Knopfler. He's also a singular force in 5.1 mixing, responsible for some of the freshest, most creative surround mixes available today. On the brutally hot July evening that Ainlay met with me, he had already completed a full day's mixing session, as well as, he proudly announced, having mowed his two-acre lawn! That he still had the energy to remain awake—much less do an in-depth two hour interview in which he carefully and articulately shared the depths of his knowledge—was nothing short of astonishing.

You're viewed primarily as a mixing expert. How do you approach a fresh mixing session? What tracks do you bring up first? What are you listening for?

I have certain things that I do straight off the bat. I'll patch in three general reverbs as a starting place. I like to use an EMT 250 for one of them, but that's not always available, so I've got a little Roland SRV-330 with a similar patch. I use it as an impact reverb, with a fairly rapid decay —between 1.5 to 2.0 seconds. It's a pretty dark, dense sound, with a good bit of chorusing. Then I usually use a Lexicon 300 for a sound that shimmers more. That one's generally got a little longer predelay on it, anywhere from 40 to 180 milliseconds, depending on the song. It's a brighter 'verb with a bit more sheen to it, more like a plate. Finally, I'll use a Lexicon 224X in a rich chamber mode. Those are kind of beginning building blocks. Then I'll have a [Lexicon] PCM70 set to a gated program and a Harmonizer that I set left/right up/down. I'll have a mono delay, and then I'll use my Ensoniq DP2 and DP4 for when I want to really expand on some 'verbs and delays. If something else comes to mind, then I'll take the time to come up with it, but in Nashville we have to move fairly rapidly, so you have to have some of this stuff ready at the get-go.

Will you put multiple instruments into the same reverb, or do you use a different reverb for each instrument?

I'll put multiple instruments into the three core reverbs. They create the ambiance of the record. One song may call for less of the shiny stuff and more of the impact stuff, while other songs may call for more airy sort of reverbs. So there are three or four reverbs that will work for the general mix. And then I'll have specific reverbs for specific instruments, like the gated things will be on percussion instruments; I may also use inverse reverbs and things like that, small room sounds.

Do you ever EQ the reverb sends or returns?

Actually, I don't much anymore. When we were using plates and real chambers and things like that years ago, yeah, you were always EQing and compressing and slapping some delay on in front of them and gating them. But with the digital reverbs, I find that by changing their response—by tweaking the high-frequency decay and the low-frequency boost in them—you can create the 'verb that fits the track.

Why is it preferable to tweak the digital EQ in an outboard processor rather than using the mixing console's EQ, which is presumably higher quality?

Well, why turn on an EQ and add an extra circuit to something when you can do it without adding that extra circuit? In general, that's my philosophy about both recording and mixing. If I can do it with less in the signal path, that's the way I'll approach it. When I record tracks, I'll generally bypass the console unless I've got a nice old discrete Neve desk that I'm tracking on. I carry a good bit of outboard gear, and I'll go through those preamps and straight to tape, using the desk just for monitoring. When I mix, in many instances I'll avoid the desk EQ and use that outboard gear instead.

You've singled out the Ensoniq DP processors, which are really semi-pro gear. Are there other semi-pro or low-end pieces of gear you regularly use?

Yeah, I like the cheapo Rolands and Yamahas like the SRV 330s and SPX90s. I've got a [Lexicon] PCM42 that I love to use for delay. It's an older digital mono delay, but because of its technology, they've put a limiting circuit on the front end of it, so if you hit it a little bit hard, it sounds like tape saturation—the frequency response isn't full-out either. Things like that, I really like. And I have no fear of using inexpensive gear if it sounds cool. The TC M2000s and 3000s aren't cheap, but they're not high end 'verbs, either, and they're great. I also like the TC 2290s for choruses and delays. With many of these inexpensive reverbs and delays, you just dial up something, and it's there; they're intended for the guy who's not going to dive into it as much. I'll use pretty much anything, as long as it's got a sound and isn't too noisy. Mind you, noise sometimes is great! (laughs)

Which faders do you bring up first when you start a mix?

I'll begin by pulling up all the faders with no effects and no reverb. I'll do some essential

panning, but just to kind of have a picture. I'll listen to the song, listen to the lyric, listen to the intent, the genre of the song; what does it emote to me from my past influences, what does it draw out of me? I may listen to it two or three times, just to understand what the song's about. Certainly after the first time through, I'm kind of focusing in on some of the problem elements of what's on tape. So I may solo the bass drum or the acoustic guitar or piano, just to see if there's a little too much honk in the acoustic or if the vocal is too thick. That will give me an idea of what I'm going to need to do as far as patching in outboard gear for each track.

Do you ever start by listening to the rough mixes, or is that a dangerous thing?

You know, I really don't like to listen to rough mixes, and I really don't like to get too much input from the artist or producer about the song prior to working on it. In fact, it's almost a negative if they say, "I love the rough mix, I just want to hear the guitar really well." Once that's in the back of your mind, you never can really find the perspective for that instrument—it's either too loud or not loud enough, and you'll just be second-guessing what that other person is hearing about the track, rather than just going by your gut. I think you really have to hear the song and to go by your past influences, to bring out from your heart and your soul what you think the music is. What I do is I kind of develop a picture of what this song is in my head, and I just start shaping it to bring it towards that. So I avoid demos; I avoid input as much as I can until I've kind of gotten into the song and found out what it is and worked awhile on it. After that is when I do like to listen to the rough to see if there is anything I'm missing. Roughs can hold some amazing insight into the original magic of the take.

Some producers like to come in midway into the mix to kind of point out problems or to discuss things like multiple tracks that need deciphering or something like that, and that's fine. Once I've gotten into it and got a handle on it, if they want to come by to comment, no problem. I just find that usually my gut idea about the song is what they're looking for. Every now and then, obviously, you have those mixes where you just don't see it the way the artist or the producer sees it, and those are really difficult mixes.

How long do you typically spend on a mix?

I always tell the producer or artist or whoever's booking me to book a day a song. Now, it doesn't always take me a day to do a song, but I don't like to work on more than one song in a day, because it's hard for me to shift modes from one song to another. The exact amount of time I spend largely depends on how problematic the track is. If there's a lot of repair work to be done— if, for example, I have to go back in and replace drums with samples and make up triggers for gates so that you can get past all the leakage—then it will take longer. To me, that's stuff that really should have been done beforehand, or it should have just been recorded better. (laughs)

If it's a reasonably recorded piece of music, then I can usually get through it in six hours. Then I'll usually do a number of versions of the mix, so there'll be a vocal up, vocal and harmony vocals up, harmony vocals only up, the solo up. We'll always do a bass version of some sort, whether it just be a bass up or bass and bass drum up or just bass drum up. When you get to mastering, sometimes there's an element that EQ doesn't necessarily fix, so they might use a different version instead—like that bass drum up version—to add a little bit of punch.

How do you know when a mix is done?

Mixing is really something that is not an intellectual experience. It comes from your heart; there's a feeling of joy. Music ought to give you an emotional response and, depending on your mood, that emotional response may be triggered or it may not. I think this is why, when you listen to an entire album in a mastering room and you go from song to song, not every one of them stands up to your expectations. When you were doing it, you thought it was great, but when you go and listen to it in retrospect, you go, "What the hell was I thinking?"

So it's a very difficult thing to decide when you're done, but what I go by is when I get a kick out of it; when I'm hearing all the elements of the record, the fills and so forth are coming out; when I can understand the lyrics; when the vocal is not blowing me away at times or too soft at other times. These are the things you work towards. You need to get through all that technical stuff to the point where the song actually gives you a kick. If it doesn't, I keep working and try and make it more exciting, make the guitars jump a bit more, maybe pan things wider—something to make it exciting to listen to. But when I'm enjoying it, I think it's done. Also, obviously, it's done when the producer thinks it's done! (laughs)

There always seems to be one track that somehow just doesn't seem to fit in the mix, though. What sort of steps do you take when you are faced with a track that just won't sit correctly?

Generally, if a track doesn't sit in the mix, it's either a performance problem or it's a dynamic or EQ problem. There's not a whole lot you can do from an engineering perspective with the performance problem other than replace it—and that's done. You can either sample a similar section from another part of the song or even fly it in from other takes if there's a chance that something like that exists.

I don't run into that much since the kind of music that's done in Nashville is performed by really seasoned session musicians who are all incredible players. People working in home studios are going to be faced more with the performance problem. I suppose that's one of the reasons I prefer to work in Nashville—I get to work with great musicians day in and day out.

If what you're facing is an equalization problem or a dynamic problem, the approach would be to decipher which you need to do, or whether you need to deal with both factors. The big thing there is to decide what kind of texturing it needs. Does it need to be warmed up, perhaps with a tube compressor or something to give it a little bit of harmonic distortion? Or do you need some sort of hard limiting in a compressor like an 1176 to put an edge to it? You have to pick your tool to do the dynamic control. Same with EQ—each equalizer has a different sonic signature.

How do you know which approach to take?

I think the tendency for the novice is to generally over-EQ and over-compress things to begin with. When I began my career, I felt the necessity to EQ everything, compress everything, and modify it. Just to put my fingerprint on it, so to speak. But I've learned that if you can let the music be, then you can get away from doing that so much. Do it where it's needed, and you'll probably find that you need to use less of it. If you don't start out by EQing the bass drum to death, then you're probably not going to have to EQ and compress the rest of the instruments as much. If you have a nice, round-sounding bass drum with a decent amount of attack and bottom, don't just start EQing until you have the perfect bass drum—let it be.

Just move through the music; move through all your tracks, and work on little bits here and there. That's my approach. Work on not just one instrument at a time in solo—try and listen to the whole thing. And when you discover a problem, think about what it is that's wrong with it. Is it too muddy? Is it too thick, or is it not bright enough? Does it need a little compression to make it stand up? If you're missing some notes, then maybe you need to compress it to make a more solid sound out of it. You can solo things to hear what you're doing, but don't sit there and work on a sound for a long time—keep popping in and out of solo, and see how it sits in the track after you've done a little bit to it. Maybe a balance change is all that's required. Mixing is more about listening overall than it is about making each element sound great.

> *"Mixing is more about listening overall than it is about making each element sound great."*

Along with that, you have to understand the principle of masking. That's when an instrument is covered up by another instrument in the same frequency range. Say, for instance, the snare drum has a lot of 5 kHz on it, a lot of brightness to it. It's going to mask the acoustic guitar that's trying to get through in the midrange too, and the tambourine, and the enunciation in the vocals. So you need to find ways to cut a little bit in one instrument to allow another instrument to jump out, or EQ an instrument so it won't interfere with another instrument. If you're having a problem where you can't hear the acoustic guitar, maybe it's the snare drum's EQ that is a little too bright. It may be better to sacrifice the snare sound and not have the best sounding snare drum in the world, because the acoustic guitar element is more important to the song.

And then there's panning, which allows you to shift things away from each other. The way I go about panning is to separate things that are of equal spectral energies but are opposing rhythmically. Say, for instance, acoustic guitar and high hat: rather than having the acoustic guitar lay on top of the high hat, I'll separate them. It's basically identifying rhythmic elements and spectral elements and separating opposing rhythmic things so that you get movement within the stereo while separating the sonic elements.

Of course, there are some tracks that are traditionally not separated: for example, kick drum and bass guitar. Do you tend to place the bass guitar frequency lower than the kick drum or vice versa?

In general, if you listen to most records, the bass drum is usually accentuated quite low—like at around 60 Hz—and then it sort of reaches a point up above where the bass would be. So I'll boost it at around 4.8 k and then maybe even 10 k to add the extreme top, then I may dish it out a little bit in the 450 Hz region to kind of take out the enormousness of the sound. That's not a very good word, is it? It's *not* a word. (laughs)

Anyway, it's dished out to give room for other instruments. Bass guitar generally lives in the 200 Hz region—the fundamentals are kind of happening from 100 Hz up, through that middle lower region of 200, 300, 400 Hz. So by dishing out the bass drum a little bit in the 450 Hz area and adding a little below and above where the bass really is, that kind of gives separation between the bass and bass drum.

Do you frequency-limit the bass guitar to get it to sit in that region?

The bass *is* a very frequency-limited instrument. You won't find much in a bass at 10 k. You'll find a good bit of energy maybe up at 3 k, but if you start adding too much upper mid to a bass guitar in that region, you're going to start wiping out everything in a snare drum and an acoustic guitar. All of a sudden, your mix will start sounding as though it's very middley and piercing. It depends on the genre of music, of course, but that element can make a mix sound bad.

That said, I may add a little bit of 2 k, 2.8 k or 3 k to the bass to give it some presence, and I may even add some air up on top in the 10 k region. If I need to enunciate notes in the bass, it's more in the 800 Hz region, to get that sort of growl happening, or I may add a little 80 Hz or 120 to add warmth.

I generally use very wide Qs on everything. I don't usually get into narrow bandwidth boosting or cutting, because it takes the music out of most instruments, unless there's some real problem element to an instrument that I need to get out. So I usually use very wide broad EQs and a lot of shelving on the top and bottom.

On the bottom, you have to make sure that you're not adding subsonic stuff that's going to cause woofer excursions. If I see a lot of excursion on the woofer, then I'll start filtering something. A lot of times, it exists in a bass guitar, which can go quite low, but what you're seeing there is a subsonic harmonic. That can be filtered out without hindering the sound of the bass at all.

Do you typically compress bass?

I usually don't compress bass when I'm tracking, because most of the guys in town come in with their own racks that usually have an LA 2 or a Tube Tech compressor, and they will do that themselves.

For mixing, I've got a JoeMeek compressor that I love—the original JoeMeek, which I think is an incredible compressor on bass. I actually have a few JoeMeeks—I've got the original one and I've got the SC3 and the SC4—and I love them all for different things.

One thing that's very important about low end is absolute phase. Maintaining absolute phase makes the biggest difference in a recording. I would suggest that everybody go out and buy a phase clicker and reader. The one that I have is made by a company called SVC, but there are a number of companies that make them. The clicker is a little transducer that emits a positive phase pulse with a built-in speaker, and you can either put it up next to a microphone, or it's got a jack that you can plug into a direct input. The reader has a built-in mic or once again a jack, plus a couple of LEDs which read the pulse as either in or out of phase. It allows you to make sure that all your mics and all your DIs are in absolute phase polarity. In the home situation, it's probably even more of a problem, and I run into it all the time in professional studios —some microphones are pin 2 hot, some microphones are pin 3 hot, some mic panels may be wired pin 2 hot or pin 3 hot. If your mic panel is wired pin 3 hot, or the piece of gear that you are going into is pin 3 hot but the mic is pin 2 hot, you have a 180 degree phase reversal! And there is definitely a difference in the way things sound— especially in low frequency sounds.

Do you generally use the bass amp signal if one has been recorded?

I think in Nashville it's generally not used, but I prefer to have a bass amp. I think it makes the sound more natural—it just kind of fills out a bass in a real way. There are a few guys that are using these boxes that are basically a road case with a speaker and a microphone built in it, and they work pretty well, adding some sort of speaker element to the bass, but it's not the real thing.

Do you compress drums during mixing?

I compress them a good bit when I mix. The tom tracks are compressed; the overheads I may limit and squash pretty good. I'll compress the high hat to try and pull up the subtleties in the playing. Usually, besides having the bass drum come up on its own channel, I'll take the same tape output and go through an 1176 and way over-compress it—maybe using a 10:1 ratio so I'm actually limiting it—and return it on another channel. I'll use a real slow attack and a very fast release so it's not grabbing the transients, but it's just smashing the sound. I'll mix that with the softer compressed signal of the original channel. Then I may actually create a drum submix and feed it to one of my other Joemeek compressors for an overall drum squeeze.

On snare drum, I do a similar thing with another 1176. If there's a cross stick played, I may mult it off to another channel. That way I can gate it out to get more level, plus I can EQ it separately. Then I'll mute the snare channel and switch on the cross stick channel at the appropriate time in the song.

A basic starting point would be to bring up the bass drum and the compressed bass drum so that the VU meters are hitting about -10. Then I balance the snare drum to that, and then I start bringing up the whole kit. By the time I get the overheads and toms and room mics up, the overall kit will be averaging somewhere around -5 VU.

Do you set the kick drum and the snare at roughly the same level?

Well, that depends on the song. You generally want a give-and-take from the snare drum and bass drum. You generally don't want the bass drum to be this soft little tap and the snare drum knocking you to the back wall, so, yeah, there's some sort of element of even sound pressure level from the snare drum and bass drum. That's a good starting point.

How do you generally record guitars?

I generally like a warmer microphone rather than a real bright microphone on acoustic guitars. For instance, I'll use a KM 84 or a 184 instead of a 451. I like to capture the purity of the tone on an acoustic guitar rather than just getting edge from the microphone. I'd prefer to roll out the bottom and add top with EQ rather than using a really bright microphone where you're not going to ever get the warmth back. I like to record acoustic guitar with the XY pattern—one capsule pointing towards the fretboard and the other one more towards the hole—placed somewhere off the 12th fret, about where the neck combines to the body of the guitar.

Do you always use matched mics for that purpose?

Generally, yes. The XY pattern is good because I can spread them out if I want to make the guitar really big, or I can get rid of the one facing the fretboard if I want just a real sort of mono-y guitar. It's nice to have the choice; when you're recording, you don't know exactly what's going to happen, so you just want to be prepared. Sometimes, if it's a solo acoustic guitar track, I'll have a distant mic either in front or behind or up above the guitar. It may be a large diaphragm microphone like a 4060 or a U 67 or C12. I usually record acoustic guitars with my Focusrite modules, and I usually will compress it with my Calrec compressors.

For electric guitars, I'll usually start with a 57 on the amp, but not straight on axis with the middle of the speaker; it's usually off-center, angled in towards the middle of the speaker and generally fairly close, just off the grill. I may also use a U 67 or 4060—I actually really like the Audio Technica 4050s on electric guitar as well. But I won't get nearly as close with those mics—maybe anywhere from a foot to three feet away. I won't generally mic the room too much, unless it's something that we're going for, as an effect. But usually it's just too imposing on the sound, too coloring—most rooms aren't really good enough, so I'll create that element with some sort of digital delay.

Do you record acoustic and electric guitars flat or with EQ?

I work with mic placement as much as possible, but with acoustic guitars I generally have to roll out a little bit of 60 Hz. I like to put a bit of 15 k on there for sparkle, and if it needs to cut more, it's usually the 4 k to 5 k element.

When I track, I'll try to not overdo the EQ. I'm not afraid to EQ, but I try to use good equalizers and, if I'm unsure, I won't go too far—I'll leave it for later. Once you commit to too much EQ or too much compression, it's very hard to get rid of it. Generally, when you mix, you're going to make it brighter, anyhow.

Have you found any low-end semi-pro preamps that do the job, or is there a big gap between the best preamps and the not-so-good ones?

There seems to be a big gap. I would say that if the home user has the opportunity to invest in something, [they should] spend a little bit of money and buy a good mic pre. I would suggest trying to find a vintage Neve module or two. I know it's a bit of dough, but your records will just be so much better.

Is it better to have a great mic and a so-so preamp or a so-so mic and a great preamp?

I would go for a good mic, I guess. It's really hard to say, because every microphone has a character to it, and no one microphone is going to work for everything. Whereas you can use a good mic preamp on just about everything. Basically, you're going to need a good microphone as well as a good preamp to make any halfway decent acoustic recordings.

But you'd start with the mic.

I think I would. Something like an Audio-Technica 4060, or this new 4047, which is a great sounding little mic. The 4060 is a great overall microphone, or their 4050, which is less expensive. I know I'm pushing Audio-Technica, but I think they're making really good products for the price, and they're very usable on lots of different things. Another option would be a good old AKG 414—you can put it on almost anything.

Are you better off buying one good microphone rather than something like six SM57s?

Well, if you don't have a number of 57s, you're crazy, because it's the greatest mic ever made. I use it on snare drum and electric guitars; you can use it on toms—it even works on a high hat. It sounds decent enough, but it's not a great vocal mic unless you're just eating it. But I think a guy in a home studio is usually going to be overdubbing one instrument at a time, and he's probably not going to be recording a drum kit, so there's less need for a whole bunch of any one kind of microphone. Home recordists should have at least two 57s, one good large diaphragm condenser microphone and one good small diaphragm condenser microphone. Then I would suggest investing in one good mic preamp or one good module like the Focusrite 215, which gives you a 4-band equalizer plus a pretty decent mic pre. Probably the most important element, though, to mixing a good record is having accurate monitoring. I'm a big fan of the KRK E8s. I know they are expensive, but you're getting high-powered amplifiers; they're bi-amped, and their low end exceeds most small speakers that I've run across.

Are you an NS10 fan?

I was the first guy in Nashville to get NS10s, and I used them for a really long time—until I couldn't stand it any more! (laughs) So I departed from NS10s probably before everybody else did. I've been through so many different esoteric speakers. For the last three or four years, I've been using the E8s, and I just love them.

Do you mix on nearfields a lot?

I use nearfields almost exclusively, because there just aren't many situations where the main monitors sound all that good. The mains in most studios are intended primarily for hyping the clients and playing real loud.

Do you monitor at low volumes?

All volumes. I actually work quite loud from time to time, but I try not to stay there very long, and will also work at low volumes and middle volumes. I don't see any way of identifying if the whole mix is really holding up unless you crank it. I don't know how you can check the bottom end and whether the vocals are poking out too much without turning it up quite loud. There are also things that you'll miss by listening loud, so you have to work at low levels, too.

Do you have any tips or techniques for recording vocals?

Well, if there's any budget at all, you might want to call up your local audio rental company and see if you can't borrow some great vocal mics. (laughs) A great vocal mic is a very expensive item that most home recordists wouldn't have the funds to buy. I'm talking about things like C12s and U 67s and U 47s and other vintage microphones. If you've got a little bit of a budget, most of these companies will loan you microphones in anticipation of a rental. They might give you five, six, seven different microphones to try out until you find the one you want to rent. Just sing in all of them, and try them out. I set them up in an array where the singer can quickly move from one microphone to the next, and it's pretty quick—it's not a painstaking process for the singer or the producer/engineer to identify the microphone that really works best for the vocalist.

The microphone is the place to start, and placement is also an important thing, but it depends on the microphone, too. Some microphones like to be really close to the singer. Large diaphragm condenser microphones are going to have a lot of proximity effect, so you may have to even get the singer to back up a little bit if it's too fat-sounding. I would avoid using any of the foam windscreens that are supplied with the microphones. Go out and get a knitting hoop and some pantyhose. Either one or two layers of pantyhose stretched very tightly in that knitting hoop will make a really good pop shield. There are companies that make pop shields, but that's essentially what they are.

How far away do you place the pop shield?

If it's right up close to the microphone, it won't be as effective, so you need to place it two to three inches away, depending on how close you want the singer to work the microphone. It's also a very good way to keep the singer off the microphone, since singers like to put their lips on something. So if you can put the pop shield a few inches off the microphone and if the sound is still too warm, then you can pull the pop shield back instead of asking the singer to move back. They probably won't know that they are not as close to the microphone, but you'll get a better sound.

If a singer is really well-trained and knows to turn their head on *p*s, no pop filter is sonically the best way to do it, because even something like panty hose messes with the phase response of high frequencies and causes a smearing in the top end which you can hear. Most singers won't do that—those days are gone. (laughs) I've worked with some singers from the 50s and 60s, and they really knew how to work a microphone. If they do that, you don't need to compress the vocal and you hardly have to ride the vocal when it's done—they've done it themselves. But you don't see that much any more.

I've heard of stuff like people taping a pencil in front of the microphone to diffuse the breath. Another trick is to slightly mic above the mouth, though you have a tendency to get more of a nasal sound if you do that. So the trade-off may be that a pop filter works best. I'll usually compress a little bit when I'm tracking—not a whole lot, because if you start compressing the vocal too much, the singer's not going to feel their natural dynamics, and then they're not going to work the mic. But you generally have to compress a little bit just so that you can listen to the singer. If you find that the singer's got no technique at all, then compress more. But first let the singer have the opportunity to work the microphone until you realize he or she has no technique! (laughs)

I like to use a tube compressor when I track, but I'll generally use a VCA compressor when I mix. My favorite for tracking is the Tube Tech compressor, set at about 2 or 3:1 ratio, with fairly slow attack and fairly quick release. Then I use a GML 8900 compressor when I mix, which just beautifully rides the vocal and doesn't destroy the high end even though it may be compressing quite a lot. That will be set to a medium attack/release setting, with a ratio of 1.8:1 to upwards of 3:1. Every now and then, I'll use an 1176 to limit vocals, depending on the voice and the kind of music you're trying to do.

My experience is more with music that has dynamic to it—country music has more dynamics [than other kinds of music]. It's losing that more and more, which is good and bad—I don't know what to say about that. You have to do what's in vogue. (laughs) I'm hoping that 5.1 is going to bring back dynamics and bring back musicality, because it's not going to be an airplay medium—at least not in the foreseeable future. From what I've seen, the more dynamic the music and the mix, the more appreciative listeners are of surround.

Do you find it easier to mix in 5.1 than in stereo?

No, I wouldn't say 5.1 mixes are easier. I would say they are certainly more fun.

Now, you're talking to a fairly jaded person here. I've been mixing for 15 years solid, and there are a lot of things that you just do over and over and over again. The procedures are all set; the models are all made. Practically everything that's been thought of has been done and you've heard it. So you can duplicate it; those models are all in the back of your mind, and it's not all that hard to conjure up an image and go for it. I don't care what kind of music it is; I listen to all kinds of music—country's not the only thing I listen to. I listen to everything, and I pretty much have models of how things ought to sound in stereo.

But in 5.1 there are no models, and it becomes a very creative, intuitive, and refreshing thing to do—it's just wide open. I think at first it's going to be a very dynamic sonic experience—people are going to mix very wild in surround just because it's a new thing, and they're going to want to impress listeners. I see nothing wrong with that. I know that there are a lot of people saying, "Oh, it's horrible, it destroys the music to do that." But I think 5.1 ought to be a fun thing to hear, at least when you first hear it, even though those kind of mixes probably aren't going to stand the test of time. Ten years from now, the stuff that's panning all around the speakers is not going to be the thing you keep pulling out to listen to; the mixes that really pull emotion out of you are going to be the ones that you'll live with the rest of your life. I don't think the gimmick element of 5.1 is going to be that significant. Not to say that it's not fun to just pan something around! (laughs) It is fun, and it does sound cool. I love all that stuff.

> *"The mixes that really pull emotion out of you are the ones that you'll live with the rest of your life."*

Do you find that you have to EQ differently when doing a surround mix?

Surround requires less EQ. We were talking earlier about ways of getting around masking, either with EQ to allow room for one instrument to sit with another instrument or by panning them and separating the spectral and rhythmic elements. So, obviously, because you have more point sources and more area to allow the sound to come from, you can pan things away from each other more, and that requires less EQ to hear everything. As a result, you don't have as many masking problems.

Do you find that you compress more or less when you are doing a surround mix?

A lot of what we do compression-wise is because we are chasing our tails and trying to make the loudest record on radio. But this format is not a radio format—it's more of a hi-fi esoteric audio listening experience, one that most people will initially experience by listening in an automobile. As a result, you'll still have to deal with ambient noise, in which case making something too dynamic is simply not going to work. In other words, I think it's more impressive to hear a multichannel mix that has a large dynamic range, but you have to be mindful of the many not-so-great situations in which it will be monitored.

Selected Listening:

Vince Gill: *Key*, MCA, 1998; *High Lonesome Sound*, MCA, 1996; *When Love Finds You*, MCA, 1994

Dixie Chicks: *Wide Open Spaces*, Sony, 1998

Trisha Yearwood: *Where Your Road Leads*, MCA, 1998; *Everybody Knows*, MCA, 1996; *Thinkin' About You*, MCA, 1996

Mark Knopfler: *Wag The Dog* (soundtrack), Polygram, 1998; *Golden Heart*, Warner Bros., 1996

Wynonna Judd: *Other Side*, Uptown/Universal, 1997; *Revelations*, Curb, 1996; *Tell Me Why*, MCA, 1993; *Wynonna*, Curb, 1992

George Strait: *One Step At A Time*, MCA, 1998; *Carrying Your Love With Me*, MCA, 1997; *Blue Clear Sky*, MCA, 1996; *Easy Come Easy Go*, MCA, 1993

Ralph Sutton

Every young recordist fantasizes at one time or another about what it must be like to land a gig with a musical legend. Ralph Sutton is one of the select few who has actually lived that dream. Currently chief engineer at Stevie Wonder's Wonderland Studios in L.A., Sutton started out assisting at City Recorders in 1979, building a client list that included Kansas, Motley Crue, and Jesse Colin Young. In 1982, he moved to Motown Hitsville, where he was at last able to focus on his musical genres of choice: funk and R&B. There, and later at Kenny Rogers' Lionshare Studios, Sutton had the opportunity to work with the aforementioned Mr. Wonder as well as superstars like Smokey Robinson, Rick James, Jeffrey Osborne, the Temptations, and the Four Tops. Along the way, he took time out to handle the technical side of seminal rap records made by artists like Grand Poobah, Rakim, and Curtis Blow. More recently, he has made the transition to producer, working with Lionel Richie, while continuing his association with Wonderland.

Lively, earnest, and clearly dedicated to his craft, Sutton shared some of his recording tips and techniques with us, as well as outlining his uniquely gridiron- and fruitbowl-oriented approach towards mixing (we kid you not). All in all, a fascinating man with a fascinating perspective.

A big problem for many people working on their own in project studios is figuring out when something is finished. How do you know when enough is enough?

When you've achieved your original idea; when you've done everything that you first thought of doing.

But what if you think of new things along the way?

You add them in, provided they do not interfere with your original concept. You have to always be careful not to walk out of the room, hear something on the radio, and think, "God, I should have used the [Antares] AutoTune because it sounds so great on Cher's voice!" You can't get caught up like that because what happens then is you've gone from creating to *re*creating—you've crossed the line.

What sort of common mistakes are people making in their demos?

A lot of times people get really anxious, and they want to rip through what they're trying to accomplish, using just any mic. Anybody who has their own studio should invest in one really good mic, whether it's a Neumann M 149 or a Sony C800, something like that. They need to have one mic which is *the* mic. They're better off buying one good mic as opposed to a bunch of the latest gizmos.

Also, it seems that a lot of people are doing their vocals in an ambient area that's uncontrolled—one with parallel walls—and then they effect it, too. So now you have a really strange tonal quality. Sometimes it's going to work out well, but for the most part it doesn't. People need to think about what they're trying to accomplish and understand that, if you're going to effect a vocal, you need that vocal to be as controlled and as dry as humanly possible for the environment that you're in. For example, you might want to put a mattress up against a wall and face it, then put the mic between you and the mattress. You don't want to do a vocal in a bathroom and then try to put more synthetic room sound on it, because you've already achieved that organically—there's going to be a conflict.

It'll be like you're in a bathroom inside a bathroom.

Exactly. Same thing with guitars. Most people would be better off tight-miking the amp or going direct, as opposed to trying to come up with something that they possibly don't yet understand how to do. People think that to get a big guitar sound, they need to put the amp in a big room and stick a mic at the other end of the room, but that's exactly the wrong way to go about it—you want to start with a tight sound and *then* make it big.

> **"People think that to get a big guitar sound, they need to put the amp in a big room and stick a mic at the other end of the room, but that's exactly the wrong way to go about it."**

When a new singer comes in for a session—someone you don't know at all—where do you start?

I put my proven mic up—the mic I know has worked before, get it in front of 'em, using my particular technique, which is three to four inches in front of the face. Don't get any closer, don't get any further away, let's hear how you sound, with no effects, no compression. I carefully set the mic pre to 3 or 4 dB under 0 so there's no danger of clipping. From that point, I then compress, and I use the output of the compressor to make up the other part of the gain because I do want to come close to 0; in the digital domain, that's plenty. I just use the compressor to knock 3 or 4 dB off at their maximum intensity, so the compressor, for me, is just something to smooth it out.

What sort of compression ratios do you use for vocals?

3:1, 4:1, somewhere in that area. But it depends on what you're trying to accomplish. If you're going for that in-your-face, Sheryl Crow type of sound, then obviously you're going to have to use a much higher ratio. That decision should be made by a combination of the artist and the engineer—it's a matter of knowing what it is you're going for, conceptualizing.

Once the compression is determined and the level is set, if there's something lacking or too much of something, then I start rolling off frequencies, beginning with the low frequency rolloff switch on the mic itself. Then you start tweaking to achieve what it is you're trying to achieve. But those are three things I focus on initially: make sure I'm using the top dog mic that I know works, then set up compression, then EQ.

Do you favor tube compressors on vocals?

I try to follow the golden rule, which is, if it's a tube mic, then you don't use a tube com-

pressor, though this doesn't always hold true. Personally, I like the way the [UREI] 1176 sounds [on vocals].

What about recording keyboards? I assume that you don't just use the plain vanilla technique of plugging into a DI box and straight into the console.

No, I don't! (laughs) For something like a Rhodes sound, the EQ might be something like 3 dB at 10 k, 2 dB at 360 Hz, and 1 or 2 dB at 100 Hz, just so I can get the "whoom." Then you might want to get into some kind of compression, but that's all stock stuff. But we also do some crazy stuff, like running a Clavinet through a stack of Marshalls; that creates a great vibe because it's an analog keyboard. I'll take the mono output from the Clav into one head and set it bright and sparkly, then daisy chain the signal into another head and leave it flat. This gives me both a killer top end and a solid bottom. I use one [Neumann] U 47 FET on the flat amp and a [Sennheiser] 421 on the one that's set to all high end, then I'll blend the two signals to taste. For organ sounds, I love the little Fender ToneMaster for its spring reverb, as well as using a Leslie. In general, it's always worth trying a keyboard signal through an amp as opposed to automatically DIing it.

Any tips for recording electric guitar?

Pretty much the same thing—DI and amp. I use the DI primarily for the attack, the picking; the amp will give you the ambience and the bottom. One guitarist I work with a lot is Michael Thompson. Mike's got all these different gizmos—retro devices, like tape slap—so all of his sound comes from the amp. But I still like to plug him in direct just so I have it. The direct sound in some cases will save your ass. If all else fails, you can feed it into an amp after the fact and create what you were trying to get initially. Maybe the room was inappropriate, or there were budget limitations and you weren't able to get access to good mics when you originally recorded it. The DI signal is a good insurance policy.

Compression with guitars, of course, is tremendously important. [A ratio of] 20:1 sounds great to me sometimes; other times, 2:1 is the right setting. It depends on how controlled the playing is.

Do you prefer tube or solid-state compression on guitars?

Generally, solid-state. Solid-state compression gives you a really controlled situation; you can depend on that signal doing exactly what you're telling it to do. With tube compression—especially with some of the older devices—it's not exactly a crapshoot, but if the guitar plays a little harder in certain sections, odd things can happen. I do like tube compression on acoustic guitar, though. It also works well on signals like the guitar that's meant to be a ghost rhythm, the one you hear only faintly in the left speaker, with all the bottom rolled off and there's nothing but top end, laid back into the track so that it's literally just ear candy.

In a project studio where you're working under a budget, an inexpensive solid-state compressor is going to beat an inexpensive tube compressor. If you can buy a tube compressor for five or six hundred dollars, believe me, it's *not* the bomb. The dbx 160x is a good, inexpensive solid-state compressor; there are a lot of affordable solid-state devices that are really very nice.

What about tips and techniques for recording bass?

I get the pleasure of recording Nathan East all the time. What works for him is a U 47 FET right up against his cabinet plus a direct signal. The 47 gives me the bottom end; I even add 6 dB at 40 Hz. I get all his fingering and top end from the DI, and that works out really well.

Do you use tube gear on bass to add warmth?

You could, but with Nate I use the solid-state stuff—an 1176 or an LA-4A. I'll use a compression ratio of 4:1, knock off 3 or 4 dB. Even though I'm almost always recording to digital multitrack [Sony 3348], in my head, I'm still thinking analog tape at +9. So I very rarely want to go over 0 VU; I'll hit it occasionally, dance around it. So when I compress, I make sure the input gain is not quite where I want to be, but close. Then the compressor will kick in when the player spikes, and I use the output gain to make up the difference. This gives me maximum volume, but with control—because the worst thing of all is to get distortion on a great take. I would rather have it too low and have to increase my noise floor than have a nasty clip. So my safety measure is to get the signal close, and then let the output of the compressor get it closer.

Let's talk about your experiences making rap records. Rap is an art form that seems to be all about breaking the rules that came before it, and it's largely based on the creative use of inexpensive gear.

We've seen that in the grunge zone, too, and in skate music. Other than the ethnicities, they're almost like first cousins to each other. But there's really no rule-breaking, because you've got to hit it on the nose. If an artist comes in with an [E-mu] SP12 drum machine, the rule has already been broken, because it's a 12-bit sampler! But that's the sound: making loops out of things sampled from vinyl, going crazy with EQ to hack up a sound and extract individual components.

What's the secret to getting that big boom in the kick drum?

You've got to start with the TR-808 kick drum—that's the king of rap. That sound happens at 60 Hz; you've usually got to add some, to taste, depending on how much boom you want. There's also a little mallet happening at 1.5 kHz.

It seems like the goal of a lot of rap records is to blow up the listener's speakers.

You're right— Curtis Blow once said he would not be happy unless people were calling to try to sue him for breaking their JVC! But it's all flavor. Some people have a predisposition for certain styles of music. I grew up in a 60-cycle domain; I was born in Chicago but we moved to the inner part of L.A. early on, right in South Central. And there's always low frequency going on, whether it's the bus going by, the airplane flying over, the jackhammer in the background. So there are certain frequencies we are exposed to for long durations of time, and, obviously I'm not a psychologist, but I think that has something to do with it. If you grow up in an inner city where this is going on all the time, that gives you a different disposition; there's music in that noise. When you hear construction noise and something falls down, there's your boom-boom right there. A different part of that noise is your snare. You can't necessarily go and capture that, but that's

"You've got to have a game plan for your mix; it can't be chaotic or haphazard, it's got to be thought out and plotted."

where a lot of the creativity comes from. I periodically ride my bike down to Venice [Beach, CA], and that's a totally different environment; there's these cats riding their bikes and on skateboards and rollerblades, so you have a different level of ambience. They live by the water, so they have that sizzle going on, that spray.

I've actually tried to figure it out myself, where this flavor comes from. When I was working with Motley Crue back in the early days, Nikki [Sixx] and Mick Mars basically said, "Ralph, make it sound black." That was the flavor. It wasn't them trying to convert me, it was us coming to a happy medium. And because we're in a techno-artistic field, there's really nothing wrong with that. It's just a perception, just somebody saying, "Put your little twist in the music."

Let's talk a little about your approach to mixing.

The big question is, who's the feature? And who's accompanying the feature? Is it a piano, a guitar, a sax? Is it background vocals, *a la* Babyface? The Babyface sound is basically riding the background vocals up as if they were the lead. That's his sound: huge, quadrupled backgrounds, four on a side, so there are eight vocals on each note. Mixing is a sport for me.

Whatever team I'm on, I need to know who the quarterback is. I need to know what the rules are—and the rules always have to be public, and the goal has to be clear. There can be no chaos; I hate chaos. You have to have a clearly defined goal in mind before you even start the mix; you can't just let it be wild.

But isn't there something to be said for creating in the studio and letting things that occur shape where you're going?

Within reason, but not with the mix. You've got to have a game plan for your mix; it can't be chaotic or haphazard, it's got to be thought out and plotted. If you're not winning with your game plan, then you alter it, but you alter it very minutely. The bassist is like your lineman; if he played a few weak notes, it's like he missed a few blocks. So what do I do? I compress him and make his ass bigger. Your guitar, he's your running back. If he's not able to get there quick enough, you increase the release time on the compressor and get him there quicker.

When you first start a mix, in what order do you bring faders up?

I always start with the rhythm section—drums, bass, keyboards, and guitar. I don't bring in the vocals until I've got everything else where it needs to be. Another thing is that I mix very soft; I very rarely listen loud. The feature is always supposed to be the feature. It's like setting up a fruitbowl, and the artist is the apple. He has to be seen, but he's still part of the bowl. Everything else is the fruit that accompanies that big red apple. That apple, it's supposed to be luscious and delicious, and the surroundings are supposed to make you just want that apple.

Sometimes I'll just start over; I'll get four or five hours into a mix and just say, fuck this, zero out the board, get my mind away from it for a little while, then come back in and start over. Get rid of all those ideas that weren't working. People sometimes try to make a dead horse run anyway; they take a bad idea and keep fucking with it until it becomes a super-bad idea!

Selected Listening:
Stevie Wonder: *Inner City Blues*, Motown, 1995
Lionel Richie: *Time*, Polygram, 1998
Michael Jackson: *You Are Not Alone* (remix), Sony, 1997
Paula Abdul: *If I Were Your Girl* (remix), Virgin, 1995; *Cry For Me* (remix), Virgin, 1995
Norman Brown: *Better Days Ahead*, MoJazz, 1996; *After The Storm*, Mojazz, 1994; *Just Between Us*, MoJazz, 1992

Sylvia Massy Shivy

Sylvia Massy Shivy has one of the most infectious laughs you'll ever hear. It's hard to imagine this bright, cheery woman—one of only a handful of female engineer/producers in the business—hanging out in the studio with the likes of angry thrashers like Tool. But clearly a synergy exists, because their partnership resulted in one of the more successful debut albums in recent memory—1993's *Undertow*.

As far back as high school, Shivy knew that music was her calling. She sang and played drums, keyboards, and guitar in local bands, performing everything from reggae to ska to punk to metal. In college, she began making radio commercials—experience that she claims has served her well by providing a theatrical view of music production. Assistantships at a number of studios in both northern and southern California followed, and she soon made the transition to engineer and then producer. Despite her early experiences working with mainstream artists like Patti LaBelle, Barbra Streisand and Prince, Shivy gravitates towards the harder edge of things, aligning herself with a variety of alternative rockers, including the aforementioned Tool and bands like Powerman 5000, System Of A Down, Machines Of Loving Grace, and Love And Rockets. Recently returned to northern California, she's currently in the process of building her own studio, where she plans to continue her work out on the bleeding edge of popular music.

Why do you think there are so few women in the music business?

You know, that is a very interesting question. When I first got into the business, I thought, well, maybe there's some kind of unfairness as far as men versus women in the business. But the more time I've spent in it, the more I realize that that is not the case. It's that women biologically have other things to do, and by the time their career really gets going, it's time to think about other things! (laughs).

That doesn't explain why there aren't more women in entry-level positions.

It's difficult when you really want to be an engineer or get into producing, and you find out that it takes everything. It takes fifteen hour days, six, sometimes seven days a week, total dedication, working for practically nothing to start. That's enough to discourage not only women, but most entry-level people.

There are also some physical demands to the job when you're starting out. As a runner, you're moving equipment, you're lifting things, you're pushing bass cabinets around. It has been difficult for some runners that I've seen at Larrabee and some other places—they can't take the physical demands.

Still, this is such a male-dominated industry.

I suppose there are some people that may feel uncomfortable working with a woman. I think that the best way for a woman to present herself in the studio is to not be noticed as much—to dress more in the uniform of a studio: jeans, really basic attire, not flashy, not dressed up. Women love to dress up, and I think it's a distraction for clients. Though some clients love it; some clients will only work with women. I was lucky to get a job in L.A. at Larrabee, which has always had a good hiring practice of starting women. But there are places that I've found to be very difficult for women to start in, and for no good reason. It is an issue. It's weird that there are not that many women in the industry.

Even if you look at the recording schools, there's a disproportionate number of male students versus female students—even at the stage _before_ they're even thinking about getting hired somewhere.

Again, I have to go back to the realization that women have other things to do, and it ultimately doesn't fit in their plans. You can't have a social life when you're working in the studio. It's very difficult to nurture relationships when you're stuck in the studio all the time, or you're traveling to England for three months at a time, or Norway, or South America, or wherever you wind up. It's just not very good for cultivating strong relationships, and I think that's important for a lot of women because of biology. That's all I can figure. It's just a natural draw towards those kind of careers that don't demand 100 percent dedication.

And yet the curious thing is that, more often than not, the studio manager is a woman.

That's true. But she can go home after 8:00 p.m. (laughs)

What experience do you feel had the greatest impact on your career?

Probably the one with the most impact was the work I did with Prince when I was assisting at Larrabee. He would have several rooms going at the same time, and he'd always be short an engineer and would just have the assistant do the project. So I got to engineer and mix for him on several different projects.

He's one of just a handful of artists that have been able to successfully produce themselves. Why do you think that is? What's the magic ingredient?

Well, the thing about Prince is that he has the final product already swimming in his head; he knows what it's going to sound like. He could get it there himself—he could engineer it, he could produce it, he could perform every part himself faster than anyone else—but he prefers to have other people put it together.

Are you saying that there's no real collaboration, that he doesn't seek input?

No, he's open to ideas, but when he walks in, he already has the finished product in his head, including every little detail. When I worked with him, this was how he worked: He would play two bars of one riff on the guitar and two bars of another riff on a guitar, and he would play a drum beat live on a drum machine with one hand and the bass line on another keyboard with the other hand. And then he would turn around and say, "OK, first riff in the verses, second riff in the choruses, there's your drum beat for the whole song, put it all together, and I'll be back." And then he'd leave, and who knows when he'd be back, but you better get

on it, 'cause it better be ready by the time he gets back.

Does he start tweaking from there, or is that the song?

He'll start adding to it. He'll lay another part down, and then he'll kick you out, and he'll have you wait for him while he records vocals. He never allowed me to be in the studio when he did vocals. The vocal mic was set up over the console so that he could do his own recording and comping for all vocal parts—I think he's very shy about his vocals in the studio. In every other sense, he certainly is an exhibitionist. When he's performing even those few little bars of guitar riffs, he's spinning on his heels, he's dancing and putting on quite a show. He's an amazing musician.

How important was the vibe of the studio to Prince?

The mood was *very* important with Prince. Larrabee went all out to make him comfortable. The first time he booked the studio, I was assigned as the assistant, and I immediately ordered the guitars and effects I thought he would want to use and had them rented and there in the studio for him. But when he walked in the door, he looked around the room and he said, "Don't you have a big Grandma's chair or anything?" And I looked at him, and I just said, "Yes, we do." Of course the studio didn't have anything like that. (laughs) But I walked out, borrowed someone's truck, drove down to Melrose, bought an overstuffed chair, threw it in the back, came back and brought it in, and he sat down on it. He wound up staying in that room for almost three years, and by the time he was done, the place was decorated with curtains and candles, with incense always going. In fact, they built a room for him upstairs called the Prince Room At Larrabee.

Did he take the chair with him when he left?

No. (laughs)

What's the oddest way that you've recorded a guitar and got a good workable track out of it?

Well, anything is workable. (laughs) The funnest moment was throwing a guitar off a cliff at Indigo Ranch while I was recording a band called Machines Of Loving Grace. There's this beautiful view of the ocean and a rocky cliff at Indigo, and it's quite a ways away from the studio, so we had to get a very, very, *very* long extension cord. I brought my portable DAT recorder up to the cliff where we set up a Marshall stack and had a sacrificial guitar that had been decorated for the occasion. We drilled a hole through the guitar and tied a long rope on it so that we could retrieve it and had a very long instrument cable going from the guitar into the Marshall stack. And then, at the precise moment of the most beautiful feedback—because we generated a feedback from the setup on the cliff—the guitar was tossed off and we recorded the sound of it crashing. It was really tremendous! (laughs) Later we retrieved the guitar and the owner of the studio framed the remains. He has it up on the wall of the studio now.

> *"When I'm working with bands, I try to get them to loosen up and to not be restrained by what they do."*

Whose idea was this—the band's or yours?

Mine. When I'm working with bands, I try to get them to loosen up and to not be restrained by what they do. So I try to think of the most insane sounds or insane things to do, for two reasons: One, to possibly get some exciting recordings to use on the record, and, secondly, to create a very memorable moment that that band will never forget. I think I manage to do that on almost every record.

It certainly sounds like you succeeded with that particular record.

Yeah.

So what did it sound like?

It was squealing and banging and crashing, with echoes off the canyon. I don't know how usable it was, but we wound up slipping it in on a segue somewhere.

So it did make it to the record.

Oh, yeah. Another odd thing I like to do is to take a cheap guitar with very microphonic pickups and set it on a guitar stand, either taping the strings quiet or tuning the guitar to an open chord in the key of the song that we're working on. Then I set it in front of the drum kit and use it as a resonator, effectively creating an ambience track.

And one of the funnest things that I've ever done—but I'll never do again—happened during the recording of the Tool *Undertow* record. I bought a couple of junker pianos, and we set them up in a garage and put some acoustic guitar contact mics on the soundboard, along with some 57s for close miking and some U 87s for room sound. Then we recorded the pianos first being shot, then destroyed with sledgehammers.

Real music lovers, aren't we?

(laughs) You know, I have to say that I'll never do that again, because after tearing apart two pianos, I really saw how they are made and the delicate pieces that go together to make these beautiful instruments. And the sounds that they made as they were being broken apart gave me a very sad feeling, so I'll never do it again. I have much more respect for pianos now.

Though obviously not as much respect for guitars.

No. (laughs)

Do these experiments really come from a search for new sounds, or is it just really a way of engaging the artist and making it a fun experience for them?

I guess the first time it was to find the most outrageous, loudest sound. There were ideas of getting a crane and dropping a thousand light bulbs from the crane and recording that, or recording in a grain silo. Those were the types of ideas we were talking about, and when the first discussions began, I found the band really getting excited. And that's what I wanted—this excitement and getting their creative juices flowing. So I think it works in both ways.

But was the purpose of the sound to enhance the music, or was it really just meant as a gimmick?

I hate to use the word "gimmick," but Tool is very angry, and it seemed to be a part of their character. We didn't have an application for the sound until after it had been created; in the end, we sequenced the noise into the last song on the Tool record. So I suppose you could call it a gimmick, but it fits the character of the band; Tool is destructive.

I guess that the fact that I came out of radio production is a factor for me. My favorite albums are the ones that are not just a collection of songs but also have a sense of humor about them and perhaps have nonsongs or little bits and pieces that can be used in radio production.

What are your favorite albums?

Let's see. XTC, *English Settlement*, and *Sgt. Pepper* and, uh...this is a very hard question. (laughs) My favorite recent record is Static X *Wisconsin Death Trip*. Flaming Lips's *Transmissions Of The Satellite Heart* is also one of my favorite records, as well as Harry Nilsson's *Nilsson Schmilsson*.

We seem to be in a very odd place in audio right now. At the same time that we're moving towards high resolution digital audio, we've also got MP3 going on, and low-fi seems to be hip these days. How do you decide which direction to take a recording?

Well, approaching any project, the first thing beyond anything technical is, are there songs? A song will shine through no matter what direction you take it—whether it's entirely recorded with machines or if there are human players. So I suppose the first thing is to find out where the song is, what it needs, and how to develop it. And, depending on where that band or artist is in their development, then the further along we'll go. If it's a brand new band with a lot of energy, it may be rawer than someone on their third record, where we'd concentrate on developing their

> **"A song will shine through no matter what direction you take it."**

singles and polishing them up. So the direction it'll take really depends on the artist and the song. I have to say that now it's easy to record with Pro Tools anyplace—not just in a commercial studio—so you don't have to sacrifice quality just because you're working with Pro Tools, as long as you use peripherals that enhance the quality of the sound as you're recording it. For example, I'll always try to get some kind of Neve preamps and some good quality mics for vocals, so there are ways to work within these new guidelines.

What is it that makes something a finished record as opposed to a demo?

I think there is a difference in the recording of a demo and of a finished album. Demos seem to have an energy that gets lost when the songs are rerecorded. Often on demos, the drum recording is unfocused, and there's usually not a lot of time spent in layering other instruments and vocal parts. If I listen to a track and notice things about it that are missing, then I would consider it a demo.

But there's a fine line between fleshing a song out sufficiently and not overdoing it. How do you know when you've crossed that line?

Well, as soon as it gets real crowded, you've gone over the line. I think a production needs negative space as much as it needs space to be filled up. As long as you have left a pocket here and there, you're doing OK. Simplicity always seems to be better when you're talking about musical parts, so as soon as it feels claustrophobic, you might want to shed a few tracks and simplify it a bit.

And there's also the all-important issue of dynamics.

Exactly—that's where the positive and negative space comes from.

That seems to be one of the hardest things for new artists to come to terms with. How can you make a new artist understand that?

You want a song to have movement and to have a payoff and hopefully a peak. If you're trying to explain that to a new artist, you might take examples of songs that they like—even though perhaps they don't know why they like it—and listen with them and discuss it. Ask them why they like it; hopefully, the song will include an example of that type of dynamic movement.

Another tough thing for home recordists is dealing with low end—getting a tight, solid bass without it becoming boomy and woofy. What kind of techniques have you come up with for dealing with that?

You have to have proper monitoring. Otherwise, you don't know what's going on with your low end; you're just flying blind. So I would recommend that in a home recording setup that you have something that translates low end real well. Even a pair of Genelecs will show you what's going on, if you can afford to put something like that together.

Assuming that you are monitoring accurately, what knobs do you start reaching for?

There's a real scary knob—the high pass filter. That allows you to trim off the sub-frequencies that are going to get you in trouble and that will help you tighten up the low end.

How do you identify what those frequencies are? For example, if you're trying to get a kick drum and a bass to lock together, how do you go about doing that?

I try to separate the frequencies and make them independent from each other, and that can be really very tricky, depending on what you're working on. I usually work on the kick drum first, putting it into a complete picture with the rest of the drum kit. Once that spectrum is worked out, then the bass comes in next. Or sometimes I'll add guitars before the bass, because the lower guitar frequencies can make the bass confused. So one way to clear the bass up is to use that high pass filter to clear up the low end on the guitar; it allows you room for the bass. I suppose the lowest frequency is the kick drum and then the bass sits right above that, and the guitars are on top of that.

So you'll roll off low frequencies in the bass so that they don't conflict with the higher end of the kick drum?

That's right.

What sort of frequency areas are you talking about?

60–100 Hz on the low part of the kick drum. And above that with the bass, depending on what key the song is in.

Do you use a lot of compression?

Most of the time I don't record with compression on the drums. I will often add compression in the mix to the kick and sometimes to the snare. If it's a real mechanical sound, I'll use a lot of compression—and very pokey sounding compression. More organic sounds will get a looser type of drum compression and more room. Bass, I usually do record with compression.

Do you record both DI and bass amp signals?

Yeah, and depending on where the bass needs to sit in the mix, I'll reverse the phase on one of the two bass tracks until it pokes out the best. Also, when recording drums, it's very important to check phase between every single mic, because there'll be some conflicting phase, and you will lose instruments and have a very difficult time later trying to hear things.

What's your favorite bass amp mic?

Sennheiser 421. Just give me a dozen 421s and I'm happy! (laughs)

What are your favorite drum mics?

I use a [Sennheiser MD] 421 for kick and toms, a [Shure SM] 57 for top and bottom snare, [AKG] 414s or 451s for high hats and individual cymbals. For overheads, a pair of [Neumann U] 87s or a C24. Sometimes I use a Neumann CMV 563 with the M7 capsule for a room mic; that's kind of an unusual mic.

I don't get too complicated with drum mics, although the last project I worked on as an engineer was difficult, because the drummer played the cymbals so loud—he was constantly riding the hat open and crashing the cymbals. I had a difficult time getting the cymbals out of the toms, so I used a Shure SM98 clip-on for the top of the toms, and that worked great. They're just little tiny things that clip on the top heads of the toms, and there's a lot of low end and very little cymbal bleed.

Do you process the rooms mics in any way?

I'll usually split them into different compressors that I carry around with me. I've got this old crusty Western Electric compressor that is maxed out, and that will go on a track. Then I've got a UA175 compressor that is slightly milder and sweeter. So I'll split the signal and have two separate mono rooms just to use as effects later.

What sort of things might you do with the room mics later?

One fun thing to do in Pro Tools is to use a gating program set to very hard gating, triggered off the kick and snare. That gives the room mics a real mechanical rhythm sound.

Is your usual electric guitar miking setup a 57 against the grille?

A 57 and a 421 against the grille, on two separate speakers. Again, you have to be very careful with phase; just check it until the signal is the strongest.

Do you ever use ambient guitar mics?

No, not unless it's for a solo. For a lot of my projects, room mics kind of cloud up my picture a little bit. I like it really in your face.

What's your setup for recording acoustic guitar?

I like recording them mono, and that could be with a 414 or even a 57 for a very dry woody sound, depending on the guitar. The 57 makes the guitar sound very percussive—it's a lot less musical and more percussive.

What about for recording piano? And don't tell me chainsaw!

(laughs) Oh, you mean without the chainsaw? That would be a pair of U 87s, or a C24 is nice, too. I'll put one far down into the low strings and one up on the high strings, just behind the hammers.

What are your favorite vocal mics?

It depends on the performance and the performer. A lot of times, to get the best performance in real hard music, I'll use a live mic like an SM58. In fact, for certain voices, it can't be beat. I'm very impressed with an SM58—isn't that silly? (laughs) I mean, I own a Telefunken U47. When I was working with the Smashing Pumpkins we set that up, plus we rented a Telefunken 251 and another, oh, $20,000 of rental tube mics, and also set up an SM58 and SM57, an 87, and some very inexpensive mics, and did the blindfold test. We listened to each individual mic and recorded a little bit of it using the same compressor, which was a UA175, and ultimately the U47 and the 58 won. And, because we could get better performance with the 58—because it can be knocked around a little bit—we went for the 58 and sent back all the tube mics.

But for intimate vocal performances, I like to use the U47 tube with a great deal of compression—usually two compressors ganged up, an LA2A with an 1176 or an RCA BA6A compressor with the UA175.

And you'll record it with double compression?

Oh, yeah, because if the performer hears his voice compressed in the headphones, he'll perform differently than if he was not hearing that compression.

So why not just do it in his headphones?

I suppose you could. But if a magical moment happens in his headphones, then dammit, we better get it on the tape just the way that it happened. I don't like to try to reproduce something after the fact.

That was the way it was with the Johnny Cash project that I engineered [*Unchained*]. There was just a star-studded group of people on that record: Tom Petty and the Heartbreakers, Flea, Carl Perkins, Mick Fleetwood, Lindsay Buckingham, and Johnny Cash. And before they even sat down, tape had better be rolling—because they're going to play, and it's going to be right the first time. So I learned big lessons with that; the tape was always rolling.

Let's talk a little more about mixing. You mentioned that you start with the kick drum, followed by the rest of the drums, and then you bring in the bass and the guitars. Where do you go from there?

Sometimes, after I get a good balance, I'll start again with just the drums, and I'll put the vocals in and then reintroduce the balance of guitars and bass to see where the vocal fits. It depends on the song. If it's an intimate song, that vocal will be very loud. If it's a very guitar-heavy song, the vocals may be right underneath the level of the guitars. The final thing is the spice—the effects; any kind of special effects will come in last.

Do you typically have two or three stock effects that multiple tracks get fed into, or do you assign discrete effects for each instrument?

I like using discrete effects. I'll usually set up a vocal plate, I like using a Cooper Timecube to thicken up drums, and a small room program on a [Lexicon] 480L for drums. Drums will have one set of effects; vocals have another set of effects.

One very common mixing problem is getting a lead vocal to sit right on top of a dense track. Any tips that you can pass on for accomplishing that?

Sure. Compress it. The more compression—without getting too spitty —the better you're going to hear it. And you might want to start with the overload of compression—see how it fits, and then back it off until it fits right. Also, along with compression, if your vocal is sonically in the same space as the guitars, you're going to have to make an adjustment, either bringing out more of a midrange or a honk out of the vocal, or likewise adjusting the guitars to make room for that vocal. That helps, but compression always seems to make things pop out.

When you say "more compression," are you talking about higher ratios or lower thresholds?

Both, but more lower thresholds than higher ratios.

What advice do you have for the reader who wants to be the next Sylvia Massy Shivy?

If you love music, stick with it. Don't be afraid when you're broke and you think the world's against you! (laughs) Use that energy, get pissed and keep going. Work with as many up-and-coming bands as you can—be out there looking for talent, and find a way to record them, whether it means buying your own home recording setup or getting a job in a commercial studio and sweeping floors. Just stick with it, and the longer you're there, the more likely you'll have success.

Selected Listening:
Johnny Cash: *Unchained*, American, 1996
Tool: *Undertow*, Zoo, 1993; *Opiate*, Zoo, 1992
Machines Of Loving Grace: *Gilt*, Mammoth, 1995
Love And Rockets: *Sweet F.A.*, American, 1996
Powerman 5000: *Tonight The Stars Revolt*, Dreamworks, 1998
System Of A Down: *System Of A Down*, American/Sony, 1998

Danny Saber

T he worlds of dance, trance, electronica, and techno may be anchored in New York and London, but there's a whole lot of remixing going on in L.A. as well, and Danny Saber is one of the central figures in that scene. An accomplished guitarist, Saber first made his mark in the mid-'90s as a member of the eclectic group Black Grape. His unortho-dox techniques soon gained him a reputation as a remixer to be reckoned with, and before long he was deconstructing and rebuilding tracks for a diverse group of artists ranging from Public Enemy to Megadeth; from David Bowie to Marilyn Manson; and from Madonna to Sheryl Crow. In 1997, word of his talents spread to the Rolling Stones, who brought him onboard for their *Bridges To Babylon* album (Saber coproduced the track "Gunface" and played bass and clavinet on the hit single "Out Of Control"). We caught up with him recently at L.A.'s fabled Record Plant studios as he was completing some tracks done in collaboration with the late Michael Hutchence. Though his conversation is liberally sprinkled with four-letter words, Saber came across as thoughtful, intelligent, and sensitive—and as someone who has clearly not lost touch with his street roots.

You're a musician who became a producer/engineer, not the other way around.

I'm an engineer by default. I'm the same guy as most of your readers who are doing shit in their house—that's how I started. I had a Tascam 8-track and one [Roland] S50 sampler and a Juno 106 [synth] and a D-50. Then I got an Atari 1040, and I was running Creator on it; then I got an [Akai] S1000 [sampler]. So, as the technology became more affordable, I just gradual-ly got stuff. I was also fortunate in that I was in the right place at the right time, because when I started, there was only one sampler—the S50—that was affordable. Before that, you were looking at a Fairlight. There was also the Ensoniq Mirage, but that thing was a piece of shit. Now it's insane—what do you buy? There's so much stuff that people can use—it must be really confusing for kids that don't know what to get.

The great mystique is that, if you have great gear, you don't need great skills—that you'll just turn the equipment on, and it will make a great record.

That's all a bunch of bullshit. Not to sound egotistical, but the reason I'm doing well is be-cause it's all about content now. Quality sound doesn't mean anything anymore, because any-body can get it. I'm a big fan of all those Steely Dan records—the records you put on not only for the writing and musicianship and performance, but for the way they sounded. Sonically,

those records are unbelievable, and it was really hard to make a record that sounded that good back then. Now, with the digital technology, anybody can do that—I'm talking purely from a technical basis, not from content, because obviously the musicianship and the songwriting and all that, nobody else can do.

But it is possible to make really bad recordings with really good gear.

You're right, but my point is that you can get a box now that gives you 800 drum sounds that are all unbelievable.

However, if you overload the console when you record them, they're still going to sound bad.

That's common sense stuff, though. I don't really think there's any trick to that. You either hear that it sounds like shit or you don't. And, sometimes, things that sound shitty are good.

What are the common mistakes that people are making in their recordings today?

I think the worst mistake people make is trying to do too much. That's a mistake I've made, and I've learned from it. When you've got something good and it's happening, you don't need to fuck with it anymore; leave it alone. That's the thing I'm really working on now: I'll spend more time doing something and do less to it. I'm being more patient, doing more listening. Not just doing shit to do it—everything has to serve a purpose, to make the song better or make the performance better.

It comes down to striking a balance. If you don't flesh out a song sufficiently, it comes out sounding like a raw demo, though maybe some songs require that. How do you know when you're doing too much and how do you know when you're doing too little?

It's all instinctive; it comes from experience and knowing what feels right when you're doing it. The way I work is totally unconscious, even on a technical level. I don't really sit down and think, "This is what I'm going to do to this." I just do it. The thing I think I want to try may not be the right thing but it will lead me to the place where the thing needs to be.

Instinct obviously plays a huge role because at the end of the day the purpose of music is to invoke emotion, but you also have to have some technical skills to make a great record.

Technically, what you need to know is how hard to hit the stereo bus, you need to know when you're putting too much compression on something, and you need to know how to EQ to create space. I didn't learn these things the way a traditional engineer learns them. I learned them by trying stuff and then picking things up from other engineers and asking people. Like compression—that's always a really, really dicey area.

So how do you know when something's overcompressed?

When the life is sucked out of it. My idea is to be conservative on those type of things when recording and save it for the mix, because you can always add more, but you can't take it off. If you overcompress shit, it'll suck the life out of stuff, especially when you're playing guitars or bass—it'll totally change your performance. It's a subtle little thing, but it can really ruin it. That gets back to what I was saying earlier: Be purposeful in your decisions.

"The key for young people starting out is to make the most of every second while they're working."

How do you know when to use a compressor and when not to use one?

I think you should almost always start with one and see if it feels right. Again, it's all about instinct, and the way that you learn about these things is by doing them. It's all about trial and error; there's no magic secret trick that you can learn that's going to sort everything out for you. It's all about experience, and all the great engineers are very experienced.

If you're an experienced musician and you come in to play on a track, you hear the chord progression and whatever the vibe of the song is, and you know there are different ways you can approach it. It's the same with engineering; it's like being in any situation in life. When you've been in that situation before, if you have half a brain, you're able to deal with it a lot better the next time it comes around. So the key for young people starting out is to make the most of every second while they're working. That way, when they get into a situation where it's important and it really means something, they're ready for it. That's the thing that I've noticed with a lot of people in life; they don't take the little shit seriously and then something a little more important comes along and they're not ready to deal with it. They're out of their depth, and maybe they could have been a little more prepared if they had worked harder on things that at the time didn't seem very important.

When I was learning, every time I got an opportunity—it didn't matter what it was—I made the most of it and learned as much as I could. And all of that stuff came back around later in a situation with the Stones or somebody like that, where you're really on your toes and you've got to use every brain cell you've got left! (laughs) That's what prepares you—the little things leading up to that. Everything goes into everything.

So what you're saying is, to learn about compression, have a compressor handy and try it on every track to see if it works or not. If it sucks the life out of the sound, kill it—if it doesn't, use it.

Exactly. Or find the middle ground. But sometimes it's good to suck the life out of shit. It's all about decisions and choices. That's why everybody's different, that's what separates the people that are really good from the people that are shit.

But those are aesthetic decisions you're talking about, not technical ones.

Yeah, but those aesthetic decisions come from technical ability. You have to have technical ability to get past that point. If you don't know how to use the fucking thing, then all you're going to be worrying about is figuring out how to use it—you're not going to be deciding whether it sounds good or not.

So if you're auditioning a compressor to decide whether to use it or not on a track, what settings would you start with?

I usually start by setting the threshold really conservatively so you're not overcompressing it, and the attack and the release really fast. I start by setting the ratio at 3:1 or 4:1 and then ease it up, going more and more until it really feels good. Guys like Tom Lord-Alge are totally the opposite; they compress the shit out of stuff. He's good at it, too—a compressor to him is like a guitar is to me. A compressor to me is something I need to use, but it's not my life.

At what point do you start changing the attack and the release?

When I start hearing what it is I'm dealing with—how it sounds and how it relates to the other things in the song. On its own, it may sound really bitching, but then you put it in the track and it's gone. Or it's too much. It's all interrelated, and that's what I think a lot of engineers miss. You've got to listen to the whole thing, and I think the problem with a lot of engineers is they listen to individual sounds. They make things sound really good individually—which is a good place to start—but then you've got to ease it back into the whole overall picture and make your adjustments.

Do you spend a lot of time setting up the headphone mix when you're recording vocals?

No, not at all. The singer gets what I got in here, deal with it. (laughs) And I've never had a problem, because, when I'm working, I'm always mixing as I go; that's the way I know what a song may be lacking. And the beauty of the Mackie Digital 8—which has totally enhanced the way I work—is that I can start with a mix and always pick up right where I left off and then dump the stuff to DA-88s, all EQ'd. So when I go into a big room, I just set all the faders at zero and I've basically got the mix. So you're constantly building, as opposed to doing things and then waiting for the mix.

This is really important for people to realize: How many times has somebody done a demo and then they go chasing the demo forever? This isn't something I thought about or worked out—it just naturally happened: The way I've always worked is I've always built on the demos, so whenever I went in somewhere, I was always starting with the demo. I don't shit-can everything on the demo and start over again when I make the record; half the record's done because the demo is the core of the record, so it's an ongoing process.

Which leads to the question: What's the difference between a demo and a record?

These days, there really isn't one. It used to be that a demo was a way for people to hear what a band was doing. It was needed because bands couldn't necessarily rely on someone coming to see them live, and because a lot of times things you do live don't translate to a record, and vice versa. The demo would give the A&R person an idea of what the band would sound like on tape, because that's ultimately what they had to sell.

Now it's totally different. You've got a bunch of kids in studios all over the place in their houses and they're throwing their ideas down. And almost every record I ever made started with that demo. I got all the stuff they did, I took it and I rebuilt the track around that. Now everything may have gotten shit-canned in the process, but that gives you the option. That's what's really important, and that's the advantage now. When you throw down your initial idea and that spark of inspiration's there, you don't have to sacrifice that anymore.

A big fear of young bands is producers coming in and changing everything. There's no excuse for that anymore, because even if there's one thing on the tape that's the essence of what that song's about—it could be a loop, it could be some vocals that somebody did in their house that maybe doesn't sound so great technically, but the vibe of it is awesome—there's no reason to get rid of that. You redo it, you try and beat it, but if you don't, you've got it. That's the real beauty of the way technology has changed. It gives you options—you've got so many more options these days then you used to have.

Someone in their own project studio theoretically can spend any amount of time on a recording. How do you know when to stop?

You've got to know when you're past the point of positive input. Again, that's something you learn by experience; there's no one defined answer to that. When you're doing a record, there's always this one song that's a bitch that you have to redo twenty times. And then there's the others that, you do them once, and they're awesome. Not only is that a problem for the guy in the project studio, I think it's an even bigger problem for the successful multi-platinum artist who all of a sudden is in a situation where he's got power. Those are the guys who shoot themselves in the foot more than anybody! I've seen it so many times, with singers especially, where the shit's happening and it sounds great, but because of their insecurity or fear or paranoia they've got to keep beating the thing into the ground until nobody can stand listening to it anymore. And if you do say "enough," sometimes you get fired! Personally, I'd rather walk, and I've done it, with big people, too. I've walked because they just beat the shit out of the song to the point where it just wasn't fun anymore.

So I guess a way you could tell when you're done is when you're not getting off on listening to it anymore. Maybe that's a point to stop and move onto something else and later come back to it with a fresh head. But you always have to remember how you felt when you first came up with the shit, because you've got to listen to stuff over and over again—that's the nature of it. And if the excitement still isn't there, you've got to differentiate between whether it's because you've heard it ten million times or because it's not good. That's a hard line to cross. Ultimately it comes down to confidence in yourself and not getting too precious about stuff and worrying. There's things I always want to keep working on, but at a certain point I just let it go.

Is it always helpful to bring in a second set of ears?

Definitely. It's nice to play finished stuff to people—or stuff that's almost finished—and say, "What do you think?" But you've got to be really careful with that, too, because half the time they're going to tell you it's great anyways. So you get this sense—it's not really so much what people say to you when you're playing them stuff, but you can look at them and tell if they're feeling it or not. That's another thing you just develop by being in those situations.

I used to go see all these A&R guys when I was nobody—somehow I got a meeting with them and they fast-forwarded through my songs, listening to ten seconds of a song and then fast-forwarding to the next one. At the time, that seemed really degrading and it sucked, but it really aids me now, because I can tell how people are reacting. When you're playing stuff to people, you can tell the vibe in the room if you're tapped into it. But ultimately it comes down to yourself; you can't rely on anybody else to tell you whether what you're doing is good or not, aside from the people you're intimately working with. Once you go outside that circle, all you're doing is inviting trouble.

How do you deal with situations where you're convinced that something is right and the artist isn't?

It depends on the artist and how genuine they are in their reasons. Sometimes the artist is saying shit because of their ego. But if they're genuinely committed to making the record and taking the musical journey, then you've got to sit there and listen to everything they say and take a hard look at what's on tape and be open.

"The best music has always come out of frictional situations."

When I'm not working, I've always got records on because I just get off on listening to music—that's my life. That's what you've got to look for, both as a producer and as an artist: people that are for real and are genuinely on that musical journey of life. But if you're a producer, you've got to listen, because the artist has to be happy—it's their record.

So you'll defer to an artist if they insist that their way is right?

Well, I won't do it just because they say it's right. But I'll listen to what they say, and we'll talk about it. And hopefully, in a good situation, we'll mutually find the place that it needs to go. And the middle ground doesn't always have to be a compromise, because sometimes compromise isn't good in music—there's got to be some friction. The best music has always come out of frictional situations. Take Mick and Keith—they may not agree on certain shit, but they still make great records. So it's not smooth all the time. But if I really believe something's right, I'll explain it to an artist and I'll tell them why. Ultimately, the final decision, well, it depends on who it is. But I really haven't had a lot of problems like that.

What's the single most important piece of gear in the project studio?

What you need these days is something to get your songs recorded with. If you're doing, say, dance music, it's imperative that you have some sort of sampler, something that you can do beats on and still be able to record some sort of vocal. People are doing instrumental music now, too, so you can do all sample-based records with just a sequencer and a sampler and run it right to DAT. But the way I started was more helping other people get their songs on tape. If you want to go that route, you need something like a DA-88 or a hard disk recorder—something that can capture whatever it is you need to record.

I think the mixer side of things is less of an issue at first. But again, it depends on what it is you're trying to accomplish. Do you want to be a producer? Do you want to just record songs? Do you want to make demos? Do you want to make records in your house? Do you want to do underground dance music type stuff? There's a million options, so you've got to go look at what's out there and figure out where you want to start. Ultimately you may end up somewhere you never thought you'd be—that's what happened to me. I just started out wanting to play guitar, and now look at what I'm doing! (laughs)

If you can pull it off, you should get some kind of mixer, buy a hard disk recorder like a Pro Tools/Logic situation, get a sampler and a couple of keyboards, and you're rocking. Then you start adding things, like different guitars for different situations. Only a few years ago, I had just two guitars, and they worked for everything, because that's all I had and they had to. You get what feels right and you can go far with stuff. But I also think it's important not to get too much shit too fast. That's why you've got a lot of producers who make one really cool record and that's it, it's over, because there's no real depth behind what they do. They just kind of get lucky or whatever, they sample some old record and put it out. There's no depth there, no experience to back it up. So the next time they get a situation, it doesn't work out—they're only capable of doing one thing because they don't have versatility. And versatility is something you get by experience—you don't just wake up one day and you're versatile.

You've talked about experience a lot, but the fact of the matter is that most people are impatient and say, "I want to do it *now*—I don't want to wait to learn what I need to know."

Well, do it now! Nobody's stopping you. Do it! The more you do now, the more experienced you'll be later. That's the whole point I'm trying to make—do as much shit as you can. But be willing to put in the work that it takes to get good at something. Look at basketball players— you don't wake up one day and get in the NBA.

But it takes a certain number of years for a basketball player to grow to be tall enough to be in the NBA. Even if they've got it all together in their head, they're still forced into waiting.

Well, that's why most guys don't make it. In music, things can happen faster. But the only people shit happens fast for are the people who are capable of writing some kind of good song or making a good record. Technical people like engineers don't really make it overnight. Engineering is not the arena you go into if you're impatient and you want to be rich tomorrow.

Because, one, you're not going to get rich from engineering—very few do—and, two, you're not going to pick up one day and know it all. It takes time to absorb all these things—you can't just wake up one day and be great at it.

I talk about this all the time to people who see where I'm at and think I just woke up one day and I was here. It doesn't work that way. This was a passion for me and something I just unconsciously did, and I knew I would succeed. In many ways, the best thing that kids that are starting out have is the naivete of not knowing what they're up against; that's their best ally. When I was a kid, the most positive thing I'd ever get was, "Yeah, you should really go for it and try it, but you need something else in case it doesn't work out, because a lot of people are trying to do what you're trying to do." In my head, I would think, "Fuck you, I'm going to make it, I'm not everybody else." *That's* what you need. That's what gets you through it.

Self-confidence is what you're talking about.

Yeah, exactly. And patience is important too. That's something that I had to learn, because I was the same way—I wanted it all right away, and it didn't happen that way. But you've got to let things come to you, you can't force the issue on everything. The things you have control over, force the issue on. But the things you don't—like if the guy who heard your tape is going to call you back—let it fucking go. Because ultimately he's not going to call you back if he's not going to call you back. And if he likes your shit, he is. You can't do anything about that. But what you *can* do is you can work on your shit and get better at what you do. That way, you give yourself the best possible chance to get in a situation where you're doing what you want to do.

Selected Listening:
Black Grape: *Stupid Stupid Stupid*, Radioactive, 1995 ; *It's Great When You're Straight*, Radioactive, 1997
Rolling Stones: *Bridges To Babylon*, Virgin, 1997
David Bowie: *Dead Man Walking*, RCA, 1997
Public Enemy: *He Got Game*, Def Jam, 1998
Michael Hutchence: *Michael Hutchence*, Sony, 1999

West Coast Producers Panel

Obsessive and Insane

Panelists: John X, Mike Clink, Danny Saber, Jack Joseph Puig, Wally Gagel

few weeks after the East Coast producer's panel that opens this book, I had the opportunity to conduct a similar discussion group in Los Angeles. In contrast, this one
was considerably more subdued—dare I say, more laid back, dude. But once again there
was a diversity in style and an interplay that yielded some fairly surprising responses. The sonic
backdrop changed—the wail of ambulance and fire engine sirens was replaced by the peri-
odic ringing of cellular phones (everyone had one in L.A.; nobody had one in New York—what
does that say about our culture?) and, at various times, participants wandered in and out of
the room while they conducted their wireless business, making for a little less continuity. But
the common ground was the panelists' eagerness to share their knowledge and experience.

Another difference was that the East Coast participants were well-acquainted with one another and so there was a comfortable familiarity in their banter. While three of the participants
on the West Coast panel (Danny Saber, John X, and Wally Gagel) knew each other well by dint
of sharing a common manager, they were meeting Mike Clink and Jack Joseph Puig for the first
time. As a result, there was a little more exploratory conversation and a little less light banter.
At the end of the proceedings (which ran uninterrupted), there were a lot of business cards being exchanged, so it's entirely possible that future collaborations were fostered through this unusual and intense meeting.

What exactly is the role of the producer? Does every artist need one?

JX: What all producers bring, as a general rule, is experience and how you bring the songs to their best position, the technical know-how of using certain pieces of gear that maybe someone at home wouldn't know about, and why it's better. And that experience and overall vision—having an objective ear—is what a producer should bring, as a general rule; everyone has their own specific ways of dealing with it, everyone has their own approach to it.

But have you ever met an artist that didn't need a producer? Someone who blew you away so much that you said, "You don't need me, you're better off doing it on your own"?

MC: I've never met anyone that doesn't need a producer. "Producer" is such a big term, anyway: it could be a friend coming in to lend an objective ear. But everybody needs to have someone that they trust to come in and give some objective opinions about what they're doing and maybe shoot a different idea out. You don't have to accept every single idea that you're given, but everybody can make a better record by getting some objective opinions.

DS: I'm an artist as well, and when you're writing, when you're working on your own stuff, you notice every little minute detail that doesn't always come across to other people. That's also what a producer helps you do—to bring out the strong points and sometimes get rid of the things that aren't really working. It kind of brings a balance and helps get your point across in a more focused way. When you've heard something you've done eight million times, you know every minute detail of it, but it's not obvious to everybody else. Having a producer helps streamline the process. When you've been in a studio for a million hours, you know all the little things and all the shortcuts, and you can save the artist a lot of time and grief, as opposed to somebody who's doing it for the first time. There's so many things going on, it can seem overwhelming to the artist at first. There's a big difference between sitting in your bedroom with an ADAT and getting in a big studio; it can be overwhelming for young artists that have never been there before. Even if the producer's not making a musical contribution, he can help create a vibe in the studio that's conducive for the artist to really be comfortable and get the most out of what they do.

JX: I think the objective side of it is also important. The fact that you can come in and not have this emotional attachment to the music and say, "That chorus does not work," or "Move this bridge completely around." When you're working on your own material, you almost don't want to do that because you're so precious about your own stuff. Speaking from experience as a songwriter, too, it's very difficult to give up something and let someone else tear it apart; it's almost painful.

JJP: Production is an insanely all-encompassing job. It has to do with so many areas: Is the song in the right key? Are the lyrics right? Is that the right image for the band? Should the song be on there? Is the album sequenced right? Is the mix right? Are we in the right studio? Should we use Pro Tools? Should we cut two inch? Should we use both? Who should play on the record? If someone in the band is not playing on the record, what does the A&R person think? Is their finger on the pulse so they know what they are doing? Does it open up good perspective? Which one's the troublemaker? It's limitless in my mind. I've worked with artists who for some reason desire to produce themselves, and I've tried to talk to them about not doing it. And I've watched all of them do it alone for a few records and come to the point of going, okay, you're right. Knowing the right perspective is fairly obvious, but I feel that one of the things we can definitely provide is to allow the artist to do what they do when they know they've got some-

From Left to Right: Jack Joseph Puig, Danny Saber, Wally Gagel, John X, Howard Massey and Mike Clink

one watching their back. So if you want to go off the cliff, fine, go off the cliff—we're watching your back. You don't have to worry about some little things that might be to your detriment, because someone who's really good is handling all those things. That's why the producer empowers the artist—because he allows them to do what they want to do. A good producer also has the ability to recognize when something is genius and right, and not fuck with it. I think an artist should never make anything less than a perfect record; that should be the absolute least. If they feel emotionally and artistically creative, and that they've got to have their reins on it, then they should at least coproduce it. But why would you want full responsibility? In the world, there's possibly five people—maybe four people—who can successfully produce a record themselves and get away with it.

WG: Or in specific genres, like some dance records, or electronic artists who really have a tunnel vision of what they do and all they care about is producing stuff in their bedroom in a very systematic way—that kind of works. I came up from learning about production from being in a band and doing demos on my own and learned that route. So, being a producer and being in a band, I can understand both sides. It can get very difficult [for an artist], because you can get too focused on the wrong things.

JX: Maybe I'll be the underdog here, because I think I should be. The old concept of producers really goes back to a time when you always had to go somewhere else to record your music. You had to go to this place, and somebody had to know how to use the gear.

WG: Engineers in lab coats.

JX: Right. The old-school discipline. There was never all this technological availability, where you could sit in your house and just freak out, learn out how to do it and write maybe 500 songs over the course of a year. We know our thing because we're trained, partially, with a lot of that old-school stuff. You can say that experience is important, but the kids are going to bring a whole new thing to the table because they don't have any of the rules that we have been taught. But it's still going to happen because they don't all need producers. As Wally said, it depends on the genre. Bubble-gum stuff is always going to have somebody like that involved with it, but not every little punk band will—there's a lot of different music that exists. The genre will evolve on its own—some of the same rules will still apply, but they're going to find their own new set, too.

DS: One thing that's already changed is this whole adversarial role, this thing of the producer being the adversary of the band. I've never felt that in all the records I've made; I've always felt like another temporary member of the band who's outside of all their internal shit, who can be objective, who can say something's not cool and get away with it because I'm not fucking the guitar player's girlfriend. If I say I don't like a guitar part, it's OK, but if the singer doesn't like it, the guitarist will say, "Oh, yeah? You're just saying that 'cause I fucked your girlfriend last night."

JJP: That's exactly right.

DS: There's records I've produced where I wrote all the music and played all the instruments— *I* need somebody. When John [X] and I work together, he'll be producing me when I'm cutting my parts, he'll be saying, "Why don't you try this?" It's just an openness. Everybody needs that, and that's the beauty of making music—the bouncing off of other people. People should be open to that and not look at it as an adversarial thing, like there's this guy who's going to come in and ruin all your shit, because it ain't about that; at least with me, it isn't.

JX: And if you have that vibe with them, you're not going to get any problems.

DS: It's not about you sitting in your room, going, "Why should I have a fucking producer? Why should I give him three points?" It isn't about that—it's about your music being taken to the best place it can be taken, and you've got to be open and willing to give a bit. And you'll find that the return is way better than sitting in your room and having your vision of things and not being open.

> **"The greatest things I've been involved with have all been a team effort."**
> **— Jack Joseph Puig.**

JJP: We're really discussing perspective and chemistry. You don't really know until you get together if the chemistry [is right]. And when the chemistry is great, nothing is better than that; it doesn't matter if it's one point or ten points or a million dollars, it's the shit. It's the best it can get. And that's something that you don't get alone; you don't get chemistry. The things I've been involved with that I think are the greatest things have all been collaborations, have all been a team effort. They're always the best.

WG: And they're the most rewarding, too.

JJP: Absolutely.

What are the qualities that an artist should look for when trying to find the ideal producer? Conversely, what are the warning signs that a producer may not be the right guy for me?

JX: Cross-dressing. (laughs)

DS: You feel it. I have friends that are in bands, and they'll talk to me as a friend, saying, "We're thinking of working with this guy; what do you think?" And I say, "Well, get in a room with him and see how it feels." This one band in particular, they had this guy, and I could have told them he was wrong. Look at the records he made and look at what they're trying to do: totally wrong. But check it out, because you never fucking know. And they got in, and it didn't feel right, so I told them, "Look, if it doesn't feel right, you shit-can it now."

MC: Right, because you get in so deep...

DS: But their thing was, "Well, the label got us this guy, and we don't want to cause any waves," but I said again, "Shit-can it *now*. Because you know what? When the record's done, it's going to be too late. You're going to be stuck with a record you don't like. It's not going to be a good record, and you're going to be through." And of course they didn't do it. They made the record, it came out like shit, it came out for fifty seconds, and it was over, and they were dropped [from the label].

WG: To start, you have to listen to the records that the producer's worked on, to see what he's done, so at least you're in an area where you know the work. And the vibe is very important, it really is. In that first meeting, if that producer's telling you exactly what he's going to do, before even hearing the band's demos, before even really knowing what the band's about—if he starts to say, "This is what we're going to do," without even discussing the band's view—you're in trouble. (laughs) Basically, there's no one way to do a record, ever. You really have to bring out what's best in the band, or in the musicians, or the songs, and there has to be a total give and take: "Have you guys ever worked in this kind of environment? Do you like this?" I have a big thing about having open light in the studio; I don't like working in dark, dingy old-school studios—I just hate it. And most of the bands that I work with really like working in places that have a little bit more space—so that's something you might want to talk about. Even the way they work on guitar sounds and how they've done it in the past—for example, if you want to be in the control room. If the producer has this vision that they don't even want to communicate, that's the first warning sign.

> **"There's no one way to do a record, ever."**
> **— Wally Gagel**

MC: I tell people that meet me, "Go talk to everybody, go talk to all these guys," because there's a vibe; I'm not going to make the same record that any of the people in this room are going to make. There has to be a vibe that happens between the band and the producer. I have to agree that too many bands never cut it off. I tell everybody, if it's not right in the beginning, it's only going to get worse, because as the record continues, tensions build, and you're just going to end up with a product that you don't like. The whole reason that we do this is because we enjoy making records, we have a good time making them. When it gets to the point where it's not fun, then who wants to be there? It becomes work, it becomes tedious. I think it's all about a vibe, and I ask the same questions when I meet the band: I say, "What kind of hours do you like to work?"

JX: "What kind of beer do you like to drink?" (laughs)

MC: I'll offer to take the artist to a bunch of different studios within the parameters of their budget; let's see what you like, and I'll see if I can make this work for you. It's all about the material and knowing if you can be the person to bring out the best in the band. I've turned down bands that I thought I wasn't right for, and I know a lot of people work just to work. But if I can't bring something to the table and make it better, then I don't want to get involved in it. And that's important.

WG: And you may also want to address just what that producer's motivation is, exactly. What is driving him towards wanting to work with your band? Is it because it's a gig that just popped up for him and that's the only reason, because he's got to make his car payments? Or is he diving on your thing because he really believes in what you're doing? That's going to make a big difference, too.

How do you handle things when an artist starts "getting creative on you"—when you see them heading down a road that you know is going to be a waste of time?

WG: Well, budgetary reasons are a good indicator. You can't let someone completely go on if you're in a two thousand dollar a day studio and you just don't have the budget. But there's definitely balance. You have to let everyone try a few things out; you have to let them have some freedom, especially if you can see they're really excited. If you say, "You know something? We don't have any more time," that's going to affect the rest of the session. But if you get to the point where you're looking over to the engineer and everyone's going [depressed voice] OK, and this is like the five hundredth time he's tried the same part out and it's really dragging, then you just stop it.

MC: It's all in the delivery, too. If you're going to shut somebody down, that's also part of the producer's gig: To not make it a nightmare when you say, "You know, you've been on this long enough..."

DS: It's a fine line—you can't not let people try stuff. But at the same time, you can't piss away a whole day on the piano sample that the guy made in his computer, and he wants it there just because he made it. It's all about the way you present things, and when—you pick your moments. When you're doing vocals and you're focused on that, you don't all of a sudden shit-can it to work on some noise. That's important for the artist to understand as well. It seems like the inexperienced artist always wants to work on the most irrelevant thing at that point in the session, when it's the least important thing at that moment. There's a time and a place. If the singer's doing vocals—and that's difficult enough—you can't interrupt it. It's important to know the artist's motivation as well, because a lot of times they're just trying to cram shit in there because they did it. So it's a weird balance, but if I had to waste a little time on something that didn't work, and the artist in the long run is going to be happy and feel good—I'd rather do that than cut him off and then never know and have him walking around with that inside him. Because that shit's going to come out later, and it'll probably cost you more time down the road.

JX: Another warning sign could be if a producer is talking about all the other bands that he's worked with and never brings up your band's demos, never discusses what the band's doing— if he doesn't have a listening capability.

There used to be a huge gap between the demo and the master—today that gap has nar-

rowed to the point where it can disappear altogether. Do you ever actually go with the demo, feel that it cannot be improved upon even if it's recorded in a better studio with better microphones?

WG: A lot of parts, certainly. Maybe not a whole song, but definitely a lot of parts.

JX: Sometimes the demo is worthy of being a master.

JJP: In that instance, the important thing is the attitude you're going for. Whether you're willing to either use elements of the demo and blend it in with the new track or whether you're actually strong enough at the end to say, "You know what? We didn't need the new track—let's just use the demo. I know we recut it, but six months from now you're not going to remember that we spent $4800 and two weeks recutting it; you're just going to know if the record's good or if it's not good. How we got there doesn't matter."

It's also a question of checking your ego at the door, because you weren't there when the demo was made.

DS: It ain't even about egos. The nature of the way records are made now, there's no reason not to use stuff. The vibe when you're writing, when you're throwing shit down—you'll never recapture that. When I write, I'm planning on using a lot of the stuff. I might take a shot at recutting the guitars or something, but nine out of ten times, I end up with the stuff from the demo.

JJP: There's no reason not to use elements of a demo, so why not? The idea of saying you can't do that is stupidity.

DS: The only time that happens is when you have a producer that's real old-school. I worked with an artist that wanted to make a record that incorporated electronica and live shit. The producer on the session was saying, "Oh, I invented loops—we'll throw loops on there, we'll loop the fuck out of it, blah, blah, blah." But he really had no actual knowledge of any of the newer technology, so it really hindered the record. He basically fucked the record up, because he wasn't capable of making the record the artist wanted to make, and he just kind of bullshitted his way through it, because he wanted the gig. In that case, a lot of things didn't get done because he didn't know how to do them and he was afraid of it.

JX: Warning sign!

DS: There's that warning sign that Wally was talking about. He was just jiving his way to get the gig because it was a big artist and he wanted the prestige of the gig so he just basically told the guy what he wanted to hear. Of course he ended up getting fired, and none of his shit got used. Mike made a really good point: If you take a gig that you're not capable of doing or isn't right for you, it's ultimately going to hurt you as much if not more than the artist. It's not fair to the artist, but it's also not fair to yourself.

JJP: It's like all relationships. If you really don't belong there, then don't go there. But you try it and see if it's going to make sense—maybe it will, maybe it won't. And usually you can tell. After you've been in production for a few days, you know. For me, I know within one day—yep, it's going to work. Or it's not. You know in preproduction, even before you get to the studio—it doesn't have to go that far.

WG: That's true. Actually, preproduction's another good thing to discuss, because I think a lot of people should have the opportunity to go through that with the producer. If they're going into the studio right off the bat, I'd say that's another warning sign.

JX: Go in and test drive on one song, and then everybody's going to know.

WG: And the technology with demos is really exciting, because you are getting the vibe. I write the same way—I try to put it down as if it's potentially something that you can keep. It's only within the last five years that you're getting stuff that's of the quality that you can keep. Now more than ever, you really can't distinguish—you know, "Bring those Pro Tools tracks over, and we'll use them."

DS: Well, it's easier now. And I don't know too many producers that are so fucked up that they won't use some shit just because they didn't record it. Unless there's another producer that did it first and there's a points issue, and there's a lot of business things, and you can't do it better. Even so, I made two records that had other producers involved, and you know what? When it came down to it, everything of mine we used, I got all the points, and if I used some of his shit, I had to split it with him. But if the shit that he did was good, I still kept it because, fuck it, the overall picture is that it's a great album. I wouldn't shit-can something someone else did because I want all the money. I wouldn't do that to the artist, and if the overall record that comes out is a hit, I'm going to look good anyway; it doesn't matter who recorded what.

Do you ever seek out new, unsigned artists? If so, how do you find them?

MC: Right now, I'm in a situation where I have two bands that have come to me through managers. Once again, if I think I can do justice to it, then I'll take it under my wing and take it on. I'm not a big guy for going out to the clubs and checking out unsigned talent; it just hasn't worked for me in particular. So it's mostly through my contacts—someone will come to me with a tape and say, what do you think? Do you think you can put it somewhere? And I'll listen to it and say yes or no, or give you a number of someone else to get it to. I love doing that—I love being able to get an artist put somewhere close.

DS: I think more important than going to clubs and trying to find stuff is just being accessible, because the stuff will find you. I'm accessible, people can get ahold of me, and people know I'm a guy they can get to. I've never, to this day, really found anything off the street that ended up being a record that came out. But there's a lot of things that I haven't worked on that I've helped people get deals or connect them with someone who'd be into it.

JX: That's a little bit of a mystery to me. I do go out and look for them, but the clubs really represent a slim percentage of what's really available to you, because there are people all over the world who get your number or mail you CDs or cassettes. I listen to all that stuff, and I've found a lot of really cool artists that I've worked with, many of them in the last couple of years. I haven't gotten to the point where there's millions of cassettes coming in each day, so it's easy to listen. If it got to that point, then I couldn't do that.

WG: I've actually gone to a couple of these conferences where I've had shopping bags filled with tapes that would break! (laughs) And you're hard-pressed to find something that really stands out—that's true even when A&R people give you tapes. It's a gift when someone sends you a really good demo.

Are there ways of getting your attention if an artist sends you an unsolicited tape in the mail?

JX: Nude photos of yourself. (laughs)

WG: Send money!

JX: No, I wouldn't judge somebody on the presentation. If they've got a great song on some reused cassette that's been marked over with a Sharpie, I'm still going to like the song.

WG: Yeah, obviously the song is important, but the big question is how to get it to us. If it comes through a friend or something like that, that tends to be the easiest way.

JJP: You pretty much have to weigh which way you can match it with us; it's limitless.

But do you listen to everything that makes it way to you?

MC: I listen to everything. I have to.

JJP: I don't listen, because I run out of time. I try; it's not arrogance, it's just time.

Once the connection has been made, what are the reasonable expectations that an artist can have of his producer? What are unreasonable expectations?

WG: The unreasonable aspect—which has always been the case—is that you can't turn shit into gold. You can't make something into something that it's not. You can certainly make a great piece into an extraordinary piece, but if the material isn't really there, then it's not going to happen.

JX: The producer does *not* have to buy dinner every day. (laughs)

MC: One of the expectations that people should have if they hire a producer is that he will make things better. If someone is spending the kind of money that they do on a producer, they're expecting to get the input and they want to see it get that much better. They're going to expect that.

JX: Then there's different sorts of producers as well. What happens if, maybe the first day, the guy doesn't even show up, saying, "I just want to get you guys going on your own." That's not cool, but I've seen a lot of them do that. But it depends on the relationship you've established, whether the artist is going to expect you to be there all the time. I've seen a lot of artists get really upset about that thing, too: "What is this? He just shows up for an hour or two a day, listens to it, throws his two cents in, and then splits."

MC: How do you keep a gig like that? I don't know...

JX: I'm not going to name any names, but some of these people are pretty major dudes; they're megadudes.

JJP: I know the people you're talking about, but I couldn't do that...

JX: That freaks out the artist—you'll see him, as the producer's walking out the door, the artist starts to tighten up and get ready to explode.

JJP: I've thought about it a lot. It's an amazing fucking perspective: The band is in there with an engineer who's really got his shit together and is actually making the record. The producer comes in eight hours later and listens and goes, "No, no, no. You should have done this..." and the band thinks, "You fucking asshole!" But you know what? He was right. Because he wasn't there in the trenches, he was able to see it right away, so he actually was right. And they corrected those things and had a hit record, so he gave a service. It's another way of looking at it. Mind you, I don't do that.

DS: But the other side of the coin is that, if he was there when the shit was going down, he could have said that at that point and then it would have gotten done the right way in the first place. Or are you saying this perspective wouldn't have been there if he was there?

JJP: Possibly not.

DS: He could have been making his phone calls in the lounge and then walked downstairs. We've all seen that. (laughs)

JX: Yeah, he's still in the building—he's within earshot. (laughs)

That actually brings up an interesting question: Do you really need to be there while the assistant engineer is moving the mic an inch and the tech is tuning up the drums?

JJP: I can't be there part-time. I feel like I owe that for the kind of money I'm paid.

MC: I can't leave anybody alone in the control room. The only thing that I don't have to be there for is the busy work, the making of the slaves. I'll set it up but then I'll go, because I hire competent people to work with me. I'll tell them, "This is how I like to do it, now you finish it up."—I don't need to be there for that kind of stuff.

JX: Well, that's different. That's not going to wind your artist up if you don't show up for that.

DS: But I think it's really insensitive to let people work for twelve straight hours and then come in and rip everything apart that they did and make them do it again. I think at least you have to be there when the creative shit's happening. If you're an engineer/producer, yeah, you need to be there for the mics. But when the creative shit is going down—when decisions are being made—it's your responsibility to be there for that, at least. You don't have to be there to make slaves, you don't have to be there to get kick drum sounds, because all that stuff is all going to change by the time you get to mix, in this day and age, anyway.

JJP: That's the way I work. But as an intelligent person, I've had to stand back and look at [the other way] and say, "I don't agree with that, but why is it working?"

DS: Because the guy's fucking lucky. (laughs)

JJP: But they're all the same!

DS: But in England, that's the way some records are made; that's a trend with English producers. And I give those guys respect because they do make really good records.

WG: The expectation then should be there, if there's a discussion with the producer before you go into it, and if the band says, "We really like to have someone who's around while we're making these decisions." If the producer says, "I don't do that. I get much more perspective this way—this is my engineer, I trust him, and he's going to be the ears for me, and I'm going to come in every now and then." If they build that relationship from the beginning and are fine with it, then great. Or if someone is incredibly meticulous during preproduction and then says, "This is the way I work—the preproduction is the most important thing to me, and then you guys are going to go into the studio, and I'm going to come in periodically and just check on how we've done." If you've established that, then I suppose that's fine. But expectations have to be somewhat given in the beginning. You still can't make something that's not there. Obviously the band and the producer have to work as a team to get the vision of the song.

JJP: I feel that producers and mixers have all become way too much like stars, and that's bullshit. It's a little bit fucked up, because it's really the artists that are the stars. My point is that the artists should just ask questions—they can ask anything they want. They're the stars, they're the commodities, they're the ones who wrote the songs, they're the diamonds in the rough. We facilitate. So ask your producer! "Why do you do this? How do you do this? How do you feel about this? What's going to happen? Will it go this fast or this slow? What will happen if this happens?" And you'll know right away. As I said, it's like any relationship. Preproduction to me is like dating, it's perfect—you go in, you know right away, before you spend any of the dough. You know this is going to work, that's not going to work; this guy is going to do nothing for my songs; this guy is going to be perfect for my songs or my songs.

DS: It's funny what you said about the producers being stars, because it seems like a lot of the artists are more conservative and straight and worried about business and that kind of shit than a lot of the producers are now. And I don't think that's necessarily a good thing—the musicians are supposed to be the ones that are out there! I myself don't really throw myself in the category of typical producer, because I always end up playing something or doing something a little more creative than just sitting there and telling them what to do. But the bands have gotten so conservative, and there's a real lack of stars out there. I think that's why producers are getting so much play—because the bands are so fucking boring most of the time! They're sitting there drinking Evian water, and a lot of the rock and roll has gone out of it—especially the young bands. It's really weird. And the producers are the ones hanging off the chandelier half the fucking time!

And presumably the producer is the senior member of the team.

JJP: My perspective is that, in the '80s, it seemed like we didn't really have a lot of artists that were really bringing things to the table—*we* were bringing it to the table. And then all of a sudden management came in; all of sudden we had to be managed, we had to have our name on the back of the CD, we had to have points. Then you had mixer guys, and they got a point. Some guys will mix a song, two, three songs in a day, and they got a point. They'd be there two fucking weeks, and they'd get a point! That's heavy.

WG: And sometimes they'd get more money than the producer.

DS: But the other side of that is this, and this just happened to me: John [X] and I just mixed two songs on a record. They didn't use the songs on the album for ego, bullshit reasons, but both of the songs were hits on radio—those songs are selling that record, and I didn't get anything. I did a lot of shit on that record, I played on it, I made a difference, I added a few things. But it's difference enough that it's this stuff that's selling their album, and people are hearing that shit on the radio with the intention of going out and buying it, and it ain't even on the record, which is a problem. My point is that, if we did something that's selling their record, I don't see why we shouldn't have a little part of it, at least on the songs we mixed.

JJP: All I'm saying is, that has caused the whole situation to get out of perspective. It's because of everything I've just described—that's put us in a funny position. You're right, you did earn, you did make that record, you should get that percentage. But you're still the star.

DS: But I'm not. And I think part of the reason it isn't on the record is that they didn't want to give us money.

JJP: I'm sure it's a big part.

DS: But they're still using it to sell their record.

What sort of business arrangements should an artist expect to have with their producer?

DS: As far as points go, it's pretty set. The producer gets between two and four points, and the artist pays that. The record company's got a great racket going, because basically everything gets paid out of the artist's share. So only their share goes towards paying us and clearing off all the costs that they incurred to make the product. And the record company takes their share right off the top, so a lot of times artists may not be recouped, but they've actually made the label a substantial amount of money. Then they get into this hole—it's like a loan shark type thing.

JX: The fee can go from zero to a million, depending on who you're talking to.

JJP: Who you're talking to and also your level of success and where you're at. But you should be flexible if you like the music and you want to make the record. As soon as you get to the place where you're saying, "I won't do it because I'm a star," you're fucked, you're fucking history. I've done it—if I think it's great, fuck it, I'll just mix it. So the other ones that maybe pay more—they make it possible for you to do that. That's the way I look at it. And it all works out, it's cool.

So depending upon the circumstances, you'll be willing to take less money.

DS: All the time, absolutely. If you're doing anything for money, or you're not doing it because of money, right there is a dangerous little road to go down. I've turned down a lot of things where there was a lot of money offered, but I hated the fucking music. It wasn't even hard. I just thought, I can't see myself working on this. And if you're really into something, even if there's not as much money as you'd get to do another thing, you'd be an idiot not to do it. If you're into it, you're going to get fulfillment out of doing it. There are some people who don't think that way, but they're doing it for the wrong reasons, anyway—they don't have a genuine motivation going on.

JX: There are more successful career options to jump into than being a music producer! (laughs)

DS: But as you start to make money and you start to get big lumps of money thrown at you, you've still got to keep your perspective and realize that's not why you got into it, and that's not where the fulfillment's going to come from. The money ain't going to do it. It doesn't matter how much money you have—I know some miserable millionaires. On the surface, they seem to have everything you could ever want, but they're so fucked up and unhappy because they're looking to the wrong place for their fulfillment. The fulfillment for me comes from making the music and the ability to get up when I want, go in and work when I want, and work on shit that I like. I'm waiting for somebody to smack me and wake me up! That's the beauty of it. The fact that I get paid money to do it is a bonus—I'd be doing it anyway, I'd be sitting in my friend's garage, that's how I started. If I wasn't getting paid to do it, I'd still be trying to do it, and I'm sure everybody else here would be, too. You've got to keep your eye on that, because that's what it's all about.

JX: I think another part of the dark stereotype of producers is the word "producer" and its association with film, which is a completely different animal. A lot of people don't really know the difference. It seems we would be more the equivalent of the director, not the producer of a film.

DS: A film producer's all about money.

The role of the record producer has evolved over the last forty years, anyway.

DS: Yeah, it can mean anything, whereas in the '50s and even in the early '60s, it was pretty much a defined role. But guys like George Martin, those were the guys that allowed us to be in the position that we're in now, and the same with a lot of bands back then. If they hadn't done what they did, it wouldn't mean what it means today, financially, socially, creatively—it wouldn't have the same importance. So there's a great deal of respect due to those people. George Martin and people of his generation that did what they did, they're a big reason why things are the way they are today. It's the same thing in sports—if it wasn't for Doctor J, I don't think there would have been a Michael Jordan, because they opened the doors up, they set the stage for the next thing to happen.

MC: Even some of the older producers who were doing stuff in the late '60s, early '70s always complained to me, "Oh, your royalty rates are so much higher; if I made what you made…" Who cares? Is that why you did it? No, you did it because you enjoyed making music and you had a great gig.

DS: We owe those guys respect because they set the stage for us to be able to do what we're doing, just like, hopefully, we'll be doing it for somebody down the road, although I don't think anything that's done now will have the impact that music had then, because it was so open—it was all being invented. There's not going to be a band like the Stones again, I don't think, that's going to have that much social impact. Or Chuck Berry, or Elvis, anything like that. Those people, they wrote history, they totally created a whole genre. It was the time they were in, socially—I mean, rock and roll had to happen. It's almost like they were victims of circumstances of the time they were in, and they seized it, and they did their thing. It's really amazing when you think about it—how did that happen? It's all the circumstances of the times.

What do you think the role of the producer is going to be 20 years from now?

WG: It's somewhat genre-specific, in the sense that someone who goes in to produce rock and roll bands and get a band vibe and work off of the live musician/song experiences going in, they're still going to probably produce records in a very similar fashion. It'll always be about creating the best vibe in the studio and getting the bands really excited and helping out with the music and the arrangement. So that's not going to change, but the thing that the home studio aspect has probably changed the most is electronic music and bands that can basically do things on their own, at home, in their bedroom. So the people who are going to come up as producers in that [genre] have to really know what they're talking about in their own world. They have to be able to use the programs that do that, and they have to be right up to speed with these bands. And then you have the Babyface types, where it's almost like the Motown days; you have these producer/songwriters coming in, and they're really dictating what happens with the artist, they're really just using a singer. It seems to be splitting a lot more, so I can't say there's any one role, because each genre has its own vibe. But most changes are definitely in the electronic stuff.

DS: It's all about one thing: versatility. Because the days of one guy doing one thing are numbered. There's less and less of that now, and there's going to be even less as time goes on. If you can mix records, record records, write songs, and program, you've got a much better shot than if you just say, I'm only going to do this. Records aren't made that way anymore. Every time a jingle was done—any time *anything* was done—it was, "Call the musicians." Now it's one guy in his room, and that guy's probably producing the thing, too. So if it's about wanting to work and have a career and earn a living within music, you have to be open and versatile. I never planned to end up where I am; I would have been happy just making a living when I first started out. I didn't have a great scheme—it turned out way beyond my wildest dreams, but the reason I'm where I'm at is because I was versatile and every time I got an opportunity I was able to make the most of it. And it didn't matter what it was—if I didn't know how to do something, I'd figure it out real quick. That's the beauty of having all this gear in your house—you can be versatile, you can write songs and record them and do all those different things. There's not going to be as much opportunity for specialty people, although they'll always be there.

Does the traditional route—assistant engineer to engineer to producer—still work?

WG: It definitely happens that way sometimes. I started in a band and assisted, then engineered, although there are some producers that don't have any engineering skills whatsoever. But that does work, although I think it helps a lot to have the music on top of it. The people who just go into it for engineering only, from a technical standpoint—a lot of the kids who come out of the engineering schools are like that—they can come out and get a little lost, because, if you want to be a producer, there is a little bit of that communication loss with the band as far as the music is concerned. But if you just want to be a great engineer, then maybe that's what you should be. I find that's actually becoming rarer and rarer—somebody who's just amazing at being an engineer, because that's what he loves.

DS: Being a great engineer doesn't really mean what it used to mean, because of the way technology has advanced. To me, the best records being made now—the most creative, interesting records—a lot of that's coming from the writing and the artist. It doesn't have the impact anymore, because you can get sounds out of a box now, so making great sounds isn't really the thing that it used to be. I think it's a good thing in the sense that you have to be more creative now, it's harder to come up with original sounds—you have to push yourself in different ways. Not to take anything away from the art of engineering—it's still an art.

JJP: You're talking about engineer/producers. To me, it's in the right perspective when you see yourself as a producer/engineer—the music's first, the other part's secondary.

What advice can you offer to the young person who's seeking to become a record producer?

DS: You've just got to get out there and hammer it. You just do everything you can to work on music.

WG: Work your strengths; know what your strengths are. If there's something that you're doing and people are always saying, "God, you're really good at that," keep working on it.

JJP: Some people have made it by going to engineering school; some people have made it because their father knew a guy who had a recording studio so they got to go in there when the guy got sick, so they stepped in. Some people have made it because they were doing the live sound for the band. You can just keep going, scenario after scenario after scenario. I don't know that there is one way.

DS: You've just got to be ready when you get an opportunity. And the way you are ready is you take every opportunity you can make for yourself to work on music, in whatever capacity it is. Then, when you get an opportunity, you're ready for it—you can do something with it. Everybody's going to get a shot. Most people that don't make it or don't do well, they get their shot and they're not ready for it.

JJP: I'll tell you what my mentor Bill Schnee said to me, early on. He said, "The thing to concern yourself with is not how you're going to get there, but making sure that, when the coach says, 'Step to the plate, grab a bat,' that you can hit the ball." There's nothing more devastating than when you get the pitch and you can't hit the ball. You've *got* to hit the ball—that's all that matters. Don't worry about your opportunities, just get your shit together.

MC: You've got to capitalize on every opportunity and be able to get your foot in the door. You may have gone to school at Berklee [College of Music] or wherever, or you may be a great musician, but if the opportunity arises to answer the phones or clean the toilets at a studio, don't be so proud that you say, "No, that's beneath me, I can't do that." Get your foot in the door and capitalize on that opportunity, because the opportunities are a little tougher these days; it's just harder to get a job in the studio and make it. Once you have your foot in the door, make yourself known as a go-getter and someone who's willing to do whatever it takes; be a fly on the wall and sit in on sessions and learn from everybody that's actually working in the business. And one day that opportunity's going to come where someone says, "I can't make it into work; can you fill in?" Then the band becomes enamored with you and, you do the next record, and so on. But you've got to capitalize on all opportunities. And that's the problem I find nowadays—people don't capitalize on the opportunities. I work in studios all around town, and I see these guys who are really talented, but they show no initiative because they're waiting for their big break to just fall into their lap. I invite everybody to my sessions: "Come on in, hang out, learn how to do this or that. Even if you don't learn specifics, just take the whole thing in and be a part of it."

> "Sometimes you have to take one step backwards to take ten forward."
> — Mike Clink

WG: I did the traditional route, getting coffee and assisting, then engineering, but I stayed in bands the whole time. I stuck with doing bands more, and I left doing studio work for awhile. When I was older, I called up a friend who was a producer and I asked if I could sit in and at least assist. It was a session where I just kind of joined in. I was there as an assistant, and the producer couldn't finish up the last day or two. I did—I engineered it. I then became the house engineer within two weeks of that time, and six months later ended up working on this top forty hit that I produced and cowrote. All just because I happened to call up this friend and humbled myself, asking him if I could just assist him, even though I'd done that when I was eighteen and nineteen. That happened so fast, but it was because I had spent all these other years doing it and trying, hitting my head against the wall. But I took the opportunity, and that's what happened.

JX: It's just timing.

MC: Sometimes you have to take one step backwards to take ten forward.

DS: It's easy to sit here and say do this and do that, but the one thing that people can do now is, get some gear somehow and start recording shit. That's how I got started. I was in a band, and I had a sampler and an 8-track, and whenever I wasn't working on the band's music, I had a little room set up, and anyone who wanted to come over could come over. I did demos with anybody. One day I was doing a demo with Miss Tennessee—a country thing. I wasn't into it, but I did it, I did the best I could. I learned something—I learned how to get a pedal steel sound out of my guitar, [so] something positive came out of it, it was a good working experience. I didn't make any money, it didn't go anywhere, but I gained something. I did demos for loads of people, and they started to get signed. That's how to make an opportunity for yourself—just start doing stuff. It's so easy now—you don't need a lot of money to get a sampler. Make your opportunities.

WG: People have to be willing to put up with the demo thing. It's never easy. I don't think people think it's going to be easy, but I guess there's a little bit of expectation that they're going to walk out of school and get paid full on. It just doesn't happen that way. If you love to do it, you just keep going, even if the money's not coming in, because your heart tells you you've got to keep doing it. And if you don't—if you give up—then you weren't meant to do it anyway. So it's one of those things where you just have to have that vision somehow beyond what you're actually in front of that day.

JX: It's pretty seductive, especially for the youngsters—you know, "Wow, I get to be with all these rock stars" and the lifestyle and the whole thing. But it takes a lot to get there. You don't walk in and end up with it; you've really got to work your ass off to get yourself to this point. Sometimes people come up to me and say, "Dude, you're really lucky, you know?" (laughs) Well, luck had nothing to do with this. You've been busting your ass for years—I've been in this for eighteen years, and that's a long time. It's only the last few years they might be able to say, yeah, you're doing really good now—I thought I was doing great the whole time! (laughs) But you're not going to just jump right in and land there, unless you are really lucky. For me, that wasn't the case—I've been just busting my ass the whole time. If you're not ready to do that, and if you don't love it enough—it's got to be just eating you from the inside, that this is what you *have* to be doing. Otherwise you won't make it—you won't survive that process. The selection process is way too brutal, and if you're not obsessive and insane about it, you're not going to do it, you're not going to get anywhere.

Obsessive and insane—you've given me the title for this chapter.

JX: That sums it up.

When it Comes to Music, We Wrote the Book.

Confessions of a Record Producer
How to Survive the Scams and Shams of the Music Business
By Moses Avalon

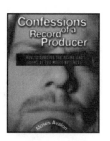

If you're involved in the music recording business—artist, producer, engineer, or any other recording professional—this practical survival guide will help you protect your rights and preserve your assets. Using real-life examples drawn from the author's 20 years of industry experience, this revealing book tells it like it is: how producers dip into budgets, artists steal songs, labels skim royalties, and other unfortunate truths—and how to succeed nonetheless.
Softcover, 241 pages, ISBN 0-87930-532-0, $17.95

The Reel World
Scoring for Pictures
By Jeff Rona

Written by one of Hollywood's leading composers, this how-to book takes you inside the world of creating music for film and television. To help you get started and succeed in scoring, it focuses on the composer's key concerns: musical aesthetics, effective technology and techniques, and the business side of things. Packed with on-the-job stories, the book reveals proven strategies plus pitfalls to avoid, drawn from actual scoring projects by industry pros.
Softcover, 256 pages, ISBN 0-98730-591-6, $24.95

Producing Great Sound for Digital Video
By Jay Rose

If your soundtracks aren't as crisp as they should be, try the pro techniques explained here. A Clio-winning sound designer offers solutions to problems throughout the entire audio process—from pre-production through mix. You get how-to tips and time-savers, plus step-by-step tutorials for making great sound with any computer or software. Including a CD of sample tracks and diagnostic tools, this is a complete audio training resource as well as a quick problem-solving guide.
Softcover with CD, 349 pages, ISBN 0-87930-597-5, $39.95

The Finale Primer
Mastering the Art of Music Notation with Finale
Second Edition
By Bill Purse

Fully updated to cover Finale 2000 for both Macintosh and Windows computers, this book flattens the learning curve of this powerful music notation software—so you can enter, edit, hear, view, lay out, and print publisher-quality music with ease. It guides you step by step through Finale's intricacies, featuring dozens of hands-on lessons, projects and drills, plus hundreds of easy-to-read illustrations.
Softcover, 247 pages, ISBN 0-87930-602-5, $24.95

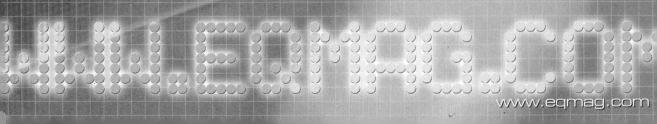

subscribe to
EQ Magazine
online…

http:

www.eqmag.com